Reconstructing Aphra

ANGELINE GOREAU

Reconstructing Aphra
A Social Biography of Aphra Behn

THE DIAL PRESS

NEW YORK

For my mother, Eloise Keaton Goreau,
whose intelligence, wit, and culture
have been both source and resource for me.

Published by The Dial Press
1 Dag Hammarskjold Plaza
New York, New York 10017

Manufactured in the United States of America
First printing
Design by Francesca Belanger

Library of Congress Cataloging in Publication Data
Goreau, Angeline.
    Reconstructing Aphra.
    Bibliography: p. 319
    Includes index.
    1. Behn, Aphra Amis, 1640–1689—Biography.
2. Authors, English—Early modern, 1500–1700—
Biography.   I. Title.
PR3317.Z5G6   822'.4[B]   80-11495
ISBN 0-8037-7478-8

Acknowledgments

Debts incurred in the writing of this book have been many more than I can properly acknowledge here: to all those who listened to my ideas, offered objections and suggestions, I owe thanks. To the National Endowment for the Humanities I owe the time and freedom I needed to begin research; to James T. Farrell and Cleo Paturis I owe a debt of gratitude for first suggesting that I apply for a grant and thereafter for their unstinting support. Louis Simpson and M. L. Rosenthal generously helped. For her kindness, for what she taught me about writing, and for her example, I also owe acknowledgment to Elizabeth Hardwick. The early encouragement and friendship of Berenice Hoffman and Joyce Johnson have meant a great deal to me. Serge Fauchereau has been important in more ways than one for a long time. Many other friends have given advice, assistance, or commiseration: Leslie Gardner, Danielle Haase-Dubosc, Julian Gloag, Gerard and Patricia Van der Leun, Robert Fine, Michael Heffernan, Pamela White, Ibsen and Sylvie Bellew, Cheryl Hart, my friends at the British Museum, and most of all Farid Chennoune, for simply being there.

I am most particularly grateful to the librarians and staff of the British Museum and the Bodleian Library, Oxford, whose unfailing help was essential to my research. Other libraries and institutions who opened their collections or offered help were the Public Record Office, the University Library, Cambridge, the Dean and Chapter Library of Canterbury Cathedral, the University of London Library, the Institute of Historical Research, the London Library, the University of Nottingham Library, the Princeton University Library, the John Carter Brown Library, the Barnard College Library, the Columbia University Library, the Folger Library, and the Bibliothèque Nationale. The National Portrait Gallery, the Pepys Library, the Museum of London, the Victoria and Albert Museum, the National Maritime Museum, the Dulwich College Picture Gallery, and the Prints and Drawings Department of the British Museum supplied pictures from their collections. The vicar of Wye permitted me to consult the parish registers, and Dr. Arthur Schlecter graciously allowed me to see his portrait of Aphra Behn.

I wish also to thank my editor, Joyce Johnson, whose sure editorial touch repaired many awkwardnesses in this book and whose critical eye steered me away from mistakes. Veronica Windholz did a fine job of copyediting. Others at Dial Press who kindly encouraged were Juris Jurjevics, Donna Schrader, and Anita Feldman. Finally, there is my mother, who gave me Charlotte Brontë and Jane Austen to read when I was very young, who ceaselessly watched over Aphra's coming into being, as she watched over mine.

Contents

Illustrations

*. . . these women have so much contradiction in 'em, that 'tis
ten to one but a man fails in the art of pleasing.*
                                        —Aphra Behn, *Sir Patient Fancy*

Reconstructing Aphra

CHAPTER ONE

Prologue: Contradictions

Aphra Behn existed.

If she had not, we would have had to invent her.

If Shakespeare could look back to Marlowe, Marlowe to Chaucer, or Chaucer to the literary forefathers whose tradition he grew out of, Mrs. Behn imposed herself on history without precedent: she was the first woman to become a professional writer.[1] Aphra had to invent herself.

The life she led would have been extraordinary in any age, but for a woman of the seventeenth century not born to fortune or position it was nearly unheard of. Aphra Behn was an adventuress who undertook the long and dangerous voyage to the West Indies, became involved in a slave rebellion there, and visited a tribe of Indians who had never before seen Europeans. She was a spy for Charles II against the Dutch. She was a debtor imprisoned for expenses incurred in the service of the King. She was a feminist who vociferously defended the right of women to an education, and the right to marry whom they pleased, or not at all. She was a sexual pioneer who contended that men and women should love freely and as equals. She was a political activist who argued the Royalist point of view at Will's Coffee House and from the stage of the Drury Lane theater. She was an early abolitionist whose novel *Oroonoko* contained the first popular portrayal of the horrors of slavery. Finally, she was a writer who not only insisted on being heard, but successfully forced the men who dominated the jealous literary world of Restoration England to recognize her as an equal. In a London that boasted only two theaters, she had seventeen plays produced in seventeen years. She wrote thirteen "novels" (thirty years before Daniel Defoe wrote *Robinson Crusoe,* generally termed the first novel) and published several collections of poems and translations.

Along with her friend and colleague John Dryden, she is buried in Westminster Abbey—Dryden in Poets' Corner; Aphra outside, at the entrance to the cloisters, where her stone has almost been worn smooth by three centuries of indifferent feet.

I began a life of Aphra and saw in her a heroine . . . for Aphra's life, though she did not and could not know it then, would signal a turning in feminine history, augur a whole new spectrum of possibility for her sex. It was she who demonstrated that a woman—if lucky, if willing to surrender respectability, comfort, approval, perhaps even love; if prepared to risk ridicule, loss of reputation, vilification or attack—might declare her autonomy and make a living by writing in an age when her only social and economic alternative was to marry or to find a wealthy "protector." She was both sign and cause: the wave of women writers that came after her would have inevitably come, but for her immediate successors the ground she gained was important. Mary Manley, Mary Pix, Eliza Haywood, Catherine Trotter, Arabella Plantin, Penelope Aubin, Elizabeth Rowe, and others could look back to Aphra as precedent, just as the next generation of aspiring young women could look back to them—though history would forget those early lady writers of the eighteenth century almost as quickly as it forgot Mrs. Behn herself. Still, they formed a tradition, if invisible, that firmly established the woman writer as a literary "fact."

"Masterpieces are not single and solitary births," wrote Virginia Woolf in *A Room of One's Own,* "they are the outcome of many years of thinking in common, of thinking by the body of the people, so that the experience of the mass is behind the single voice. Jane Austen should have laid a wreath upon the grave of Fanny Burney, and George Eliot done homage to the shade of Eliza Carter . . . all women together ought to let flowers fall upon the tomb of Aphra Behn, for it was she who earned them the right to speak their minds."[2]

————·

A feminist heroine . . . but she was not the heroine I had thought first to discover; for the Aphra who so well understood, articulated, and raged against the oppression of women nevertheless found herself reenacting what she so opposed. The woman and the writer in her contradicted: *"I see no reason why women should not write as well as men,"* she said in a manifesto and then, in another, entered this plea: *"All I ask, is the privilege for my masculine part, the poet in me."* One Aphra could not live without independence, the other could not give up her dependence. She would not be a *"slave to love,"* she said, but still wrote to her lover begging him not to leave her, promising humility.

Aphra's dilemma proceeded precisely from her radical attempt to be free; for new roles do not replace old ones in a single moment of realization, or even over centuries. The struggle for freedom is not linear but dialectic; the price of change is doubleness, and out of the contradiction emerges a new self. In this sense Aphra's life is as much the biography of our own times as it is the history of her age. From our three hundred years' difference, we see ourselves in the tattered fabric of her life. Across the shock of centuries, her autobiography is ours. Her weakness, her desperate need for approval, are ours too. Her need for independence, equally strong now. Her aloneness that prevailed, though she surrounded herself with all Grub Street, we also understand. Her conflict, her uncertainties, her anger, her pain, her doubts, her feminism, her double bind.

CHAPTER TWO

"Birth"

Aphra Behn, in the history of English letters, is something more than a mere harlot. The fact that she wrote is much more important than the quality of what she wrote. The importance of Aphra Behn is that she was the first woman in England to earn her living by her pen.

—Vita Sackville-West, 1927

Intellectually, Mrs. Behn was qualified to lead the playwrights of her day through pure and bright ways; but she was a mere harlot, who danced through uncleanness, and dared them to follow. Remonstrance was useless with this wanton hussy.

—Dr. Doran, 1888

Mrs. Behn allow'd herself of writing loosely and giving some scandal to the modesty of her sex.

—John Dryden, c. 1690

I

Ordinarily, the biography of a famous writer begins with the tracing of genealogies:

A writer's literary genealogy establishes what tradition he has grown out of, either as inheritor or rebel; what predecessors have influenced his work; what his place in history is; what "school" he belongs to.

His family genealogy discovers what physical, psychological, and cultural inheritance the writer has begun life with: what family resemblances, what knowledge or profession, fortune or title have passed on from father to son. He may have from his father a fluent pen, an eye for color or form, a logical acuity, a passion for the Greeks . . . or perhaps none of these. Perhaps only a dogmatic and stubborn ignorance that, by indirection, sharpens all the more the young man's hunger for a life of the mind.

It is from these beginnings, out of these chronologies, that biographers establish the identity of the writer who, before he was a famous man of letters, was also a young man, a child, an idea in the back of his father's mind, who of course assumed he would have a son to carry on the family name. . . .

Aphra Behn's beginnings, however, present a considerable obstacle to her biographer. Her literary genealogy starts with herself: for as the first woman to enter literature as a writer, rather than as a lady who occasionally scribbled verses, she had no predecessors or examples to follow. If she emerges from any tradition at all, it is one of anonymity and silences, apologies and equivocations.

She is not, finally, a famous writer. In fact, she is almost unknown. Outside of a few literary specialists in the Restoration and, more recently, feminist scholars and writers beginning to uncover history's "lost women," few people have heard of her at all, though in her own time she was as well known as Dryden or Wycherley.[1] For nearly two hundred years after her death, she disappeared almost entirely from the pages of biography, of literature, of history itself; by the time her works were reprinted in the nineteenth century, they had long been unobtainable, and the almost unanimous response of the reviewers and critics was that they should remain so.[2]

The search for Aphra's "identity," then, must begin with the recognition of the paradox that the first woman to forcibly emerge from anonymity by claiming an identity as a writer has been rendered anonymous by history. For while Aphra's biography lay buried all those years under the weight of history's dismissal and then forgetfulness, the facts of her birth, parentage, and ancestry gradually grew into a tangled fiction. When the buried biography was finally unearthed by scholars at the end of the nineteenth century, it was firmly embedded in a mass of contradictory claims. Every new attempt on

Aphra's life, it seemed, only succeeded in further obscuring her identity.

Aphra herself spoke of her father, mother, sisters, and brother in her autobiographical novel *Oroonoko,* but gave little specific information about them, except to say that her father had been appointed Lieutenant General of Surinam, a British colony on the coast of South America. Her first biographer, in a brief "History of the Life and Memoirs of Mrs. Behn," published shortly after Aphra died, confirmed her autobiographical statements and added that she was a "gentlewoman by birth, of a good family in the city of Canterbury in Kent." Her name was Johnson, and her father's "relation to Lord Willoughby drew him, for the advantageous post of Lieutenant General of Surinam, from his quiet retreat at Canterbury, to run the hazardous voyage of the West-Indies." [3]

The author of Aphra's biography was a woman, a contemporary who claimed to have known her intimately but chose to remain anonymous herself, revealing only that she was "One of the Fair Sex." She justified the withholding of her name by asserting that she could thus more daringly defend Aphra's: "This I may venture to say because I'm unknown, and the revengeful censures of my sex will not reach me, since they will never be able to draw the veil, and discover the speaker of these bold truths." One of the Fair Sex was, however, of two minds about how to defend Aphra's reputation. First, she claimed that the scandal surrounding Aphra's name was unwarranted: "I knew her intimately, and never saw aught unbecoming the just modesty of our sex." But then she admitted that Aphra was, after all, "a little more gay and free than the folly of the precise will allow." Finally, she returned to Aphra's defense with the argument that if Aphra wasn't "modest," she was at least honest and deserved to be remembered for her achievement: "She was, I'm satisfied, a greater honour to our sex, than all the canting tribe of dissemblers, that die with the false reputation of saints." [4]

Since One of the Fair Sex was Aphra's first and last biographer for more than two hundred years, there was no one to question her version of the story or to add new material until the end of the nineteenth century, when Sir Edmund Gosse happened on an unexpected reference to Mrs. Behn. Perusing a recently discovered manuscript of

Anne Finch, the Countess of Winchelsea (another "lost" woman poet who was a younger contemporary of Aphra's), he came across these lines:

> And standing where sadly we might decry
> From the banks of the Stour the desolate Wye
> He lamented for Behn, o'er that place of her birth,
> And said amongst women there was none on earth
> Her superior in fancy, in language, or wit,
> Yet owned that a little too loosely she writ.[5]

In the margin of the manuscript, Mr. Gosse noticed a hastily scribbled note: "Mrs. Behn was daughter to a barber, who lived formerly in Wye, a little market town in Kent. Though the account of her life before her works pretends otherwise, some persons now alive do testify upon their knowledge that to be her original." Edmund Gosse did not merely take the Countess at her word, but sent a letter to the parish priest at Wye asking him to verify the information. The vicar, copying the appropriate entry in the parish register, corroborated her statement: "On July 1640, were baptised at Wye, Ayfara the daughter and Peter the son of John and Amy Johnson." The profession column, said the vicar, had "barber" recorded in it. Satisfied with the new "facts," Gosse published his discovery of Mrs. Behn's "identity," commenting that Aphra was guilty of the "pardonable vanity" of pretending that she was born at Canterbury in order to conceal the fact that she was a barber's daughter.[6]

This discovery was challenged a few years later by a Restoration scholar who checked the very same parish register again and found that the Aphra in question was the daughter of *John and Amy Amis,* not *Johnson.* Oddly enough, there was no profession column at all where "barber" might have been recorded.

The matter was further complicated by the publication in 1913 of an article by Ernest Bernbaum entitled "Mrs. Behn's Biography, a Fiction." Mr. Bernbaum contended in this essay that One of the Fair Sex was not indeed one of the fair sex; that Aphra never went to Surinam at all, but copied her description of the colony from a contemporary account; that no Mr. Behn had ever existed; and that Aphra never warned the King of the Dutch attack on the English fleet when she was a spy.[7]

This was not the first time such an attack had been leveled at Aphra. In her own lifetime there were constant rumors that she had not written her own works; that the true author of the plays that appeared under her name was a man, an "ingenious gentleman" who was her lover. One of Bernbaum's reasons for disbelieving Aphra and her friend One of the Fair Sex is his conviction that the anonymous biographer was really Charles Gildon, who remarked in the preface to a play of Aphra's published after her death that "to draw Mrs. Behn to the life one must write like her, that is, with all the softness of her sex and all the fire of ours."[8] It is not impossible that Gildon disguised himself as One of the Fair Sex, but as there is no external evidence or indication in the first biography that he wrote it, there seems no reason to believe that he did. It seems more logical to believe that it was precisely *because* she was a member of the fair sex that Aphra's biographer chose to "veil" her identity. She would have been, after all, only acting as countless other women had before her who chose to protect their "modesty" with anonymity.

In any case, why did Bernbaum want to discredit Aphra? Why insist that her first biographer was a man and not a woman? Why dismantle her history? The evidence he gave for doubting her word was primarily speculative—he had discovered no new "facts" that established an alternative version of her story. "Mrs. Behn's Biography, a Fiction," it seems, was based more on an unwillingness to believe that a woman of Aphra's time could have lived the life she did than on any compelling evidence to the contrary.

The final chapter was added by an Englishman named A. Purvis, who had the idea of consulting the Wye burial register.[9] Written in the same clear hand as Aphra's entry in the birth register was:

	1640	
Afara ye daughter	July ye 12th	
		of John Amis.
Peter ye son	July ye 16th	

Here was incontrovertible evidence that Aphra Behn died soon after she was born. Mr. Bernbaum need not have gone to the trouble to prove that she could not have done all the things she claimed to have done. Conveniently, she never existed. Her de-biographers had finally returned her to the silence thought proper for a woman of her time.

II

How, then, to restore Aphra's "birth"? Finding a name in a parish register without any corroborating evidence is likely to be misleading. The version of Aphra's birth and parentage retailed by One of the Fair Sex and by Aphra herself is disputed by the Countess of Winchelsea. There is, moreover, yet another contemporary account which seems to support both sides. Colonel Thomas Culpepper, a well-known eccentric, noted in his manuscript "Adversaria" that "Mrs. Aphra Bhen [sic] was born at Canterbury or Sturry [and] her name was Johnson. She was foster sister to the Colonel [i.e., Culpepper himself], her mother being the Colonel's nurse."[10] Culpepper substantiates One of the Fair Sex's claim that Aphra's maiden name was Johnson, but implies, with the Countess of Winchelsea, that Aphra was not born a gentlewoman. The three accounts do not greatly differ on Aphra's birthplace: Wye and Sturry are very near Canterbury, Kent, and whatever the exact place, it may be safely said that she was born somewhere in the neighborhood of that city. Culpepper's information also helps to establish approximately the date of Aphra's birth. He was born in December 1637 and had a sister born in 1640. As a "foster sister," Aphra might have been nursed at the same time as either, but the later date seems more likely, given the subsequent chronology of Aphra's life.

The question of what class Aphra Johnson (?) belonged to is much more difficult to resolve. There is one fact that argues definitively against Aphra's having grown up the daughter of a barber or a wet nurse: her education. If she had been a boy, she might, like Shakespeare or Ben Jonson, have been educated to the level of the aristocracy at one of the very good public schools; but there was no way that a lower-class girl could receive the kind of education Aphra manifestly had. It was available to women only among the gentry or nobility. A girl of the lower classes probably would not even have had access to books.

Another piece of evidence not to be ignored is that Aphra, her mother, and sisters were called "ladies" by the steward of the plantation they stayed on in Surinam in a letter he wrote to his employer. Several details of Aphra's autobiographical account of her stay in that country seem to confirm that she was indeed a "lady"—her dress, her residence, her servants, and other casually mentioned particulars. Furthermore, she seems to have been introduced into court circles through some family connection: Sir Thomas Killigrew, Groom of the Bedchamber to Charles II, apparently knew her mother well.

Aphra's connection to the Willoughby family forms an insistent theme. One of the Fair Sex claimed that Aphra's father was appointed Lieutenant General of Surinam because he was related to Lord Willoughby, who was both founder and Governor of that colony. Her contention seems supported by the fact that, when it became known that Aphra and her family were staying at St. John's Hill (in Surinam), local rumor assumed that the plantation had been sold to Lord Willoughby. There was another association, however, that connected Aphra with the Willoughby family in a most unlikely way: a few years before Aphra went to Surinam, Lady Willoughby informed on Lord Willoughby to Thomas Scot, who was then in charge of intelligence operations under the Commonwealth. Thomas Scot was the father of William, who was Aphra's lover in Surinam and later her spying partner in Antwerp. Another odd coincidence was that Lady Willoughby's daughter Diana, who had married the Earl of Winchelsea, lived a few miles outside Wye, Kent, during the years Aphra was growing up. Thomas Culpepper, Aphra's "foster brother," lived on the same estate at the same time, with his guardian, who was the Earl of Winchelsea's steward.

Between all the connections there seems to be a strangely missing link. One clue might explain the discrepancy between the humble origins ascribed to Aphra and her "gentle" upbringing and connections: a nineteenth-century history of Surinam notes that Lord Willoughby deputed a relation of his named Johnson as Lieutenant General of that colony and that this Johnson "took with him his wife and children, and in that number, an adopted daughter Aphra."[11] There is one strong objection, though, to the theory that Aphra, though lowly born, had been adopted into a gentle family: such things almost never happened in the seventeenth century. Even if a child had been taken in for some reason or another, it would probably have been in some menial capacity. For her to be educated with the other children of the household would be almost inconceivable. A possible exception to this rule of class might have been an illegitimate child passed off as a relative of some sort. The fact that Aphra's mother was said to have been a wet nurse makes this possibility even more likely, as illegitimate children were often deposited with nurses who were instructed to claim them as their own. Lord Willoughby resided for long periods in the West Indies at just about the time Aphra was born: is it possible that she could have been the "natural" daughter of his Lady? If this were true, it would illuminate still another mysterious aspect of Aphra's upbringing: she mentioned, much later in life, that she had once been "designed a nun." Lady Willoughby, as Thomas Scot tells us, was also a Catholic, a religion which generations of persecution had made relatively rare in England then.

The suggestion that Aphra may have been illegitimate can be no more than speculation, but it is the only theory that explains the seeming contradiction of Aphra's birth. Of course the nature of the claim itself dictates that proof cannot be found. Outside of the discovery of some more candid (and verifiable) account than any we now have, it is not likely that at this distance the truth about Aphra will come out.

III

The story of Mrs. Behn's missing "birth" might well belong to the biography of a male writer of the seventeenth century; it hardly seems fair to blame the loss of her "facts" on the tradition of anonymity that covered her sex. The loss of her historical identity, however, is another matter: from the very beginning, the way critics and historians talked about Aphra suggested that it was precisely because she was a woman and a writer and the first to venture into what was seen as male preserve that she was for so long dismissed and ignored. A literary fantasy published in the popular *Gentleman's Magazine* fifty years after her death indicates the intensity of resentment and resistance that could still be evoked by a lady who, already two generations before, had forced herself into the ranks of male writers. In the fantasy, there is a convocation of writers buried in the Poets' Corner of Westminster Abbey, the purpose of which is to admit Milton into the society of Great Writers. Aphra Behn attempts to join the group and is repulsed. The narrator comments: "Observe that lady dressed in the loose robe de chambre with her neck and breasts bare . . . what an indignant look she bestows on the President [Chaucer] who is telling her that none of her sex has a right to a seat there. How she throws her eyes about, to see if she can find out any of the assembly who inclines to take her part. No! No one stirs . . . she flings out of the assembly."[12]

The very act of publishing her writing would have been sufficient to destroy a lady's reputation in the seventeenth century; exposing oneself in print was a violation of feminine propriety. But Aphra offended the modesty of her sex still further by writing as her fellow playwrights did—bawdy. She obviously enjoyed it, but in any case she admitted that in order to succeed she had to write "to the taste of the age." Unfortunately, in the century that followed, the principle that what was not decent ought not to be read came to dominate. And Aphra, who had written about sex with the same openness as her male contemporaries, was seen as infinitely more indecent, immoral, immodest, and unreadable because a woman.

When she finally was republished at the end of the nineteenth century, it was in a prohibitively expensive edition of only five hundred copies. The critics' response to the reappearance of a lady writer whom they had properly forgotten was not encouraging. "Mrs. Behn is still to be found here and there in the dusty, worm-eaten libraries of old country houses," wrote the reviewer from *The Saturday Review*, "but, as a rule, we imagine, she has been ejected from all *decent* society for more than a generation or two. If Mrs. Behn is read at all, it can only be from a love of impurity for its own sake, for rank indecency . . . even in her own day, Mrs. Behn's works had a scandalous reputation . . . it is true that this did not prevent her from attaining honourable burial in Westminster Abbey, but it is a pity her books did not rot with her bones. That they should now be disinterred from the obscurity into which they have happily fallen is surely inexcusable."[13]

Despite the recommendation of the critic from *The Saturday Review*, Aphra's name did finally begin to appear in print more often. Mrs. Behn was "rediscovered" by several different literary historians, but hardly in eulogistic terms: not one of them fails to mention her unwomanliness. A *Dictionary of English Literature* compiled near the end of the nineteenth century emphasized that "the licentiousness of Mrs. Behn's pen is a disgrace to her sex and to the language."[14] Dr. Doran, the dramatic scholar, was hardly more generous: "She might have been an honour to womanhood—she was its disgrace. She might have gained glory by her labours—but she chose to reap infamy. Her pleasures were not those which became an honest woman."[15]

Even Miss Julia Kavanaugh, in her *English Women of Letters,* felt compelled to take the obligatory moral stance toward her sister of letters: "The inveterate coarseness of her mind sullied Aphra Behn's noblest gifts; beauty, sincerity, wit, an eloquent tongue and a ready pen, perished in the wreck of all that is delicate and refined in woman." Perhaps Miss Kavanaugh felt that as a writer who might run the risk of being identified with Mrs. Behn for no other reason than her sex she had to express disapproval of Aphra's "unfemininity." At the same time, though, she could not resist admiring her courage and independence and recognizing the fact that Aphra's "indecency" was not unconnected to the fact that she was a woman. She admitted, almost unwillingly, "Aphra Behn wrote dramas, which, though no worse than those of her contemporaries, revolted the public as proceeding from a woman, yet, braving censure and reproof, with an independence worthy a better cause, she persisted in her course."[16]

It was not until the beginning of the twentieth century that any work of Aphra's came reasonably within the reach of a curious reader who might have come across her name and wished to read something she had written. In 1905, Ernest Baker published some of Mrs. Behn's novels under the imprint of a collection called "Half-Forgotten Books." Ironically, most of the titles in this collection were by women. Mr. Baker's preface to Aphra's novels explained that since the relaxing of moral strictures had made Mrs. Behn's work "less offensive to modern taste," it could now be reprinted without creating great scandal. Baker can hardly be described as a champion of Aphra's reputation, however. This was his introduction to her work: "To most people nowadays the name of Aphra Behn conveys nothing more than vague associations of license and impropriety. She is dimly remembered as the author of plays and novels, now unread, that embodied the immorality of Restoration times, and were all the more scandalous in that they were written by a woman. Her works are to be found in few libraries, and are rarely to be met with at the booksellers'. Although they were republished in an expensive form and in a limited edition in 1871, they have now been many years out of print . . . nor is this much to be regretted."[17]

As the history of Aphra's posthumous demise illustrates, the loss of her "identity" is very much tied to the sexual politics implicit in the repeated assertions that she ought not to be read or even published; over and over, the connection between her femaleness and her "indecency" was drawn. To suggest that she was deliberately and systematically lost by history is to oversimplify: it was not merely the *Dictionary of English Literature,* Dr. Doran, the critic from *The Saturday Review,* or Julia Kavanaugh who were responsible for Aphra's disappearance, but a whole climate of social opinion, convention, and myth which operated on women as a class for centuries. This tradition of anonymity made the privilege of individual identity almost an exclusively male prerogative.

The text of Aphra Behn's life, then, cannot be understood outside the context of her feminine status: her biographer must reconstruct the collective experience in order to distinguish Aphra as an individual. This reconstruction forces us into a new kind of biography—an archaeology of the passed over, the stillborn. For if Aphra's genealogy is to begin in the lives of her foremothers, it is among the shadowy figures of the unremembered women. From the shards that remain of women's lives, from letters, from sermons, from etiquette books and anecdotes, we gradually piece together what it must have been like for Aphra to be a woman in the seventeenth century.

CHAPTER THREE

Childhood: The World Turned Upside Down

The old world . . . is running up like parchment in the fire.
—Gerrard Winstanley, 1647

Oh, these are the men that would turn the world upside down, that make the nation full of tumults and uproars, that work all the disturbance in church and state.
—William Dell, 1646

I

Aphra. Saint Aphra.

The name has been obscured with its owner: strange, unused, now unremembered. It must have had a foreign sound even to a seventeenth-century ear. The original Aphra was a martyr, the patron saint of female penitents. She had been a sacred prostitute in the temple of Venus in Augsburg on the Rhine in the third century A.D., until converted to Christianity by Saint Narcissus. One legend says she was beheaded for her conversion, another that she was burned on a fire of vine leaves. How the girl child born at Wye or Canterbury or Sturry sometime around 1640 came by "Aphra" will remain undiscovered and undiscoverable, but her superstitious century might have held, for no other reason than her name, that she was beginning life at a prophetic disadvantage.

Aphra's immediate world, the universe that was about to take up her education, was Kent: everywhere stretching into the distance were gentle hills green in winter and summer; grazing sheep; the pleasant sound of scythes cutting long grass, and the smell of it. Kent in the seventeenth century was little different from Kent of the preceding centuries. Most of its parish churches had stood in the same spot for at least a few hundred years and, except for changing fashion in architecture, the little towns in the vicinity of Canterbury had remained the same for as long as anyone—or anyone's grandfather—could remember. The same families inhabited the same timbered houses for generations; it was rare for anyone to marry outside the county. The principal clans intermarried and then intermarried further until almost all the Kentish gentry were in one way or another related.

Despite its proximity to London, Kent had remained for centuries principally a rural county. Its rich soil made it ideal for agriculture, and its essentially conservative population resisted the expansion that trade and industry would bring. William Lambarde, in *The Perambulation of Kent,* written in 1656, described its largely unspoiled landscape: "Wood occupies the greatest proportion even 'till this day. In fertile and fruitful woods and trees, this country is most flourishing . . . whether you respect the most of oak, beech and chestnut for cattle, or the fruit of apples, pears, cherries and plums for men." [1]

Aphra's spirit of adventure that was later to lead her to visit an Indian tribe in Surinam who had never before seen Europeans may have longed for wider horizons than stable, unchanging Kent, but there must have been something reassuring too about the continuity of life there. Aphra may have remembered her rural childhood with affection; later she would put forth a theory that it was only in a pure state of nature that man's essential goodness could be expressed. Perhaps a part of her conviction grew out of an image of youthful innocence in timeless green groves and pastures, removed from the "business" of the world.

II

. . . these distempered times . . .

If Kent's invariable landscape remained firmly rooted in the past, the world outside, of London, of Parliament and the King, of Cavaliers and Puritans, traditionalists and dissenters, was a place in which there were no longer any givens, in which nothing could be counted upon.

In the first ten years of Aphra's life, the world as her father had known it turned upside down: between 1640 and 1650, England underwent the first revolution in its history, fought a civil war, and beheaded a king. What had been unthinkable suddenly became possible. Ideas, rights, and privileges held for as long as the country had existed as a state came under attack. The relationships of King to subject, governed to government, church to individual, master to servant, parent to child were uprooted and transformed. The Puritan's rejection of the authority of King and Church opened the way for this questioning of the very structure of society, though a great many of the godly fathers who fought for and set up the Commonwealth were horrified at the logical extensions of their doctrine being drawn by the more radical wing of the party. The principle of individual conscience gave birth to innumerable dissenting groups within the Puritan movement, and ideas like the priesthood of all believers became the basis for radical democratic ideals. Religious sects like the Diggers and Levelers, Ranters, Seekers, and Quakers proposed revolutionary concepts of liberty. Gerrard Winstanley professed that the earth belonged to all men and none had the right to deny another free use of it. The Ranters proclaimed that sin and hell did not exist. Women preached; some of them even prophesied.

Kent came under the control of Parliament at the very beginning of the Civil War. Strategically, it was important. It was close to London, which was also in the hands of the rebel forces, and lay across the main routes to the Continent. In August 1642, even before the war was officially declared, a Colonel Sandys was dispatched with a troop of soldiers to quell any possible resistance. His band went through the countryside seizing arms, ammunition, money, plundering the houses of known Royalists. Aphra's adopted "family" may well have been among them. Suspected supporters of the King, if they had not already left for the army or fled into exile, were arrested and imprisoned. Dover Castle, Rochester Castle, and other strongholds were captured and fortified against attack. Parliamentary troops broke into the "idolatrous" Canterbury Cathedral, destroyed the organ, ripped up the Communion rails, sawed the image of Christ out of the altar cloth, and smashed as many stained-glass windows as they could. Traffic on all the roads was strictly controlled: travelers, or even ordinary citizens walking to the market in the next town, might be stopped and harassed or questioned by soldiers. A great many had their horses confiscated for the cavalry. A gentleman who lived not far from Wye complained that his letters to his sweetheart were being seized and censored. Royalist or Puritan, no one remained unaffected by the upheaval. Aphra was no doubt too young to remember when the world turned upside down in the summer of 1642, but the feeling of displacement must have been communicated to her.

It cannot be said for certain under whose care or protection Aphra lived during those years, nor can it be said with certainty what their political sympathies were. By the mid-1650s, Aphra would have been old enough to hold some idea of party, but she may well have found herself caught in a net of conflicting loyalties. One of the events that ultimately led to the restoration of the King brought together a confusing concatenation of Aphra's friends, relations, and later connections—both Royalist and republican. In the spring of 1659, the exiled King was at Breda, in Holland, attempting to organize a Royalist rebellion to further his return to England. One of his principal advisers was Lord Willoughby. A series of simultaneous uprisings in strategic counties was planned, and Lord Willoughby was appointed to lead the Royalists in Kent. Among the Cavaliers whose aid he enlisted in this project was Colonel Thomas Culpepper, Aphra's "foster brother," who was to raise a cavalry troop in Canterbury.

On July 9, Willoughby, Culpepper, and a number of other Royalist conspirators met in London and decided that the uprising would take place on August 1. Thomas Scot, who was in charge of intelligence for the Parliamentarian Committee of Safety, seems to have received very detailed information about this meeting, which allowed the republicans to prepare for and ultimately quell the rebellion. The source of this information, Scot later confessed, was Lady Willoughby: "She spoke very particularly with respect to the intended day of rising, and mentioned a meeting that the King's party had near Gray's Inn."[2] As a result of her betrayal, several Royalists were arrested, but there is no evidence that any of them ever suspected Lady Willoughby until after the Restoration, which she did not long survive. She died in 1661. Thomas Scot was executed as a regicide at about the same time, and his son William fled to Surinam and then to Holland, where he would later be Aphra Behn's partner in spying.

III

The events that convulsed the England of Aphra's childhood affected her life in a material, everyday sense, but they also acted indirectly to shape her vision of the world, of what was possible and not possible, of herself in relation to that world. She was being educated in the signs, the figures, the images, of her time.

Whether she was brought up Royalist or Puritan, the very fact that she was born on the eve of an age of unprecedented political and social revolution was important to Aphra's learning her part in the world. It was, in a sense, the very disordering of her world and the disruption of the established order that formed her sense of what might be attempted. It was no doubt through these cracks and reversals that a young girl of imagination was able to invent a future for herself inimical to that which her society might have determined for her in the past. Moreover, certain characteristics of Puritanism itself might well have proven useful to Aphra. She was growing up in a society controlled by men committed to a strong individualism and to a revolutionary vision of an ideal world, qualities which, though she used them to another purpose, were indispensable to the stand she was later to make against convention. The very suggestion that an individual might choose to live *otherwise* must have been important to her radical departure from the identity that a woman of her time might be expected to live out.

To describe Aphra's character and future imagination as influenced by the spirit, if not the text, of Puritanism is not, of course, to distinguish her from other women of her time. But it is essential to an understanding of what made it possible for her to break with history and a tradition that had confined the lives of her foremothers to the domestic circle. What, after all, was the special conjunction of opportunity and character that allowed Aphra to prevail where others before her, with equal gifts and equal courage, had demurred?

To understand, we must first examine the nature of the feminine education that she violated.

CHAPTER FOUR

Educations: Woman's Sphere

> *Women are from their very infancy debarred those advantages (of education) with the want of which they are afterwards reproached, and nursed up in those vices with which will hereafter be upbraided them. So partial are men as to expect bricks when they afford no straw.*
>
> —Mary Astell,
> *A Serious Proposal to the Ladies for the*
> *Advancement of their True and Greatest Interest,*
> 1694

> *That sex, which heretofore was not allowed,*
> *To understand more than a beast, or crowd;*
> *Of which problems were made, whether or no*
> *Women had souls, but to be damned, if so;*
> *Whose highest contemplation could not pass,*
> *In mens esteem, no higher than the glass;*
> *And all the painful labours of their brain,*
> *Was only how to dress and entertain:*
> *Or, if they ventured to speak sense, the wise*
> *Made that, and speaking ox, like prodigies.*

> —Anonymous (female)
> "To the Excellent Orinda," 1669

I

How to describe Aphra's education?

The names of most of her literary colleagues may be found in records like the *Alumni Cantabrigensis* or the rolls of the Middle Temple. The nature of the classical instruction a young man enrolled in these institutions benefited from is well documented, and we could list with some accuracy what he learned or failed to learn, depending on his application to studies. Aphra's sex, however, complicates the question of her literary training, for one of the principal objects of women's education in the seventeenth century was the assimilation of the idea that what was then considered "learning" was utterly out of women's sphere.

During the Elizabethan era, feminine education had enjoyed a brief renaissance in which women were both respected and admired for intellectual accomplishment; but by the time Aphra Behn came of age, a reaction had set in and the standard of instruction for her sex was far inferior to that of young men. A feminist tract written by an anonymous woman in 1640 gives a depressing picture of contemporary practice: "When a father has a numerous issue of sons and daughters, the sons must be first put to the Grammar School, and after perchance sent to the University and trained up in the liberal arts and sciences, and there (if they prove not blockheads) they may in time be book-learned. . . . [But we daughters] are set only to the needle to prick our fingers; or else to the wheel to spin a fair thread for our own undoings, or perchance to some dirty and debased drudgery. If we be taught to read, they then confine us within the compass of the mother tongue, and that limit we are not suffered to pass. . . . If we be weak by nature, they strive to make us more weak by our nurture. And if in degree of place low, they strive by their policy to keep us more under."[1] It is possible that the author of *The Women's Sharpe Revenge* is exaggerating the dismal state of women's education to further her purpose—which may be inferred from the title of her tract—but countless contemporary references, both published and unpublished, indicate that her account is for the most part accurate. Lady Damaris Masham, a friend of the philosopher Locke, daughter of a Cambridge professor, alludes to frequent conversations among her lady friends in which "they expressed much displeasure at the too general neglect of the instruction of their sex."[2]

What instruction was thought proper for a young woman of Aphra Behn's generation might be administered in three different ways: she could be taught at home by tutors; she could be sent to a girls' boarding school; or, if her family was poor, she might learn her ABCs from the parish priest, were he so inclined. Of course among the lower classes, it was more often the case that both girls and boys were needed for work to help support the family by the age of seven or earlier. There is evidence that in rare instances girls may have been permitted to attend Grammar School (where the pupils learned Latin), but only for a few early years. But according to the anonymous feminine author of the *Essay in Defense of the Female Sex* (1696), the usual circumstance was that "after children can talk, they are promiscuously taught to read and write by the same persons, and at the same time. When these are acquitted, which is generally about the age of six or seven years, they begin to be separated, and the boys sent to Grammar School, and the girls to boarding schools, or other places, to learn needlework, dancing, singing, music, drawing, painting, and other accomplishments. . . . Here then, lies the main defect, that we are taught only our mother tongue, or perhaps French."[3]

John Lyon, when he founded Harrow in the seventeenth century, specifically stated in that eminent school's charter that girls were not to be admitted under any circumstances.[4] Clearly no daughters ever made their way into the traditionally masculine domain of the university—there could be no question of admittance to Oxford or Cambridge. When the poet Abraham Cowley, whom Aphra Behn greatly admired, proposed the creation of a new college for the study of philosophy, the only females mentioned in his prospectus were "four old women to tend the chambers and such like services." These poor souls were to be paid the least of any of the other (male) servants and scholars: "To the four necessary women," Cowley specified in the projected budget, "ten pounds."[5] The ten pounds per annum were to be divided *among* them. This despite the fact that Abraham Cowley frequented the literary circle of the poet Katherine Philips and had expressed great admiration for her intellectual and poetic gifts. But even if it had occurred to an enlightened man of the seventeenth century to suggest that women students be included in such a college, all the available evidence indicates that the social opposition would have been overwhelming.

Girls themselves, for the most part, were far from imagining such possibilities. Among the model letters Hannah Woolley printed in her manual for letter writing of the day was a plaintive missive from a young lady to her brother at Oxford asking for more frequent communications from him, but adding, "I fear that your studies will not admit you such idle time as to think of me long, your genius being wholly employed to hear the sage philosophers and Muses, which I do imagine cannot choose but be very delightful." [6] Probably Hannah Woolley's "model" young lady had been left behind to the boredom and isolation of a country estate while her brother not only expanded his mental horizons, but was meeting the next generation of scholars, poets, politicians, and courtiers who would make England's future. His sister's sense of her own importance—or, more properly, lack of it—did not allow her to question the status quo, but only to envy the sex that benefited from it. [7]

The educational establishments that *were* designed for young gentlewomen of Aphra Behn's time laid emphasis on practical rather than intellectual achievement. As the future occupation of the great majority of their scholars was to be marriage, the schools prepared them accordingly. They usually learned reading and writing: reading, because a pious education required being able to read the Bible; writing, because it was necessary often to communicate with absent husbands regarding domestic affairs. Sometimes the girls were instructed in accounting, which was important to the complex operation of a seventeenth-century household; and customarily they also had lessons in singing, dancing, playing the flute, French and "curious work"— all the social graces needed first to catch a husband and later to ornament his ancestral quarters. The "curious work" so often mentioned in the curricula of girls' schools comprised all sorts of needlework, shell-work, moss-work, "transparent works," all manner of pretty toys, rocks made with shells, frames for mirrors, and other "household-arts" designed to occupy the idle hours of a gentlewoman. [8]

Of all the "female academies" that we have any description of, only Mrs. Bathusa Makin's school seems to have attempted a more serious academic program. Mrs. Makin expressed disdain for the standard schools of the day: they existed, she said, "merely to teach gentlewomen to frisk and dance, to paint their faces, to curl their hair, to put on a whisk, to wear gay clothes." [9] The young ladies who attended her school on Tottenham High Road in London studied grammar and rhetoric, logic, languages—especially Greek and Hebrew, "as these will enable the better understanding of the Scriptures"—as well as mathematics, geography, music, painting, and poetry, among other subjects.

There were at least three boarding schools for girls in the neighborhood of Kent when Aphra Behn was growing up. One was at Westerham; another at Ashford, next to Wye, kept by a Mr. Beven; and a third, kept by Margaret Jackson, in Canterbury, not far from the Cathedral. In 1652, a young girl of about Aphra's age, Kitty Oxinden, was sent to Mrs. Jackson's school to learn her letters. The school mistress reported to her father after a few months that it would take a while for his daughter to master her own "character" (i.e., handwriting), but soon enough she would be writing herself to report on her own progress: "I hope her owne lines will speake her: your dutifull daughter;" promised Mrs. Jackson, "in the meantime: she humbly presents her promise of obedience: to yourselfe and her mother."[10] Mrs. Jackson's spelling and erratic punctuation would hardly seem to recommend her as a pedagogue for Miss Kitty, but Mr. Oxinden was apparently well satisfied when some time later he received a brief communication from the pupil herself signed "your most dutifull and obedient daughter." Mrs. Jackson had been true to her word: Katherine's character was well on its way to being educated in the proper manner.

Duty and meek behavior also figured large in the curriculum of Mr. Beven's school for girls in Ashford. Lady Unton Dering wrote to Mr. Oxinden highly commending the education her daughter had received there and suggesting that he send his daughters also: "Besides the qualities of musick, both for virginals and singing, writing, and to cast account which will be useful to them hereafter, Mr. Beven will be careful also that their behavior be modest and such as becomes their quality [i.e., class]."[11] How much more appropriate it would have been for an aspiring poet—One of the Fair Sex tells us that Aphra began writing verses at a very early age—to have gone to the boys' Grammar School at Wye. The headmaster, Henry Bradshaw, wrote to the parent of one of his new pupils that the first lesson he would learn would be the composition of poetry, and then the correct pronunciation of Latin. The literary training that would have been useful for Aphra went unappreciated by its actual recipient, however, for the young man in question was so dull that later his wife, who had been to Mr. Beven's school, was obliged to do all the letter writing for the family.

Most of the girls who stayed home and were taught by tutors fared little better than their contemporaries at the female academies. There are records of a few, like Susannah Evelyn or the girls of Little Gidding, who had the benefit of enlightened parents, but there are many more testimonies to the frustration a young girl of exceptional gifts might suffer from the censorship parents felt it their duty to exercise. In 1652, Sir Ralph Verney, hearing of his goddaughter's desire to study Latin, Greek, and Hebrew, confessed, "I did not think you had been guilty of so much learning as I see you are," and urged her to give up such unfeminine ambitions and confine her studies to a Bible in her mother tongue. "Be confident your husband will be of the same opinion," he added.[12]

Lady Anne Clifford was fortunate enough to have the poet Samuel Daniel for her tutor, but her father, the Earl of Cumberland, was careful to warn him that she should under no circumstances be taught Latin. Lady Mary Wortley Montagu, under the same parental restriction, was forced to buy Latin books secretly and hide them in her closet. Lucy Hutchinson had a Puritan father who gave her studies unusual encouragement—particularly her Biblical scholarship; yet when she really began to conceive intellectual aspirations, she was physically prevented from pursuing them. "My genius was quite averse to all but my book," she wrote, "[so that] my mother, thinking it prejudiced my health, would moderate me in it; yet this rather animated me than kept me back, and every moment I could steal from my play I would employ in any book I could find, when my own were locked up from me."[13] The real fear, of course, behind her mother's severity was that her daughter would make herself a social outcast. A learned woman in that day was at best a figure of ridicule and derision and at worst regarded as only slightly less dangerous than one practiced in the Black Arts. "A learned women," asserted Bathusa Makin, "is thought to be a comet that bodes mischief whenever it appears."[14]

Lucy Hutchinson had the good fortune to happen on a man who married her precisely because he adored her intellectual curiosity, but she herself acknowledged this was extremely rare. Parents, complained Lady Masham, were not eager to educate their daughters, "from an apprehension that, should they be perceived to understand any learned language, or be conversant in books, they might be in danger of not finding husbands: so few men . . . relishing these accomplishments in a lady."[15]

The practical result of this social prejudice was that ladies even highly born could not write a sentence without the most atrocious errors in usage and spelling. The correspondence of the period stands as a testament to the systematic neglect of the education of women. There are no quantitative figures available to measure the level of female literacy in the seventeenth century, but when Lord Hardwicke's Marriage Act was passed in 1753, only one in three women could even sign her name to the marriage register. It seems unlikely that matters were much better a hundred years earlier.

II

Good breeding, fashion, dancing, dressing, play
Are the accomplishments we should desire;
To write, to read, or think, or to enquire
Would cloud our beauty, and exhaust our time,
And interrupt the conquests of our prime;
Whilst the dull manage, of a servile house,
Is held by some, our utmost art, and use.
　　　　　　　　—Anne Finch, Countess of Winchelsea, ca. 1690

Aphra Behn seems to have received, more or less, a conventional gentlewoman's instruction: she played on the flute, she says, spoke French, and was *"mistress of all sorts of pretty works."* Her reading, however, was not only confined to the fashionable romances that were standard feminine fare; unlike most young women of her day, Aphra also evidently attempted a much more general range of history, philosophy, and literature. There are numerous references to Greek and Roman mythology, to classical philosophy, poetry, and drama in her later literary work. French, Italian, and occasional Spanish phrases are sprinkled throughout her plays, and her familiarity with much of the literature in those languages is clear. Countless other details casually dropped into her writing belie an educated knowledge of the world.

Nevertheless, Aphra often referred with some bitterness to what she regarded as a deficient education. She strongly felt that it put her at a considerable disadvantage in her struggle to take her place in the male-dominated literary world of her day and defend herself against a host of critics. Among the playwrights, poets, translators, and literary dabblers who formed her circle there was hardly one who had not had some sort of classical training: William Wycherley, Elkannah Settle, Lord Rochester, Sir Charles Sedley, Thomas Creech, Thomas Sprat, and Thomas Otway went to Oxford; Thomas Shadwell, John Dryden, Nathaniel Lee, the Duke of Buckingham, Lord Lansdowne, and Sir Robert Howard attended Cambridge, where Etherege was also said to have gone; Nahum Tate was educated at Trinity College, Dublin; Henry Higden and Edward Ravenscroft are to be found in the rolls of the Middle Temple; and finally Aphra Behn's lover, John Hoyle, was a member of Gray's Inn and later the Inner Temple. He read Latin, Greek, and several European languages. Part of the fascination he held for her over such a long time was clearly rooted in her admiration of his erudition.

Aside from the benefits of exposure to literary tradition and the discipline of academic training that a university afforded, the institution had other advantages for an aspiring playwright or poet. It provided a chance to establish literary friendships and ties to future patrons which could prove at least useful, if not crucial, to a later career. Charles Gildon, who edited Aphra Behn's works after her death, dedicated his work to a patron whose friendship he had cultivated at university: "Honoured Sir," he wrote, "I am extremely pleased with this opportunity of renewing that acquaintance, which I had the honour and happiness to begin with you at college (where you laid the foundation of that fine gentleman you have since proved and where you gave such early and certain promises of your future merit)."[16] Such an acquaintance could well determine whether a struggling young artist survived. Equally important was the sense of community of letters and exchange of ideas that a gentlewoman educated in the privacy of her home could never know.

Aphra particularly resented not having had the opportunity to learn Latin. Literary translation of the classics was very much in vogue in her day, and her colleagues were busy turning out new versions of poems, satires, and essays from both Latin and Greek literature. Abraham Cowley translated odes from Pindar and Horace; Edmund Waller, part of Virgil's *Aeneid;* Thomas Creech, Lucretius's *De Rerum Natura;* Henry Higden, Juvenal's *Satires;* and John Dryden, Ovid and Homer. Aphra Behn, determined not to be left out, had to "translate" Ovid's *Epistle of Oenone to Paris* and other works by paraphrasing a literal rendering of the original. She attempted to make a virtue of her lack by arguing that this process gave her greater poetic freedom, that it allowed her to make the poem her own. But her fundamental resentment of the handicap she was forced to work under is demonstrated in the congratulatory poem she wrote for her friend Thomas Creech to preface his translation of Lucretius. Here Aphra reflects that since she is *"unlearned in schools,"* she has not until now been able to satisfy her appetite for the inaccessible Greek and Latin literature which remained untranslated. She is hardly apologetic for her limitation, however:

> *Till now, I curst my birth, my education,*
> *And more the scanted customs of the nation:*
> *Permitting not the female sex to tread,*
> *The mighty paths of learned heroes dead.*
> *The God-like Virgil, and great Homers verse,*
> *Like divine mysteries are concealed from us.*
> *   We are forbid all grateful themes,*
> *   No ravishing thoughts approach our ear,*
> *   The fulsome gingle of the times,*
> *Is all we are allowed to understand or hear.*
> *   So thou by this translation dost advance*
> *Our knowledge from the state of ignorance,*
> *And equals us to man! . . .*

The strength of Aphra's indignation over the educational double standard her sex suffered under is clear in this statement. Latin, of course, was the great dividing line between the sexes. Until the seventeenth century, much of what was considered knowledge was written in Latin and therefore effectively locked away from women. Though things had changed a great deal by the time Aphra came of age—she was able to read a good deal, in fact, in translation—the residual sense of inferiority remained. In 1696, the author of the *Essay in Defense of the Female Sex* could still write: "The other sex, by means of a more extensive education to the knowledge of Greek and Roman languages, have a vaster field for their imaginations to rove in, and their capacities thereby enlarged." [17]

Behind Aphra Behn's anger at her exclusion from classical tradition is the hint of a still larger sense of injustice: she is clearly preoccupied with the fact that the *"customs of the nation"* had also denied her sex a part in the great literary tradition in the English language. That female thoughts as well as tongues or pens should be *"forbid all grateful themes"* was reason enough to curse one's birth, according to Aphra.

III

Everything she sees or hears serves to fix impressions, call forth emotions, and associate ideas, that give a sexual character to the mind. . . . Besides, the books professedly written for her instruction all inculcate the same opinions.

—Mary Wollstonecraft,
A Vindication of the Rights of Women, 1792

As the advertised curricula of the female academies in Kent directed by Mr. Beven and Mrs. Jackson indicate, schooling in proper deportment was a central element of the instruction young women of Aphra Behn's generation were exposed to. This education in the "feminine virtues" would prove to be at least as important to the evolution of Aphra's literary career as her initiation into the realm of learning, and would, through a complex and elusive set of connections, determine her relation to the act of writing itself.

Most men and women of Aphra's century thought of male and female spheres of experience as two contiguous but irreconcilable universes. The phrase "the feminine sphere" comes up repeatedly in letters, diaries, etiquette manuals, sermons, literary texts, and even political tracts; it is used synonomously with the "private domain," or "the home," while the male province delineates "the world." Any foray into what was seen as male preserve, whether real or imagined, verbal or actual, written or merely dreamed, was seen as a negation of "femininity." The sexual symbolism of this language is implicit: woman's "sphere" confines her to her "inner space," while man's projecting sex naturally propels him into a larger, aggressive theater of activity. That, of course, is reading a twentieth-century point of view into what Aphra's contemporaries accepted as an inherent division ordained by divine wisdom. The sharp line that separated the two domains seems to cut across the deep political, social, and religious divisions that fragmented the seventeenth century. Although between Cavalier and Puritan notions of the "ideal" woman might differ, there seemed to be, except for certain religious dissident opinion, general agreement on her "proper sphere."

The dialectic of masculine/feminine translated into oppositions of public/private, "world"/domestic circle, active/passive, prerogative/obedience. The Duchess of Newcastle, in a "Preface to the Reader" written in 1655, outlined masculine and feminine territories: "Men and women may be compared to the sun and the moon, according to the description in the Holy Writ, which says, 'God made two great lights, one to rule the day, the other the night.' So man is made to govern commonwealths and women their private families . . . the moon has no strength nor light of understanding, but what is given them from men. This is the reason why we are not mathematicians, arithmeticians, logicians, geometricians, cosmographers, and the like. This is the reason we are not witty poets, eloquent orators, subtle schoolmen, subtracting chemists, rare musicians, curious limners. This is the reason we are not navigators, architects, exact surveyors, inventive artisans. This is the reason why we are not skillful soldiers, politic statesmen, dispatchful secretaries, or conquering Caesars."[18]

The Duchess of Newcastle, who passionately longed for literary fame, was far from conforming to her own image of what was properly feminine; nevertheless, she could not rid herself of the classification. "Business" was a male prerogative and women's place was in the home. Richard Brathwaite, in *The English Gentlewoman* (1631), instructs young women to limit their discourse to subjects "as may best improve your knowledge in household affairs, and other *private* * employments. To discourse of state-matters, will not become your auditory."[19] Mrs. Pepys complained that her husband deliberately dirtied the house in order to keep her employed at home, which accusation Pepys, in the diary he kept secret from her, admitted "is true enough in a great degree." The author of the *Essay in Defense of the Female Sex* confirms that Mrs. Pepys's domestic confinement was typical: "Men look upon us to have very little interest in the public affairs of the world . . . our sedentary life and the narrow limits to which our acquaintance, and business are circumscribed, afford us so little variety, so regular a face of things."[20]

* my italics

————·

Knowledge itself was considered a part of masculine tenure; it was encompassed in the property of "the world." It was also understood in the Biblical (sexual) sense: a woman "known" was one whose chastity had been violated, which helps to explain how women's intellectual activity came to be connected to their sexuality, a logic which would later play a crucial part in Aphra's reputation as a writer.

"Books are a part of man's prerogative," Sir Thomas Overbury wrote in his poem "The Wife." Women, he insisted, ought at most to pretend to a "passive understanding" and ideally not seek to understand at all: "domestic charge doth best that sex befit." [21] This attitude was stated still more explicitly by a character in Thomas D'Urfey's *Richmond Heiress* (1693). Sophronia, a young lady whose love of philosophy has led to her fiancé's desertion, is observed by him reading a book. He comments mockingly, "What, always reading, Madam, still affronting mankind by invading their province of knowledge, fye this is unnatural; a Lady should no more pretend to a book, than a sword, neither of 'em are proper to her sphere of activity." [22] The remark was intended to be caricature, but its comic effect depends on the conventional language it burlesques. No doubt the audience had only too often encountered the same phrases.

Women themselves had so internalized this masculine-feminine dichotomy and its restrictions that they perpetuated it by teaching their daughters to behave accordingly. Elizabeth Jocelyn, who wrote a *Treatise of Education* for her husband just before the birth of her first child (1662), instructed him, in the event of her death, to teach the child, if it were a daughter, "the Bible . . . good housewifery, writing, and good work; other learning a woman needs not." [23] Mrs. Jocelyn's premonition of her own death by childbirth was timely; it would serve as a first lesson for her infant daughter in what one's duty as a woman was. Mary Evelyn was even more adamant in insisting that knowledge and "domestic charge" were mutually exclusive and that women had no right to desire the former or neglect the latter: "Women were not born to read authors and censure the learned," she wrote, "to compare lives and judge of virtues, to give rules of mortality and sacrifice to the Muses. . . . We are willing to acknowledge all time borrowed from family duties is misspent: the care of children's education, observing a husband's commands, assisting the sick, relieving the poor and being serviceable to our friends are of sufficient weight to employ the most improved capacities amongst us. If sometimes it happens by accident that one of a thousand aspires a little higher, her fate commonly exposes her to wonder but adds little esteem. . . . A heroine is a kind of prodigy; the influence of a blazing star is not more dangerous or more to be avoided."[24] A comet was, in that century, believed to bode ill.

Even Anna van Schurman, who was one of the first women to argue in print that her sex ought to have access to classical education, justified it in terms of women's proper sphere. "The study of letters is convenient for them," she argued, "for whom it is more decent to find themselves both business and recreation *at home* and in private, than abroad among others"—precisely the situation of women, she pointed out, as "the Apostle requireth women to be 'keepers at home.'" Furthermore, stated the "virgin" scholar (as she called herself), allowing women to engage in studies would even help keep them at home, a consideration not to be ignored by parents, as "experience testifies, whose tongues, ears, eyes often travail abroad, hunting after pleasures, their faith, diligence, and modesty too, is generally called into question."[25] In recommending a program of subjects to be undertaken by young women, Anna van Schurman counseled against those studies which pertained to the practice of law, military discipline, the court, the church, or the university, since they were, she said, less "proper" for women. But she would not "yield" that a maid be excluded from a "scholastic" knowledge or theory of those subjects. What she implied was that a woman may have a theoretical or passive knowledge of masculine theaters, but not a practical or active one. That would be inappropriate to her lot—as ordained by God.

If Aphra herself, as a young girl, had expressed a desire to become a spy, an adventuress, a playwright, poet, or political actvist, she most likely would have had something like the foregoing wisdom about women's proper sphere repeated to her, if she were not thought altogether mad to begin with for even conceiving such ambitions. Any doubts a young girl might have about her sex's inherent inferiority could be referred to the supreme authority of the Bible. Most often quoted by seventeenth-century parents was Saint Paul, whose injunctions fall into three categories: silence, submission, obedience.

Let all women learn in silence with all subjection.

But I suffer not a woman to teach, nor to usurp authority over a man, but to be in silence.

—1 Timothy 2:11

Wives, submit yourselves unto your own husbands, as unto the Lord.

—Ephesians 5:22

Let your women keep silence in the churches; for it is not permitted unto them to speak. . . . And if they will learn anything, let them ask their husbands at home.

—1 Corinthians 14:34

A woman's education in piety was thought much more important in Aphra Behn's time than a man's—partly because she was believed more vulnerable to carnal temptation.

If she were not fully convinced of her *duty* to keep to her place, the belief that her intrinsic abilities were inferior might give a young woman of Aphra's age second thoughts about attempting masculine ground. Lady Mary Wortley Montagu, sending the august Bishop Burnet a translation she had done from Epictetus for his opinion of it, protested vigorously that her sex was usually "forbid studies of this nature," but then added: "I am not now arguing for an equality for the sexes; I do not doubt God and nature has thrown us into an inferior rank. We are a lower part of the creation; we owe obedience and submission to the superior sex; and any woman who suffers her vanity and folly to deny this, rebels against the law of the creator and indisputable order of nature." [26]

The notion of the feminine sphere made it difficult enough for a woman of the seventeenth century to imagine herself a writer or intellectual without feeling guiltily that she was trespassing on masculine territory; but there was a still more powerful mythology behind that which would almost certainly put an end to literary ambitions, and that was chastity: "modesty," "reputation," "honor," and "virtue." Chastity had then, says Virginia Woolf, "almost a religious importance in a woman's life, and had so wrapped itself round with nerves and instincts that to cut it free and bring it to the light of day demands the courage of the rarest. . . . It was the relic of the sense of chastity that dictated anonymity to women even late in the nineteenth century." [27]

The absolute requirement of continence in women has been a precept shared by many different civilizations in history, but in England of the seventeenth century it was very much connected to the whole economic and social structure of that society. The principle of chastity was reinforced by the patriarchal, primogenital system of inheritance and by the idea, then law, that men had absolute property in women. Since the aristocracy's chief means of consolidating and perpetuating its power was through marriage, the "honor" of its ladies acquired a property value. To be of value on the marriage market, girls had to preserve their maidenheads, for in the words of a contemporary, "Wives, if once known, lose their value." A maid who had lost her virginity was described by another seventeenth-century commentator as "unthrifty." A deflowered heiress could be disinherited, since her maidenhead was an essential part of her dowry and she had deprived her father of the possibility of "selling" her to a husband whose family line she would carry on. *The Whole Duty of Man,* a mid-seventeenth-century tract that documents the conventional morality, states: "The corrupting of a man's wife, enticing her to a strange bed, is by all acknowledged to be the worst sort of theft, infinitely beyond that of goods."

Not only was a woman of Aphra Behn's era considered a property, belonging first to her father and then to her husband, but she did not even have the right to dispose of her own "goods." "A woman hath no power of her own body, but her husband does," stated *The Instruction of a Christian Woman,* which further warned: "Thou dost the more wrong to give away that thing which is another body's without the owner's licence."[28]

The connection between the feminine sphere, knowledge, chastity, and property was clearly drawn by the Duchess of Newcastle, whose understanding of the structure that governed the lives of women of her time was equalled only by the ambivalence of her attitudes toward them: "The education and liberty of conversation which men have is both unfit and dangerous to our sex, knowing we may bear and bring forth branches from a wrong stock, by which every man would come to lose the property of their own children."[29]

The social pressure on Aphra Behn's female contemporaries to hold a chaste posture not only in reality but in every social manifestation was enormous. The fact that survival for a woman was contingent on absolute modesty and unquestioned virginity imposed a far greater censorship on her actions than the watchful eye of a father could hope to. A woman who protested against the system might pay a terrible price: she would either lose her reputation, be in fact considered nothing less than a prostitute, or be viewed simply as a madwoman, unfit for a wife, and live out her days as an old maid. Lady Anne Twisden, who lived in Kent between Canterbury and Wye during the time Aphra Behn was growing up, was so careful of her reputation, even when she had been married for years and her children were grown, that she never permitted herself any society that might cast doubt on her virtue. "Her maxim was," wrote her husband, "that the woman was to blame of whom there could be any suspicion, and therefore she was never with any man (except her husband) but she had some woman by in the room, or at least the doors open, and in sight of her." Lady Twisden knew four languages—Latin, Italian, French, and Spanish—"but never obtruded her knowledge." [30] For her husband she embodied the feminine ideal. Her contemporary and neighbor, Dorothy Oxinden, who lived a few miles away in Barham, Kent, testified to the necessity of such behavior. In a letter, she reminded her lover that "a woman which has lost her good name is dead while she lives." [31]

Modesty had its roots in the prescription of chastity, but its sexual politics went much further: the principle expanded to cover every aspect of a woman's life, and the requirements for honor became so abstract that they dictated a woman's way of speaking, looking, walking, imagining, thinking. Discretion was carried to the point of invisibility. *The Whole Duty of a Woman* specified that "*Modesty* confines itself not to the face only . . . but spreads itself in life, motions and words. . . . Your looks, your speech, and the course of your whole behaviour should own a humble distrust of yourselves; rather being willing to learn and observe, than to dictate and prescribe. . . . As you value your reputation, keep us to the strictures of this virtue . . . give no occasion for scandal or reproach; but let your conversation set an example to others . . . in all public assemblies behave yourselves with all reverence and modesty and becoming decency. *Let neither your thoughts nor eyes wander.*" [32] Manifestly, wandering eyes or even thoughts came to stand for unchastity. As the seventeenth-century proverb went: "Discreet women have neither eyes, nor ears."

The symbolic split that such instruction might occasion in a young girl of Aphra's sensibilities and aspirations becomes plain when one remembers that a writer's first training must necessarily be in observation, and that her ability to reproduce reality in her own imagined form of course depends on knowledge of and intercourse with "the world"—territory not properly her own.

IV

Aphra, though she frankly rejected the appearance of modesty in her own life and in her writing created heroines who took for themselves the same swaggering sexual freedom that Restoration men in Cavalier circles enjoyed, bitterly resented being accused of immodesty by her detractors. She defended her feminine "reputation" by denying accusations—which, but for the exaggerations characteristic of slandering gossip, were more or less true. Her poems, however, like "On Desire" or "The Willing Mistress" or "The Disappointment" (on impotence), published her sexual stance for all who cared to see.

Despite her rebellion and defiant remarks about the odious burden of feminine honor, Aphra did not seem to be able to fully rid herself of its domination. She still viewed it as an essential part of what makes a woman—particularly a young woman—attractive and desirable. In her adaptation of *The Lover's Watch,* a French etiquette book describing the contemporary stylized manner of making love, she referred to modesty as *"so commendable a virtue in the fair."* This virtue is exhibited in high degree in her heroine Cleonte (*The Dutch Lover*): when informed that she may marry the man she loves, she replies, "Sir, I must own a joy greater than is fit for a virgin to express." There is no hint of irony or distance from the character in the lines; Aphra seems to feel that this was a perfectly normal way for young women to talk. Women who talked otherwise were asking for trouble.

The most striking illustration of Aphra Behn's attachment to modesty as a positive value, however, is in the description of the heroines who belong to the later period of her novels. Gracelove, the hero of *The Unfortunate Happy Lady,* falls in love with Philadelphia, partly because she steadfastly maintains her virtue in a situation where everything threatens it, her brother having imprisoned her in a brothel. Aphra recounts: *"Here Gracelove . . . saluted Philadelphia, and acquitted himself like a person of good Sense and Education, in his first addresses to her; which she returned with all the Modesty and ingenuous simplicity that was still proper to her.*" Later, when two men are discussing whether to help her escape, it is implied that she deserves their aid only if her chastity is verifiable: "*A very beautiful lady 'tis, (returned the Counsellor) and very modest, I believe. That I can witness (replied the other). Also, Sir: (said the fair unfortunate) I have nothing but my Modesty and honest education to recommend me to your Regard.*" She was not far from the mark.

In the story *The Fair Jilt,* the heroine/villainess Miranda's attractions are enumerated in the following order: her physical beauty, her modesty, and last, her wit. The priority is characteristic of Aphra's fictional ladies. The two heroines of *The Lucky Mistake* are described similarly: their "*extreme beauty,*" innocence, modesty, and birth are duly noted. Finally, Aphra's most moving and sympathetic female protagonist, Imoinda, Oroonoko's bride, is hardly ever referred to without mention of her modesty. On her first appearance in the novel, the characteristics Aphra chooses to emphasize are the beauty of her "*face and person,*" her "*lovely modesty,*" and the "*softness in her look and sighs.*"

Aphra Behn also created heroines of a very different sort, who rejected this image of passive femininity; but the fact that she could evoke two voices of such contrasting tenor is testimony to the ambivalent attitudes that she herself held toward the feminine behavior prescribed by her upbringing and her own instinct for freedom, which pressed toward the evolution of a new kind of heroine.

CHAPTER FIVE

Surinam

Guiana is a country that hath yet her maidenhead, never sacked, turned or wrought, the face of the earth hath not been torn, nor the vertue and salt of the soil spent by manurance, the graves have not been opened for gold, the mines not broken with sledges, nor their images pulled down out of their temples. It hath never been entered by any army or strength, and never conquered or possessed by any Christian Prince.

—Sir Walter Ralegh,
*The Discoverie of the Large, Rich and Beautiful
Empire of Guiana,* 1595

. . . his misfortune was to fall into an obscure world, that afforded only a female pen to celebrate his fame. . . .

—Aphra Behn,
Oroonoko, 1688

I

In 1660 Charles II was restored to the throne and the Puritan experiment was over. Upheaval subsided, at least for a while, into the passive relief of tradition regained. In those first few years of the Restoration, it seemed England wished only to be rescued from uncertainty, to return to the "old" world before the Commonwealth.

Aphra, now a young woman in her early twenties, was on her way elsewhere—to the wilderness of Surinam, a newly established colony on the coast of South America, then belonging to the British.* Her father, as she later said, had been appointed Lieutenant General

*later to become Dutch Guiana

of that tropical outpost, but *"dy'd at sea, and never arrived to possess the honour designed for him . . . nor the advantages he hoped to reap by them."*

What can have been her thoughts as she watched the wrapped body of her father lowered from the side of the ship that was irreversibly carrying her to an unfamiliar continent, a colony only half carved out of a virtually unexplored wilderness.

Whatever her feelings about her father, his death unquestionably freed her from one restraint: his presence would no longer ensure that her behavior corresponded to that expected of a young lady of marriageable age, a young lady with a reputation to protect. Her father's death may have altered the spectrum of possibilities open to Aphra in another way as well: he could not now see to it that a dowry assured her a suitable marriage. Apparently, he did not make any provision for his adopted (?) daughter in his will, though perhaps he did not think to make a will and certainly did not expect to die on the way to Surinam where, as Aphra tells us, he had hoped to make his fortune. It seems that in any case his means were probably somewhat reduced, as it appears he had little to leave his widow and children.[1]

Their more powerful relative, Lord Willoughby, cannot have been much of a resource, since even his fortunes seem to have reached a surprisingly low ebb. He was drowned in a hurricane not long after Aphra left Surinam, and when the will was read, his estate was discovered to be negligible. According to Governor Sir Jonathan Atkins, he had been compelled to mortgage and sell his English lands and had ruined his fortune by spending fifty thousand pounds, a stupendous sum in those days, on "fruitless designs"—his colonization schemes.[2] Henry Willoughby, his brother and heir, complained to the King of his predecessor's management of financial affairs: "My brother hath dealt unkindly with me, but I forgive him. . . . His accounts are confused, both as to your Majesty's concerns and his own; I shall only say he was honest and careless, for he hath left little behind him."[3]

Whatever the actual circumstances in which her father's death left Aphra, one thing is clear: her economic survival, her future, her life, now depended on no one but herself. She was ultimately, as she later says, "forced to write for bread."

Aphra's narrative of her adventures in Surinam is the first detailed account of her life that we have from the author herself, though it was not written until more than twenty years later and was cast in the form of an autobiographical "novel" or "history" called *Oroonoko,* published the year before she died. Although the principal focus of this history is not Aphra herself but Oroonoko, a black slave she met in Surinam, she nevertheless tells us a great deal of her own life in explaining how she came to be in that place and what she observed. *"I was an eyewitness to a great part of what you will find here set down,"* she wrote at the beginning of the book, and then continued to drop fragments of her own story into that of her friend.[4]

How much of the book may be taken for fact was for a long while one of the most debated issues of Aphra's biography. Her contemporary One of the Fair Sex seconded Aphra's autobiographical information, and that account of her experiences in Surinam became the accepted version until 1913, when Ernest Bernbaum wrote an article attempting to prove that Aphra was "lying." Deliberately, he said. Bernbaum argued that Mrs. Behn had never been to Surinam at all, but had copied her description of that country from a book by one George Warren, published in 1667. Since Mr. Bernbaum was operating on the newly discovered "fact" that Aphra's father was a barber, his initial skepticism regarding Aphra's account is at least understandable; but how he could argue that her description of Surinam was copied from a text that in fact does not give as many details concerning that country as Aphra did, or how he could have reasonable ground for even assuming that she had ever read it in the first place, is more difficult to see. Bernbaum's attack on Aphra's biography was considered definitive by many critics, however, and those who chose to argue with him concentrated on comparison of the two texts, a technique which, as H. L. Mencken pointed out in a review of one of the essays, could not possibly lead to settling the question: "Both More and his antagonist base their arguments upon intuition, word-juggling and the doctrine of probabilities. It seems to have occurred to neither of them to inspect the colonial records of Surinam, probably easily accessible in London. There is no sign that either has ever made the attempt. A good deal of so-called scholarship . . . is grounded upon just such stupidity. It is simply medieval text-chewing. It gets nowhere, and is not even amusing."[5]

Some years later, a scholar named Harrison Gray Platt took Mencken's advice and looked further into the external evidence, which turned out to be abundant. He uncovered several references in a private correspondence between Sir Robert Harley and his representatives in Surinam which testified to Aphra's presence there. Subsequent scholars have found still more substantiating evidence in the State Papers and other contemporary documents: countless details verify Aphra's description of the colonial army in Surinam, the governing council, the colonists, the terrain, the Indians, the slave revolts.[6] The historical existence of some of the people she mentions—obscure people, by no means public figures who might be known in London—has been proven through references in letters and official papers she cannot possibly have had access to. One of them was Colonel Martin, whom she named a character for in a play she seems to have written about the same time as *Oroonoko*. Colonel Martin died shortly after Aphra left Surinam, never having returned to England, so she could not have met him later in London. Her casual mention of the location of his plantation is verifiable on a contemporary map of Surinam.[7]

Though twentieth-century scholars have found it necessary to prove Aphra's statements about herself, none of her contemporaries, who were in a position to know, objected that she was "lying"—and certainly few of her enemies lost an opportunity to attack. Strangely enough, in the critical argument over "evidence," the importance of a statement Aphra made outside the text of *Oroonoko* has been ignored. The first edition of the novel was dedicated to Richard Maitland, fourth Earl of Lauderdale, who was Privy Councillor to James II, and in that dedication, Aphra wrote: *"I had the honour to know [Oroonoko] in my travels to the other world; and though I had none above me in that country yet I wanted power to preserve this just man. If there be anything that seems romantic I beseech your Lordship to consider these countries do, in all things, so far differ from ours that they produce unconceivable wonders, at least, so they appear to us, because new and strange. What I have mentioned I have taken care should be truth."*[8] It was possible that Aphra's saying, at the beginning of *Oroonoko*, that she was telling a true story might have been no more than fictional convention, but it was very unlikely that she would put forth such a claim in a dedication addressed to one of the most powerful men in England, whose patronage she was courting. There would have been a number of people still alive to contest her statement had it been suspect—not the least of whom was Lawrence Hyde, first Earl of Rochester, who was also an adviser to James II and had shared the Royal Patent for Surinam with Lord

Willoughby at the time Aphra's story took place. She had dedicated a play to him only two years before *Oroonoko* was published.

Aphra referred to her South American experience as though it were common knowledge among her friends in the dedication to her play *The Young King,* written nearly ten years before *Oroonoko.* *"She feared the reproach of being an American,"* Aphra wrote tongue in cheek of herself, explaining that she had written the play itself many years before that, *"having measured three thousand leagues of spacious ocean."* Thomas Southerne, who adapted *Oroonoko* for the stage, indicated that Aphra had told the story many times before making it a novel. As he remarks in the preface, "She always told the story more feelingly than she writ it." [9]

The "history" of Aphra's experience in Surinam can be reconstructed from her own account and from contemporary letters and documents that help to date her stay and fill in details where she is reticent.

II

Aphra described the passage to Surinam as a *"tedious voyage"* across weeks and weeks of *"spacious ocean"*—three thousand leagues of what must have seemed endless watery space to travelers whose familiar unit of measurement was the English Channel. But finally the coast of South America: the palms; the "drowned land" along the shore; the velocity of the muddy rivers intersecting blue-green water as they emptied into the sea. An adventurer who came to Surinam fifty years before Aphra noted in his log fresh water as far as twenty leagues out; such was the swiftness of the current.

Ships arriving in the colony sailed along the coast to the mouth of the Surinam River, where it is joined by the Commewyne River. There was a harbor there, where ships anchored from other colonies in the West Indies, from Europe and New England, from the African Guinea Coast, bringing slaves and supplies, taking away sugar. Miles of grassy savannahs stretched into the distance, interrupted by clusters of palms and tangled undergrowth. Since the air at the mouth of the river was thought unhealthy, no plantation or any other sign of civilization was to be seen. The only visible structure was a deserted Indian village. It is said that Paramaribo, the modern city that stands in that place, capital of present Surinam, took its name from the Indian village that had already retreated to what was still wilderness when Aphra's ship sailed into the harbor. It is also said that the Indians avenged their loss by periodically setting fire to the wooden fortress Lord Willoughby built there a year later to defend the English colony against its Dutch rivals in the slave trade, against the privateers who were their own countrymen, and against the Indians themselves.

Surinam did not give itself over easily to Europe. Columbus, on his first voyage to America, passed very nearby but decided not to venture the shore, having heard from the Indians of Trinidad that the continent which lay directly to the south was inhabited by monstrous cannibals, who devoured not only each other but also any stranger. Explorers came after Columbus, nevertheless, and the first to penetrate the hitherto untouched land found what they described as a paradise. They met friendly Indians who traded with them and guided them through the mysteries of the jungle; but they soon found that not only were the rumors about cannibals true, but that the climate itself was also one of the most unhealthy for Europeans in the entire then-discovered world.

As early as 1530, there had been attempts to start a colony in Surinam, but the would-be settlers lasted no more than a few years. They went home in despair, died in droves from tropical diseases, or were killed and sometimes eaten by Indians. By 1650, when Lord Willoughby sent three hundred men to found a settlement, there had already been thirteen attempted and failed colonies—only three had survived. The land Willoughby's party chose to build on had been occupied formerly by French settlers, who came to a ghastly end in that place. Captain John Scott, whom Lord Willoughby later employed to attack the Dutch colony in Surinam, related their story in his manuscript "Description of Guyana": "They lived peaceably until the year 1642 at what time they grew careless, had difference with the Indians, and were cut up in one day." [10] There were 370 men with their families in the French settlement, all killed in a single attack.

Lord Willoughby's colony, however, had managed not only to survive but to prosper for more than ten years by the time Aphra came there. Even so, the threat of Indian attack remained imminent: *"About this time,"* Aphra wrote, *"we were in many mortal fears, about some disputes the English had with the Indians; so that we could scarcely trust ourselves, without great numbers, to go to any Indian towns, or place where they abode, for fear they should fall upon us, as they did immediately after my coming away; and the place being in the possession of the Dutch, they used them not so civilly as the English; so that they cut in pieces all they could take, getting into houses and hanging up the mother, and all her children about her; and cut a footman I left behind me all in joints, and nailed him to trees."*

In addition to the natural dangers of Surinam—tropics, natives, accident—the seventeenth-century settler in that country might justifiably feel that his fellow colonists posed no small hazard themselves. Certainly some respectable men chose to try their fortunes there, but for the most part the population consisted of transported criminals, prostitutes, ruffians, paupers, political dissidents, and fanatics, and others who were either forced to go there or had a compelling enough reason to chance the manifold dangers of the frontier.

Henry Adys, writing to Lord Willoughby from Toorarica, the capital and indeed the only town of Surinam, on December 10, 1663 (while Aphra was in the colony), protested the "violence" of its inhabitants and complained of "seeing, by the rude rabble, drunkenness and so much debauchery; and hearing, to the great trouble of my soul, so many bitter oaths, horrid execrations, and lascivious abominations." Lord Willoughby answered him that there was very little he could do to remedy the situation, adding: "You know what sort of people generally all new colonies are made of." [11] Sir Josiah Child further characterized these first settlers of the West Indies as "a sort of loose vagrant people, vicious and destitute of means to live at home, (being either unfit for labour, or such as could find none to employ themselves about, or had so misbehaved themselves by whoring, thieving or other debauchery, that none would set them on work) which merchants and masters of ships by their agents gathered up about the streets of London, and other places, clothed and transported, to be employed upon plantations." [12]

Aphra Behn, describing the men who governed Surinam, presumably among its most respectable citizens, confirms these stories: *"The Council consisted of such notorious villains as Newgate never transported; and possibly originally were such who understood neither the laws of God or man, and had no sort of principles to make them worthy of the name of men; but at the very Council-table would contradict and fight with one another, and swear so bloodily, that 'twas terrible to hear and see 'em."* Her play *The Widow Ranter*, which draws heavily on her colonial experience (though set in Virginia), gives a vivid picture of the scoundrels who had become "aristocracy": *"Transported criminals who having acquired great estates, are now become your Honour and Rightful Worshipful, and possess all places of authority."* On arriving in the colony from England, Hazard, a gentleman, is confronted with an insulting, crude group of men who claim to be *"of the honourable Council."* Obviously, standards of conduct differed considerably from those of polite society in the parent country. *"Is it your custom to affront strangers?"* Hazard asks a lady who has witnessed the scene (a former prostitute, he later discovers). *"Alas, Sir, 'tis a familiar way they have, Sir,"* she answers.[13]

It was hardly a place for a lady—not, at least, a lady as the seventeenth century thought of her—and a gentlewoman's arriving in Surinam alone (that is to say, unaccompanied by either husband or father or master) was not the usual circumstance. There were women who had been brought along as servants; there were prostitutes who had been forced to leave England; and there were criminals who had been transported from Newgate—thieves or even murderesses. But for the most part, the gentlewomen who were there were the sisters, wives, and daughters of planters or military officials, and there were few enough of those. Men greatly outnumbered women in the colonies and, unless a family moved permanently to Surinam or one of the islands, most husbands who had business in that part of the world did not bring their wives along. Lord Willoughby, even when gone for as long as two years in his capacity as Governor, left his Lady safely at home in England. Aphra herself does not mention any other women in her narrative of events that took place in Surinam except her mother, sister, serving woman, and the female slaves on the plantation. The resident ladies evidently did not take part in the sort of adventures that Aphra embarked on: going out *"tyger-hunting,"* visiting savage Indian tribes, befriending Negro slaves, and involving herself in their rebellions scarcely fell within the sphere of "feminine" activity. Madam Margaret Heathcote, a gentlewoman living in Antigua at the time, wrote to her cousin John Winthrop in Massachusetts that she was virtually confined to the house by the lack of proper society and the roughness of the country. She dared not "go much abroad," she said, for "they be all a company of sodomists that live here."[14] It seems probable that had Aphra's father been present, her unladylike doings might have been considerably curtailed.

Aphra's mother must have been a rather ineffectual replacement for paternal authority. More or less in the background of Aphra's narrative, she seems not to have been able to exercise restraint on her already unconventional, strong-willed daughter, if Aphra is to be believed. The first time she appears in *Oroonoko* is on the last page. Of course Aphra's version may not have been entirely accurate on that point; she perhaps exaggerated her own role or romanticized details in order to make the narrative more interesting. As the widow of the Lieutenant General who never arrived to take up his post, her mother may well have felt overwhelmed by the circumfluence of events that had thrust her alone on the shore of a strange continent. Aphra does not tell us what her mother's feelings or reactions were, but very little in her education can have prepared her to cope with such a situation.

Aphra does not specifically say in *Oroonoko* when she arrived in Surinam, but the reference to her father's official appointment indicates that it was probably some time early in the fall of 1663. Lord Willoughby and Laurence Hyde, second son of the Earl of Clarendon, were jointly appointed Lord Proprietors of Barbados, Surinam, and other Caribbean possessions on June 2, 1663, by Royal Patent.[15] Clarendon was a close friend of Willoughby's, and Aphra either knew his son from this period of her life or met him afterward through the connection, for it was to him that she dedicated her play *The Lucky Chance* shortly before *Oroonoko* was written.

On June 16, 1663, Lord Willoughby had received an urgent request from the King to "repair with all convenient speed to his government."[16] Under the patent newly granted him, he had the power to appoint a Lieutenant General (a military post), and as he had business in Barbados to take care of first, it seems likely that he would send a relative—Aphra's father, who died on the voyage—to take care of matters in Surinam until he could arrive. Most ships coming to Surinam stopped off at Barbados, the "parent colony," both a center of government and source of supply for the newer settlement in Surinam.

Since the journey from England normally took from six to nine weeks and sometimes longer, Aphra's party could not have landed before the middle of August. Lord Willoughby himself reached Barbados on August 10; perhaps they came on the same ship. On August 15, John Treffry, not having had time to hear of Lord Willoughby's arrival in Barbados, wrote from Surinam: "We have been long in expectation of my Lord Willoughby, who by his last told me that he would soon be ready to sail, having fully agreed with His Majesty concerning Barbadoes and this place."[17] He was evidently referring to Lord Willoughby's patent of June 2 and subsequent instructions from the King. Further in the letter Treffry mentioned that the planters in Surinam were daily watching for the arrival of a ship from Barbados, the *Guiana,* carrying sixty passengers and planters. A man named Renatus Enys wrote to Secretary of State Arlington, whose intelligence network Aphra was later a part of, to say that he had arrived in Surinam on August 27, after a voyage of nine weeks from England, having stopped off at Barbados.[18] This may very well have been the ship Aphra came on, as arrivals were not frequent.

Aphra's immediate party probably consisted of her mother, sister, younger brother, and at least two servants—all of whom she mentions in her account. As she speaks of *my* footman and *my* maid, the family may have brought several more in different capacities; it would have been consonant with her father's position. Alternatively, claiming the servants as her own may simply have been egotism on Aphra's part. She also mentions a kinsman in Surinam, who either accompanied the party on the boat or was already in the colony. Lord Willoughby had indeed generously sprinkled his relatives in various capacities throughout his domain: there were Sir Martin Noël and his son Thomas, related to Lady Willoughby's mother; there were representatives of the Finch family, which Willoughby's daughter, like the Countess of Winchelsea, married into; there was Brereton Creek, named for the Lords Brereton, whose family his third daughter had married into. The colonies were a perfect syphon for younger sons or other members of the family in need of employment or patronage, and family connections naturally provided a ready-made administrative network for overseeing far-flung investments. Lord Willoughby himself had originally obtained the lease of the Caribee Islands in 1647 from his wife's uncle, the Earl of Carlisle. There were also numbers of people in the colonies of Surinam and Barbados whom Aphra was quite likely to know, if she was not actually related to them, as Kentish families were well represented: Crispes from Canterbury, Thornhills from Wye, and members of several branches of the Culpepper family.[19]

The ship Aphra's family came on would in all likelihood have been met by Major Byam, then Deputy Governor of Surinam, and by John Treffry, overseer of Lord Willoughby's plantation. Perhaps there were also other important men of the colony who had come on board to meet the new Lieutenant General. Byam, at least, cannot have been unhappy to hear of the latter's death on shipboard, as he was a few months later promoted to the post that Aphra's father was to have occupied. This, among other reasons, may have been the source of the later friction between Byam and Aphra.

The party would have been conveyed from the ship to smaller river boats and rowed by slaves up the Surinam River to Noëlia Wharf. From there it was another three days' journey to Toorarica, the metropolis of the colony: a hundred houses, a chapel, and a government building called Parham House, after Lord Willoughby of Parham. Along the way, Aphra and her party *"put in at several houses for refreshment."* There were about five hundred plantations in the whole of Surinam at the time, scattered thirty miles above the town and thirty miles below, all along the two rivers. Lord Willoughby's plantation, Parham Hill, the largest estate in the colony, was another twenty miles beyond Toorarica. Parham House stood on a hill overlooking the river.

From Parham Hill, it was only a short distance farther to the house Aphra was to occupy for the duration of her stay in Surinam: *"As soon as I came into the country, the best house in it was presented to me, called St. John's Hill"* she says in *Oroonoko*. Rowing up the river, she saw, as if in a dream, a house built of cedar: *"It stood on a vast rock of white marble, at the foot of which, the river ran a vast depth down, and not to be descended on that side: the little waves still dashing and washing the foot of this rock, made the softest murmurs and purlings in the world; and the opposite bank was adorn'd with such vast quantities of different flowers eternally blowing, and every day and hour new, fenc'd behind 'em with lofty trees of a thousand rare forms and colours, that the prospect was the most ravishing that sands can create."*

On the edge of the white rock, between the house and the river, was a grove of lemon and orange trees intersected by a walk that was more than half the length of the Mall in London. The leafy branches arched over the path and met at the top, so that not even the fierce noonday sun could penetrate its thickness of green. One could walk there, Aphra says, and entertain people *"at all the hottest hours of the day."* Cool air came in from the river. The orange fragrance dizzied one with its sweetness. Not all the gardens of Italy, she thinks, can *"Out-vie"* this: *"The whole globe of the world cannot shew so delightful a place."* Perhaps she was never again to feel so completely happy, so completely given to the world that surrounded her as she did here. For the rest of her life she would harbor an intense longing for a pastoral paradise that she believed existed only in a pure state of nature untouched by "the world."

Why, or on whose authority, Aphra's party was offered the house on St. John's Hill remains unclear. It belonged not to Lord Willoughby but to his friend Sir Robert Harley. Probably it had been arranged in advance that Aphra's father and his family would stay on Harley's plantation; but the steward, William Yearworth, seems to have been somewhat confused by what was going on. He wrote to Harley on January 27, 1664, to inform him of their presence: "The Ladies that are here live at St. John's Hill. It is reported here that your Honour have sold that plantation to Lord Willoughby." [20]

Yearworth's comment would seem to imply that Aphra's relation to Lord Willoughby was common knowledge: common enough for the steward to assume that if she was staying at St. John's Hill, Lord Willoughby had bought it. She herself clearly says that *"there was none above me in that country"*—a statement appropriate to the daughter of the Lieutenant Governor related to the Lord Governor. Further, Aphra maintains that *"I had authority and Interest enough* [in the colony] *to prevent Oroonoko's being whipped,"* if she had not been absent from Parham Hill at the time, having gone down river for a visit. She seems to feel certain enough of her influence with Lord Willoughby to *"assure* [Oroonoko] *his liberty as soon as the Lord Governor arrived."* Aphra and her family were also frequent visitors to Parham Hill, Willoughby's plantation, where the slave Oroonoko is brought and a great part of the action of her story takes place.

III

Autumn, 1663, arriving in Surinam. What was Aphra like at this point in her life?

Colonel Culpepper tells us Aphra was a beautiful woman, now about twenty-three, if she was indeed born some time around 1640. She had regular features, large brown eyes, chestnut hair, and a high color. Her shoulders were fashionably plump, lips full. She described herself and her brother as *"dressed very glittering and rich, so that we appeared extremely fine,"* but her appearance, on elaboration, seems more eccentric than elegant: *"My hair was cut short, and I had a taffety cap with black feathers on my head."* Perhaps this was the fashion that year, but graphic evidence from the period does not seem to indicate so. Her brother was dressed more conventionally in a stuff suit with silver loops and buttons and, says Aphra, *"an abundance of green ribbon."*

One of the Fair Sex described her thus: "She was of the generous and open temper, something passionate, very serviceable to her friends in all that was in her power; and could sooner forgive an injury than do one. She had wit, honour, good humour, and judgment. She was mistress of all the pleasing arts of conversation, but used 'em not to any but those who love plain-dealing. She was a woman of sense, and by consequence a lover of pleasure."[21] In her early twenties, she was already given to the romantic imagination, disregard for convention, intense curiosity, and delight in discourse that were to characterize her later life. She was propelled into all sorts of "improper" activities by her love of adventure and yet saw herself as fragile at the same time. *"I was persuaded to leave* [Parham Hill] *for some time,"* she tells us, *"being . . . but sickly, and very apt to fall into fits of dangerous illness upon any extraordinary melancholy."* The resources of strength and energy that Aphra displays in her narrative of the events in Surinam, though no doubt somewhat exaggerated, seem to contradict this picture of herself, but her feeling that she was controlled, even tyrannized, by her emotions later in her life confirms it. That she was a "passionate woman" is remembered by several of her contemporaries as her most striking trait.

Her response to Surinam, too, was intense. It was the New World. Not only was it unknown to her and therefore discoverable, but it was utterly unlike anything she had ever seen before. She explored, marveled, observed, tried, listened, saw . . . Surinam intoxicated her; Surinam filled her senses, fevered her already excited imagination. In every way it corresponded to the romantic in her nature. "*'Tis a continent whose vast extent was never known; they say it reaches from East to West one way as far as China, the other to Peru,*" she wrote. The extremist in her loved it even for its violence; it seemed to intensify her experience. In such a place one could feel free of the restrictions of England and the Old World.

It were endless to give an account of all the divers wonderful and strange things that country affords, and which we took a great delight to go in search of, though these adventures are oftentimes fatal, and at least dangerous. . . .

But she was never afraid, she said. Never once hesitated; though her memory may have colored her original experience. She drank in every detail; remembered it, recorded it:

'Tis there eternal Spring, always the very months of April, May, and June; the shades are perpetual, the trees bearing at once all degrees of leaves, and fruit, from blooming buds to ripe autumn: groves of oranges, lemons, citrons, figs, nutmegs, and noble aromaticks, continually bearing their fragrancies: The trees appearing all like nosegays, adorn'd with flowers of different kinds; some are all white, some purple, some scarlet, some blue, some yellow; bearing at the same time ripe fruit, and blooming young, or producing every day new.

She was already writing. One of the Fair Sex says that "besides the vivacity and wit of her conversation, . . . she would write the prettiest, soft-engaging verses in the world." [22] No doubt they were characteristic of the pastoral poetry that dominated the fashion of her generation. She was evidently also much given to another fashionable pastime, the voracious consumption of endless historical romances. Like other young women of her age (Dorothy Osborne and Mrs. Pepys among those whose habit was recorded), she read La Calprenède's *Cléopâtre*, Mlle de Scudéry's *Le Grand Cyrus*, Honoré d'Urfé's *L'Astrée*. She was so taken with the last that she adopted the name of the heroine, Astrea, as her pen name and even, as will later be seen, carried on a gallantry with a man she called Celladon, after the hero of that romance—to the great amusement of some of the observers in

Surinam. That these high-flown romances were taken quite seriously, even literally, by Aphra's contemporaries as patterns for social behavior and ideals to live one's life by is testified to by Dorothy Osborne's letters to her fiancé, William Temple, in which she requested his opinion of the actions of various fictional characters and analyzed their relationships as though they were like those of anyone else she knew or knew of from gossip.

Aphra may well have been writing her first play in Surinam, whose plot was taken from an incident in *Cléopâtre,* though it was not to be produced until fifteen years later. Perhaps Aphra had also already begun at this point to keep the "Journal-Observations" she says she was writing in Antwerp two years later. The very unfamiliarity of Surinam gave her a perfect opportunity to develop her literary skills, to sharpen her powers of observation and description. Already her mind was collecting, classifying, noting. She gathered every particular; the writer in her was beginning to see the world as material. Systematically, she inventoried:

> *Fish, venison, buffaloes skins, and little rarities; as marmosets, a sort of monkey, as big as a rat or weasel, but of a marvellous and delicate shape, having face and hands like a human creature; and cousheries, a little beast in the form and fashion of a lion, as big as a kitten, but so exactly made in all parts like that noble beast, that it is it in miniature: Then for little paraketoes, great parrots, muckaws, and a thousand other birds and beasts of wonderful and surprizing forms, shapes, and colours: for skins of prodigious snakes, of which there are some three-score yards in length.*

Aphra described the flora and fauna, geography, inhabitants, politics, economy, slave trade, hunting, sport, food, and houses of Surinam in *Oroonoko.* What she had understood before the majority of her literary contemporaries was how to construct a fictional world that mirrored the real one; or perhaps it was that she merely transformed her experience into fiction.

IV

The validity of Mrs. Behn's *Oroonoko* as autobiographical statement has now been generally accepted, but some literary critics still contend that the hero himself is a romantic fiction inserted into an otherwise historically accurate narrative. Aphra's description of Oroonoko's "royal" upbringing is merely borrowed, it has been argued, from chivalric tradition and belongs more properly to a European court than the uncivilized country of Coromantien on the barbaric Gold Coast of Africa.[23] It was an historian of slavery, Professor David Brion Davis, who recently pointed out that *Oroonoko* is in fact "more realistic than critics have imagined." He attests to the verisimilitude of Aphra's "fictional" reproduction of West African customs and further confirms that some African princes did receive the kind of European education that she said Oroonoko had. What is more, Mrs. Behn's account of the way slaves were sold is correct, and contemporary records indicate that there were a number of African princes who, like Oroonoko, had been kidnapped by independent slave traders.[24] More than half a century later, in 1749, when two such captured princes were brought to see a dramatic adaptation of *Oroonoko*, they so visibly identified with the hero that one, overwhelmed with emotion, was forced to depart before the end of the play, leaving the other weeping through the entire last act.[25]

In the same letter in which William Yearworth reported the presence of the "Ladies" at St. John's Hill, he also informed Sir Robert Harley that "There is a genney man [a slave ship from the Guinea coast] arrived here in this river on the 24th [of January] this instant at Sand Point. She has 130 negroes on board; the commander's name [is] Joseph John Woode; she has lost 54 negroes in the voyage."[26]

The description fits precisely the circumstances of Oroonoko's arrival in Surinam as Aphra tells of it. Oroonoko's ship landed a few months after she had settled in the colony; he was captured and transported by an English captain; he came from the Guinea coast of Africa; and he told her that a great many fellow slaves had perished on board ship, or rather in the dark hold where they were chained, during the voyage. There cannot have been many English ships coming from the Guinea coast at the time, as the Dutch Admiral De Ruyter had virtually driven out the English merchants and established a monopoly for his country over the slave trade in that part of the world. The records are full of complaints by English merchants that testify to this circumstance, and it was one of the major reasons for the subsequent outbreak of the second Anglo-Dutch War (which Aphra would play her part in too).[27]

Aphra describes in great detail the operation of the slave trade. Those who want slaves, she says, make a bargain with a master or captain of a ship and contract to pay him about twenty pounds a head for an agreed-upon number of blacks, the sum to be handed over upon delivery of the goods. When the ship arrives, the overseers of the plantations who have contracts go aboard and receive the number of slaves they have ordered by "lot." A typical lot, Aphra tells us, would be made up of a few male slaves, the most desirable for the hard physical labor on the plantations, and the rest women and children, in varying proportions. Out of a lot of ten, there might be three or four men at the most. It was the Captain who made up the lots and, puns Aphra, you were simply *"obliged to be contented with your lot."*

The planters of Surinam were forced to import slaves from Africa, according to Mrs. Behn, because they dared not "command" the native South American Indians who, not being Christians, would have been equally eligible for slave status. The reasons for this generous treatment, Aphra noted sarcastically, were first, that the Indians vastly outnumbered the settlers in Surinam; and second, that they had access to the secrets of survival in that foreign place which the Europeans were eager to acquire. They knew all the places to get the best food in the country and were experienced in tracking down animals through almost impassable places; they knew how to navigate the treacherous rivers and falls; and they could be exploited in trading valuable goods for trinkets. So it was not out of respect for the Indians as fellow human beings, Aphra states, but a combination of fear and greed that engendered the Englishmen's hypocritical attitude. *"They being on all occasions very useful to us, we find it absolutely necessary to caress 'em as friends, and not to treat 'em as slaves; nor dare we do otherwise, their numbers far surpassing ours on that continent."* Slavery, then, as Aphra saw it, was a matter of power. It had nothing to do with natural superiority, Christianity, or any of the other justifications that were commonly assumed at the time—assumed rather than argued because there was not as yet any real debate over the defensibility of slavery. It was unworthy of a society that claimed to be based on Christian ideals. This was quite a radical position to put forth when the English had just begun to enjoy the profits of the slave trade and had not even yet questioned its inhumanity.

Aphra makes her position quite clear in the narrative of Oroonoko's capture and enslavement. She describes the sea captain who betrays him as well-bred, eloquent, and more mannerly than others of his profession. He therefore is no barbarian himself, but a good middle-class citizen whose moral education could hardly have failed to teach him the meaning of "honor." Because Oroonoko finds this Englishman a "man of Parts and Wit" whose conversation is not only engaging but instructive, he, as Prince of the African country Coromantien, invites the Captain to court, where he is entertained in great splendor. Oroonoko, as successor to the throne, has been well educated and knows both French and English. The Captain, seemingly honored by this attention, entertains *"the Prince every day with globes and maps, and mathematical discourses and instruments"* and so gains his affection and trust. It is significant that Aphra sees such activities as "entertaining"; she herself very much shared Oroonoko's intellectual curiosity and delight in everything that might be called "learning." It is also interesting that it is precisely because of this predilection that Oroonoko is captured; his desire for mental improvement is the trap. By a strange twist of symbolism, his position mirrors that of young women of European society, whose desire for knowledge—if they were unfortunate enough to possess such longings—was most often a sure route to downfall.

At any rate, the Captain, in return for Oroonoko's many favors, invites him on board ship and entertains him royally: there are carpets and velvet cushions, music and trumpets, several kinds of wine, and quantities of punch. When Oroonoko and his numerous entourage are thoroughly inebriated, they are given a tour of the ship and, on reaching the hold, are clapped in irons, secured with chains, and *"betrayed to slavery."* The suddenness and surprise of the attack precludes defense, and by the time the Africans realize what has happened, the English ship has hoisted sail for the West Indies.

"Some have commended this act, as brave in the Captain," Aphra comments sarcastically at this point, *"but I will spare my sense of it. It may be easily guessed, in what manner the Prince* [Oroonoko] *resented this indignity."*

Oroonoko rages and struggles to free himself, but soon realizing that it is useless, resolves to escape slavery by starving himself. His companions are of the same mettle. The Captain, determined not to lose so much valuable property, sends a messenger to inform Oroon- · oko that he has already begun to regret his rash act, but it is too late to return the Africans to their native country, as the ships have gone too far to turn back. The Captain is afraid, the messenger says, to set the captured party free on board ship for fear they will take revenge. He pledges his word of honor that he will set Oroonoko and his companions free on the next shore sighted if they will end their hunger strike. Oroonoko, whose *"honour was such that he had never violated a word in his life,"* accepts the Captain's oath uncritically, but demands release from his shameful fetters.

The Captain, Aphra relates, *"could not resolve to trust a heathen, he said, upon his parole, a man that had no sense or notion of the God that he worshipped. Oroonoko then replied, he was very sorry to hear that the Captain pretended to the knowledge and worship of any Gods, who had taught him no better principles, than not to credit as he would be credited."* Finally, the Captain realizes that he has no alternative but to set Oroonoko free if he does not wish to see his entire booty slip away before he can reap a profit from it. He succeeds in persuading Oroonoko of his sincerity and releases him from his chains. Oroonoko, who cannot conceive of a man's breaking his word of honor, is confident of impending liberty.

When he is betrayed a second time by the treacherous slaver on arrival in Surinam, Oroonoko gives him a look of profound disdain and only comments: *"Farewell, Sir, 'tis worth my suffering to gain a true knowledge both of you and your Gods, by whom you swear. . . . 'Come, my fellow-slaves,' he cried out, 'let us descend, and see if we can meet with more honour and honesty in the next world we shall touch upon.' "*

The whole transaction between Oroonoko and the slavers turns on the question of honor, which, as Professor Lawrence Stone points out, had a very specific definition in the seventeenth century, significantly different from its current usage. The most severe accusation one could make against a man was that he was a liar—slander that most often resulted in a duel. A man's honor was synonomous with the reliability of his word, and its violation the greatest shame imaginable.[28] Oroonoko, for Aphra, embodies an ideal of honor and truth now lost in the corruption of her own society. Though a slave, he repeatedly proves himself more noble than his white owners. It is, in fact, his savagery that saves him from what Aphra sees as the moral degeneracy of European society. In every instance of the adventures Aphra says she lived through with the slave, his essential superiority is confirmed.

———·

Oroonoko, as the prize slave, is the first sold when the slave ship anchors in Surinam, in a lot of eighteen of which he is the only man. The Captain, for fear that the slaves may join forces to carry off a rebellion, scrupulously separates Oroonoko's companions. The man who purchases Oroonoko is John Treffry, Lord Willoughby's overseer. Treffry, Aphra says, is a man of great learning and wit—a very good mathematician and a linguist who can speak both French and Spanish. (As always, intellectual accomplishments are what Aphra finds most impressive in a man.) It takes a man of such intelligence no time at all to perceive that Oroonoko is no ordinary slave, neither barbarous nor ignorant. During the course of their voyage up river to Parham Hill, Treffry extracts the entire history of Oroonoko's capture and his previous life. Oroonoko, delighted to find his new master a "man of wit," nevertheless informs him that, despite the affection he feels for Treffry, he has no intention of remaining a slave for long. Treffry, however, is sympathetic to Oroonoko's position and outraged by the "dishonour" of his treatment. He would sooner have died, he affirms, "than have been the author of such a perfidy." Treffry assures the wronged Oroonoko that he will do everything in his power to procure his liberty, but that of course the matter must wait for the arrival of Lord Willoughby, without whose authority he cannot act. Until then, Oroonoko must accept the temporary role of slave. As is the custom, he is renamed "Caesar" (slaves ordinarily received new names with new masters), assigned his portion of land, his house, and his work on the plantation.

Aphra loses no time in meeting this most interesting addition to the company at Parham Hill, where she is visiting when he arrives, and hearing the entire story from Oroonoko himself. As ever, she is enthralled by any good story, but an incident that follows shortly afterward adds the romantic interest she thrives on. Oroonoko, in relating the history of his life in Africa, has told Aphra of an almost-fatal love affair that became his tragedy. He had been hopelessly smitten by the orphaned daughter of a great general, who died by his side in battle. Her name was Imoinda. She had returned his affections, and they had contracted to be married when the King, Oroonoko's grandfather, took possession of her for his own. She managed to hold him at arm's length while intriguing with Oroonoko to elope. Meanwhile, they were discovered, and the King revenged himself by telling Oroonoko that he had had Imoinda executed for her betrayal, while secretly selling her into slavery. Oroonoko, as he tells Aphra, nearly perished from grief.

He is still under the illusion that his Imoinda is dead when Treffry tells him of a beautiful young slave girl, *"adorned with the most graceful modesty that ever beautified youth,"* whom he himself is in love with, as is the greater part of the male slave population on the plantation. She has refused all, however, including her master. When Oroonoko asks Treffry why, since the girl is his slave, he does not force her to yield, Treffry replied that she has utterly disarmed him by her *"modesty and weeping"*—so that, to his relief, he has been prevented from violating her. The company, Aphra says, laughs at such courtesy to a slave, but Oroonoko applauds Treffry's recognition and appreciation of *"true notions of honour and virtue"* in her.

The slave girl is, of course, Oroonoko's Imoinda. They recognize each other in a moment, and Treffry rushes off to Parham House to give Aphra an account of what has happened. She immediately pays the lovers a visit, and from then on they are her inseparable companions: "[they] *were scarce an hour in a day from my lodgings; . . . they ate with me, and I obliged them in all things I was capable. I entertained them with the lives of the Romans, and great men, which charmed him to my company; and her, with teaching her all the pretty works that I was mistress of* [needlework and "curious" work], *and telling her stories of nuns, and endeavouring to bring her to the knowledge of the true God; But of all discourses, Caesar liked that the worst. . . . However, these conversations failed not altogether so well to divert him, that he liked the company of us women much above the men."* Aphra's telling Imoinda stories of nuns and attempting to convert her to the "true" religion seem once more to suggest that she was either then a Catholic or had had a Catholic upbringing. Two decades later, the stories told to Imoinda metamorphosed into "novels": *The History of the Nun; or the Fair Vow-Breaker* and *The Nun; or the Perjured Beauty,* among others.

Aphra and her new companions also amuse themselves by venturing into the wild parts of Surinam. They make several trips into the jungle looking for "tyger" cubs to steal while the "dam" is out of the den—why, Aphra doesn't say, but certainly there must have been the excitement of the danger.[29] On one occasion, their party is too small for such a risky outing: there are only four women—probably Aphra, her sister, her woman servant (*"a maid of good courage"*), and

Imoinda—accompanied by Oroonoko and an English gentleman named Colonel George Martin, *"a man of great gallantry, wit and goodness, whom I have celebrated in a character of my new comedy* [The Younger Brother]," says Aphra, *"by his own name, in memory of so brave a man."* (Colonel Martin died soon after Aphra left Surinam, a victim of the plague that ravaged the colony.)

The scouting party is surprised, cub in hands, by an enormous "tyger," who drops the bloody buttock of a cow that she has in her mouth and lunges for the interlopers. Oroonoko snatches Colonel Martin's sword before anyone knows what is happening, grapples a moment, and runs the weapon through the heart of the animal up to the hilt. She has dug her huge claws into his thigh, but was too enfeebled to tear the flesh away. Oroonoko unconcernedly walks over to Aphra and places the cub at her feet, without any sense of victory or pride, she relates, or indeed that his action is at all out of the ordinary.

Aphra also tells of several other impressive feats of Oroonoko. He kills a "tyger" that no one else has been able to destroy; he picks up an electric eel (which Aphra calls a "numb-eel") as an experiment and is nearly electrocuted; he is, in short, valor itself. Afraid of nothing, he seeks danger merely to try his powers. He is the perfect Arthurian knight (dragon-killer) in the guise of a black slave.

How does Aphra define herself in relation to this? The narration of these deeds is evidently to the purpose of demonstrating Oroonoko's "manliness"—in the same way a knight's honor is proven by his physical prowess. She portrays herself as sharing many of his adventures, but never implies any doubt of the propriety of her actions. Her motivation seems to be curiosity: the writer's systematic collection of experience. Still, she is conscious that her willingness to take risks is out of the ordinary and feels a certain pride in it.

Though wars with the Indians have begun to make penetration into the Amazon territory hazardous, Aphra nevertheless is determined to visit some Indian towns in the interior. Oroonoko volunteers to escort her and whoever else will venture on this expedition. They manage to gather a party of eighteen and set out on a barge up river. After eight days' journey, they finally arrive at an Indian town, whereupon *"the hearts of some of our company failed,"* and they decline to go any farther. Aphra says she is determined to go ashore no matter what if Oroonoko will go with her, and she is seconded by her brother and her womanservant. Having met a fisherman who has lived at the mouth of the river for some years, traded with the Indians and learned their language, the four persuade him to act as their translator. Because of his long residence in that part of the world, the fisherman has become *"a perfect Indian in colour"* and warns the party that the Indians have never seen white people before. Wishing to surprise them, Aphra, her brother, and her maid approach the village alone while the fisherman and Oroonoko hide on the bank of the river behind some reeds and flowers. The effect of their appearance is even greater than Aphra and her friends have calculated, for the Indians set up such a cry on seeing them that the interlopers are sure they are about to be killed. They encircle the three Europeans, taking their hair in their hands and spreading it wide—a sign, Aphra learns later, to indicate "Numberless Wonders" to the others, who come running from all parts of the village. *"By degrees they grew more bold,"* Aphra relates, *"and from gazing upon us round, they touched us, laying their hands upon all the features of our faces, feeling our breasts and arms, taking up one petticoat, then wondering to see another; admiring our shoes and stockings, but more our garters, which we gave 'em, and they tied about their legs, being laced with silver lace at the ends; for they much esteem any shining things. In fine, we suffered 'em to survey us as they pleased, and we thought they would never have done admiring us."*

Oroonoko and the fisherman, seeing that the Indians' reaction is one of amazement rather than hostility, come out of their hiding place and are immediately surrounded by the tribesmen, who are eager to know whether these strange creatures can speak, and if so, have they *"sense and wit"?*

Aphra and her brother oblige them by playing on their flutes, which they have carried with them, and performing other tricks like setting paper on fire with a magnifying glass. The Indians are so impressed by the latter that they treat their guests almost like gods. After a few similar trials of cultural exchange, the Indians invite them to a very peppery dinner, served on a giant Sarumbo leaf, and demonstrate a few of their own customs.

Oroonoko is diverted for some time by these adventures, but when Imoinda, who is now his wife, finds herself pregnant, his determination to be released from the bondage of slavery increases acutely. Finally, he decides to take matters into his own hands. One Sunday, when, as is their custom on that day, all the whites on the plantation have drunk themselves into a stupor, Oroonoko gathers all the black slaves and makes a rousing speech against the evils of their condition. As Aphra tells it, he *"made an harangue to 'em, of the miseries and ignominies of slavery; counting up all their toils and sufferings, under such loads, burdens and drudgeries, as were fitter for beasts than men; senseless brutes, than human souls. He told 'em, it was not for days, months or years, but for eternity; there was no end to be of their misfortunes: They suffered not like men, who might find a glory and fortitude in oppression; but like dogs, that loved the whip and bell, and fawned the more they were beaten: That they had lost the divine quality of men, and were become insensible asses, fit only to bear: Nay, worse; an ass, or dog, or horse, having done his duty, could lie down in retreat, and rise to work again, and while he did his duty, endured no stripes, but men, villainous, senseless men, such as they, toiled on all the tedious week 'till black Friday; and then whether they worked or not, whether they were faulty or meriting, they, promiscuously, the innocent with the guilty, suffered the infamous whip, the sordid stripes, from their fellow-slaves, 'till their blood trickled from all parts of their body; blood, whose every drop ought to be revenged with a life of some of those tyrants that impose it."*

Fierce with this rhetoric, the united slaves move to flee toward the sea, where the dense jungle and swamps will render pursuit extremely difficult; hoping to establish a colony there and build ships that can return them to their homeland. Their absence is discovered Monday morning, when the overseers come to collect them for work, and the news spreads rapidly over the whole country.

A militia of about six hundred men is assembled by noon, led by the Deputy Governor, William Byam, described by Aphra as the *"most fawning fair-tongued fellow in the world . . . whose character is not fit to be mentioned with the worst of slaves."* Unfortunately for Oroonoko and his companions, the army is able to follow the runaways with relative ease, because the latter have been forced to cut their way through the heavy undergrowth. The English catch up to them after only a few days and attack so savagely that gradually the other slaves fall away until only Oroonoko, his trusted friend Tuscan, and Imoinda—who, though pregnant, is very skillful with poisoned arrows and bow—are left fighting. Oroonoko is resolved to die rather than surrender, but finally he is persuaded by Treffry to do so out of consideration for his wife and unborn child—on the promise of his freedom, guaranteed by Byam. But of course both Oroonoko and Treffry are betrayed immediately by the devious Deputy Governor, and the rebel is whipped *"in a most deplorable and inhumane manner, rending the very flesh from [his] Bones."* To complete the indignity, his wounds are rubbed with Indian pepper, which nearly drives him mad with pain.

Aphra tries to nurse her friend and comfort him as best she can, but he is inconsolable. Treffry attempts to hinder further action by Byam by declaring that his authority does not extend to the Lord Governor's plantation. But Oroonoko is convinced that the only remedy for his dishonor is revenge, followed by his own death. In preparation, he determines to kill Imoinda so that she will not fall victim to his persecutors when he is no longer there to protect her. When he announces his plans, she readily agrees, and feigning a need for fresh air to speed his recovery, they walk out into the woods, where he stabs her. Having accomplished this, he grieves so intensely that he is unable to leave her and remains holding her corpse in his arms for more than a week without stirring. A scouting party sent to look for him easily finds the spot by the overwhelming stench of her decomposing body. An almost unrecognizable Oroonoko meets their eyes: weakened to the point of immobility, he falls into their hands at once.

This time his execution is assured and, as Aphra tells it, he calmly smokes a pipeful of tobacco while ears, nose, and arms are hacked off one by one with a dull knife. Aphra, unable to bear the scene, has gone down river to Colonel Martin's, but *"my mother and sister were by him all the while, but not suffered to save him; so rude and wild were the rabble, and so inhuman were the justices who stood by to see the execution."* Oroonoko is then cut into quarters, and the parts are sent to all the neighboring plantation owners to exhibit as an example to other rebellious slaves.

So ends Aphra's hero, whose "barbarity" is so far outdistanced by his masters'. Deputy Governor Byam, naturally enough, told a different version of the story. In a manuscript report on the state of Surinam that he wrote a little over a year later, he referred to "the insolencies of our Negroes, killing our stock, breaking open houses, threatening our women, and some flying into the woods in rebellion."[30] Whether Byam was blackening the reputation of the Negro slaves or simply relating a truth that Aphra chose to romanticize for her own purposes is impossible to tell. But her description of his character does not encourage us to believe his word is likely to be entirely unprejudiced.

V

There was one encounter important to her stay in Surinam and still more important to her life later which Aphra does not mention in her narrative. That was with William Scot. He was then about thirty-five or thirty-six—twelve years or so older than Aphra—a political exile and a rebel: the perfect combination to appeal to her sympathies and romantic imaginings. He had been a spy in the intelligence service managed by his father, Thomas Scot, under the Commonwealth, but had gotten into some kind of trouble in 1659–1660, and on March 5, 1660, a warrant for his arrest was issued.[31] A Sergeant Norfolk was instructed to bring Scot into custody before the Council of State, of which his father, ironically enough, was a member, though apparently helpless to prevent the move against his son. Edmund Ludlow, also on the Council of State, recounts in his *Memoirs* a debate held in the House of Commons at the end of February in which it was intimated by certain members that Scot's son might be guilty of high treason. Thomas Scot leaped to William's defense, but Ludlow rebutted the portrait Scot painted of his son as loyal servant to the cause: "I assured them [the House] they could not think to be much a person as he [Thomas Scot] had represented him, unless they esteemed the insurrection of Sir George Booth to have been for their service, he having attempted to justify the lawfulness of it in my presence."[32]

Four days after the first warrant, a second one was issued authorizing Auditor Roberts to pay one thousand pounds to William Jessop, clerk of the Council, for intelligence. This sum was to be taken from the proceeds of the Post Office paid to William Scot and Isaac Dorislaus while they managed it under Thomas Scot. What happened to the money is not clear; but it seems that it was no longer in the possession of either when the warrant for arrest was issued. Was William Scot guilty of embezzlement in addition to the suspicions of treason held against him? The fact that he seems to have disappeared just then points to the affirmative. Isaac Dorislaus fled to Holland and was assassinated by Royalists; but Scot, who was more wary of reprisals, trusted his fate to distant Surinam. His brother Richard had a plantation there and the Scot family had been involved in the colonial administration of the West Indies all through the Commonwealth. He therefore knew the territory well.

There were also a number of political and religious refugees in the colonies; most of them had arrived after the Restoration, when they were no longer welcome in England. But even before, the relative newness of the colonial governments had allowed dissidents much more freedom to determine their own lives and structure their surroundings to their politics than they had in England. There was a colony of Quakers in Surinam and even a plantation called "Pilgrim" on the Para River not far from Noëlia Wharf. Colonel George Martin was the brother of Harry Martin, whom Aphra calls "the Great Oliverian." * Robert Sanford, who owned the plantation next door to St. John's Hill, also seems to have had republican leanings.

The presence of two conflicting groups in the colony—Royalists and Parliamentarians—gave rise to a more or less continuous state of civil war fought in small skirmishes over authority. The republican sympathizers resented William Byam, who had been elected Governor of the colony for two consecutive terms in the 1650s but, at the Restoration, had seized power for himself and dissolved the election. Byam, who was a violent Royalist, wrote to the King in 1662 to say that Surinam was divided into camps and rebellion was rife: "On the 28th of October at the meeting of inhabitants of the division of Toorarica," he attested, "Mr. William Sanford (one of the confederacy) did very insolently spit in the face of authority, stirring up the people to sedition; and was uncontrolled by his brother, Lieutenant Colonel Robert Sanford, then present; a Magistrate and one of my Council; who afterwards appeared to head the faction." This group was resolved, Byam reported, "to unhinge the frame of authority and bring all things into a confused disorder." [33] The conspiracy was supported, according to him, by a group of scoundrels whose position in the colony had fallen through their own "sloth and drunkenness" and who hoped to repair their fortunes by gaining control of the government.

Robert Sanford, incensed, denied the charges and riposted, publishing a pamphlet entitled *Surinam Justice* (1662). "The colony," he

---

* referring to Oliver Cromwell

wrote, "was full of discontents and fears." [34] But it was Byam's fault—and the result of the repressive measures he had instituted against respectable citizens, which included imprisoning them in the hold of a ship anchored offshore.

The King's response to the reports of dissent and rebellion was to make Lord Willoughby's de facto government official and inform him that he was to take ship for Surinam as quickly as possible. His instructions were to defend, by force if he thought necessary, the rights, privileges, and prerogatives of the Crown; to prevent and suppress all factions and seditions; and especially to ensure that the Gospel was preached and propagated according to the doctrine of the Church of England—not to be distorted by Puritan fanatics. When Lord Willoughby was finally able to survey the situation for himself, he concluded that Byam's report indeed had some truth in it. He wrote to the King that the people were "rebellious and not to be governed by an easy hand." As if in proof, he was attacked by a madman who managed to cut two fingers off his right hand. As soon as he had recovered, the bewildered Willoughby returned to Barbados, and as Byam reported, "no sooner was his Excellency gone, but strange jealousies possessed the inhabitants which broke out into great discontents." [35]

The atmosphere was one William Scot thrived on, but his residence in Surinam was abruptly to come to an end, for it seems that the debt he had left behind him in England had finally caught up with him.

William Byam had sufficient reason to dislike Aphra Behn for her involvement in the slave rebellion and her championship of Oroonoko, but he was also keeping a suspicious eye on her relationship with the infamous republican exile, William Scot. Their affair seems to have been general gossip among the inhabitants of the place and of sufficient interest for Byam to write to Sir Robert Harley in England of its romantic ending:

"I need not enlarge but to advise you of the sympathetical passion of the Grand Shepheard Celedon who is fled after Astrea, being resolved to espouse all distress or felicities of fortune with her. But the more certaine cause of his flight (waving the arrow and services he had for the lodger [of St. John's Hill]) was a regiment of protests to the number of 1000 pounds sterling drawne up against him.* And he being a tender gentleman and unable to keep the field hath betaken himself to the other element as fleeting as himself, but whether for certain I cannot yet resolve you. Truly the Brethren [Puritans] are much startled that the Governor of the Reformation should turne tayle on the day of battle."[36]

Scot had his revenge, however, for Byam's sarcastic remarks about his gallantry with Aphra: in another letter to Harley, written four years later, Byam reported that the Dutch fleet that captured Surinam in 1667 was "sent out by the advice of Scot."[37]

Byam's letter telling of Aphra's departure is dated March 14, 1664, so she must have left Surinam shortly before. Another, undated, letter from Byam to Harley, probably written from Barbados, says that he had managed to find a ship "full freighted bound for London, on whom I sent off the fair Shepherdess and Devouring Gorge, but with what reluctancy and regret you may well conjecture."[38] The Shepherdess is of course Aphra, and Devouring Gorge seems to have been a reference to Captain Arthur Gorges, since Byam wrote to Harley again on May 14, saying, "I suppose Capt. Gorges is with you."[39] If Aphra departed in early March, she would have arrived in London, after a voyage of six to nine weeks, around the middle of May. She had clearly been long gone from St. John's Hill in July, when one William Gwilt wrote to his father in England, saying that he was staying there "with one negro for a companion."[40]

It would have, in fact, been difficult for Aphra to stay at St. John's Hill any longer than she did. Lord Willoughby and Sir Robert Harley (who owned St. John's Hill) had been once the closest of friends, but they had come to a parting of the ways in Barbados over a matter of government, and Willoughby had him arrested on February 11 (1664). The news would have reached Surinam about a week later. Lord Willoughby humiliated Harley by having him thrown into jail and then sent home in disgrace. Aphra would hardly have felt under the circumstances that she could continue to enjoy his hospitality. So she went back to England and William Scot went to Holland, where they would meet again a little more than two years later.

---

*This was the debt Scot had left behind in England.

CHAPTER SIX

London; Marriage; Plague

The extent of wives' subjection doth stretch itself very far, even unto all things. . . .

— William Gouge, *Of Domestical Duties*, 1622

> *Wife and servant are the same,*
> *But only differ in the name . . .*
> *When she the word 'obey' has said,*
> *And man by law supreme has made, . . .*
> *Fierce as an Eastern Prince he grows*
> *And all his innate rigor shows.*
> *Then but to look, to laugh, or speak*
> *Will the nuptial contract break.*
> *Like mutes she signs alone must make,*
> *And never any freedom take,*
> *But still be governed by a nod*
> *And fear her husband as her God.*

— Lady Mary Chudleigh, 1703

Hymen and priest wait still upon Portion and Jointure; Love and Beauty have their own ceremonies. Marriage is as certain a bane to Love as lending money is to friendship.

— Aphra Behn, 1677

I

Women's wants are their most importunate solicitors to marriage.
—William Wycherley, 1677

Late spring or early summer of 1664 found Aphra Behn returned to England with no father to rely on and, it would seem, no inheritance, no dowry, no income, and no imminent prospect of any. What was she to do? What alternatives did London of that time offer to a young woman of Aphra's gifts, resourcefulness, and independence of spirit more than amply demonstrated by her experience in Surinam?

She could marry. She could attach herself to some great household as a lady-in-waiting (the upper-class of servant) or a chamber maid. She could be "kept" as a mistress or descend still further to the streets as a prostitute. Or she could work to support herself.

The normal expectation of course was that she would find a husband: the idea of a gentlewoman's working was not merely socially unacceptable, but almost unthinkable. Most young women of Aphra's age and class who were lucky enough to "catch" a husband, and they were indeed considered lucky, had already been married a few years. But given the extraordinary character that Aphra had thus far manifested, it could hardly be counted upon that she would behave in the normal way. If she had chosen the freedom of shifting for herself rather than the necessarily dependent position of any of the foregoing possibilities, what could she do? Careers in the church, the law, the university, and the government were closed to her sex, and crafts and trades, which were tightly controlled, for the most part admitted women only as their husband's partners—though widows who had inherited a business might be permitted to continue operating alone if there was no male heir to take over. Although a few merchants were women, it required capital that not many had access to, to set up a trade.

William Davenant, in his play *The Wits*, expresses the options available to a single woman of the seventeenth century who wished to support herself "honestly"—that is, avoid prostitution: "I must teach children in a dark cellar,/ Or work coifs for cracked groats and broken meats."

The great majority of women who kept themselves were wage earners: teachers, agricultural laborers or other menial workers, and spinsters (women employed in spinning—a usage coined around 1617 and subsequently denoting any unmarried woman). The working conditions for most wage earners meant hardship; but for the poor unmarried woman, at the bottom of the ladder, they entailed a slowly degrading state of semistarvation. Labor was cheap and easily available, for in this period England was relatively overpopulated—that is to say, the population was greater than the economy as it was then organized could absorb.[1] Furthermore, rapid inflation drove up prices; and as a consequence, real wages fell during the century, driving a terrifying number of people into utter poverty. Gregory King, a seventeenth-century statistician, estimated in 1696 that over half the people then in England were unable to live on the wages they brought home.[2] How they survived is a mystery to historians. Poor Relief, a government agency hardly known for its charity and not likely to overestimate, calculated five shillings as the minimum amount for the maintenance of an adult for a week. One may imagine just how minimal this was. A report of the Justices of the Peace in 1638 stated that "when they have work the wages given them is so small that it hardly suffices to buy the poor man and his family bread, for they pay six shillings for one bushel of grain and receive but eight pence for their day's work."[3] (At twelve pence to the shilling, four shillings a week for six days' work.)

Spinsters usually earned about four pence a day, without meat or drink, working full time, which adds up to two shillings a week if they worked six days, or two shillings, four pence if they worked seven: considerably less than the minimal five shillings thought necessary by the Poor Relief. Sometimes spinsters made even less than four pence: the Quarters Sessions' Wage Assessments for Devon in 1654 specified that they should be paid no more than six pence *per week* with meat and drink or one shilling, four pence without them (wages were set by the court).[4] In 1658, a quart of milk cost one pence; a pair of gloves, from four pence to ten pence; four faggots of wood for heating, twelve pence; a turkey, one shilling; and a hat, four shillings. A piece of cotton cloth was thirty shillings.[5]

Women teachers were a little better off than the multitudes of beggared spinsters, but only comparatively. In 1672, Mary Sutton was paid five shillings by the overseers of the poor for teaching workhouse children lace making, probably her week's wages. "It's little they pay, and it's little we learn 'em," commented another schoolmistress.[6]

For agricultural labor, women commonly received just a little more than half what men got for the same work. In Bedfordshire in 1684, wages for a male haymaker were fixed at ten pence a day without meat and drink and six pence a day with. The women who worked alongside them were paid only six pence a day without food and three pence with—the difference between the wages with and without nourishment proceeding from the fact that the food allowance for women was always considerably smaller, sometimes by half, than that for men, though both worked the same number of hours.[7] Under such conditions, the women who worked in the fields quickly lost their health, beauty, and often their children too: by thirty, they were old women, skin and bones. The Devon Justices of the Peace fixed wages only for women between the ages of eighteen and thirty, as if no woman over thirty was likely to be capable of working in the fields.[8]

Countless women came to the city hoping to find better conditions, but matters were equally bad there, if not worse. A visitor to England from America wondered "how possibly a livelihood could be exacted out of" such predominantly female trades "as to cry matches, small-coal, blacking, pen & ink, thread-laced, and a hundred more such kind of trifling merchandises. . . ."[9] The lack of even such starvation-level employment is signaled by the growing number of girls forced into prostitution toward the end of the seventeenth century.

Hannah Woolley, in *The Gentlewoman's Companion* (1675), advised young women to try to find places as waiting-maids. Otherwise, she cautions, they might well end in "bawdyhouses," or be tempted to steal.[10] But they could hardly be blamed for resisting servitude. Although the lot of the seventeenth-century servant was better than that of the wage earner in that she was part of a household and usually did not starve, her wages did not permit her to entertain any hopes of extricating herself from her position. A washmaid, cook, or dairymaid received about two pounds a year in 1685, and a ladies' maid about seven pounds or so, depending on her accomplishments. Samuel Pepys spent more buying a new suit of clothes for his servant girl so that she would look minimally respectable than her entire year's salary amounted to. The hours were long and the work back-breaking, as the functions of a seventeenth-century household were much more extensive than the relatively mechanized ones of today. In addition, servant girls were frequently maltreated, severely beaten, and often subject to sexual harassment by their masters. Samuel Pepys's continual fingering of his female servants was not in the least uncommon. Of course if the girl was so unfortunate as to get pregnant, she was immediately discharged, often with no security, no funds to keep herself and her child, and no possibility of getting other work.

It was rare for a young woman to persist in believing that she could survive independently. Jane Martindale, who preceded Aphra by a generation, left her home in Yorkshire with the idea of making a living in London, but after only a short time, according to her brother, "her money grew so near to an end, that she had thoughts to sell her hair, which was very lovely both for length and color." Instead, another means of survival presented itself: "At [that] instant, a gentleman . . . being fallen in love with her, (suspecting what her condition might be), supplied her for the present, and shortly after married her." [11]

Such experiences were a strong argument for marriage. If one had to choose between wage slavery and the slavery of marriage for money, at least the latter kept the wolves from the door, in one sense if not the other.

II

A woman . . . has been taught to think preferment the sum total of her endeavours, the completion of all her hopes.

—Mary Astell,
Reflections on Marriage, 1700

If financial exigency were not persuasion enough to marry, there were plenty of other inducements that could be brought to bear on a young woman in Aphra Behn's position. One was age. A girl in those times began to be uncomfortable if she had passed eighteen without finding a husband, anxious by her early twenties, and frantic by her mid-twenties. Aphra Behn was about twenty-four when she arrived in London. Twenty-five was the dividing line: a woman unmarried by then was seen as a lost cause, "a living confession of failure," as one writer put it. Jane Barker, a poet who published a book of verse the year before Aphra died (1688), included a poem in praise of "A Virgin Life," entreating fate to let her remain in this "happy life . . . Fearless of twenty-five and all its train,/ Of slights and scorns, or being called old maid . . . Ah lovely state how strange it is to see,/ What mad conceptions some have made of thee,/ As though thy being was all wretchedness,/ Or foul deformity in the ugliest dress." Jane Barker also included in her collection, however, a poem by a man friend of hers called "Farther Advice to the Ladies," which counseled: "Be prudent, Ladies; marry while you may,/ Lest, when too late, you do repent and say,/ You wish you had, whilst the sun had shone, made hay."[12] By twenty-one, he advises, a young lady had better take any husband who will still have her.[13]

The Countess of Winchelsea was apparently so ashamed of her advanced years at marriage that she lied about her age on her marriage license. It read: "14 May, 1684: Appeared personally Colonel Heneage Finch [later the Earl of Winchelsea] of Eastwell in ye county of Kent, Batchelor, aged about twenty-seven years alleged that he intends to marry Madam Anne Kingsmill . . . a spinster aged about eighteen years."[14] The future Countess of Winchelsea was in fact twenty-three, not eighteen.

The specter of old maid hung over young women as a sort of nightmare that inevitably awaited their failure to acquire a man. There was simply no place in society for women who remained unattached past a certain age; they were the subject of ridicule and derision, a disgrace to their families, shunned as outcasts and freaks. "An old maid," wrote the author of *The Ladies Calling* (1673), "is now thought such a curse as no poetic fury can exceed, looked on as the most calamitous creature in nature."[15] Mary Astell, in *A Serious Proposal to the Ladies* (1694), described the desperation suffered by women confronted with the prospect of passing the "climacteric" of twenty-five without the stamp of matrimony: "The poor lady, having past the prime of her years in gaity and company, in running the circles of all the vanities of the town, having spread all her nets and used all her arts for conquest, and finding that the bait fails where she would have it take; and having all this while been so over-careful of her body, that she had no time to improve her mind, which therefore affords her no safe retreat, now she meets with disappointments abroad, and growing every day more and more sensible that the respect which used to be paid her decays as fast as her beauty; quite terrified with the dreadful name of old maid, which yet none but fools will reproach her with, nor any wise woman be afraid of, to avoid this terrible *Mormo,* and the scoffs that are thrown on superannuated virgins, she flies to some dishonourable match as her last, tho' much mistaken refuge, to the disgrace of her family, and her own irreparable ruin." [16]

Moreover, there was simply nowhere for old maids to go. In former times, families had placed them in nunneries—"convenient stowage for withered daughters," as Milton put it—but with the Reformation those institutions had disappeared from England. Governesses were not yet as common as they became in the eighteenth century, so that option was not yet as fully available as it was to the unhappy Brontë sisters two centuries later. In the seventeenth century, after the death of the father, the eldest son or closest male relative normally inherited the family house, and the unmarried daughters who remained with nowhere else to go were not usually welcome members of the new family. They were an embarrassment and a burden. In some cases, they were kept on in the household in the reduced capacity of domestic help. Mary and Ralph Josselin's father died when she was twenty-one and he was about fifteen. In the beginning, he helped her out financially, but when after twelve years on the marriage market she was still unmarried, he took her into his house as a servant, though promising that "my respect is, and shall always be towards her as a sister." [17] It may have been that the situation was awkward for Mary, since, after only eight months, she went to work for neighbors. In the next twenty years, her brother only mentioned her twice in the diary he kept: once to complain that she rarely came to see him. Mary's relations with her employers do not seem to have been without difficulty, for after thirteen years of service, her brother wrote that she had complained to him and described her as "my poor sister Mary, whose heart is broken with grief and trouble." He exhorted her "to submit to God in his providence to her," but records no other offer of help. [18] Finally, Mary was released from her long servitude when she married a widower at fifty.

Legally, any woman over twelve—the age of consent for marriage—could be forced into service if she was without a husband. *The Lawes Resolution of the Rights of Women* (1632) stated that "two Justices of the Peace in the country, or the head officer and two Burgesses in the cities, may appoint any woman of the age of twelve years, and under forty, being unmarried, and out of service, to serve and be retained by year, week, or day, in such cost and for such wages as they shall think meet, and if she refuse, they may commit her to prison, till she shall be bound to serve." [19] This, of course, would not apply to any women of position or fortune who had "protectors."

Single people generally were regarded with suspicion and mistrust by their contemporaries. At a time when most people belonged to some sort of family group, those who did not were considered oddities. Gregory King calculated that in London at the end of the century thirty-seven percent of the inhabitants were husbands or wives, two percent widowers, seven percent widows, thirty-three percent children, thirteen percent servants, and only *eight* percent sojourners and single persons (sojourners might include a mother-in-law who lived with the family). In the major towns outside London, single people accounted for only five percent of the population, and in villages and hamlets, only three percent. [20] For a woman to deliberately choose to remain unmarried was to place herself in the position of an outsider. For most, the embarrassment of a prolonged single state was a misery equalled only by that of the many women who had been married off to husbands they positively loathed.

The pressure to "catch" a husband before it was too late was further intensified by another factor: as the seventeenth century progressed, the search was getting more and more difficult. The combination of several elements, such as a difference in mortality rates and greater masculine vulnerability to the plague, led to an imbalance between the sexes. At the end of the century there were thirteen women to every ten men in London.

The extent to which the marriage market was weighted against women is evidenced by the widening differential between dowry and jointure: the dowry, also called a "portion," was the cash sum a father handed over to the husband upon marriage in exchange for his signing over the jointure, an agreed-upon income guaranteed his wife if she survived him. In the mid-sixteenth century, a girl's family had to give four or five hundred pounds to every one hundred made over to her as a jointure, but by the end of the seventeenth century, that ratio had become ten to one. A woman's rateable value, then, had plummeted to half of what it had been in just a little over half a century.[21] The inflation, as may well be imagined, caused a certain measure of matrimonial panic.

In the 1640s, Henry Oxinden, who lived in the neighborhood of Kent that Aphra grew up in, wrote to his mother, who was staying in London at the time: "Pray if my sister Elizabeth may marry well in London, not to neglect it, for good husbands are hard to be got here."[22]

If none of the foregoing could propel a girl into the arms of the first eligible man who wooed her, there was still another consideration that might decide her: that was sex. In an age without any effective contraception, there were three alternatives for a sexually active unmarried woman: she could, like Middleton's *Roaring Girl,* remain chaste; she could lie-in secretly or somehow dispose of the child; or she could openly take on the social stigma and financial burden of a bastard child. But for the most part, only the very poor or the mistresses of Charles II, who were exempted from the general rule by their royal connection, dared the last. (And even they came under fire in anonymous lampoons and satires.) For the rest of the population, it was against the law: a woman could be heavily fined and even imprisoned for giving birth to a bastard child. In Hertfordshire in 1659, according to the Court Records, a woman was sentenced to one year in prison for that crime and lost her child to the parish authorities.[23] The Court Records are also full of women arrested and even executed for murdering their illegitimate children.

Given the penalties, it is not surprising that many women who found themselves pregnant either blackmailed the father into marrying them or laid their hands on the first man they could persuade to do the honors before their "term" was up.

III

All of them [women] *are understood either married or to be married. . . . The Common Law here shaketh hand with divinitie. . . .*
—*The Lawes Resolution of the Rights of Women,* 1632

A story that Aphra Behn wrote at the end of her life, called *The Black Lady,* perfectly illustrates the way in which these circumstances acted to force young women with minds of their own to conform to the marital conventions of their day. Though the characters are disguised by typically Restoration literary names like Bellamora and her Fondlove, they are in fact realistically drawn and very much creatures of Aphra Behn's London, presented by her as though she were simply gossiping to a friend about another acquaintance rather than creating a fiction. Aphra begins the narrative thus: *"About the beginning of last June (as near as I can remember) Bellamora came to town from Hampshire, and was obliged to lodge the first night at the same inn where the stage-coach set up. The next day she took coach for Covent-Garden, where she thought to find Madam Brightly, a relation of hers, with whom she designed to continue for about half a year undiscovered, if possible, by her friends* [i.e., relatives] *in the country: and ordered therefore her trunk, with her clothes, and most of her money and jewels, to be brought after her to Madame Brightly's by a strange porter, whom she spoke to in the street as she was taking coach; being utterly unacquainted with the neat* [i.e., dishonest] *practices of this fine city. When she came to Bridges-Street, where indeed her cousin had lodged near three or four years since, she was strangely surprised that she could not learn anything of her . . . till, at last, describing Madam Brightly to one of the housekeepers in that place, he told her that there was such a kind of lady, whom he had sometimes seen there about a year and a half ago, but that he believed she was married and removed towards Soho."*

The unfortunate Bellamora, Aphra goes on, having forgotten all her jewels and money, hires a hackney coach and wanders all through St. Anne's parish, looking for her cousin Mrs. Brightly. Finally, just when the fugitive is about to despair of finding her female friend, she happens on a private house owned by an elderly gentlewoman who, having no other means of supporting herself, lets lodgings in the house she has inherited from her husband. In Bellamora's description of her cousin the older gentlewoman recognizes a lady currently lodging with her; so she invites the younger woman, who seems most distracted, to make herself comfortable until the lady she is looking for returns. A good while passes before the cousin appears, and in the interim Bellamora and the old gentlewoman talk, first politely, then more and more intimately. Bellamora ultimately confesses the cause of her flight from the country: *"to avoid the hated importunities of a gentleman, whose pretended love to her she feared had been her eternal ruin."*

Eventually the lady they are waiting for returns, and Bellamora finds to her horror that it is not her cousin Mrs. Brightly. The lady, however, recognizes the country girl, who remembers only that she has seen her some years ago. She is delighted to find a friend in any case and readily accepts the lady's offer to shelter her until she is able to recover her money and jewels. This lady, unbeknownst to Bellamora, happens to be the sister of the very gentleman she wishes to escape. Given the fact that the upper classes in England of that time lived in a very small world, the coincidence is not altogether impossible, but such plot devices were also a convention of Restoration literature.

At any rate, it is the elderly gentlewoman with whom Bellamora establishes the closest rapport; the next day she confides her secret to her, *"almost drowned in tears."* Bellamora's situation is this: for some time, she had been courted by Mr. Fondlove, who, she had reason to believe, loved her sincerely and even passionately. Her mother, however, had in mind a more ambitious marriage for her, to a gentleman of greater estate, whom Bellamora thoroughly disliked. As an act of rebellion, she has acceded to Fondlove's sexual advances and, as she puts it, *"ruined herself."* Her double attitude toward the sexual initiation is interesting: evidently her own choice, actively decided, it is nevertheless understood and expressed by her in passive terms. She cannot, in the context of acceptable feminine behavior, take responsibility for her own decision. Nor does she feel free to acknowledge her own sexuality. Nor does she want to give up her independence. Nor does she wish to marry. She is caught in a complicated web of double binds that function both externally and internally. She at once internalizes and rejects the dominant sexual conventions of her society.

The "antient" gentlewoman, who has not yet understood the full implications of Bellamora's intentions, asks her why she imagines herself ruined: *"To which she answered, I am great with child by him, Madam, and wonder you did not perceive it last night. Alas: I have not a month to go: I am ashamed, ruined, and damned, I fear, forever lost. Oh: fie, Madam, think not so (said the other), for the gentleman may yet prove true and marry you."* Bellamora replies that indeed he has repeatedly entreated her to marry him and continues to solicit her earnestly to do so. The original obstacle of her mother's hopes for a more financially advantageous marriage has been removed by the favored suitor's death. But, insists Bellamora, she herself cannot bear the idea of marrying. Her reasons are twofold: first, she does not wish to be in the position that wives ordinarily occupied in the Restoration—objects whose principal value lay in the production of an heir and a dowry, deserted in the solitude and boredom of country estates while husbands pursued pleasures and mistresses and "business" in the capital. Bellamora of course does not articulate her fears, but mournfully declares to the gentlewoman that she is sure that Fondlove *"can never love me after* [they marry]." Her second objection to him as a husband lies in the fact that he has been the agent of her disgrace: her sexual guilt is so overwhelming that she is compelled to displace it to him and translate herself to the role of the helplessly seduced—evidently not the case.

The old gentlewoman does not question her reasoning but raises the practical question of what provision she intends to make for her child. Bellamora admits herself at a loss, and the older woman says that she will do everything she can to help, though her resources are quite meager. She immediately goes to the second lady, her lodger and Fondlove's sister, to recount the story and take consultation. The two women are sympathetic to Bellamora's position and understand her aversion to marriage; but, having more experience in the world than she, they realize that her alternatives are very limited, if not nonexistent. They agree to notify Fondlove, who rushes to the scene. He is advised not to signal his presence, however, until Bellamora has fully comprehended the dimensions of her situation. The landlady tells her that *"she had but a little money herself, and if the overseers of the poor (justly so called from their overlooking 'em) should have the least suspicion of a strange and unmarried person, who was entertained in her house big with child, and so near her time as Bellamora was, she should be troubled, if they could not give security to the parish of twenty or thirty pounds, that they should not suffer by her, which she could not; or otherwise she must be sent to the House of Correction, and her child to the parish nurse."*

Bellamora, Aphra relates, is sufficiently impressed by this warning, but still insists that she would rather undergo all this than be exposed to the scorn of her friends and relations in the country. The landlady continues to represent to Bellamora the cul-de-sac she faces, but the young lady holds out for three weeks under the barrage of persuasion. Her pregnancy has been kept as secret as possible, even from the servants (who are not allowed to enter Bellamora's room), but a chambermaid overhears a conversation, and eventually word *"reached the long ears of the wolves of the parish (the overseers), who next day designed to pay her a visit."* That evening, however, Fondlove makes his presence known, and the lovers fall into each other's arms. But Bella-mora still refuses to marry him. He begs her to reconsider *"if not for his, nor her own, yet for the child's sake, which she hourly expected; that it might not be born out of wedlock, and so be made incapable of inheriting ei-ther of their estates; with a great worry, more pressing arguments on all sides."* Finally she relents and is forthwith rewarded by a trip to the Exchange, where she is provided with *"several pretty businesses that la-dies in her condition want."* She has bartered her ideal of love-out-of-marriage for traditional baubles. The story ends on a menacing note: while they are all gone to the Exchange, the *"vermin of the parish, (I mean the overseers of the poor, who eat the bread from 'em)* [came] *to search for a young black-haired lady (for so was Bellamora) who was either brought to bed, or just ready to lie down."*

Aphra herself well understood the dilemma that young women of her time faced: the contradiction between independence and desire, the oppression of the system of arranged marriages, the bankruptcy of the institution itself, and the disastrous position in which it placed women were all recurrent themes in her writing—the articulation of her own life and the lives of the men and women she knew.

IV

> *Oh how fatal are forced marriages!*
> *How many ruins one such match pulls on!*
>
> —Aphra Behn,
> *The Lucky Chance,* 1686

If a young woman of Aphra Behn's generation had few choices outside of marriage, once married she had fewer. Under Common Law, she became a *femme covert,* which meant that she had no legal rights or identity outside her spouse's: she could own no property, make no contract, and have no right to her own children. She did not even have guardianship of her sons and daughters if her husband died unless he so specified in his will—otherwise, they automatically be-came the wards of her father-in-law. Some families in the seventeenth century had begun to make marriage settlements that protected a daughter's inheritance to some extent from a possibly irresponsible husband's dissipating it. But the purpose in so doing was primarily to assure that the fortune would pass to blood heirs, rather than to establish the wife's financial independence during marriage. Even so, such measures could provide only limited protection, and they were for the most part confined to those with great fortunes to dispose of.

The Lawes Resolution of the Rights of Women (1632) described the legal principle that governed women's position in the courts: "This consolidation which we call wedlock is a locking together. It is true that man and wife are one person, but understand in what manner: when a small brook or a little river incorporatith with the . . . Thames, the poor rivulet looseth her name; it is carried and recarried with the new associate; it beareth no sway; it possesseth nothing during coverture. A woman, as soon as she is married, is called *covert,* in Latin *nupta,* that is "veiled," as it were, clouded and overshadowed; she hath lost her stream. . . . I may more truly say to a married woman, her new self is her superior, her companion, her master."[24]

Under these conditions, opposition to a husband was at best difficult: even if he beat his wife or threatened her life, she had no legal recourse. If she left him, he could by law force her to return; she could take no property with her, and any money she might be able to earn or that might be given her automatically became her husband's property—to dispose of as he wished. If a husband chose to do so, it was in his power to literally prevent his wife from surviving if she had left home without his consent. An anonymous woman writer who was one of Aphra Behn's literary successors complained in 1688 of the "unbounded arbitrary power" that a man had over his wife: "If custom we accuse as too severe,/ In impositions when we virgins are;/ What yokes and fetters choose,/ Who enters the matrimonial noose?/ To be the partner of another's flame,/ Gives up her self, her fortune, and her name,/ Her hours of soft repose and liberty,/ Nay, her own will then cease[s] to be free;/ For what commands may not a husband lay,/ When the wife's part, *is only to obey?*"[25]

Even if a woman were fortunate enough to have a husband she really loved, whose companionship she enjoyed—which, as diaries and letters indicate, was uncommon enough in the seventeenth century, given the marriage system—his upbringing would still in all likelihood have led him to expect the unconditional feminine submission that tradition dictated. Nor could he ignore the social pressure to protect family "honor."

———·

Aphra's marriage to Mr. Behn occupied no more than a brief interlude in her affairs—probably at most a year and a half—but it might reasonably be assumed that had it lasted longer, her life almost certainly would have taken a different direction. First, the question of supporting herself by writing would never have come up; and second, unless Mr. Behn were a man of singular liberality, he probably would have shrunk from allowing his wife to endanger her reputation by associating herself with the seamy theatrical world of London. Last, the minimal material conditions for writing professionally simply did not exist for most married women. In the absence of birth control, it was not unusual for wives to remain pregnant almost constantly: in seventeen years, Lady Anne Fanshawe gave birth to no fewer than twenty children.[26] Even though she suffered severe physical pain and increasingly serious illness, Alice Thornton saw it as her God-imposed duty to produce children. Dreading each new pregnancy, she nevertheless passively accepted her condition: "It is not a Christian's part to choose anything of this nature," she wrote in her autobiography, "be it ever so contrary to our own desires."[27] Aside from the fact that a wife's chief responsibility was to produce an heir, it was also, wrote the Duchess of Newcastle, a social disgrace to remain childless: "Many times married women desire children, as maids do husbands, more for honour than for comfort or happiness, thinking it a disgrace to live old maids, and so likewise to be barren."[28] In addition to the physical discomfort and hazard to health that repeated pregnancies caused, the management of a seventeenth-century household was considerably more cumbersome than its present-day counterpart. Soap, medicines, and all sorts of necessaries had to be produced at home; fires had to be kept going, children looked after. Even great ladies who had a staff of servants had to devote a great deal of time simply to organizing, keeping accounts, and making sure all went as it should. Only very unusual circumstances would give a wife with a large household the time to write that a single woman might have at her disposal.

What marriage to Mr. Behn was like must remain a matter of speculation, since very little is known about him. Charles Gildon, in his preface to Aphra's play *The Younger Brother* (1696), stated that Mr. Behn was an "eminent" London merchant of Dutch ancestry. One of the Fair Sex furnished the same information, adding that Aphra married Mr. Behn after her return from Surinam. She was apparently no longer married to him when she went to Antwerp in July 1666. He was scarcely more than a fleeting episode in her life.

Though Mr. Behn, like many other "facts" of Aphra's biography, has been held to be merely another invention of Aphra's—to make her seem more respectable—there is substantial ground for believing that he was more than merely a figment of her imagination. She used the name Aphra Behn on official correspondence sent to the Secretary of State from Antwerp and also on letters to the Groom of the Bedchamber, Thomas Killigrew, who seems to have known both her and her family well. Both sets of letters, in her handwriting, are preserved among the State Papers in the Public Record Office. She also used the name Behn on two petitions to the King, written by a lawyer or legal clerk when she was about to go to debtor's prison— not a situation in which she would use a recently assumed name when there were many witnesses who could testify to its falseness. In all the hostile satires written about her there is no questioning of her right to call herself Mrs. Behn, and one lampoon refers to her as "the lewd widow." The fact that she was buried in Westminster Abbey as Mrs. Behn further confirms that there was no doubt of her marriage among her contemporaries. Finally, Thomas Culpepper quite clearly says that Aphra had a foster sister who married a Colonel Write (*sic*) and "Aphra mary'd Mr. Beene." [29] He makes a joke about Aphra "Beene" as "Ben Johnson," since her maiden name was Johnson and her married name Behn (presumably pronounced "Ben").

The circumstances surrounding Aphra's marriage can only be speculated on. As a young woman with charm, wit, and beauty but no dowry, Aphra must have had severely limited marital possibilities. Sons of the aristocracy who had not yet inherited their estates were generally compelled by parents to make financially advantageous alliances, and girls in Aphra's position were often forced into matches with older merchants, who were at liberty to trade fortune for beauty if they wished. There is a hint in Gildon's description of Mr. Behn as an "eminent" London merchant that suggests just such an arrangement. It hardly sounds like a love match: unless Aphra knew Mr. Behn before she went to Surinam—where, it will be remembered, she carried on a gallantry with William Scot—she cannot have had time to build up much of an acquaintance before she married him.

No characters in all Aphra Behn's literary work are described with so much antipathy as older City merchants who have the vanity to marry young girls, forced into the match by financial necessity or by tyrannical parents. Ordinarily, Aphra amusedly mocks people whose shortcomings she finds ridiculous, but her portrayal of these "trading" husbands is vituperative. If her marriage to Mr. Behn was indeed one of those "forced" alliances, it would at least in part explain some of the feeling behind Aphra's violent attack on the institution and its thematic domination of so much of her work. Unfortunately, such inference must remain conjecture, as Mr. Behn seems likely to continue an enigma: extensive research has thus far failed to produce a more than randomly likely candidate. There is no record of the marriage extant and, as Mr. Behn's given name is not known—nor any facts such as his place of residence or business or his birthplace or parents' names—there are no clues to provide corroborating evidence for any name that might appear in parish registers or other records.[30]

As divorce was more or less out of the question for all but the very rich—and even then obtainable only through a lengthy process culminating in an act of Parliament—Aphra's marriage to Mr. Behn must have been ended by his death. It seems probable that he was one of the victims of the Great Plague (1665–1666), as he died during the year that visitation swept London. Merchants were particularly vulnerable to the contagion, because they could not leave their businesses in the City without great loss and so were not able to spend most of the year in the country, as the aristocracy and courtiers did.

If Aphra spent any part of the plague year in London, she was lucky to have survived. Samuel Pepys noticed the first signs of plague—red crosses upon the doors of a few houses in Drury Lane, quarantining those within—on June 7, 1665: "the hottest day that I ever felt in my life," he wrote in his *Diary*. By the end of June, the rapid spread of the disease had created such a panic that everyone who could was leaving London. Carts and wagons crowded the roads out of town, and the Mayor's office was besieged with requests for passes and permission to travel. Every available boat was commandeered, and the river was full of fugitives and their possessions. The court removed on July 9 to Hampton Court, at the end of July to Salisbury, and then in September to Oxford, where it remained until January. Parliament also retired to Oxford. In London, those who remained were dying by the thousands: in the week of August 4, 2,010 died; August 18,

3,880; August 23, 4,237; and August 31, 6,012. There seemed no end to mortality. Church bells rang constantly in discordant requiem, and furious crowds ran to brothels in the hope of contracting syphilis, which was rumored to prevent the more immediately fatal disease. Quack doctors, witches, astrologers, and medicine men extracted outrageous sums for cures; dissident preachers blamed the visitation on the Pope and on the restoration of the popish Church of England. Corpses were to be buried at night, but so many were beginning to pile up that on August 12 Pepys recorded: "The people did so, that now it seems they are fain to carry the dead to be buried by daylight, the nights not sufficing to do it in." The plague had undermined any humanity or social conscience in people's behavior toward one another, "the plague making us cruel as dogs to each other," according to Pepys.[31]

September was the worst month of all. A thousand corpses were added to the lists every day: 6,988 the first week, 6,544 the second, and 7,165 the third—thirty thousand in one month. The dimensions of the disaster were staggering: out of a population of five hundred thousand, nearly seventy thousand died. It was the last great plague to ravage England.

London, marriage, plague, in little more than two years: Aphra's education in life's adversity was proceeding at a formidable rate. Poverty was to be her next lesson, as it seems that Mr. Behn either did not include her in his will or his affairs fell victim to the disaster that took his life. When Aphra went to Antwerp, her entire means consisted of no more than forty pounds and a few rings to pawn. Perhaps Mr. Behn's will was contested, too: when his fellow merchant Sir Martin Noël died, the confusion was so great that no one could determine his worth or the state of his investments, which Pepys says was not unusual for eminent merchants: "It seems that nobody can make anything of his estate, as nobody can understand whereabouts his estate is—which is the fate of those great dealers in everything."[32]

Aphra's brief experiment with marriage seems to have left her with a more or less permanent distaste for the institution: it was an experience she was never to repeat. She had, however, to find a way to support herself if she was to eschew the financial security of matrimony. She barely had time to cast about before an interesting opportunity presented itself: she was asked to spy for Charles II.

CHAPTER SEVEN

Spying

Public matters in a most sad condition. Seamen discouraged for want of pay, and are become not to be governed. Our enemies, the French and Dutch, great, and grow more, by our poverty. The Parliament backward in raising, because jealous of the spending of the money. The City less and less likely to be built again, everybody settling elsewhere, and nobody encouraged to trade. A sad, vicious, negligent court, and all sober men there fearful of the ruin of the whole kingdom this next year.

—Samuel Pepys,
Diary, December 31, 1666

. . . London, Empress of the Northern Clime,
By an high fate thou greatly didst expire;
Great as the worlds, which at the death of time
Must fall, and rise a nobler frame by fire.

Such was the rise of this prodigious fire,
Which in mean buildings first obscurely bred,
From thence did soon to open streets aspire,
And straight to Palaces and Temples spread.

The next to danger, hot pursued by fate,
Half clothed, half naked, hastily retire:
And frighted Mothers strike their breasts, too late,
For helpless Infants left amidst the fire.

—John Dryden, *Annus Mirabilis,* 1666

I

"Public employments in the field and courts are usually denied to women," wrote Bathusa Makin during the reign of Charles II.[1] And indeed, outside the office of mistress or household servant, there were virtually no women in the King's employ in Aphra Behn's time. Aside from the fact that women were not legally empowered to act independently of their husbands (and few women had either the education or exposure to the world of business or empire to pretend to any position of political responsibility) involvement in "state-matters" was considered simply out of their sphere—foreign both to their innate capacities and to the modesty that was properly and naturally "feminine." Women of royal blood were of course exempt from this dictum by birthright.

Ordinary women who meddled in politics were considered dangerously out of order. Katherine Philips, the Matchless Orinda, felt compelled to justify her only political poem, written upon the execution of Charles I, by claiming that the circumstance was extraordinary enough to warrant such a departure from the subject matter proper to her sex:

> *I think not on the State, nor am concerned*
> *Which way soever the great helm is turned:*
> *But as that son whose Father's danger nigh*
> *Did force his native dumbness, and untie*
> *The fettered organs; so this is a cause*
> *That will excuse the breach of Nature's laws.*[2]

Katherine Philips's defensiveness about her political "intervention" hardly seems necessary, but her desire to protect herself from criticism accurately reflects the hostility that women who did wish to make some political impact might reasonably expect.

During the Commonwealth, such radically dissenting groups as the Levellers, the Ranters, and the Diggers, advocating unheard-of propositions, produced a series of collective political actions carried out by women—the presentation to Parliament of protesting petitions signed by thousands of women (in 1642, 1643, 1649, and 1653), accompanied by what were called "violent" demonstrations outside the House. The petitioners nevertheless referred to themselves as the "weaker sex" and spoke of their "frail condition," which evidently was exaggerated. Their petition of 1649 carefully stated: "We confess it is not our custom to address ourselves to this House in the public behalf . . ." and indeed to do so "may be thought strange and unbeseeming to our sex."[3] Even a revolutionary Parliament thought their action so "unbeseeming" that it at first categorically refused even to accept the petition, but two days later finally did so and forwarded the following answer: "The matter you petition about, is of an higher concernment than you understand. The House gave an answer to your husbands; and therefore you are desired to go home, and look after your own business, and meddle with your huswifery." A newspaper that reported the event quoted the statement and interpreted it as meaning "in effect, that they should go home and spin; it being the usuall work of women either to spin or knit and not to meddle with state affairs." A second newspaper added: "It can never be a good world, when women meddle in state matters . . . their husbands are to blame, that they have no fitter employment for them."[4]

Aphra Behn, who entered King Charles's intelligence service in July 1666, was perfectly conscious of the extraordinary nature of her position as a woman acting in an official capacity. Years later, she spoke of her mission in a poem addressed to John, son of William Howard, Viscount Stafford, recalling having known him while in Antwerp when

> . . . *by the Arcadian King's Commands* [Charles II]
> *I left these Shades, to visit Foreign Lands;*
> *Employed in public toils of State Affairs,*
> *Unusual with my Sex, or to my Years.*

She was hardly apologetic, however. She made no statements about her feminine "weakness" or unsuitability for the difficult and dangerous job of espionage.

The second Anglo-Dutch War, which Aphra was to play her part in, began while she was still in Surinam, though it was not formally declared until February 1665, about a year after she returned to England. In the Battle of Lowestoft, the first encounter between the two fleets, there were heavy losses on both sides; but in the end the English gained ascendency and the Dutch took flight. What might have been a complete victory was spoiled by an incident that was to prove characteristic of the English efforts throughout the war. James, Duke of York, Lord High Admiral of the Navy in command of the fleet, had retired to his cabin after a hard day's fighting, leaving the crew with orders to pursue the Dutch retreat. Henry Brouncker, his secretary, a reputed "wit" and gambler, decided that he had seen more than enough action already and pretended to have gotten a change of command from the Duke. The Captain, having no reason to doubt the counterfeit orders to shorten sail, did so, and the Duke awoke next morning to see the Dutch fleet far in the distance, escaping to the safety of Texel.

The war, though fought on sea, must have seemed very immediate to the English people, for the guns could be heard clearly in London itself. Dryden recalled that the "noise of the cannon from both navies reached our ears about the city, so that all men being alarmed with it, and in a dreadful suspense of the event which we knew was then deciding, everyone went following the sound as his fancy led him; and, leaving the town almost empty, some took towards the park, some across the river, others down it all seeking the noise in the depth of silence."[5] Aphra Behn may very well have been among the listening crowds, either recently married to the London merchant Mr. Behn or already his early widow. That she shared their anxiety and patriotism is clear from her later statements.

During that summer, 1665, the Duke of York went to Yorkshire to investigate rumors of an imminent uprising of republican dissidents in the west and north, to be carried out with the aid of Holland. Republicans themselves, the Dutch had offered sanctuary to a great number of political refugees at the Restoration; the latter, in turn, had organized a standing army with the intention of sparking an internal rebellion in England, then invading with the Dutch, and reinstating the Commonwealth. Shortly after the English victory at Lowestoft, Sir William Davidson, then in Holland, wrote to Lord Arlington, Secretary of State in charge of intelligence, to forward a letter "from a person in Rotterdam, who has promised to discover a plot for a rising in the west and north of England, to be aided from Holland, and is son to one of the King's judges who was quartered."[6] The informer, as other sources confirm, could have been no one else but William Scot. Scot, who had gone to Holland shortly after leaving Surinam—perhaps directly, since he could not safely return to England—was in a very good position to inform on such plots, as he had lost no time in joining the regiment of English Parliamentarian officers and other "disaffected persons" who were meeting in the Netherlands. This army in exile was commanded by Colonel Bampfield, an ex-spy in Thomas Scot's Commonwealth intelligence service, and included a number of high officials of the Puritan regime.

The information that Scot sent Arlington about a republican uprising in the north and west of England was soon confirmed by domestic sources, who also reported that one of the connections between the republicans in Holland and the plotters in Yorkshire was Richard Sykes, "Scot's brother-in-law and correspondent." [7]

William Scot was therefore a most useful connection for the English intelligence service to establish. Arlington evidently considered his information valuable enough to instruct Thomas Corney and Nicholas Oudart, two of his agents already in the Netherlands, to find out more about Scot and to negotiate with him. On August 3, however, an anonymous agent reported: "Thomas Corney thinks that by means of William Scot he can discover all actions of the discontented party, both there and in England, but he is filled with untruths by Scot, Colonel Bampfield, and Lord Nieuport, late ambassador in England; they plotted together and took Corney prisoner and had his papers searched: Oudart, who corresponded with Corney, was also taken and his papers; the latter will die, but Corney will be spared. Sands Temple, lieutenant of the *Charity,* was called in on pretence of giving bail, and taken close prisoner." [8]

Spying could be dangerous. The price for discovery was heavy, and sources like William Scot could not always be counted upon not to double-cross in favor of the highest bidder.

Scot later explained to Aphra Behn that he was forced to betray Corney to the Dutch because the latter's indiscretion had placed both of them in danger. Whether Scot was telling the truth in this instance is debatable; but it is without question that he was perfectly capable of double-dealing. The fact that John De Witt, Pensionary of the Dutch States General, gave William Scot a post at a thousand rixdollars* a year at the Hague immediately after Thomas Corney's apprehension makes Scot look still more suspect.

The dissident exiles in Holland were decisively important in the carrying on of the business of the Anglo-Dutch war. Not only did

*Dutch currency

they provide an extremely efficient intelligence network, but they encouraged the Dutch to entertain schemes of invading England and effecting a coup d'etat—an ambition they would have been unlikely to harbor without the aid of Englishmen themselves. Even De Ruyter's spectacular attack on the Thames depended heavily on the information supplied by sea captains who had been in Cromwell's navy and denied promotion at the Restoration. Both the Thames and the Medway were difficult rivers to navigate, the former because of sandbanks in the estuary and the latter because of its winding course and many mud flats. De Witt had also been informed by his intelligence sources of the exact location and number of English men-of-war laid up on the Medway, as well as the dockyard installations and the state of the defenses. Conversely, it was a renegade Dutch captain, Heemskerk, who helped Sir Robert Holmes carry out his raid on the islands of Vlieland and Ter Schelling, with disastrous losses for the Dutch.

Intelligence also played an essential part in the next major battle of the war after Lowestoft—six weeks before Aphra Behn was sent spying. The English navy suffered heavy losses in what is remembered as the Four Days' Battle (June 1–4, 1668) because Arlington's spies had furnished inaccurate information. There was great public outcry over the intelligence service's incompetence. Samuel Pepys remarked in his diary on June 4: "how bad we are at intelligence"; and his naval superior Sir William Coventry confided to Pepys a few weeks later that "he was under the lash of people's discourse," but "as to the business of intelligence, the want whereof the world [does] much complain of, that it was not his business."[9] The responsibility, of course, rested on Arlington.

Given his delicate political position and the need for strengthening the intelligence services, Lord Arlington may well have decided at this point that it was worth trying a second time to persuade the wily William Scot to transfer his allegiance to the King. Scot was unlikely, however, after his initial experience with the clumsy Thomas Corney, to trust another professional spy sent by the Secretary of State. Perhaps Scot himself suggested that Aphra Behn be recruited for the job; or maybe Arlington discovered through his own sources Aphra's gallantry in Surinam with Scot and hit on the idea of sending an ambassador to treat with him whom he would be certain to trust and less likely to betray.

Though Arlington could have known of Aphra through several connections, it was not he but Thomas Killigrew who introduced her into the spying network. She wrote to him with a familiarity very different in tone from the letters she wrote to the officials who were in Arlington's service. Killigrew evidently knew her mother as well as the "Sir Thomas" who seems to be closely associated with her mother. Killigrew was also a friend of the Willoughby family. About the time Aphra was returning from Antwerp, William Willoughby (who had succeeded Francis, Lord Willoughby in the title after the death of the latter in a hurricane) wrote to the King to give news of some business dealings he had in Barbados with Arlington, Clarendon, (Lord Chancellor Hyde) and Thomas Killigrew. He presumed, the letter said, that the first two would acquaint the King with the particulars, and added that "if Tom Killigrew fails on his part, I shall him of his sugar. Found his two sons here [in Barbados]. They are loyal subjects, and had not Harry stuck close to Nevis [the island] it had been lost."[10]

Exactly how long Aphra had known Killigrew is difficult to determine, but that she had some sort of personal tie to him before he asked her to spy for the King is clear. Officially, he was Groom of the Bedchamber to the King and unofficially, court jester. Someone once told Pepys that Killigrew had "a fee out of the wardrobe for cap and bells under the title of King's jester, and may revile or jeer anybody, the greatest person without offence, by the privilege of his place."[11] Killigrew had a reputation for wit, debauchery, promiscuity, and irreverence. The King was so fond of him that he allowed the most scathing criticism from him, as long as it was amusing. On one occasion, Killigrew told Charles that he was going to hell to bring back Oliver Cromwell "that he may take some care of the affairs of England, for his successor takes none."

II

You must pardon me if I do not give my judgment or opinion in a publick letter, concerning publick affairs, in which I ought not to meddle, being a woman.

—Margaret Cavendish, Duchess of
Newcastle

Aphra's apprenticeship in her first career was just beginning at the end of July 1666, when, as a spy in the King's service, she sailed from Gravesend aboard the *Castel Rodrigo* with the Flanders fleet—two small frigates and ninety merchantmen. The *Castel Rodrigo* probably left England on Friday, July 27, or Saturday, July 28. It first landed at Ostend, but the crew was afraid to enter the town, finding the plague rife there, so went on directly to Bruges.

Aphra wrote in her first spy report that she had met on board Sir Anthony Desmarches, who took great care of her on the voyage—so much so that he afterward became one of her principal "advisers" in Antwerp. She was traveling with her brother and possibly a servant or two; a remark in a letter of August 25 to Killigrew suggests that there were four in her party, three financially dependent on her. On board also were William Howard, Lord Stafford, and his son John, with whom Aphra maintained a friendship for many years.

Somewhere on her person or in her baggage was a set of written instructions from someone in Arlington's employ, under the heading of *Memorialls for Mrs. Affora*.[12] The imperatives of her mission were these: she was first to contact "Mr. S." and to persuade him to "become a convert" and serve his King and country. In return, she was to promise him not only a pardon from His Majesty, but a substantial reward for his services, to be forwarded punctually. Through Scot, Aphra was supposed to find out exactly how many men and ships the Dutch had lost in "the late engagement"—the Battle of St. James's Day, which had taken place on July 25–26. She was to discover whether the Dutch had any plans for landing troops in any of the King's dominions; when the fleet would be out; what spies the Dutch had sent into England and who their correspondents were; which of the dissidents then in Holland were the most actively involved with the Dutch; and what merchant fleets were expected either to depart or return to Holland. She was to choose names for herself and Scot to correspond under, and "to use all secresy imaginable in the management of this business."[13] Her official supervisor was to be James Halsall, Cupbearer to the King.

The ground for persuading William Scot to cooperate and "become a convert" had been prepared by a proclamation issued by Parliament of April 9, 1666, warning twelve dissidents to return to England to stand trial under pain of being attainted for high treason and forfeiting their property.[14] William Scot's name came before any other on the list. Among the others were Colonel John Desborough, who had been on the Committee of Safety in 1659 with Thomas Scot; Thomas Kelsey, who had been the most important Parliamentary official in Kent during the Interregnum; and Sir Robert Honeywood, another republican from an old Kentish family, brother-in-law to Sir Henry Vane, and colleague of Thomas Culpepper's uncle, Algernon Sidney. Both Kelsey and Honeywood had had extensive dealings with Culpepper—on different occasions each had been responsible for his arrest and imprisonment. If these men knew who Aphra was when she arrived in Antwerp, she would be under suspicion. They were probably already anxious because of the desertion of an important member of their ranks; Colonel John Desborough had given up and returned to England. At the time Aphra was abroad, he was still in the Tower. William Scot was too crafty to let himself fall into the same trap. He would negotiate from safe territory.

Aphra's first report was written on Monday, August 6, about a week after her arrival in Antwerp. Since letters then took at least three days to get to London, Arlington's office probably received it by the end of the week. She was rushing to make the post and so had to apologize for the spelling, grammatical errors, and general "disorder," though these seem to characterize most of her letters; so one wonders whether she was always forced to write in haste, or whether these elements were not in fact inevitable in her epistolary composition. When compared to other women's letters of the time, nevertheless, they seem above average in execution. What is most striking is how natural they sound, clearly in Aphra's own voice. *"Sir,"* she begins. *"My time is very short in thear fore posibly you will find disorder; yesterday morning came Celladon: but in so much hast that he could not stay an hower so yt I was forcd to get a coach and go a days jorney wth him to have an opertunity to speak wth him, wch I did and tould him wt I had to say to him and though at first he was very shy yet affter I had usd all Ye arguments to him that weare fitt for me:* * *he became so extreamly willing to under take ye service yt he saide more to conferme me then I could expect but first I must go to Holland: for he had no time at all, he is so extreamly watch by Bampfield* [this name is in code], *that he is not suffered to go out of his sight hardly expesially into fflanders wheare I now am: because he is ye most jealous creature alive; and so he is upon most of ye English offisers about him,*

---

*Aphra seems to wish to clear herself of the suspicion that she has used "feminine wiles" to extract information from Scot.

so yt if it should be knowne to him that Celladon was in fflanders he would suspect som thing: and as he is ye most closly cuning ffellow in the world: he would doubtless do him a mischiff." [15] The scarcity of punctuation is due in part to Aphra's having used the edge of the paper as a kind of natural limit to her phrasing. She had chosen as code names Astrea and Celladon to cover herself and Scot, perhaps remembering Surinam days.

Aphra's letter goes on to remind Arlington that Scot had made a previous attempt to set up a spying correspondence with him, *"but was prevented by som body."* She affirms that he now hates his employer, Bampfield, commander of the exiled rebel troops, so much that he is now entirely ready to cooperate with the other side—though Bampfield, on his part, *"has no secret unhid from him,"* according to Scot. Astrea seems to have her own reservations about Celladon's trustworthiness. She says she must venture into Holland to meet him, despite the great danger to herself: *"Yet I will leave him without excuses, rather than have him lay a fault on me."* She also underlines the necessity for giving some proofs of the seriousness of Arlington's offers, for Scot has expressed doubts that they will materialize.

Aphra was worried too, because she had learned that Bampfield had already heard of her arrival, which sent him into *"a jealous pate concerning me."* Apparently Bampfield knew her well enough to recognize her from the description someone she calls *"the old man"* has given him. He also was quite aware of her connection with Scot and had questioned him at length about what she was doing in Antwerp.[16] Scot's denial of responsibility for her presence only increased Bampfield's misgivings. Scot had already given Aphra information about another of his agents, *"ye man in Ludgate, a base rogue,"* so Bampfield's suspicions were well founded. The rogue had been sent to visit all the English seaports, to recruit informers who would let the Dutch know the comings and goings and destinations of merchant ships that might be attacked and taken prize.

The dissidents were not the only ones watching Aphra, however. It seems from the next part of her letter that Arlington had instructed another one of his agents, Sir Anthony Desmarches, to keep an eye on her—either because he thought she might be tempted to act in Scot's interest rather than his own or because he was afraid she might commit some indiscretion. That the latter fear was grounded is evidenced by the fact that when Desmarches questioned her about her purpose in going to Antwerp, she told him everything and then innocently wrote her employer that she had done so.

The last matter that Aphra took up in her first letter was that of finances. She said she had brought only fifty pounds with her upon bill and had lost ten just in exchange. As Sir Anthony Desmarches would testify, she had been as frugal as possible, but Flanders was extremely expensive. In addition to her own expenses, she had been obliged to pay Scot's as well. She was to go to Dortrecht on Thursday next to meet Scot and needed the funds to travel if she was to be of any use to Arlington. Could he please send her some as soon as possible?

In the postscript, Aphra informed her correspondent that she had invented a new "character" or cipher, as the code used by Halsall took up too much room. His had two characters for one letter of the alphabet, and hers only one. She would continue to use, however, the other system they had agreed upon, in which a number stands for a whole word: 26 is Amsterdam; 27, Army; 38, Bampfield; 60, Fanatics (dissidents); 62, Fleet; 71, Holland, or the Dutch; 101, the Prince of Orange; 156, England, or the English; 158, France, or the French; 159, Scot; 160, herself. It seems ridiculously simple, but Arlington's office evidently considered it adequately obscure, which either reveals something about the state of seventeenth-century "technology," or more likely remarks the clumsiness and inefficiency the intelligence service was notorious for.

Aphra's second spy report was written on August 17, 1666. Since the first letter, the English commander Sir Robert Holmes had sailed up to the entrance of the Vlie, surprised 150 Dutch merchant ships, and entirely destroyed them. The next day, a landing party discovered a number of warehouses and stores on the islands of Vlieland and Ter Schelling, which they swiftly set about burning. Although Dutch losses were estimated at more than one million pounds, the English lost no more than twelve men. The attack came as a complete surprise to Aphra and certainly must have been an unpleasant one, whatever her feelings of patriotism might have been, as her business was considerably complicated by it and the danger attached to her presence in enemy territory much increased. In Holland, feeling against the English was running so high that no citizen of that country was free from suspicion. Aphra had to remain in Antwerp. She wrote to her employers: *"I am very un hapy that it is not*

yet in my power to do som thing more then hether to I have dun: but I know
you would not impute it to neglect if you knew how imposible it yet is for me
to send [to Scot] . . . *in Holland I dare as well be hanged as go and theare*
is such great doings now that they will not suffer him [Scot] *to com a way:*
and have upon the burning of these ships comanded all the companyes and
troops that went for Germany to come back again; I would venture to Dor-
trecht [in Holland] *at the hazard of my life but I am very much perswaided*
to the contrary . . . I can by no means yet saffly speak to this Rogue [Scot],
who expresses the greatest desire to serve you in the world: but I must not trust
him in Holland: when once I can see him: I shall soon settle a way of
corispondence with you and him." [17]

Anxious to prove herself, Aphra was frustrated by her own powerlessness to act. She seems eager to establish a professional objec-
tivity and distance herself from Scot, calling him "this Rogue" and
saying she cannot trust him in Holland. Her letter betrays some concern about the volatile political situation, but gives the impression
that she is more annoyed than afraid. Sir Anthony Desmarches and
another of Arlington's agents, Hieronymous Nipho, have both
strongly advised her that it is too dangerous at the moment to consider crossing the border into Holland to meet Scot. Therefore she has
written to Scot to come to her. They are to meet at a little house, in
the greatest secrecy, just outside Antwerp. She has promised to pay
his traveling expenses and whatever charges he incurs in the course of
his visit. To this purpose, she again reminds Halsall that she is out of
funds and has been forced to pawn one of her rings just to pay daily
expenses. *"Pray do not let me want for that which is the reall support of*
all," she concludes her letter, *"for I really am sick till I give you som*
good acompt of

> *Sr*
> *your most humble and faithful servant:*
> *ABehne."*

Celladon kept his rendezvous with Astrea on August 18 despite
the jealous Bampfield and brought with him a detailed answer, in his
own handwriting, to each question in Arlington's *Memorialls for Mrs.*
Affora. His information about the Dutch losses and the movements of
the merchant fleet cannot have added much to what the English already knew, but he was in an ideal position to provide news of the activities of the "fanatics" exiled in Holland. Though rather vague on

the exact number of ships the Dutch had lost in Holmes's recent raid, Scot was able to forward information which ultimately (though Arlington cannot have fully realized it then) would prove much more important. The Dutch, Scot said, were eager to avenge the insult of Sir Robert Holmes's attack on the Vlie. They had been encouraged by the Englishman Samuel Raven to believe that if a landing at Harwich could be effected, there was a significant network of English republicans who could be depended upon to support the Dutch invasion from within. Though this plan had been laid aside for the time being because of De Ruyter's ill health, Scot cautioned, "it may yet be judg'd (reasonably enough) especially upon their fond and over forward listeninge to and engageinge with soe inconsiderable a fellow as Raven, that they are really greedy of harkeninge to any such overtures." [18]

As far as remaining documents indicate, Scot appears to have been Arlington's unique source of information about Samuel Raven and no doubt several others. The circumstance put Scot in a tricky position: some of the details he revealed were known only to one or two other people—Bampfield, for instance—and if it were discovered that the information had become known to the English, the informer would be immediately identifiable. It was therefore in Scot's interest to parcel out enough intelligence to make himself valuable to Arlington without giving himself away.

Promise of a pardon from the King and a "plentiful" financial reward seem to have been a sufficient lure, even so, for Scot to risk betraying several of his fellow conspirators to the enemy. Sands Temple, an English naval officer who had a reputation among the Dutch as a "perfect Englishman," had been seduced by Bampfield, according to Scot, and persuaded to make a secret pledge of loyalty to the States General. He had promised to bring over his own ship to the Dutch and, if possible, to induce other English commanders to do likewise, in exchange for a reward and the command of a foot company in Holland. Scot's was most probably the first warning Arlington had of Sands Temple's defection. Scot also identified two other dissidents who had been sent into England to spy for the Dutch. These were subsequently arrested and imprisoned there on charges of espionage as a result of his information, and Aphra cautioned Arlington to make certain that both remained in prison, for if they escaped again to

Holland, they would be certain to denounce Scot's treachery to all his fellow radicals.

The covering letter Aphra sent with Scot's report shows incipient strain. A series of conflicting pressures bound her: first, she had to demonstrate to her employers that she was capable of using Scot for her purposes rather than letting herself be used for his; furthermore, she had to show that her first loyalties lay with the Royal cause. These preoccupations were manifest in the first reports she wrote to Halsall. On the other hand, if Scot's information was to be of any use, Arlington had to be persuaded of his sincerity and capabilities. Aphra had to do this without making herself seem gullible. She was also beginning to be nervous because she had had neither word nor additional funds from Halsall. Perhaps her anxiousness on this point led her to take up Scot's defense: *"I really do believe that his intentt is very reall and well be very diligent in the way of doing you all the service in the world for the ffuter* [future]: *he expresses him self very hansomly: and I beleeve him in all things: I am sure he wants no witt nor adress: nor any thing to manage this affaire with, but money."* [19] Halsall may not have appreciated Scot's "wit and address" as Aphra did and perhaps he thought she protested overmuch, but he had put her in an impossible position. Scot was in debt and insisted that he could not return to Amsterdam, where he could be of most use to Arlington, until he was furnished with some money. On the other hand, it was beginning to look as though Halsall was waiting to see exactly how useful Scot would prove to be. Aphra, of course, was caught in the middle. She could not know whether to attribute Halsall's failure to reply to her letters to indifference, mismanagement, or deliberate manipulation.

In desperation, she wrote to Thomas Killigrew at his lodgings in Whitehall Palace. Addressing him as a friend, she apologized for not having written before: *"I have not presented my service to you ever since I came: nor will you now give me thanks when you know tis not that alone that obleges my now writing, but to give you a trouble which I can not abide to give an other."* [20] Despite the fact that she had written often to Mr. Halsall, she explained, there had been no answer and her financial situation was becoming acute. Antwerp was an excessively expensive city, and she could not go into Holland because of Bampfield's *"damnable jealousy."* Scot's coming to Antwerp had cost her more than ten pounds each time; she had to pay for a special messenger to carry all his letters and hers; and her daily expenses came to no less than ten guilders. To make matters worse, Thomas Corney had arrived in Antwerp. Lord Stafford had written to Corney to advise him of Scot's presence, and Corney, still determined to avenge his betrayal by Scot to the Dutch, immediately came, threatening to kill Aphra's "friend" if he found him. Corney missed Scot, but was watching Aphra closely in case he should return. It was therefore impossible for Scot to come back to Antwerp, and Aphra had determined, she told Killigrew, to go to Holland no matter what the danger might be. But she could not leave until she had paid her debts. Would Killigrew intercede in her favor with the dilatory Halsall, she asked, and added: *"I presume to take affreedom with you more then any, and the sooner because twas from you as well as any I receavd my buseness: and from you I shall expect a favor."* [21]

Five days later (September 4)—before Killigrew could possibly have had a chance to answer her—she wrote him a second letter repeating the same information and complaining that she had been forced to pawn all her rings and was left without even the money to buy herself shoes to travel in. Other agents in the King's service had begun to protest similar treatment, and she was afraid the royal cause was being damaged through this "insouciance": *"I see what other of his Majestys servants heare are forcd to do allso if they will do any good."* [22]

If she was already feeling worried over the dead silence from her employers in England, the news that the next post brought must have made her despair. London had burned. What was afterward known as the Great Fire had started in Pudding Lane early on Sunday morning, September 2. Within a matter of hours the conflagration had spread a mile, and the high wind that carried the flames showed no signs of abating. Thames Street, Fish Street, Canning Street, Cornhill, and Fenchurch Street swiftly fell under the blaze, and it was only at the Inner Temple that the authorities were able to stop the fire. It burned for four days. At the end, all old London within the city walls had been consumed. All that was left of the magnificent St. Paul's was a blackened rubble of stone. Thousands of people were without food or shelter, camping out in the open fields surrounding the ruins.

Rumor blamed the Dutch for the disaster. Gossip had it that a Dutchman had lurked in the neighborhood where the fire started. Lady Hobart wrote to Ralph Verney in the country: "O dear Ralph, I am sorry to be the messenger of so dismal news, for poor London is almost burnt down. It began on Saturday night and has burnt ever since and is at this time more fierce than ever. It did begin in Pudding Lane at a bakers, where a Dutch rogue lay, and burnt to the bridge . . . and it is thought Fleet Street will be burnt by tomorrow. There is nothing left of any house there, nor in the Temple, there was never so sad a sight, nor so doleful a cry heard, my heart is not able to express the tenth, nay the thousandth part of it." [23]

Perhaps Aphra got a letter like this, or perhaps she merely heard the news cried in the streets of Antwerp. However it was, her heart must have sunk: the London she had known was gone forever, and immediate relief for her in Antwerp seemed even less likely than before. Her misfortunes had been dwarfed by the mass of homeless, needy people in London looking to the King and Parliament for aid. And now troubles of another order were added to her worries over money. She had received letters from her mother and the man she called "Sir Thomas"—apparently well known to Killigrew and closely associated with Aphra's mother. [24] According to the letters, Killigrew, Halsall, and even His Majesty himself were furious with Aphra because she had sent a messenger to ask for money. Their objection seemed to lie in the fact that she had employed so "base a fellow" as a messenger and risked letting him into her secret affairs. Aphra, very much upset, wrote a third time to Killigrew attempting to justify herself: "*I hope* [trust] *he is neither cheat nor traytor,*" she said, but claimed that "*I had none besides (except Sir Thomas) that I could send . . . my mother was not so fitt, being a woman: and posibly I should be loath to have her have it, for another reason and Sir Thomas: I did not know but you might scruple at, as much as any: besides he is selldom in towne: and I was sure that none of you would do it for feare of suspition: so pray Sir tell me what I was to do in such a case: Sir Thomas is angry since he saw the letter I sent to you: and says, I say he* [the messenger Aphra sent to Killigrew] *is that only man in the world I could trust: tis true Sir: he is so: except himself: and so he might have tould you too: but I find every on has a pregudice to do me if they can: but for my part, you may beleeve what you please: you shall find still this that how great a child soever I am in other matters: I shall mind dilligently what I am now about: and doubt not but to aquitt my self as becoms me, and is my duty. . . ." [25] Her envoy, Aphra insisted, knew nothing whatsoever of her business. She hoped that, having considered the circumstances, Killigrew would not continue to believe that she had been indiscreet or managed her assignment ineptly. Above all, she was terrified that the King would think badly of her. The postscript to the letter pleaded: *"For christ his sake Sir let me receave no ill opinion from his Majesty who would give my poore life to serve him in never so little a degree: and really Sir in this I have not merritted it."* [26]

Aphra reveals in this letter certain aspects of her character that have not yet been explored. One statement in particular is fascinating: what does she mean by *"how great a child soever I am in other matters"*? Does she view herself as a precocious child entrusted with a responsibility beyond her years? That seems rather improbable, given the fact that she was already in her mid-twenties—a mature age in that century. Perhaps she had in mind the traditional feminine incapacity for "business," an interpretation given weight by Aphra's saying she could not send her mother on business because she is *"unfit, being a woman."* She is careful not to mention her sex in any of her communications. Perhaps she did not want to draw attention to it; perhaps she already felt that she was working at a disadvantage. Not very long after, when she started to write for the stage, she attempted to disarm her critics by openly stating the fact of her sex and arguing her right to engage in a masculine activity. Her spying experience may have contributed to the evolution of her attitude. Certainly she deeply resented not being taken seriously and smarted from the critical skepticism that focused on her sex.

There are a few other biographically interesting details in this third letter to Killigrew. The "Sir Thomas" mentioned is a tantalizing reference—never accompanied, unfortunately, by a surname. From what Aphra says, it may be ascertained that he was a country squire who did not often come up to London; that he had court connections and was well known to Killigrew; and that he was close to Aphra's mother—a relative, or maybe even a second husband. It can also be assumed that, despite his title, he did not have sufficient disposable fortune to extricate Aphra from her painful dilemma. The absence of corroborating evidence makes it impossible to identify "Sir Thomas," but the very fact that someone who was either in or close to her family frequented the Court might help explain how she came by her appointment in the first place.

Despite the lack of encouragement, Mrs. Behn continued to send Arlington intelligence by nearly every post all through September 1666, as she had during the month of August. Killigrew may well have spoken to Halsall, who seems to have sent her some money at about the beginning of September, but apparently not enough to pay her debts and allow her to go to Holland to meet Scot. She corresponded faithfully with him, still, and was able to furnish the Secretary of State with details about the Dutch fleet, Orangist intrigues, republican spies in England, the activities of the "brethren" and other English rebels in exile, the general atmosphere in Holland, and the public humor.

Aphra was even able to provide useful information about another of his agents in Antwerp—the bumbling Thomas Corney. She brought her literary abilities to bear on a characterization that might well have been the portrait of one of the ridiculous town fops who peopled her plays: *"Mr. Corney came to Antwerp: and came (like the impudent fellow he is) wheare I was: and affter he had raild against Scot and vowd his death a thousand times, though in the Church he began to see what he could gett out of me: and seeing himself no wiser then he was before: affter his usiall custom: he went behind my back and spoke many thing of Scot and I: as that he beleevd I would be clapd up if you should know in England that I held corispondancy with a Rogue: and a thousand things more and Mr. nepho presantly saide, this prating ffelow would spoyle all: In fine Sir, since he can not guess at my buseness, he has writ into Holland to every creature he knows: and has given them an acoumpt of my being heare . . . in fine Sir he talks so much of the King and what great buseniss he had to do . . . that I am very confident he will ruen all if he be trusted for you never heard [one] talke so in your life, and that before any body, and tells how my Lord Arlington writs to him . . . every body dreads him and none abids [abides] him, he is so insufferable a scandalous Lying prating ffellow: and I am sure they do not love his Majesty's intrest that trust him with the least of secritt Sir Pardon this long no ration [narration], ocationed by a true desire I have to serve you: which forces me to asure you that if som speedy cheek [check] be not given to his tongue he will not only ruen all he has to do: but all other. He was very like to be killd last weeke for his prating and saying that on Mr. Hartup had hird men for the service of the statts [Dutch States General] and because he denyde it affter it was sufficiently provd he was like to have run him through: he coms with the ffairest face in the world to see me every day: and theare talks at such a rate of the courtiers of his imploys heare: and of the Ladyes at court that I have hardly patience to heare such damnable rodmantos [rodomontade]."*[27] Poor Thomas Corney. William Scot had first conspired with him, then turned him in to the Dutch, cost-

ing him six months in prison and the loss of most of his property—
his desire to revenge himself on the traitor was perfectly understandable. Corney's behavior was, however, as Aphra rightly pointed
out, at best unprofessional and worse, dangerous to others. Arlington
apparently found Aphra's account interesting enough to pass on to Sir
William Temple, who also employed Corney.[28]

Even in the face of what seemed either indifference or criminal
neglect by Arlington's office, Aphra obviously felt that personal in-
tegrity required her to carry out her assignment. Her financial dilemma continued to worsen: *"I am almost out of my witts I heare not
ffrom you,"* she wrote to Halsall September 21. *"Sir I am worse than
dead till I am out of this expensive hous wheare I vow to god I do not rest
with continuall thoughts of my debts and fears of displeasing you."* The
pleas for money grew more and more desperate. Although Halsall apparently sent her funds once or twice, they were not enough to
meet her expenses or begin to pay her now very pressing debts. The
last extant letter Aphra sent Arlington's office giving intelligence was
dated October 5, 1666. It is possible that other intelligence letters
were intercepted, but it seems more likely that she now did not even
have the money to send messengers either to Scot or to England. The
next communication from her, written a month later, on November
3, was for the first time addressed to Arlington himself rather than to
one of his underlings or to Killigrew. The tone alternated sheer desperation and resentment over the unfairness of the treatment she has
received. *"My Lord,"* it began, *"I humbly beg pardon for the boldness my
extreame nesesityes forces me to take; I did beleeve when I came out of England
that it was in order to a service to your Lordship: when I did indeavor, with
all the power of my life, as ffar as time, and my want of money, would give
me leave: I am very confident that no person in the world could have drawn
him [Scot] to a resolution of that kind, besides my self: I promis'd him all
what I had in charge to do: which because he saw no effects off: he knew not
what to think: but I still keep'd him up with the confidence I had that all
should be as was saide. I sent to your Lordship from time to time not missing
a post, wheare in I did not beg your Lordship to give him som incouragement:
but t'was all in vaine I never could get that, nor a poore answer of all I sent
. . . Being so long with out any money: I was forcd to be at very great charge
where I had credit so that when I ow'd 100 and 20 pownds I had a bill of
50: which only served to pay as ffar as it would go . . . all my trunks, and*

all that little I brought with me is ingagd ffor: which being so little a pawne
for so great a debt I am dayly, and howerly, abusd and threatened by them
. . . I am in extreame want and necessity . . . I beg your Lordship: will also
let me know what I shall say or do to the poore man [Scot]: I have pawnd all
my rings, and little things I had: for him all ready; which made but ffew
pownds: however I had rather starve than be worse then my word . . . I
beseech you, take some pitty on a poore strainger whose life or death is in your
hands." [29]

It is not known exactly what Arlington's response to Aphra's
passionate demands was; her next letter makes it clear, however, that
she had received orders to return home but no funds to meet a debt of
a hundred pounds or even pay her passage home. Writing the day
after what must have been a cold and miserable Christmas, she told
the Secretary of State that she is *"wild with my heard treatment"* and
reminded him that *"I neither petitioned ffor nor desird the place I now have*
nor have I in the least bin prodigall more then what your delays have occa-
tiond: and I am all most killd with the griefe I have to be so Ill thought
on." [30] This was a bold letter for a woman in her mid-twenties to
write to one of the most powerful ministers of the King. Aphra had
already proved, however, that she was no ordinary young woman and
had been placed in a circumstance intolerable to her sense of justice.
Aside from the very real suffering caused by her money troubles, she
seemed most preoccupied with the idea that her capacity to carry out
"business" was in question. She was eager to justify herself.

Aphra had to borrow one hundred fifty pounds from one Edward
Butler to get back to England. She says in her last letter that if she
missed the convoy she would have to wait two months for the next,
and probably in fact she had to wait much longer. Her biographer of
the fair sex says that she traveled from Ostend on the same boat as Sir
Bernard Gascoigne, a merchant who, according to the State Papers,
was issued a pass to go to England on May 1 but did not leave until
May 11 (he was, incidently, another agent of Arlington's). One of
the Fair Sex relates that in concert with her other difficulties, Aphra's
ship was caught in a storm and crashed the rocks, the passengers
being forced to row ashore in small rescue boats.[31] A report in the
Calendar of State Papers dated May 1, 1667, confirms this—a fleet of
sixty Ostenders bound for London had run into bad weather and some
had foundered; Sir Bernard Gascoigne was among those who arrived
in this convoy.[32]

————·

Little more than a month later, on the afternoon of June 7, a fleet of fifty or sixty Dutch ships was sighted off the English coast. By evening, they had anchored at the mouth of the Thames in the King's Channel. Admirals De Ruyter, De Witt, and Van Ghent were in command, and Colonel Thomas Dolman, Colonel Ludlow, and "many of the discontented"[33] were with them—all rebel exiles William Scot had reported on. Perhaps even Scot himself was aboard. The republicans knew the English waters well—Dolman had been a Naval officer during the Commonwealth, and the "fanatick" spies had provided the Dutch with exact information as to the state of defenses and the number and location of English ships laid up in harbor.

For three days the Dutch fleet blocked the Thames while the English floundered helplessly trying to muster last-minute defenses. Then a smaller force of seventeen warships was sent up the river Medway. The Dutch had little difficulty penetrating the huge chain that was one of the river's principal defenses, and the naval commanders who rushed to the scene found very few cannons mounted, with no powder—or only moldered powder—to load those that were. The seamen, who had been unpaid and in rebellion for months, refused to lift a finger. Workmen in the naval yards, also starving for want of pay, had pilfered so many supplies that there were no oak planks to support the guns. At each firing, they sank farther into the ground. The Dutch were able to proceed unimpeded straight up the Medway to Chatham, where most of the English fleet was in dock. Unmanned and unarmed, the *Royal James* was easily destroyed by the Dutch fire ships; many others followed. When the last fire ship had been used, the Dutch tied a rope to the flagship—the *Royal Charles*—and led it away in triumph. It was on the *Royal Charles* that Charles II himself had returned in triumph when he was restored to the throne in 1660. The symbolic effect of the Dutch victory was devastating—to say nothing of the material damage. The English had been made the laughingstock of Europe. The Dutch, had they wished, could easily have sailed up the Thames and bombarded London; such was the English unreadiness for attack. Recriminations flew: "There is much whispering of bad persons," an anonymous agent reported to Arlington, "and the King and Council are blamed that the ships were left without defence, and that there was no intelligence of the mischief nor care to prevent it."[34] Arlington also had no warning of the final Dutch attack, when Thomas Dolman landed at Harwich with a troop of 1,200 men—many of them renegade Englishmen—and executed great damage.

Aphra must have felt vindicated, for among the articles of information she had forwarded to Arlington the previous September was the following: *"Their is one thomas woodman formerly a Captain both by sea and land for the Parliament, hath lived at Bruges, but is now in Holland, and much with Dolman and De Witt, hee undertakes to sincke shipps, and block upp the river of thames."* [35] She had given advance warning, too, of the Dutch ambitions to carry out a landing at Harwich, and probably would have been privy to much more detailed information had Arlington supplied her with the means to function efficiently.

The Secretary of State's dealings with Aphra, however, were generally characteristic of the royal administration of affairs. The King always seemed to have money for his mistresses, but there was a fear of insurrection in London because the sailors had been unpaid for so long. In October 1666, Samuel Pepys had recorded in his diary that "to all our complaints for want of money, the Duke [of York] only tells us that he is sorry for it, and hath spoke to the King of it, and money we shall have as soon as it can be found; and though all the issue of the war lies upon it, yet that is all the answer we can get, and that is as bad or worse than nothing." [36] Perhaps Killigrew did at some point attempt to solicit the King on Aphra's behalf or chide him, because on December 8 the gossip reached Pepys that Abraham Cowley had overheard Tom Killigrew "publicly tell the King that his matters were coming into a very ill state, but that there was a way to help all—which is, says he, 'There is a good honest able man that I could name, that if your Majesty would employ and command to see all things well executed, all things would soon be mended; and this is our Charles Stuart—who now spends his time employing his lips and prick at Court, and hath no other employment. But if you would give him this employment, he were the fittest man in the world to perform it.' " Pepys, a more cautious man, commented privately, that "the King doth not profit by any of this, but lays all aside and remembers nothing but his pleasures again." [37] An unhappy sequel was that a few days later, Pepys heard that one of the King's most gifted musicians had died "for mere want," his wages five years behind in payment.

———.

The version of Aphra's experiences as a spy related by One of the Fair Sex in her biography is an extravagant romance, but the basic facts she presents correspond quite closely to those delineated by the reports preserved in the Public Record Office and elsewhere. One of the Fair Sex includes a long relation of a rivalry for Aphra's attention and affection between two Dutchmen: Van der Albert, thirty-two years old and "an irreconcilable enemy to monarchy," and his friend Van Bruin, a foppish old fool who comes to see her every day. William Scot and Thomas Corney, thinly disguised, are immediately recognizable.

What is interesting about the account is that the authoress says she was told the story by Aphra herself—and indeed there are certain details that only people actually involved could have known. The story as repeated may therefore give some hint of Aphra's point of view outside the official correspondence. According to One of the Fair Sex, Aphra had been severely disappointed by the fact that her intelligence had not been credited and that "all the encouragement she met with, was to be laughed at by the Minister she wrote to, and her letter showed by way of a contempt." [38] A friend of Aphra's, the fair biographer says, reported this wretched behavior to her and suggested that since her services were so little valued, she ought to "lay aside her politick negotiation, and divert her friends with some pleasant adventures of Antwerp, either as to her lovers, or those of any other lady of her acquaintance." Aphra accordingly gave over all thoughts of "business" and complied with her friend's request by writing a series of letters which One of the Fair Sex reprinted. The letters read very much like the novels that Aphra wrote at the end of her life. It seems quite possible that they were part of her literary remains—a rough form of something she had been working on when she died. She had, after all, used her own experience in the same way in *Oroonoko,* written the year before.

The advice that Aphra's friend was said to have offered reflected what was probably the general attitude toward her spying. "Business" and politics were a part of the masculine domain, where a woman could quite naturally be expected to fail. Aphra herself subscribed to that dichotomy later on in some of her writings, where the vocabulary of "business" and "love" as masculine and feminine principles clearly informs the work. But in this instance, if we are to believe the authenticity of the friend's letter, she took strong exception to the implication that she was not capable of acting in the world as well as any man: *"Your remarks upon my politick capacity, though they are sharp, touch me not, but recoil on those that have not made use of the advantages they might have drawn from thence."* [39] The conflict between her subscription to traditional views of masculine and feminine spheres and her own desire to act along with her male contemporaries in "the world" was to recur continually in the course of her career.

III

They say that women are not fit to govern, Betray their weakness, and their want of knowledge.

—Thomas D'Urfey, 1685

It has been urged by certain of Aphra Behn's biographers that she was not entirely justified in her anger against Arlington and Halsall—after all, they had sent her the substantial sum of one hundred twenty-five pounds in exchange for information of very little value. Aphra overestimated her own usefulness, argues William Cameron; and furthermore, she was extravagant. Ernest Bernbaum, in his article "Mrs. Behn's Biography, a Fiction," even goes so far as to point out that the assertion made by One of the Fair Sex that Aphra warned of the Dutch attack ahead of time was false. Professor Bernbaum also, it will be remembered, maintains that Aphra never went to Surinam. Another thesis, put forth by Harrison Gray Platt, is that Aphra went to Surinam and Antwerp as Scot's mistress—"If we can follow Aphra's men, we can follow Aphra," he states. The spying business, he says, was merely a cover for an elaborate plot to obtain a pardon for Scot and extract money from the King. Aphra, it seems, is destined to be denied credit for her intelligence posthumously as well as in her own time. Her biographers are no more willing to let her act "in the world"—the man's world—than her contemporaries were. [40]

Bernbaum, unfortunately, simply overlooked the letter in the State Papers in which Mrs. Behn warned of the proposal to block up the Thames and burn ships. Platt's and Cameron's arguments, however, deserve consideration. First, Platt's contention that Aphra tricked Arlington into sending her to contact Scot seems difficult to believe in the face of her repeated assertions to both Killigrew and Arlington that she had not sought her place, but had been *sought out* by them to undertake the job. Second, Aphra's intelligence can hardly be said to have been peripheral to Arlington's principal concerns: as Peter Fraser's recent book, *The Intelligence of the Secretaries of State, 1660–1668*, confirms, the two major threats to the kingdom in the early years of the Restoration were the remaining "fanatic" dissenters within and the potential Dutch invaders without.[41] Aphra's information was important with regard to both. It seems at least as valuable as the intelligence coming into Arlington's office from his other agents in Flanders and Holland. Nor were Aphra's expenses out of line with other agents'. Hieronymus Nipho, who was also in Antwerp, received seven hundred fifty pounds from Arlington from December 1664 to December 1666 for his expenses, about the same rate that Aphra was paid.[42] In addition, Aphra had to pay for her voyage to Antwerp and all of Scot's expenses as well. Her account of how she spent her money seems reasonable. Given the fact that Arlington failed to provide her with the money even to go to Holland as she wished, Aphra in fact carried out her mission remarkably well.

Whether her treatment was just or not, she was without the funds requisite to pay back the one hundred fifty pounds she borrowed from Mr. Butler in order to return to England. For more than a year, she unsuccessfully attempted to get the King to pay her what *"Mr. Halsall and Mr. Killigrew know is so justly due."* [43] Two of her petitions are among the State Papers of 1668, but there may have been others. Mr. Butler was more and more insistent. Finally, he threatened her with prison. At her wits' end, Aphra wrote to Killigrew once again: *"If you could guess at the affliction of my soule you would I am sure pity me, 'tis to morrow that I must submitt my self to a prison the time being expired though I indeavoured all day yesterday to get a few days more: I can not because they say, they see I am dallied with all and so they say I shall be for ever: so I can not revoke my doome I have cryd my self dead and could find my hart to break through all and get to the King and never rise 'till he weare pleased to pay this; but I am sick and weake and unfitt for it; or a prison; I shall go tomorrow. But I will send my mother to the King with a petition for I see everybody are words: and I will not perish in a prison: from whence he swears I shall not stirr til the uttmost farthing be payd. and oh god; who considers my misery and charges too; this is my reward for all my great promises, and my endeavours. Sir if I have not the money to night you must send me som thing to keepe me in prison for I will not starve."* [44]

It is not certain which prison Aphra went to, for Ludgate and the Fleet, where debtors had been traditionally kept until someone paid their debts or they simply expired, had been destroyed in the Great Fire. Newgate was summarily repaired to accommodate the homeless prisoners and apparently the Marshalsea, which appears to have been still standing, and the newly acquired Caronne House, in South Lambeth, managed as best they could to take up the overflowing population of ragged beggars who had been left homeless by the fire. The filth, lice, cruelty, and corruption of seventeenth-century prisons was notorious in the best of times, but in the year after London burned, thousands of ruined citizens added to the already unbearably crowded conditions.

Whether the King ultimately paid her debt or some alternative measure was finally managed by friends, Aphra somehow extricated herself from her painful situation. The experience made a strong impression on her. Her instinct for independence must have been reinforced by the feeling that dependence on others could have dangerous consequences. She must also have begun to understand that real independence required a financial base.

CHAPTER EIGHT

Profession of Letters: From Beauty to Wit

> Who is't that to women's beauty would submit,
>   And yet refuse the fetters of their wit?

—Aphra Behn,
prologue to *The Forced Marriage*, 1671

> 'Tis beauty that to womankind
>   Gives all the rule and sway,
> Which once declining, or declin'd,
>   Men afterwards unwillingly obey;
> Your beauty 'twas at first did awe me,
> And into bondage, woeful bondage draw me;
>   It was your cheek, your eye, your lip
> Which rais'd you first to the dictatorship:
>
> But your six months are now expir'd,
>   'Tis time I now should reign,
> And if from you obedience be requir'd
>   You must not to submit disdain
>
> Consult your glass, and see
> If I ha'n't reason on my side.

—Charles Cotton,
"To Chloris"

scene

I

Aphra Behn was nearly thirty, an ex-spy out of debtor's prison, a widow with no evident prospect of getting a living when, at the end of the 1660s, she sat down at her table in the crowded quarters of the rooms she let, probably in one of the semislums like the proverbial Grub Street that professional writers of that time commonly inhabited, and became a playwright: the first woman to live by her pen.

Exactly how long Aphra remained in debtor's prison is difficult to determine, but three petitions in the Calendar of State Papers of 1668 suggest that it was not until the end of that year that she was imprisoned. It is to be hoped that her experience as an inmate was short-lived, since Aphra said in her last extant letter to Killigrew that she was "weak and unfit for prison." Perhaps the concrete fact of her incarceration moved Aphra's friends and former employers to act when her desperate letters could not. One piece of evidence may indicate, if it may be correctly attributed to Aphra, that she was already free by the middle of 1669 and at the door of the theater with a play. Sometime around May, a young woman named Elizabeth Cottington, writing to her cousin in the country to give the latest playhouse gossip and news about town, passed on the following curiosity: "There is a bold woman hath offered [a play]: my cousin Aston can give you a better account of her than I can. Some verses I have seen are not ill; that is commendation enough: she will think so too, I believe, when it come upon the stage. I shall tremble for the poor woman exposed among the critics." [1]

As Aphra Behn's dramatic debut came not long afterward—in 1670—it seems quite likely that she was in fact the "bold woman" Elizabeth Cottington was referring to. There were, however, two other shadowy figures who might also have fit the description. Almost exactly a year before Aphra's first work was staged, a woman named Frances Boothby had a play produced by the King's Company. *Marcelia; or, the Treacherous Friend* was licensed for publication on October 9, 1669, and probably performed the summer before. Very little is known about Frances Boothby after this one bold stroke; as far as I have been able to discover, she was never heard of again.

Elizabeth Polwhele was another young woman trying to break into the theater at the time. She had apparently managed to have a tragedy called *The Faithful Virgins* performed sometime in the 1660s, but it was never published and there is no record of any contemporary comment on it. The only evidence that it was actually staged is a license issued to the Duke's Theater. If the manuscript had not somehow come under the protection of the Bodleian Library at Oxford, it would be another "lost" play.[2] Elizabeth Polwhele also wrote a second play, a comedy called *The Frolicks,* which she must have been urging on the theater managers and sending around in manuscript in 1670 or 1671. The dedication, addressed to Prince Rupert, no doubt in the hope of finding a patron powerful enough to get her play put on, seems painfully conscious of the impediments created by the author's sex: her sense of illegitimacy, of transgression, of powerlessness, are only too clear. "Mighty Prince," she begins, "Encouraged by Mistress Fame I have for some minutes thrown my foolish modesty aside, with a boldness that does not well become a virgin, presume to offer this comedy at your grace's feet, from whence you may spurn it into nothing, if in anything it can offend you . . . I am young, no scholar, and what I write I write by nature, not by art . . . I implore your Highness's pardon for my unparalleled boldness, as I am a woman."[3] Elizabeth Polwhele's uncertainties were not without substance: *The Frolicks* never got beyond manuscript stage and foundered in obscurity for more than three hundred years until two scholars discovered the yellowing pages in a library and published it in 1977.

The existence of Frances Boothby and Elizabeth Polwhele is evidence that Aphra was not an entirely isolated phenomenon; that neither of them ever succeeded in having more than a single play performed before lapsing back into obscurity is a measure of just how difficult it was "to oppose the censuring world, upon this uncommon action [playwriting] in my sex," as Frances Boothby put it.[4] The very fact that Aphra Behn managed not only to endure, but prevail in the face of this hardship is a tribute to her courage, perseverance, and force of character—which is not to discount the role that luck or the possible influence of friends may have played. It must also be noted that the play Aphra made her literary debut with, though in many ways awkward, nevertheless showed more promise than either Boothby's or Polwhele's, and Aphra's progress thereafter was astoundingly rapid. Perhaps the necessary catalyst to perfecting her style was simply the experience of dealing with the practical problems of staging, or maybe it was simply that having tried several different dramatic forms, she finally hit on the one which suited her best; but in any case it was clear that by the time Aphra wrote her third play, less than two years later, she had already gained considerable mastery over her craft.

Aphra seems to have been one of those naturally prolific writers for whom setting pen to paper was instinctive; a fundamental element of temperament. Apparently her propensity for composition manifested itself very early. One of the Fair Sex says that Aphra had been writing verses since "the first use almost of reason in discourse." There is no evidence to indicate from what time or how long Aphra might have kept the "Journal-Observations" she says she wrote while in Antwerp, but the way she speaks of it, as though it were a *given* in her life, hints that the diary may have been a habit of some duration. According to her contemporaries, writing came almost as easily to Aphra as talking. "Her muse was never subject to bringing forth with pain," testified her friend and literary executor Charles Gildon, "for she always writ with the greatest ease in the world, and that in the midst of company, and discourse of other matters." [5] Writing for the theater seems to have perfectly suited Aphra's character: she was evidently not a writer who wished or needed to isolate herself. Mrs. Behn's love of conversation was remembered by many, and the facility with which she handled dialogue may have had its source at least partly in an extraordinary natural gift for repartee. "She had a ready command of pertinent expressions," reported William Oldys, "and was of a fancy pregnant and fluent. I am told, moreover, by one who knew her, that she had a happy vein in determining any disputes or controversies that might arise in her company; having such agreeable repartees at hand upon all occasions, and so much discretion in the timing of them, that she played them off like winning cards." [6]

How Aphra actually managed to introduce herself into the theater world to observe and learn her craft remains a matter of speculation. One possible route of course was through Thomas Killigrew. Killigrew was a playwright himself, and his obsession with the theater went back to his boyhood in the 1620s, when he was reputed to have gone to the Red Bull Playhouse and volunteered to "personate" devils so that he could see the play for nothing. After the Restoration, he and Sir William Davenant had been given patents for two new theaters and permission to establish companies of players: Killigrew's became the King's Company at the Theater Royal, and Davenant's, the Duke's Company at Dorset Garden. Whether it was through Killigrew or by other means, Aphra seems to have had some sort of introduction to the King's Company, for in *Oroonoko* she claims that she presented them with a set of Indian feathers from Surinam that was worn by the heroine of Sir Robert Howard's *The Indian Queen*—"infinitely admired by persons of quality," according to Aphra. The play was first produced in January 1664, while Aphra was still in Surinam, but was revived frequently thereafter and it was probably one of these revivals that sported her feathers. Shortly after the production of her first play, Mrs. Behn wrote some commendatory verses for a drama by Sir Robert Howard's brother Edward, who was also a playwright. Since Aphra dates her connection to the Howard family from her childhood, it is quite as likely that she gained entry to the theatrical milieu through them as through Killigrew. In any case, knowing either would necessarily lead to the other, as Killigrew and Sir Robert Howard were the two principal shareholders of the King's Company and directed it together.

It would be reassuring to discover that Thomas Killigrew, guilty about his role in Aphra's imprisonment, had tried to redress the injury by accepting her play for production at his theater, but this was not the case. Though Killigrew or Howard may have initially introduced her to the theatrical milieu, it was the Duke's Company, directed by Thomas Betterton after Sir William Davenant's death in 1668, that staged her first play and afterward made her a "house" playwright. Whether Aphra had a supporter within the Duke's Company who encouraged Betterton to take her on is not known, but it seems entirely possible, given her independent spirit, that she may have known no one at all, but simply persisted in demanding a hearing for her play until someone listened.

Despite the traditional prejudice that Aphra had to face as a woman, there were also several historical circumstances that favored her emergence as a playwright. The theaters had been closed by the Puritans for nearly twenty years when Charles II reopened them in 1660. The break in continuity provided an opening for all sorts of innovations: among them a new design for the playhouse, the increasingly sophisticated use of scenery, elaborate machines for flying, and other visual or auditory effects. The change that was most important to Aphra, however, was the introduction of actresses to the stage—before the Restoration, all the female parts had been played by young boys. From that innovation, it was only a logical step to a woman playwright. The Duke's Company, at an initial disadvantage because the King's Company was given exclusive rights to a greater stock of old plays, was more adventurous in seeking out new attractions to draw playgoers away from its competitors, and Thomas Betterton may well have seized on Mrs. Behn as a novelty that might have a salutary effect on his box-office receipts.

Another historical development that permitted Aphra to make a career as a dramatist was the advent of the professional writers. Before the second half of the seventeenth century, most writers who did not have independent fortunes depended upon patrons or positions at court for financial support. Even Shakespeare had not lived by his pen. Of course he derived a substantial income from his plays, but they were only one part of his theatrical activities: he was also an actor, director, and manager. Like the other actors, he had a share in the company and was remunerated as part owner of the theater. Ben Jonson, whose livelihood was more completely dependent on his plays, was not able to eke out a living from their production or publication alone and had to rely heavily on patronage. The Civil War, however, exiled or impoverished many patrons, and writers like John Taylor, the Water-Poet, found it was possible to replace them with the collective patronage of publication by subscription. When the theaters were reorganized at the Restoration, allowance was made for an author's "benefit," and the professional writer became a permanent fixture of the literary scene with Dryden's generation. By the time Aphra Behn came to the stage in 1670, playwriting had become at least a viable, if not always reliable, means of supporting oneself.

Aphra may well have eventually taken her place alongside the male playwrights no matter what her circumstances, but the fact that she was newly out of debtor's prison and desperate for a way to live may well have given her the impetus to impose herself where other women had failed.

The new theater of the Restoration that Aphra was writing for had to begin almost from scratch: most of the old players from the days of James I or Charles I had died, most of the theaters had been destroyed or converted, and few playwrights of the former age were still writing. There was a whole generation of Londoners who had never been to a play or seen a playhouse. Even the audiences had to be recreated.

The Duke's Company had initially established itself in Lisle's tennis court, Lincoln's Inn Fields, which was converted to a playhouse. It was here that Aphra's first two plays were produced, very close together. Her third play opened in the new Dorset Garden Theater (sometimes called the Duke's Theater), which was to be the permanent home of the company. Dorset Garden was built along the Thames, and the steps that descended all the way down to the river permitted access by boat as well as by carriage or on foot. It was said to have been designed by Sir Christopher Wren and was one hundred forty feet long and fifty-seven feet wide, an intimate theatrical space. The audience was divided into two classes: prostitutes ("vizard masks"), fops, sparks, and ordinary citizens, who sat on the straight-backed benches of the pit; and the higher nobility, who occupied the three tiers of boxes that comprised the lower, middle, and upper galleries. A visitor to the theater in 1676 observed that the amphitheater pit sloped upward toward the boxes, and reported that the two lower tiers of the gallery were divided into seven boxes, each seating twenty persons.[7] It is difficult to estimate accurately the size of the audience, however, as the benches of the pit were designed to permit maximum capacity for a successful play. The jostling and overcrowding that resulted are well documented by contemporaries.

Under the new design, the stage extended far into the pit so that the players were surrounded on three sides by the audience, often so close as to find each other face to face. Conversation above a whisper in the pit risked drowning out the actors, and from the frequent complaints of Pepys and other theatergoers, as well as the playwrights themselves, it seems this was not an unusual occurrence. On February 18, 1667, Pepys was entertained for the entire duration of the play by a lively conversation between two ladies and Sir Charles Sedley; although he greatly admired Sedley's wit, Pepys confessed that he had, in consequence, "lost the pleasure of the play wholly," not having heard a single line of the dialogue.[8]

An anonymous satirist complained that "a playhouse is become a meer beer-garden where everyone enjoys his liberty and property of noise."[9] Numerous prologues and epilogues to plays mentioned the loud inattention of the audience. The prologue to *The Debauchee,* an anonymous play produced in 1677 which has been attributed to Aphra Behn, protests the interruptions occasioned by the self-advertisement of would-be "rakes":

> You come bawling in with broken French,
> Roaring out oaths aloud, from bench to bench,
> And bellowing bawdy to the orange-wench,
> Quarrel with masques, and to be brisk and free,
> You'll sell 'em bargains for a repartee,
> And then cry Damn 'em whores, whoere they be. [10]

People went to the theater to see and be seen, to gossip and be talked about. For a great many of them, the play was incidental. Those who were interested in what was happening on the stage found it hard to concentrate in the midst of so much else going on: the orange-wenches cried their oranges; the prostitutes of the pit plied their trade; gentlemen and ladies carried on flirtations and discussed the latest scandals; wits and fops combed their blond periwigs, shouted insults at each other, and told bawdy jokes; numbers of spectators arrived in the middle of acts; and the general coming and going, pushing and shoving, kept up a constant bustle. The crowding of so many bodies, in an age when baths were still very much out of the ordinary and lice were not, into such a small space must have produced a memorable smell—though seventeenth-century sensibilities were very much less particular on this point than today's. There were no facilities: Mrs. Pepys, when suddenly seized with an intestinal disorder in the middle of a play performed by the Duke's Company, had to run out into the adjacent Lincoln's Inn Fields to do her "business." Apparently not everyone took the trouble to depart upon such an emergency.

The author of *The Young Gallants' Academy* (1674) describes in detail, if ironically, the currently fashionable behavior that young men must ape if they aspire to be "wits" of the playhouse: "Let our gallant (having paid his half-crown, and given the doorkeeper his ticket) presently advance himself into the pit, where, having made his honour to the rest of the company, but especially to the vizard-masks, let him pull out his comb and manage his flaxen wig with all the grace he can. Having so done, the next step is to give a hum to the China-orange wench, and give her her own rate for the oranges (for 'tis below a gentleman to stand haggling like a citizen's wife) and then to present the fairest to the next vizard-mask. . . . It shall crown you with rich commendations to laugh aloud in the midst of the most serious and sudden scene of the terriblest tragedy, and to let the clapper (your tongue) be tossed so high that all the house may ring of it, for by talking and laughing you keep Pelion upon Ossa, glory upon glory: as first, all the eyes in the galleries will leave walking after the players, and will follow you: the most pedantick person in the house snatches up your name, and when he meets you in the street, he'll say, he is such a gallant, and the people admire you."[11]

Thus were plays and playwrights sacrificed to the acquisition of a reputation for wit.

The audience Aphra Behn was writing for when she made her literary debut in 1670 was, then, captious, rowdy, and fickle; it was difficult enough to capture their attention, but to hold it successfully was a rare feat. One had to be spectacular, outrageous, or extraordinary in some way. It is no wonder that the age eventually came to be dominated by burlesque and caricature. The rival companies vied to mirror the latest fashion, catch up the most recent slang, and invent the most amusing improvement to play or theater. The playwrights struggled to divine the next swing of audience taste and wrote to anticipate it, for the new professionals were more dependent on the box office than ever before. Shakespeare had been a permanent sharer in his company, so that the success or failure of any single play did not determine whether he would eat or starve.[12] Playwrights' royalties in the Restoration theater, however, were the receipts of the box office on the third day's performance. On an exceptionally good night, this could be as much as one hundred pounds, a very respectable sum in the seventeenth century. The most a playwright ever earned from the admissions alone of a single night was one hundred twenty pounds, but some authors occasionally sold seats themselves to rich patrons as an extra benefit.[13] A play that was booed, hissed, and damned at the premiere might not even last as long as three performances. In that case, the writer received nothing at all for his or her labors. A poorly attended third day could mean a starving season. Playwrights who, like Aphra Behn, had no known independent income were very much hostage to the dictates of audience approval. When she later said that she had been forced to write to the taste of the age, she was not exaggerating.

Literary politics could also play a great part in determining a playwright's fate: a cabal of wits could make or break a play. If someone like Lady Castlemaine, one of the King's mistresses, wished to support a certain author, she had only to announce publicly that she planned to attend on the third day and the playhouse would be filled to capacity by curious onlookers. If a court wit like Rochester or Buckingham or Dorset applauded a play, a great many others would follow suit; if they hissed, fashion did too. In fact, any interested person who could marshal a group of supporters could effectively ruin a play on its first night, thereby cutting short its run. George Granville, Lord Lansdowne (an amateur dramatist who was a great admirer of Aphra), described the standard method of undermining a play: "They spread themselves in parties all over the house; some in the pit, some in boxes, others in the galleries, but principally on the stage; they cough, sneeze, talk loud, and break silly jests; the house is an uproar; some laugh and clap, some hiss and are angry; swords are drawn, the actors interrupted, the scene broken off, and so the play's sent to the devil."[14] *The Young Gallants' Academy* advised the following means of sabotage: "mew at passionate speeches, blare at merry, find fault with the musick, whistle at the songs. . . ."[15]

II

The first recorded production of Aphra Behn's work was the play *The Forced Marriage; or, the Jealous Bridegroom,* which was performed on Tuesday, September 20, 1670, at Lincoln's Inn Fields. The director and manager of the Duke's Company, Thomas Betterton, played one of the leading parts. It is not certain whether or not this was the premiere, but the fact that it was the first performance entered on the Lord Chamberlain's records seems to indicate so.

Under the inscription, *"Va mon enfant! Prend ta fortune,"* the prologue to this first effort frankly declared the author's sex:

> *Women those charming victors, in whose eyes*
> *Lie all their arts, and their artilleries,*
> *Not being contented with the wounds they made,*
> *Would by new stratagems our lives invade.*
> *Beauty alone goes now at too cheap rates;*
> *And therefore they, like wise and politic states,*

Court a new power that may the old supply,
To keep as well as gain the victory:
They'll join the force of wit to beauty now,*
And so maintain the right they have in you.
If the vain sex this privilege should boast,
Past cure of a declining face we're lost.
You'll never know the bliss of change; this art
Retrieves (when beauty fades) the wandring heart;
And though the airy spirits move no more,
Wit still invites, as beauty did before.
Today one of their party ventures out,
Not with design to conquer, but to scout.
Discourage but this first attempt, and then
They'll hardly dare to sally out again.

Both author and audience were well aware that *The Forced Marriage* represented a break from tradition: Aphra is transgressing and chooses to acknowledge it openly. She has also chosen not to present herself as an exception to the rule but as speaking *on behalf* of her sex, declaring her entry into the hitherto masculine domain of literature as a step for all women. She is aware of the symbolic significance of her act. The statement delineates the spheres thought proper to masculine and feminine enterprise—"wit" and "beauty"—and justifies the woman writer's "invading" property historically not her own. The language of the statement borrows "masculine" metaphors of battle: artilleries, wounds, stratagems, politic states, power, victory.[16] But at the same time, the borrowed aggression is contradicted by "feminine" retreat—the offensive has its source in women's desire to please, to retain masculine affection and desire rather then infringe upon prerogative. The deliberate ambiguity is no doubt in part a device to attract the attention of a fickle audience and to disarm her ready critics, but it also seems to represent a fundamental division in Aphra's attitude. Her fighting declaration of entry into the sphere of the wits is equivocated by her reluctance to risk being considered unfeminine. Her desire to be taken seriously is countered by her wish to charm.

Though unwise to read material of this sort as direct autobiographical statement, it is at least arguable that Aphra's preoccupation

---

* my emphasis

here with the ephemerality of feminine beauty is not uninfluenced by her being nearly thirty in a world where women's attractiveness supposedly ended at twenty-five. This does not seem to have prevented Aphra from carrying on a love life that was thought of by some as scandalous, and not a few of her contemporaries testified that she was still beautiful and charming. Nevertheless, she felt and resented the pressure that the double standard of sexual aging imposed on women. *"You'll never know the bliss of change,"* she warns the men of the audience, implying that by depriving women of mind in favor of body, they condemn themselves to endless repetition.

Behind the burlesque of the teasing prologue, another more general problem is raised: that of the increasingly vulnerable and contingent position of women in Restoration society. *"Beauty alone goes now at too cheap rates"* accurately describes the world of the wits and rakes who frequented the theater. The easy availability of sex took its toll on the way women were treated in general. Aphra's argument is economic: if the value of women's one commodity is debased, they must find a new way to attract men. Aphra's way would be to establish the base for her own autonomy. With difficulty.

If the prologue to *The Forced Marriage* constituted a kind of blind declaration of independence, the epilogue denied what had been advanced. It was "by a woman" who is not further identified, as though a return to the anonymity that Aphra had denied were signaled. The woman reverses the proposition of her predecessor:

> *We charg'd you boldly in our first advance,*
> *And gave the onset* à la mode *de France,*
> *As each had been a* Joan *of* Orleance . . .
>
> *The trial though will recompense the pain,*
> *It having wisely taught us how to reign;*
> *'Tis beauty only can our power maintain.*
>
> *But yet, as tributary kings, we own*
> *It is by you that we possess that throne,*
> *Where had we victors been, we'd reign'd alone.*
>
> *And we have promis'd what we could not do;*
> *A fault, me thinks, might be forgiven too,*
> *Since 'tis what we learnt of some of you.*

But we are upon equal treatment yet,
For neither conquer, since we both submit;
You to our beauty bow, we to your wit.

Whether or not this "charming" piece of coquetry represented Aphra's true sentiments on the subject, she allowed it to be affixed to her play, if she did not indeed write it herself. The apology did not, in any case, hide the fact that a woman had produced a play on the English stage under her own name without any pretense that someone had done it without her knowledge and consent.[17]

The Forced Marriage was a traditional romantic tragicomedy of the sort that Beaumont and Fletcher had first popularized in the Jacobean era and which Dryden, Sir Robert Howard, Sir William Davenant, the Earl of Orrery, and others had turned out so prolifically in the first decade after the reopening of the theaters. Its subject is the fashionable conflict between love and honor—so clichéd by that time that it provided a target for satire. Aphra's vision of the mode is superficially conventional: the language of bombast, the Petrarchan conceits, the one-dimensional characters, the rhymed couplets, the moral direction of the plot, and the overblown tragic gesture had all appeared frequently before. Aphra, however, brings a distinctly feminine viewpoint to bear on the familiar form by introducing a double perspective on the concept of honor. The plot centers on the thwarted love of Erminia and Philander; the latter the son of the King of France and the former the daughter of Orgulius, the retiring general of the army. Alcippius, favorite of the King and hero of a recent battle, is rewarded with the command of the army, willingly handed over by the aging Orgulius, and with the hand of his daughter as well, also willingly proffered—without her knowledge. Both Prince Philander and Erminia despair over this turn of events, but no degree of persuasion, tears, or reasoning can move the King and Orgulius, who have given their respective "words of honor." To renounce their contract would be to bring their honor into question, under the code. Erminia is forced to marry Alcippius, whose honor is in turn threatened because she refuses to sleep with him.

As the play unfolds, a parallel structure becomes apparent: honor for the King, the father, and the husband lies in defending an obligation they have freely taken upon themselves; whereas honor for Erminia means carrying out a promise that has been made in her absence, without her approval. She is blackmailed by their contention that their honor depends on hers; *she* must protect their "name." Even her lover, the Prince, subscribes to the belief that a man's reputation is in the safekeeping of his wife; he rushes off to defend *his* honor by killing Alcippius, saying *"I kill a man that has undone my fame/ Ravish'd my mistress, and contemn'd my name."* The idea even extends to inner thoughts; Erminia swears to Alcippius that she will protect his honor in every way except by fulfilling her wifely duty to share his bed: *"Whilst I'm your wife I'll not allow birth to a thought that tends to injuring you."* For Erminia, honor must be defined as virtue, duty, obedience. . . . Her own instincts, love and desire, are opposed.

Aphra's heroine is paralyzed by the conflict. She cannot conceive of violating the duty she feels she owes her father, yet she cannot accede to his wishes either. Instead, she thinks of death. Rebellion or direct opposition to her father does not seem to occur to Erminia. She pleads for indulgence, but when her father refuses and reminds her of her "duty" she is overwhelmed by guilt and shame. Rather than oppose him, she splits into two entirely incompatible selves. She is conscious of being entangled in a structure foreign to her own desires or conception of justice, yet still cannot envisage any other possibility than acting out her predetermined role:

> *Ungrateful duty, whose uncivil pride*
> *By reason is not to be satisfied;*
> *Who even love's almighty power overthrows,*
> *Or does in it too rigorous laws impose;*
> *Who bindest up our virtue too straight,*
> *And on our honour lays too great a weight.*

Her lover, in despair, replies:

> *—Oh Gods, shall duty to a king and father*
> *Make thee commit murder on thy self,*
> *Thy sacred self, and me that do adore thee?*

Aphra ends the play with an unlikely "happy" conclusion. The lovers are united; opposition reconciled; conflicts dissolved—but only because the unwanted husband chooses to renounce his claim and cede to the greater force of true love. The heroine never acts; the fundamental structures are undisturbed. She remains suspended in passive agony while her father, her husband, and her lover unravel her fate. Her one positive step is a negative one: she refuses to sleep with the man her father has forced her to marry. She clearly sees and understands the nature of the structure that oppresses her, but is blind to the possibility of rebelling against it.

The Forced Marriage evokes the violence that the custom of arranged marriage wrought on the lives of Aphra's contemporaries and demonstrates the terrible effects of "the interest of a father" on his daughter's fate, but it does not present the female characters with a way out. The only alternative to Erminia's model is a comic character, Aminta, whose irreverent attitude toward love, honor, and fate provides dramatic relief from the grand tragedy of the others. Still, her presence in the play is not without interest. She is in love with another minor character, Alcander, who returns her affection, but she cannot accept the terms:

> *Hang love, for I will never pine*
> *For any man alive;*
> *Nor shall this jolly heart of mine*
> *The thoughts of it receive;*
> *I will not purchase slavery*
> *At such a dangerous rate;*
> *But glory in my liberty,*
> *And laugh at love and fate.*

Finally disgusted by Aminta's refusal to capitulate, Alcander bids her farewell and cautions, *"Mayst thou want a lover, when I shall hate both thee and thy whole sex."* In the grand reconciliation at the "happy" ending, however, pressure is brought to bear on her from all sides, and she is persuaded that the only way a woman can rule is through submission. She is warned that her determination to retain independence will lead only to finding herself without a man at all in the end:

ERMINIA: *Aminta, be persuaded.*
AMINTA: *He'd use me scurvily then.*
ALCANDER: *That's according as you behaved yourself, Aminta.*
AMINTA: *I should domineer.*
ALCANDER: *Then I should make love elsewhere.*
AMINTA: *Well, I find we shall not agree then.*

ALCANDER: *Faith—now we have disputed a point I never thought on*
before, I would willingly pursue it for the humor on't, not that I think
I shall much approve on't.
PISARO: *Give him your hand, Aminta, and conclude,*
'Tis time this haughty humor were subdued.
By your submission, whatsoe'er he seem,
In time you'll make the greater slave of him.
AMINTA: *Well—not from the hope of that, but from my love,*
His change of humor I'm content to prove.
Here take me, Alcander;
Whilst to inconstancy I bid adieu,
I find variety enough in you.

The logic of this scene echoes the epilogue "by a woman." But
Aminta's character is to be developed into the witty heroines that
dominate Aphra Behn's later work. The helpless Erminia will give
way to female characters who regard the parental fiat, especially in
matters of marriage, with a much more rebellious eye; who are willing to do battle with the men they love in order to get what they
want. *The Forced Marriage* imitated a tradition whose conventions
were well established, but at the same time carried a dissenting voice
that points elsewhere.[18]

According to John Downes, then prompter of the Duke's Theater, *The Forced Marriage* was a "good play," and it ran six nights. Either a sizeable part of the theater audience agreed with him or the
anomaly of a woman author attracted a curious public, because six
nights was a very good run at that time. A play that lasted more than
eight days would have to draw a good part of the theater-going public
twice. Downes also noted a mishap that occurred in the course of the
performance, which must have brought down the house and made it
difficult for the actors to proceed. A young man named Thomas
Otway, who was not yet twenty, had come up from Oxford to London, where he hoped to enter into the world of the wits and the theater. Someone sent him to Aphra Behn, who was persuaded to give
him the part of the King in her play. The King had only a few lines
to deliver at the beginning of the play and in the first scene, which
apparently Otway managed to get through; but when he came to his
grand scene in the fifth act, he was overcome with stage fright and

unable to utter a word. "He being not used to the stage," the prompter recorded, "the full house put him into such a sweat and tremendous agony, being dash't, spoilt him for an actor." [19]

Aphra Behn was described by one of her contemporaries as generous almost to a fault, a claim amply borne out by the fact that she had entrusted a part in her first play to an inexperienced young man who, like her, harbored dramatic aspirations. Thomas Otway never attempted the stage again, but became one of the best writers of his generation. Apparently Aphra easily forgave him; a close friendship between them continued for the remainder of Otway's life.

The relative success of her first play encouraged Aphra to submit a second. Only six months later, on February 24, 1671, *The Amorous Prince* went on the boards. [20] It was another romantic tragicomedy, but this time the comic element dominated. The prologue assumes more confidence than that of the first play, and indeed takes on a bantering tone of assault:

> *Well! you expect a prologue to the play,*
> *And you expect it to petition-way;*
> *With chapeau bas* beseeching you t'excuse*
> *A damn'd intrigue of an unpractised muse.*

Aphra goes on to tally up the objections that will be brought against her play. One group of critics, she says, will condemn it because it does not conform to the classical rule for heroic tragedy but is defiled by comic action: *"You grave Dons,"* she writes, *"who love no play/ But what is regular, great Jonson's way;/ Who hate monsieur with the farce and droll,/ But are for things well said with spirit and soul."* [21] The opposing party of critics, the fops and cullies and "wits," only want "a smutty jest," and she sends them off with *"You too are quite undone, for here's no farce;/ Damn me! you'll cry, this play will be mine A[rse]."*

Aphra ends the prologue with a half apology, by no means as deferent as that of *The Forced Marriage:*

> *Not serious, nor yet comic, what is't then?*
> *Th' imperfect issue of a lukewarm brain:*
> *Bait it then as ye please, we'll not defend it,*
> *But he who dis-approve it, let him mend it.*

*hat in hand

In the guise of a sardonic prologue, Aphra was taking her position in the war of opinions, as Dryden called it, that divided the theatrical coterie as well as the learned critics of her day. The factions were the "Ancients" and the "Moderns": for "regular" plays that kept to the Aristotelian unities of time, place, and action or for "natural" ones that did not; for rhymed verse or for prose; for tragedy or for comedy, for moral instruction or for amusement. The quarrel went back to Jonson and Shakespeare and before, but at the Restoration, spurred on by the influence of the French Academy, it reappeared with new virulence and acquired a tone of pompous solemnity. In the early 1660s, a Frenchman who belonged to the newly formed Royal Society had attacked the English theater for its lack of adherence to the classical rules, and another member had published a reply. A lengthy exchange of opinion on the issue followed between Dryden and Sir Robert Howard in a series of critical prefaces to plays, which led to the composition of Dryden's famous *Essay of Dramatic Poesy* (1668), where four different points of view are argued by four characters. In his last assault, Howard had taxed Dryden with arrogance of opinion, to which the latter answered: "Those propositions . . . are not mine, nor were ever pretended to be, but derived from the authority of Aristotle and Horace, and from the rules and examples of Ben Jonson and Corneille." [22]

The purists of the Royal Society looked down particularly on tragicomedy as a bastard genre. Articulated by a character in Dryden's *Essay of Dramatic Poesy,* their argument went thus: "The end of tragedies or serious plays, says Aristotle, is to beget admiration, compassion, or concernment, but are not mirth and compassion things incompatible?" [23] Although Dryden's essay presented the counter-argument as well and he himself later wrote tragicomedies, his defense of Jonson and the classical unities placed him generally in the camp of the "Ancients." Aphra's mockery of *"You Grave Dons who love no play but what is regular, Great Jonson's way,"* in the prologue to *The Amorous Prince,* was at least in part, then, an attack on Dryden. He had been made Poet Laureate the year before (1670) and Aphra was a beginning playwright—worse still, of the wrong sex. Even if Dryden was only partly a target of her parody, the attack must still have seemed effrontery.

———·

Apparently she herself was under fire because her third play, *The Dutch Lover*, produced on February 6, 1673, carried an "Epistle to the Reader" which ridiculed her detractors and further defended the position she had taken in the ideological fray going on in the theater. *"Good Sweet, Honey, Sugar-Candied Reader,"* she began in a sarcastic imitation of current literary flattery, *"Which I think is more than anyone has called you yet, I must have a word or two with you before you do advance into the treatise; but 'tis not to beg your pardon for diverting you from your affairs by such an idle pamphlet as this is . . . for I have dealt pretty fairly in the matter, told you in the title-page what you are to expect within."*

Having taken a dig at her literary colleagues, Aphra goes on to ridicule the ponderous logic and pretentious language that academic pronouncements on drama were couched in: *"Indeed, had I hung a sign of the immortality of the soul, or the mystery of godliness, or of eccle-·astical policie, and then had treated you with indiscerpibility and essential spissitude (words, which though I am no competent judge of, for want of languages, yet I fancy strongly ought to mean just nothing) . . . or had presented you with two or three of the worst principles transcribed out of the peremptory and ill-natured (though prettily ingenious) Doctor of Malmsbury [Hobbes] . . . I were then indeed sufficiently in fault; but having inscribed comedy on the beginning of my book, you may guess pretty near what penny-worths you are like to have, and ware your money and your time accordingly."*

Next, she lampoons certain members of the Royal Society who disparaged plays as a lesser art: *"I would not yet be understood to lessen the dignity of plays, for surely they deserve among the middle if not the better sort of books; for I have heard the most of that which bears the name of learning, and which has abused such quantities of ink and paper, and continually employs so many ignorant, unhappy souls for ten, twelve, twenty years in the University (who yet poor wretches think they are doing something all the while) as logick etc. and several other things (that shall be nameless lest I misspell them) are much more absolutely nothing than the errantest play that e'er was writ."*

Finally, pretending to apologize for her presumption in joining an argument outside her "sphere," Aphra attacks the new science of literature that pretended to classify both literature and language into a system of rules: *"Take notice, reader, I do not assert this purely upon my own knowledge, but I think I have known it very fully proved, both sides being fairly heard, and even some ingenious opposers of it most abominably baffled in the argument: Some of which I have got so perfectly by rote, that if this were a proper place for it, I am apt to think myself could almost make it clear; and as I would not undervalue poetry, so neither am I altogether of their judgment who believe no wisdom in the world beyond it. I have often heard indeed (and read) how much the world was anciently obliged to it for most of that which they called science, which my want of letters makes me less assured of than others happily may be: but I have heard some wise men say that no considerable part of useful knowledge was this way communicated, and on the other way, that it hath served to propagate so many idle superstitions, as all the benefits it that or can be guilty of, can never make sufficient amends for; which unaided by the unlucky charms of poetry, could never have possessed a thinking creature such as man."*

Literature in the English language had rarely, if ever, seen such a diatribe in print with a woman's name signed at the bottom. Something had made Aphra very angry indeed, and from the text, one might guess that she had been told that her "want of language" or "want of letters" disqualified her from taking a position in the dispute over the rules that ought to govern the writing of plays. Of course it was true that her sex had excluded her from the academies, and it was also true that, unlike Dryden, she could not read Aristotle and the "Ancients" for herself. She insists, however, that she is not asserting her position *"purely on my own knowledge,"* but has listened very carefully to both parties presenting their platforms and has memorized the arguments. Defiantly sarcastic, she is first of all refusing to be intimidated into a sense of inferiority because of her sex's ignorance, and second, dismissing the much-vaunted "learning" that she has been denied as so much "academic frippery." This stance, as comments she later made would prove, did in fact mask a certain sense of deprivation, but she was at this point determined to hold her own among her male colleagues no matter at what disadvantage.

Aphra's deliberately flippant attitude had another purpose, however. She was setting the stage for a manifesto: a declaration against those critics and writers who wished to burden plays with the task of the *"reformation of men's minds or manners."* As early as 1664, a minor writer named Richard Flecknoe wrote in a "Discourse of the English Stage," published at the end of his play *Love's Kingdom*, that "a dramatic poet [ought to be] a good moral philosopher . . . the chiefest end [of drama] is to render folly ridiculous, vice odious, and virtue and nobleness so amiable and lovely, as everyone should be delighted and enamoured with it."[24] Dryden specified in *Of Dramatic Poesy* that the purpose of theater ought to be "the delight and instruction of mankind," as the Elizabethans before him had held; but Thomas Shadwell accused him of a little too much emphasis on delight, claiming that he himself aimed in his plays to "reprehend some of the vices and follies of the age."[25] A short time later, Dryden slightly modified the emphasis of his position, allowing that "examples of piety" in plays ought not to be omitted by dramatists. That this point of view had at least some support in the audience is evidenced by a letter Mary Evelyn wrote after seeing Mr. Dryden's *The Conquest of Granada.* Inspired by the moral virtue exemplified in this heroic tragedy, she told her correspondent: "as poetic fiction has been instructive in former ages, I wish this same event in ours."[26]

But what constituted "virtue" in the seventeenth century was precisely what Aphra detested most in her society—the virtue that had led the heroine of *The Forced Marriage* to marry a man she did not love in obedience to her father's wishes; the virtue that dictated that all relations between men and women must be sanctified by an oppressive set of legal conditions—marriage, which rendered women utterly helpless. Such a morality did not in the least correspond to Aphra's beliefs or desires, and she was not going to be persuaded to illustrate or uphold it in her plays: *"In my judgement,"* she wrote in the "Epistle to the Reader," *"the increasing number of our latter plays have not done much more towards the amending of men's morals, or their wit, than hath the frequent preaching which this last age hath been pestered with, (indeed without all controversy they have done less harm) nor can I once imagine what temptation anyone can have to expect it from them; for sure I am no play was ever writ with that design. . . . In short, I think a play the best divertisement that wise men have; but do also think them nothing so who do discourse as formally about the rules of it, as if 'twere the grand affair of human life."*

Aphra was never one to fail to appreciate pleasure, but another consideration may have influenced her statement: sex comedy was beginning to dominate popular taste. Any writer who wanted to survive had to follow the trend. Dryden himself, a professional with a living to make, had to acknowledge the fact and accordingly bend his talents to please. If her only purpose had been to cater to fashion, however, Aphra would not have felt compelled to write such a preface. Her position was, in its own way, as moral a denial of the morality she could not accept as "virtue" itself.

———·

The Dutch Lover was Aphra's third play. The wits and fops and critics and writers might have been amused and titillated by the innovation of a woman writing for the stage when she produced her first play, but when a second appeared in rapid succession and then a third, it must have become apparent that she intended to establish herself as a permanent competitor. To make matters worse, she had dared to throw herself into a debate over the function and nature of theater that was beyond her education or proper sphere. According to Aphra, a deliberate effort was made to sabotage, discourage, and eliminate her from the stage. The "Epistle to the Reader" recounts:

"Indeed that day 'twas acted first, there comes me into the pit, a long, lither, phlegmatick, white, ill-favour'd, wretched fop, an officer in masquerade newly transported with a scarf and feather out of France, a sorry animal that has nought else to shield it from the uttermost contempt of all mankind, but that respect which we afford to rats and toads, which though we do not well allow to live, yet when considered as a part of God's creation, we make honourable mention of them. A thing, reader—but no more of such a smelt: This thing, I tell ye, opening that which serves it for a mouth, out issued such a noise as this to those that sat about it, that they were to expect a woeful play, God damn him, for it was a woman's.* *Now how this came about I am not sure, but I suppose he brought it piping hot from some who had with him the reputation of a villanous wit: for creatures of his size of sense talk without all imagination, such scraps as they pick up from other folks. I would not for a world be taken arguing with such a propertie as this: but if I thought there were a man of any tolerable parts, who could upon mature deliberation distinguish well his right hand from his left, and justly state the difference between the number of sixteen and two, yet had this prejudice upon him; I would take a little pains to make him know how much he errs.* For waving the examination why women having equal education with men, were not as capable of knowledge, of whatsoever sort as well as they: I'll only say as I have touched before, that plays have no great room for that which is men's great advantage over women, that is learning.* *We all well know that the immortal Shakespeare's plays (who was not guilty of much more of this* [learning] *than often falls to women's share) have better pleased the world than Jonson's works, though by the way 'tis said that Benjamin was no such Rabbi neither, for I am in-*

* my emphasis

formed that his learning was but Grammar high (sufficient indeed to rob poor Salust of his best orations) . . . and for our modern [dramatists], except our more unimitable Laureat, I dare to say I know of none that write at such a formidable rate, but that a woman may hope to reach their greatest heights. Then for their musty rules of unity, and God knows what besides, if they meant anything, they are enough intelligible and as practible by a woman."[27]

All pretense of apology or feminine coquetry has evaporated in the heat of Aphra's fury at being discriminated against because of her sex. Her anger at the reception of *The Dutch Lover* finally outweighs the hesitant sense of transgression that tempered her boldness at her literary debut. The sense of the argument is twofold: first, Aphra implies that it is not any lack in women's innate capacity for knowledge that has kept them from the pen but a double standard in access to learning; but secondly, she asserts that the "learning" denied to her sex is in no way essential to the writing of plays. As before, in the same breath that she protests women's exclusion from the possession of "knowledge," she denies that her present activity requires it. There is some confusion between her stated position against the writing of plays being governed by erudition and the separate issue of women's relation to knowledge. Apparently, the criticisms that had had such a radicalizing effect on her had further entrenched her self-doubt at the same time that they had strengthened and given the force of anger to her nascent feminism. Whatever the contradictions of "Epistle to the Reader," it was as close to a manifesto as a female author writing for a popular audience had come.

In addition to the aspersions cast on the sex of its author, *The Dutch Lover* was sabotaged on another ground: according to Aphra, it was *"hugely injured in the acting."* The actor who played the Dutch lover, she says, had forgotten his lines and simply ad-libbed for most of the play, so that what she heard little resembled what she had written. The complicated intrigue of the plot too was completely ruined by the *"intolerable negligence"* of some of the other actors. Lastly, the costumes did not at all correspond to her instructions, with the result that one scene, which depended on a character's being mistaken for another because their dress was alike, was undermined. Aphra had attained, by the time she wrote her third play, a considerable technical mastery of her craft. The dialogue moves quickly, the repartee is sharp and witty, the intricate plot is handled with ease and skill, the timing is perfect—with the result that *The Dutch Lover* is a thoroughly entertaining play, even for a twentieth-century audience. To have her work destroyed by the unprofessionalism of the actors *"did vex me so,"* she says, *"I could almost be angry."*

The final insult was that the fellow writer who had promised her an epilogue found himself indisposed and deputed an inferior to supply it. Aphra duly had it printed in the published version anyway, but the epilogue was *"by misfortune"* lost.

III

If there was a literary cabal determined to humiliate Aphra and force her from the stage, there was also a party of wits and writers who sought and enjoyed her company. She had a reputation for lively intellectual conversation, said a friend of hers: "Mrs. Behn, in the nicest metaphysical points, would argue with judgment, and extremely happy distinctions; she would, with an engaging air, enforce her notions, with all the justness of the most able philosopher, tho' not with his magical roughness."[28]

A number of new dramatists clustered around the Duke's Company and made their debut about the same time Aphra did: Henry Neville (Payne), who would remain a loyal supporter all her life and to whom she would dedicate *The Fair Jilt* in 1688 (the year before she died), produced his first play, *The Fatal Jealousy,* in August 1672.[29] Edward Ravenscroft, a rakehell lawyer of the Middle Temple, "beguiled a fortnight's illness" with the composition of *Mamamouchi; or The Citizen turned Gentleman,* which was an immediate success when staged in July of 1672. Ravenscroft, it seems likely, was probably the *"brother of the pen"* whose indisposition prevented him from supplying the epilogue to *The Dutch Lover.* If he was indeed guilty, however, he made his word good for a prologue at the next opportunity. In any case, they kept up a friendship for many years that contemporary gossip held was more than merely literary.[30]

Both Aphra and Ravenscroft contributed verses to *The Six Days' Adventure; or The New Utopia,* acted also by the Duke's Company in March 1671. The author was Edward Howard, brother to Sir Robert Howard, brother-in-law to Dryden, and a member of the powerful Howard clan whose importance to Aphra's childhood she acknowledged in the dedication of her play *The City Heiress* (1682) (addressed to Henry Howard, Duke of Norfolk). Edward Howard was also related to Viscount Stafford, whom Aphra had known in Antwerp. Apparently their tie was to be a long-standing one, as Edward Howard returned the favor of her verses many years later when he sent her a commendatory poem for the publication of her *Miscellany* in 1685.

Another literary friendship that had its beginning at this early period and continued for a lifetime was that with Thomas Otway, the young man whose rendition of the part of the King in *The Forced Marriage* ended his career as an actor and set him on writing. Aphra must already have had the reputation of a wit even before her first play was produced, since Otway sought her out as one whose foothold in the literary world was sufficiently established to enable her to help a younger aspirant.

If the "bold woman" that Elizabeth Cottington referred to in 1669 was in fact Aphra, her poetry had begun to be passed around outside the immediate circle of her personal acquaintances. Given the fact that usually more than half of the poems published in the popular collections of the time were unsigned, it is extremely difficult to identify any of Aphra's definitively. The modern editor of a miscellany first published in 1671, *The Westminster Drollery*, attributes one of the poems to her.[31] If it was indeed hers, she had rewritten it from a poem published earlier in another collection—quite a common practice. The hero of her play *The Rover II* (1681) sings a verse from this poem to a prostitute whose mercenary spirit contradicts his vision of love. Interestingly enough, the poem is an argument against the quantification of relationships between men and women and for free love—a position Aphra would elaborate throughout her career, whether in opposition to marriage for material gain or the prostitution of desire.

Aphra may well have been the editor of another volume of verse that came out the following year (1672); it was called *The Covent Garden Drollery; or a Collection of all the Choice Songs, Poems, Prologues, and Epilogues, (Sung and Spoken at Courts and Theaters) never in print before. Written by the refined'st Witts of the Age. And Collected by A. B.* Thorn-Drury, prefacing a twentieth-century reprint of *The Covent Garden Drollery* argues convincingly that A. B. is in fact Aphra Behn, and though others have disputed that claim, no other suitable alternative has been suggested.[32] The collection contains at least twenty-six unpublished epilogues and prologues, and Aphra would have been in an ideal position to solicit these from her friends and colleagues in the theater. There are pieces by Dryden, Wycherley, the Earl of Rochester, Thomas Killigrew, and four poems by Aphra herself that were printed for the first time. One of her poems, "I Led my Silvia to a Grove," which later appeared in *The Dutch Lover,* was shortly after reprinted in *Choice Airs and Dialogues* (1673) under a slightly different title; it was finally published in Aphra's *Poems upon Several Occasions* (1684) under still a third title. One piece of evidence seems to indicate that Aphra's contemporaries were quite well aware of who A. B. was: the anonymous N. C., who collected a *Bristol Drollery* appearing shortly after *The Covent Garden Drollery,* counsels his muse, "Humbly to cast herself on Mrs. Behn." [33] A number of Mrs. Behn's poems appeared in the miscellany *Choice Airs and Dialogues* (1673), keeping company with the wits of the day: Dryden, Wycherley, Crowne, Shadwell, Ravenscroft, Henry Neville (Payne), Thomas Duffett, Joseph Arrowsmith, and others.

Several other poems that Aphra Behn later published in collections of her work seem to belong to this early period when her career was just beginning. One, "To My Lady Morland at Tunbridge," can be dated to the years between 1670 and 1674. It was addressed to a young woman named Carola, who in 1670 had married Sir Samuel Morland. Her maiden name was Harsnett, and she was the daughter of a knight. In 1674, on October 10, she died in childbirth. She was evidently part of a group of friends close to Aphra, and the poem is an affectionate piece of advice about a man from one woman to another. [34]

Aphra's gallant has, it appears, abruptly transferred his attentions to the younger beauty—Mrs. Behn was twelve years older than Carola Morland. But Aphra maintains that she too has been struck by the younger woman's beauty and finds it *"just that you should out-rival me. Amyntas,"* she says, has betrayed her many times before—but among *"all his perjuries to me,"* this is the first involving a woman whose charms she admits surpass her own. The gallant in question however, Aphra warns, is too cynical to merit Carola's love: *"You too meanly prize . . .* [your beauty] *if you permit him on an amorous score,/ To be your slave, who was my slave before./ He oft has fetters worn, and can with ease / Admit 'em or dismiss 'em when he please."* Aphra advises Lady Morland to give her heart only to a man whose passion is deeper than the superficial Restoration wit or gallant. The advice is from a woman of experience to a woman of innocence: cautioning her to beware the wiles of men who use women and then discard them.

Another poem of Aphra's published in her *Poems Upon Several Occasions* (1685) whose composition seems to fall naturally into this early period is "Our Cabal," another play of love games disguised as pastoral frolic. Aphra and a group of her friends—identified by initials—have set out on a holiday to "wanton" in the green hills and pastures of the countryside. The company consists of Mr. V. U., Mr. G. V., *My dear Brother J. C., My dear Amoret, Mris. B.,* Mr. Je. B., Mr. E. B. and Mrs. F. M., Mr. J. H., and Mr. Ed. Bed. *The Muses Mercury,* which reprinted a part of the poem in 1708, identified E. B. and F. M. as Edward Butler and Mrs. Masters; "My dear Amoret," tradition has it, was the actress Elizabeth Barry; "My dear brother J. C." remains an intriguing mystery; Mr. J. H. was the man Aphra Behn would fall deeply in love with later on; and Mr. Je. B. was, at the time the poem was written, *"the author of my sighs and flame."* [35]

Any identification from initials such as these must necessarily be tentative, but an external document suggests that the young man whom Aphra had given her affections to might well have been a certain Jeffrey Boys, a lawyer of Gray's Inn, who was about Aphra's age. In his pocket diary for 1671, he recorded that he went to see "Astrea's play," *The Forced Marriage,* and on July 1 of that year, he wrote: "Astrea's boy brought me her play of *Ye Amorous Prince."* [36] They may have known each other from a very early age: Boys belonged to an old Kentish family whose principal branches lived around Canterbury and spread out into the surrounding countryside. The Boyses had intermarried extensively with other important families of the gentry in that neighborhood. Thomas Culpepper speaks of his cousin "John Boys," who was either first or second cousin to Aphra's Jeffrey Boys. [37]

Jeffrey Boys was the son of John Boys of Betshanger, who at the outbreak of the Civil War declared for Parliament and held various military posts for the length of the conflict, to the chagrin of some of his Cavalier relatives. In the early 1640s, John Boys and Algernon Sidney (Thomas Culpepper's uncle, whom Aphra later spied on in Antwerp) replaced Thomas Culpepper, Sr., as lieutenants of Dover Castle. Jeffrey Boys notes frequent returns to visit his father at the family estate in Kent during 1671, and among the errands he carried out in London for his father was supplying the Puritan rebel Edward Calamy with funds. Calamy was one of the men Aphra had informed on in her spying days. Along with Algernon Sidney and others, he had been close to Thomas Scot in the days of the Commonwealth. Another branch of the Boys family had, however, been involved with Lord Willoughby in the secret committee appointed by the King to bring off Booth's Rebellion in 1659.

Despite his Puritan background, Aphra's Jeffrey seems to have been the mirror of a fashionable man-about-town of his age. He frequented the theaters, took coaches in Hyde Park—which was then a rendezvous for what is in modern terms called a "pick-up"—drank a great deal, and dined out nearly every night in company. He spent June 19 (1671) at the King's Arms in Highgate, February 14 at the Vulture Tavern, September 25 at the Sun Tavern, March 3 at the Castle in Chancery Lane, February 2 at the King's Arms in Bow Street (Covent Garden); he went to the Pageant Tavern, the Paradise Tavern, the Cock Ale Tavern, the Pope's Head Tavern, the Reindeer, the Say "Chicken" Tavern, the Three Tuns Tavern, and many others. He must have met the wits at the Rose Tavern in Covent Garden (next to Rose Alley, where Dryden was later mugged for a literary offense), and at Mason's Coffeehouse. More than once he dined at the notorious Oxford Kate's, where a few years before the witty Sir Charles Sedley had been arrested for disporting himself naked on the balcony and shouting insults and obscenities to the gathered crowd. July 17, the sociable Jeffrey spent at Mother Damnable's, a tavern at Highgate. He was constantly in the company of his numerous cousins and was regularly at the Kentish Club, where he might well have seen Thomas Culpepper.

Mr. Jeffrey Boys of Gray's Inn wore laced cuffs and a laced crop, suits made from stuff and silk, a hat with ribbons, brunitty gloves, silk stockings, a sword, and a periwig of a very light color.[38] He smoked tobacco from "Virginy" and was inordinately fond of the Northdown Ale that came from Kent. The young man's reading ranged from the *Histoire des amours de Lysandre et de Caliste* (1670) to Calvin's *Institutes* (in Latin) and included: Robert Boyle's *Essay on Seraphic Love* (1660); *Letters of Advice to a Young Gentleman*, by Richard Lingard (1670); Trenchfield's *Advice to a Son* (?); and finally a *Discourse of Natural and Moral Impotency*, published anonymously in that year (1671).

It is impossible to know whether or not Jeffrey Boys was ever actually Aphra Behn's beau, but that he was her friend is certain. There is one remark he made in his diary that sheds a rather enigmatic light on her state of mind at the time: next to the date May 29, he entered: "give Astrea 5s. for a Guiny if she live halfe a year."[39] Perhaps Aphra was burning the candle at both ends. Perhaps she was leading the extravagant, drunken, violent life of the wits and the denizens of the theater world.

Another explanation of Jeffrey Boys's remark, though, may have been that Aphra was finding that the struggle to hold her own in such a world, to stand up to the critics and assert her right to the pen, was taking its toll on her. After the disaster of *The Dutch Lover,* she did not stage another play for three years. Whatever the reason was, she was unable herself to follow that advice she had so confidently given Edward Howard in 1671 when his play *The New Utopia* was a miserable failure:

> *Write on! and let not after ages say,*
> *The whistle or rude hiss could lay*
> *Thy mighty spright of poetry . . .*
> *Silence will like submission show:*
> *And give advantage to the foe!*

CHAPTER NINE

Literary Foremothers

Wit in women is apt to have had consequences; like a sword without a scabbard, it wounds the wearer and provokes assailants. I am sorry to say the generality of women who have excelled in wit have failed in chastity. . . .

—Elizabeth Montagu, 1750

It is curious that the first woman to write professionally for the English Stage began her career when the morality of English Drama was at its lowest.

—*Cambridge History of English Literature*, on Aphra Behn.

Women make poems? burn them, burn them,
Let them make bone-lace, let them make bone-lace. . . .

—Margaret Cavendish, Duchess of Newcastle, 1662

I

Currer Bell, George Eliot, George Sand, all the victims of inner strife as their writings prove, sought ineffectively to veil themselves by using the name of a man. They did homage to the convention, which if not implanted by the other sex, was liberally encouraged by them (the chief glory of a woman is not to be talked of, said Pericles, himself a much-talked-of man) that publicity in women is detestable. Anonymity runs in their blood.

—Virginia Woolf

The full risk and radical nature of the literary stance Aphra Behn had taken from the very beginning of her career can only be realized when understood in the context of what other women wrote, how they viewed their own writing in relation to the world, and what significance they chose to give the act itself. In the generation just before Aphra's, two women writers emerged who published literary work under their own names, breaking with the long tradition of feminine anonymity. They were Katherine Philips, the "Matchless Orinda" (1631–1664), and Margaret Cavendish, the Duchess of Newcastle (1624?–1664), with whom the reader is already acquainted.

Katherine Philips was part of a literary "society of friends" which included the poets Jeremy Taylor and Henry Vaughn, Sir Edward Dering, Katherine's husband, and several ladies under pastoral pseudonyms. They wrote each other elevated verse celebrating honor, virtue, and the modest life, and espoused platonic friendship. Katherine's poems were handed about in manuscript and had acquired quite a reputation when, at the encouragement of the Earl of Orrery, she began the translation of Corneille's *Pompey*. Though it was widely known among her friends to be her work, she shrank from the idea of signing her name to a published text: she wrote to Sir Charles Cotterel, whom she called "Poliarchus": "I would beg leave publickly to address it [*Pompey*] to the Duchess, but that then I must put my name to it, which I can never resolve to do; for I shall scarce ever pardon myself the confidence of having permitted it to see the light at all, tho' it was purely in my own defence that I did; for had I not furnished a true copy, it had been printed from one that was very false and imperfect. But should I once own it publicly, I think I should never be able to show my face again."[1] Not wishing to involve herself directly in the business of publication, Orinda confided the affair to Sir Charles Cotterel, with only one stipulation: "I consent to whatever you think fit to do about printing it," she wrote a little later, "but conjure you by all our mutual friendship, not to put my name to it, nay, not so much as the least mark or hint whereby the public may guess from whence it came."[2]

A few months later, an edition of Katherine Philips's poems was published in London, without her knowledge, according to the indignant letter she wrote to Poliarchus: "The injury done me by that printer and publisher surpasses all the troubles that to my remembrance I ever had . . . who never writ a line in my life with the intention to have it printed . . . you know me, Sir, to have been all along sufficiently distrustful of whatever my own want of company and better employment, or the commands of others have seduced me to write, and that I have rather endeavoured never to have those trifles seen at all, than that they should be exposed to all the world . . . sometimes I think that to make verses is so much above my reach, and a diversion so unfit for the sex to which I belong, that I am about to resolve against it forever; and could I have recovered those fugitive papers that have escaped my hands, I had long since, I believe, made a sacrifice of them all to the flames. The truth is, I have always had an incorrigible inclination to the vanity of rhyming, but intended the effects of that humour only for my own amusement in a retired life, and therefore did not so much resist it as a wise woman would have done."[3]

There was hardly anything shocking in the published verses. The people the poems were addressed to were disguised under names like Lucasia and Silvander, the subject matter of the highest virtue, and the style so literary that one wonders if they were in fact *not* written with publication in mind. Katherine Philips unquestionably harbored literary aspirations and found it perfectly natural that the male poets of her group should publish their works; but whether or not she really believed it was unthinkable for a woman to make herself "public" in this way, she nevertheless wrote to all her friends to disclaim responsibility for the publication and ask them to spread the word. To Dorothy Osborne she complained: "I must never show any face among any reasonable people again, for some most dishonest person hath got some collection of my poems as I hear, and hath delivered them to a printer who I hear is just upon putting them out and this hath so extreamly disturbed me, both to have my private folly so unhandsomely exposed and the belief that I believe the most part of the world are apt enough to believe that I connived at this ugly accident that I have been on the rack ever since I heard it, though I have written to Col. Jeffries who first sent me word of it to get the printer punished, the book called in, and me some way publickly vindicated; yet I shall need all my friends to be my champions to the critical and malicious that I am so innocent of the pitiful design of a knave to get a groat that I never was more vexed at anything and that I utterly disclaime whatever he hath so unhandsomely exposed." [4]

Mrs. Philips even went so far as to claim that this event had thrown her into a "fit of sickness." She finally succeeded in having the edition suppressed, and forced the printer, Marriott, to apologize and publicly announce his intention to withdraw the book in an advertisement in the London *Intelligencer* of January 18, 1664. Six months later, Mrs. Philips died of smallpox. Her poems were posthumously reedited, with her disclaimer of responsibility and her assertion that the activity of writing verses was "unfit for her sex" prefacing the new edition. She was thereafter held up as an example to her sex, a proof that women might have wit. She was often referred to as the "Chaste Orinda," and future defenders of women's right to the muse would cite her as the paragon for imitation, passing over Aphra Behn. Mrs. Philips had, in fact, succeeded in preserving the character Sir Edward Dering had given of her in his epilogue to her translation of *Pompey:* "No bolder thought can tax, those rhymes of blemish to the blushing sex; As chaste the lines, as harmless is the sense, as the first smiles of infant innocence." [5]

Margaret Cavendish, the Duchess of Newcastle, was equally eager to guard her reputation for virtue, and in her autobiography, appended to the life of her husband, plainly told the reader: "I am chaste, both by nature, and education, inasmuch as I do abhor an unchaste thought." [6] She does not seem to have regarded the publishing of her writings as a blight on her reputation, however, and even went so far as to insist that she wrote for "fame" and "eternity itself." At the same time, she constantly reminded the reader not only of her own incompetence in the field of "learning," but of her sex's general incapacity in that field of endeavor: "Women's minds are like shops of small-wares," she commented to another lady, "wherein some have pretty toys, but nothing of any great value." [7]

A young lady, apparently encouraged by seeing another woman venture into print, wrote to the Duchess and received the following reply: "Madam, you wrote in your letter that I had given our sex courage and confidence to write, and to divulge what they writ in print; but give me leave humbly to tell you, that it is no commendation to give them courage and confidence, if I cannot give them wit." [8]

Margaret Cavendish was married to the powerful and wealthy Duke of Newcastle. It seems she was strikingly pretty. He was many years older than she, and they lived in a great, empty country estate and had no children. To keep her occupied, and doubtless also away from other men, he encouraged her, as she tells it, "in my harmless pastime of writing." [9] He paid printers to publish lavish editions of her writings and protected her by writing introductions for nearly all of them, defending her. His commendation would be followed by a letter from her thanking him for permission to publish—a favor, she noted, few men allowed their wives. She was always careful to signal her proper position of inferiority and wrote of her husband: "He creates himself with his pen, writing what his wit dictates to him, but I pass my time rather with scribbling than with writing, with words than with wit . . . I am so far from thinking my self able, to teach, as I am afraid I have not capacity to learn, yet I must tell the world, that I think that not any hath a more abler master to learn from, than I have, for if I had never married the person I have, I do believe I should never have writ so, as to have adventured to divulge my works." [10] Despite the Duchess's humility about her own abilities, her evident desire for recognition and eagerness for literary fame scandalized her contemporaries. She was thought bold even to madness: when her first book of poems was published in 1653, Dorothy Osborne wrote to her fiancé, William Temple, to ask him to send her the curiosity, commenting, "Sure the poor woman is a little distracted, she could never be so ridiculous else as to venture at writing books and in verse too. If I could not sleep this fortnight I should not come to that." [11]

Dorothy Osborne was a young woman with an evident gift and urge to write—for seven whole years she kept up a steady stream of letters to her lover, articulate with descriptions of the countryside around her, of her reading, of whatever gossip she could garner in her isolated corner. The idea of a woman's employing her pen for a public, however, seemed outrageous to her: "You need not send me my Lady Newcastle's book," she wrote to William Temple a few weeks after she had asked him to get her a copy of the newly published work, "for I have seen it, and am satisfied that there are many soberer people in Bedlam, I'll swear her friends are much to blame to let her go abroad . . . there are certain things that custom has made almost of absolute necessity, and reputation I take to be one of those; *if one could be invisible I should choose that,* * but since all people are seen and known, and shall be talked of in spite of their teeth's, who is it that does not desire at least that nothing of ill may be said of them . . . no not [even] my Lady Newcastle with all her philosophy." [12]

Dorothy Osborne was, at the time this letter was written, avidly consuming volume after volume of Mlle. de Scudéry's *Artamène, or the Grand Cyrus,* seemingly under the impression that the author was a man. A translation into English had been published in that year (1653), with the inscription "written by Monsieur de Scudéry" on the title page. The translator, who dedicated the book to a Lady, tells her in the preface that had the book been a learned treatise written in Greek or Hebrew, he would have dedicated it to her Lord, but as it was only a romance, he thought her a more appropriate patron. He further says that he allows himself to compliment her on her learning only "because your modesty is transcendent over the rest." [13] Dorothy sent each volume to William Temple as she finished it, eagerly requesting his opinion of the events therein. In the course of her reading, she heard that the gentleman who had written the romances lived with his sister, a spinster, who furnished him "with all the little stories that come between," and was possessed with a great deal of wit, but had the misfortune (so Dorothy Osborne told her lover) to be ugly. Mlle de Scudéry had indeed initially published under her brother's name, and the romances that she so unflaggingly produced were not generally known in England to have been her work until much later. It is interesting to speculate whether Dorothy Osborne, had she known the truth, would have thought the author Mlle. de Scudéry mad for publishing her work, as she did the Duchess of Newcastle.

Dorothy Osborne was, however, only expressing the general opinion of her day in condemning Margaret Cavendish's rash adventure: her act of publication earned her the title "Mad Madge," and

* my emphasis

she shut herself away in the countryside, receiving only visitors who flattered and approved her, often in hopes of finding a generous patron. The Duchess's eccentricities did in fact become more and more pronounced, though whether it was a natural evolution or the effects of the conflict of her ambitions and her sex is not clear. Her husband might subsidize the publication of her philosophical works or poems, but her plays, which were all intended for the stage, went unacted. She wrote nineteen of them, but among all the extant dramatic records, there is no evidence of a single performance, with the possible exception of a play performed under the Duke of Newcastle's name and rumored to have been written by his wife.

The intensity of Katherine Philips's anguish over having her name attached to a published work and the violence of the reaction to the Duchess of Newcastle's publicly acknowledging the authorship serve as an index of the strength of opposition a woman writer of that time might encounter. Orinda had the support of a circle of friends, the Duchess of Newcastle had the privilege of great wealth, and both had the approval and encouragement of affectionate husbands. Aphra Behn, of course, had none of these advantages: she was alone and had a living to make. Perhaps, though, necessity freed her. If she had no one to protect her or to fall back on, she also was the guardian of no one's honor but her own.

II

The tyranny of custom hath hindered many [women] *from publishing their works, in which, in our nation, that great mirror of her sex, and of our age, the Duchess of Newcastle is only happy, by leaving the benefit of her writings to posterity.*
—Robert Codrington, *Youth's Behaviour or Decency in Conversation Amongst Women,* 1661

The two principal inhibitions, it seems, that kept women from writing and from publishing their writing in the seventeenth century and before were the sense that wit belonged to the masculine province and the fear of violating feminine "modesty." The first is clear enough, but the second, less immediately evident.[14] Its source lies in the complex interaction of symbolic and concrete interpretation of the concept of feminine sphere. As has been stated earlier, this division of masculine and feminine spheres of experience separated "the world" from the "domestic circle," the public from the private arena; women were denied access to the former and confined to the latter by "custom." The social hegemony of modesty and its attributes—virtue, honor, name, fame, and reputation—served to police the segregation by ascribing a sexual significance to any penetration, either from within or from without, of a woman's "private circle." To publish one's work, then, was to make oneself "public": to expose oneself to "the world." Women who did so violated their feminine modesty both by egressing from the private sphere which was their proper domain and by permitting foreign eyes access to what ought to remain hidden and anonymous.

In an age that generally agreed a gentleman's reputation was in his wife's keeping, a woman's shame was also her husband's. It was not merely out of a desire to please that the Duchess of Newcastle thanked her husband for permission to publish. As a woman was legally the property of her husband, she could not under the law own anything independently (with a few exceptions having to do with dowry agreements) as long as she was married to him, even a book published under her own name. Interestingly enough, at that time publication had a second meaning that has since been dropped from circulation: when a citizen went bankrupt, publication of his goods was made; that is to say, his property was distributed to the public whom he was indebted to. The way in which feminine chastity played a central role in the transmission of wealth in a primogenital, patrilinear inheritance system and was therefore assigned an independent material value has already been discussed: in this light, a wife's "publication" might in one sense be described as a publication of her husband's goods.

The symbolic violation of feminine modesty by seeking fame or publishing oneself to "the world" is described in the language of verses written by a Lady Elizabeth Carey at the beginning of the seventeenth century:

> 'Tis not enough for one that is a wife
>   To keep her spotless from an act of ill:
> But from suspicion she should free her life,
>   And bare herself of power as well as will.
> 'Tis not so glorious for her to be free,
>   As by her proper self restrain'd to be.

When she hath spacious ground to walk upon,
  Why on the ridge should she desire to go?
It is no glory to forbear alone
  Those things that may her honour overthrow:
But 'tis thankworthy, if she will not take
All lawful liberties for honour's sake.

That wife her hand against her fame doth rear,
  That more than to her lord alone will give
A private word to any second ear;
  And though she may with reputation live,
Yet tho' most chaste, she doth her glory blot,
And wounds her honour, tho' she kills it not.

When to their husbands they themselves do bind,
  Do they not wholly give themselves away?
Or give they but their body, not their mind,
  Reserving that, tho' best, for other's prey?
No, sure, their thought no more can be their own,
And therefore to none but one be known.

Then she usurps upon another's right,
  That seeks to be by public language graced;
And tho' her thoughts reflect with purest light
  Her mind, if not peculiar, is not chaste.
For in a wife it is no worse to find
A common body, than a common mind.[15]

Paradoxically, this explicit statement of the incompatibility of feminine chastity and publicity of thought came from a lady who may have been, though the records are too incomplete to be considered definitive, the author of the first published play in the English language by a woman. In 1613, Lady Carey, who was married to Sir Henry Carey, later Viscount Falkland, published a work called *The Tragedie of Mariam, the Faire Queen of Jewry*. Its author was identified only by the initials E. C., but even so, the act was very much at odds with the principles expressed in the foregoing verses, which came in the Chorus at the end of Act III. It cannot be said for certain whether or not the play was ever performed.

Characters in Aphra Behn's early plays may be found repeating the same language: Erminia, the heroine of *The Forced Marriage*, promises her husband that *"whilst I'm your wife I'll not allow birth to a thought that tends to injuring you* [meaning his honor]." In *The*

Amorous Prince, Clarinda tells her friend Ismena, who is utterly ignorant of social convention, as she has been brought up in the isolation
of a convent, that "*'Tis not the custom here for men to expose their wives to
the view of any.*"

Katherine Philips's near-frantic fear of being "exposed" to the
world in the publication of her poems takes on a more logical aspect
in this perspective. Dorothy Osborne's casual wish to become invisible in order to protect her reputation unwittingly expresses the impulse that must have made countless women choose anonymity over
publicity. The unidentified female author of a feminist tract published in 1696 states quite explicitly her reasons for keeping her name
a secret: "I presume not so far upon the merits of what I have written,
as to make my name public with it," she said, adding, "nothing
could induce me to bring my name upon the *public stage of the world* *
. . . the tenderness of reputation in our sex . . . made me very cautious, how I exposed mine to such poisonous vapours. I was not ignorant, how liberal men are of their scandal, whenever provoked,
especially by a woman."[16] Anna van Schurman, in a letter she reprinted in her book *The Learned Maid or, Whether a Maid may be a
Scholar?,* specifically asks her fellow-scholar Johannes Beverovicious
(author of *The Excellency of the Female Sex,* 1639) not to dedicate his
book to her because it might damage her reputation: "I do heartily
entreat you, yea by our inviolable friendship I beseech you, that you
would not dedicate his book to me," she writes, "for, as you are not
ignorant, with what evil eyes the greatest part of men do behold what
tendeth to our praise."[17] She was afraid that malicious tongues would
call her his mistress. The title page of Anna van Schurman's learned
treatise announces that it was written by "a Virgin," and the author
of the prefatory Epistle to the Reader praises her extensive mastery of
learning, but further states that "these gifts are far inferiour to those
which she accounteth chief: piety without ostentation, modesty
beyond example, and most exemplary holiness of life and conversation."[18] It seems that even those women who were strong enough and
educated enough to argue against male prerogative in the domain of
knowledge still felt they had to protect the reputation for modesty
that was such an important reinforcement of the "feminine sphere."

Anne Wharton, whom Aphra Behn exchanged verses with,

* my emphasis

showed a similar concern when she dedicated a play she wrote to another woman friend, Mrs. Mary Howe, apologizing: "Forgive me for offering to you a play which never deserved, nor was ever designed to be publick, and therefore cannot aspire to the name of a dedication." [19] The play indeed was never performed and never printed and remains an obscure manuscript preserved in the British Museum. Anne Wharton retained her chaste posture even in the face of the inordinate promiscuity of her husband, well known to everyone, which caused her great suffering, and she criticized Aphra, of whom she was nevertheless personally fond, for the "immodesty" of her verses.

Anne Finch, the Countess of Winchelsea, who also respected Aphra Behn, nevertheless "owned that a little too loosely she writ," and unhappily acknowledged the necessary obscurity of a woman writer of her time:

> Did I, my lines intend for public view
> How many censures would their faults persue,
> Some would, because such words they do affect,
> Cry they're insipid, empty, uncorrect.
> And many, have attained, dull and untaught
> The name of wit, only by finding fault.
> True judges, might condemn their want of wit,
> And all might say, they're by a woman writ.
> Alas! a woman that attempts the pen,
> Such an intruder on the rights of men,
> Such a presumptuous creature, is esteemed,
> The fault can by no virtue be redeemed.
> They tell us, we mistake our sex and way . . .
> Be cautioned then my muse, and still retired;
> Nor be despised, aiming to be admired;
> Conscious of wants, still with contracted wing,
> To some friends, and to thy sorrows sing;
> For groves of laurel, thou wert never meant;
> Be dark enough the shades, and be thou there content. [20]

It is not surprising that a good deal of the earliest writing by women should have taken the form of letters, diaries, or autobiographies. They are entirely private forms of writing, not destined for publication and dealing only with what limited experience might come within the circumference of a lady's life. Because they were not meant for the eyes of "the world" or the public, diaries did not abrogate the all-powerful feminine modesty. The Duchess of Newcastle recorded that she wrote her autobiography "for my own sake . . . to tell the truth, lest after-ages should mistake, in not knowing I was daughter to one Master Lucas of St. Johns, near Colchester, in Essex, second wife to the Lord Marquis of Newcastle; for my Lord having had two wives, I might easily have been mistaken, especially if I should die and my Lord marry again."[21] What is most painful about these few lines is the Duchess's recognition of her own historical invisibility: "after-ages" do not concern themselves with her sex or care to distinguish between the interchangeable wives of the great Lord. As Mary Astell reminded her female readers a few years later: "You yourselves (as great a figure as you make) must be buried in silence and forgetfulness."[22]

The question of literary "identity" for a woman writing in the seventeenth century could not but be affected by the fact that a woman's "name" was literally not her own. The Duchess of Newcastle writes that a woman's "name is lost as to her particular in her marrying, for she quits her own and is named as her husband; also her family, for neither name nor estate goes to her family according to the laws and customs of this country . . . she hazards her life by bringing [children] into the world, and has the greatest share of trouble in bringing them up [but cannot] assure themselves of comfort or happiness by them, when they are grown to be men, for their name only lives in sons, who continue the line of succession, whereas daughters are but branches which by marriage are broken off from the root from whence they sprang, and ingrafted into the stock of another family, so that daughters are but moveable goods or furnitures that wear out; and though sometimes they carry the lands with them, for want of male-heirs, yet the name is not kept nor the line continued with them, for the line, name, and life of a family ends with the male issue . . ."[23] As Sir Thomas Overbury put it, "My wife is my adopted self."[24]

Feminine modesty, it seems, naturally entailed namelessness. Hannah Woolley, at the beginning of *The Gentlewoman's Companion* (1675), rejected the seeking of a "name" as a proper motive for publishing her book: "It is no ambitious design of gaining a name in print (a thing as rare for a woman to endeavour, as obtain) that puts me on this bold undertaking," she wrote, explaining that her purpose was only to give other women the benefit of her practical experience.[25] William Walsh, in the course of an argument defending women's right to the pen, commended ladies who took this attitude (citing Orinda as England's patron muse, while failing to mention Aphra Behn, though he was writing after she died) and contended that his country might boast of many female poets except that "modesty too often hinders them from making their vertues known; that they are not of those eternal scribblers who are continually plaguing the world with their works; and that it is not the vanity of getting a name, which several of the greatest men of the world have owned to be the cause of their writing."[26] In these last, he was most unfortunately not far from the truth.

The double meaning of "name" in Aphra Behn's century—"name" for modesty and "name" for renown—created a split in women of literary ambitions that forced some into anonymity, others into denial of responsibility for publication, and still others into constant apology and humble appeal. It is this tradition of invisibility that makes Aphra's virulent attack on those who criticised her as a woman writing impressive.

III

An honest man, being troubled with a scold,
Told her, if she continued so bold,
That he would have a case made out of hand,
To keep her tongue in, under his command.
                    —*Anatomy of a Woman's Tongue,* 1638

In addition to the problem that the implication of her sexuality in the act of writing might pose for a literary woman, there was still another difficulty: she was inevitably seen as a threat, viewed as competing with her male contemporaries whether or not they were writers themselves. The prologue to Aphra's *The Forced Marriage* makes this abundantly clear. She had initially attempted to circumvent hostile reaction by a sleight of "feminine" coquetry: claiming that her invasion of the masculine territory of wit was only the better to charm. But her subsequent remarks make it evident that the evasion was to no purpose. Men might compete among each other on professional ground, sometimes even savagely, but a female wit was, by the very fact of her existence, felt to be a direct challenge to male supremacy as a whole.

———— .

A woman poet who apparently frequented the literary and theatrical circles of Aphra Behn's day, but whose historical identity goes no further than "Sylvia," was pilloried—primarily on the grounds of immodesty—by hack-writer Robert Gould, who advised her to give up the pen and leave the writing to her male contemporaries. The language of her answer quite clearly articulates the restrictions of masculine and feminine spheres and defines the threatened feelings that women wits aroused:

> *Must men be blessed with intellectual light,*
> *Whilst we remain in ignorances night?*
>   *We've noble souls as well as they,*
>   *And we've retentive memories too.*
> *But I suppose, they think we'll best obey,*
>   *And best our servile business do,*
>   *If nothing else we know*
> *But what concerns a kitchen or a field,*
>   *And those low things they yield:*
>   *As if a rational unbounded mind*
> *Should be to such low worthless sordid things confined;*
>
> *They'll let us learn to work,* to dance, to sing,*
>   *Or any other trivial thing;*
>   *But they're unwilling we should know*
>   *What sacred science can impart:*
> *Nor would they have us dive into the abyss of art,*
>   *Nor in the labyrinths of learning go,*
>   *Nor have us know the languages of the schools,*
>   *As if they thought to keep us fools. . .*
>
> *But should we know as much as they,*
>   *They fear their empire would decay;*
>   *For they know women heretofore*
> *Gained victories, and envied laurels wore.†*
>   *And now they fear we'll once again*
>   *Ambitious be to reign,*
> *And so invade the territories of the brain.*[27]

* Work means needlework here.

† She is referring to the Amazons, Sappho, Joan of Arc, etc., who were often cited in tracts of the period defending the idea that women had historically proven their inherent capabilities.

Apparently Sylvia published no more; at least her style is not recognizable in the work of any women whose publications were recorded in the *Term Catalogues* or the *Stationer's Register* of the time. She was not alone, however, among the early feminists who followed in Aphra's footsteps to argue that men had excluded her sex from learning out of envy and fear that they themselves would be dominated. The woman who wrote the *Defense of the Female Sex* (1696) said: "Nothing made one party slavishly depress another, but their fear that they may at one time or other become strong or courageous enough to make themselves equal to, if not superior to their masters. This is our case; for men being sensible as well of the abilities of mind in our sex . . . began to grow jealous, that we, who in the infancy of the world were their equals and partners in dominion, might in process of time, by subtlety and stratagem, become their superiors . . . from that time they have endeavoured to train us up altogether to ease and ignorance, as conquerors use to do to those, they reduce by force, so that they may disarm 'em both of courage and wit." [28]

Another unidentified woman, who prefixed commendatory verses to the posthumous edition of Katherine Philips's poetry, equated knowledge with power in the same military terms: "Ask me not then, why jealous men debar/ Our sex from books in peace, from arms in war;/ It is because our parts will soon demand/ Tribunals for our persons, and command." [29] Lady Mary Chudleigh also believed that part of the impulse behind male suppression of women came from a sense of their own frailty and a horror of the female strength they perceived underneath the exterior weakness. In *The Ladies Defence* (1701), a dialogue in which two men represent the masculine point of view to a young lady who opposes them, Lady Chudleigh connects domination in love with domination in knowledge: one of the men declares that if women succeeded in obtaining the learning they so desired, then men would never dare to court any maid above a chambermaid. . . .

> Then blame us not if we our interest mind,
> And would have knowledge to ourselves confined,
> Since that alone pre-eminence does give,
> And robbed of it we should unvalued live.
> While you are ignorant, we are secure,
> A little pain will your esteem procure. [30]

The perspicacious Lady Chudleigh, despite her feminist leanings, chose to live in silent retreat in order to practice her knowledge in private: "There uncontrolled I can myself survey,/ And from observers free, my intellectual powers display."[31]

It is an historical commonplace that women writers suffered from prejudice against their sex; to comprehend the tangled network of that reaction in its confusion of figurative and literal is far more elusive. The problem women who wrote in that century had in defining themselves in relation to a tradition of anonymity, in establishing a feminine literary identity, and in struggling with the sexual implications of their act cannot have failed to influence Aphra Behn. The fact that from the moment a woman set pen to paper her sexuality came into question is important to understanding why, as one of Aphra's contemporaries couched it, "whore's the like reproachful name, as poetess—the luckless twins of shame."[32] The principal criticism flung at Aphra in the course of her career was lack of modesty, an accusation she savagely resented. Had she never written a line that was bawdy she would still have been at fault, but her freely expressed sexuality, though no worse than any other playwright's of her age, damned her beyond repair. Though she chose public scandal over modest retreat, she still suffered the same divided consciousness that the women who had chosen differently also felt. The imperative of reputation could not be eradicated from the feminine mind in a single leap of conviction or desire.

IV

Another group of women who suffered from the taint of immodesty were the actresses, who exposed not only mind but body in "the public stage of the world." Women actors had been common in France for years, but the English reacted violently to the idea of this perversion. When, in 1629, French actresses appeared on the stage in a play performed at Black-Friars, an observer recorded that these "women, or monsters rather," had only just begun their performance when they were "hissed, hooted, and pippin-pelted from the stage, so that I do not think they will soon be ready to try the same again."[33] He further noted that the very act of performing before an audience was "unwomanish and graceless."

No actress ventured the forbidden territory for more than thirty years after that. Their historical advent on the English stage very nearly coincided with Aphra Behn's introduction of the female playwright. Both, as previously pointed out, benefited from the vehement reaction to the strictures of Puritanism and the consequent "new immorality" that was a fashionable *sine qua non* for the Cavalier who wished to demonstrate his distance from that party and loyalty to the royal cause. Though it affected only a small segment of Restoration society, it created an atmosphere in which actress and female playwright might survive, if with difficulty, and a coterie which accepted them—though not necessarily on the most desirable terms.

No young lady of good family who had a name to protect—and a father or husband or family to enforce that protection—could seriously consider becoming an actress.[34] Even a lady who, as Colley Cibber relates, had already been abandoned by her family because of her "female indiscretions" was prevented by them from going on the stage. Her attempt to support herself by "getting bread from the stage was looked upon as an addition of new scandal to her former dishonour," says Cibber.[35] Her relations put pressure on the owner of the theater, and the young lady's application to join the company was rejected. Most of the women who did take up the profession were in some sort of irregular position: Moll Davis was the illegitimate daughter of a gentleman; Elizabeth Barry, the orphaned daughter of a barrister ruined in the Civil War; Charlotte Butler's father was a "decayed knight"; Sarah Cooke's, a widowed shop-keeper; Anne Bracegirdle was the daughter of a Staffordshire yeoman who had more children than he could feed and was happy to give her to Thomas Betterton, at the age of six, to be brought up in his family. Finally, the famous Nell Gwyn, who became the King's mistress, was the daughter of a disgraced Welsh soldier and a slatternly alcoholic mother who, in 1679, fell while drunk into a pond in Chelsea and drowned.

The noblemen and fops and wits who frequented the theater arrogantly viewed the actresses as their personal playthings, whether the latter wished it or not. They crowded into the tyring-rooms (dressing rooms) where the actresses were changing and carried on a continual bantering "amorous discourse"—before, after, and even *during* the play. Often the bantering did not merely stop at discourse, and the actresses complained more than once to the King of being harassed and manhandled behind the scenes. In 1664, the King issued a proclamation ordering that "no person of what quality soever do presume to enter at the door of the attiring house, but such as do belong to the company and are employed by them."[36] The order seems to have had little effect on the rakes who viewed actresses as below this nicety of discretion. The actress who declined the privilege of a wit's attentions risked vilification. Colley Cibber tells the story of a young actress who, sitting in the upper box of the theater, was joined by a nobleman. When he began to compliment her extravagantly, she informed him that she preferred the music to his conversation; he sneered at her and finally cursed her "in a style too grossly insulting for the meanest female ear to endure unresented." At her next performance, he stood up in the middle of her most dramatic speech, threw trash at her, and treated her to the most degrading slander.

Rebecca Marshall, an actress of the King's Company, formally petitioned the King in 1667 to defend her against a gentleman who had revenged himself on her because she had dared to object to his behavior. He had, the petition claimed, "assaulted her violently in a coach and after many horrid oaths and threats said that he would be revenged of her for complaining to my Lord Chamberlain formerly of him, pursued her with the sword in his hand. And when by flight she had secured herself in a house he continued his abusive language and he broke the windows of the adjoining house."[37] A few years later, the same Rebecca Marshall brought more trouble on herself. Sir Hugh Middleton, who had made some obscene and derogatory remarks about the actresses of her company, came sauntering into the tyring-room with the idea of seducing the very women he had just been detracting, only to find himself attacked by an infuriated Mrs. Marshall. At first he was too much taken by surprise to react, but soon replied by calling her every name that came to mind and informing her of his intention to kick her and have her beaten soundly by his footman. Rebecca Marshall ran to King Charles to extract a promise that he would prevent the gentleman in question from doing so; but the next evening found Sir Hugh Middleton waiting for her as she came out the stage door to Drury Lane. He merely smiled as she passed by, but a few steps later she realized a scurrilous-looking man was following her. When she had almost reached her lodgings, he rushed up to her and smeared excrement all over her face. Such was the hostility toward these women who were seen as little more than whores.

Most of the actresses, however, were not in any position to reject such advances. The salaries were no more than a pittance, and most of them were glad to accept the "protection" of a gentleman; in a society which provided few financial possibilities for a woman, the alternative was grim. As most of the actresses were without dowry or portion, and by their profession already rendered ineligible for the marriage market, reputation was not a matter of necessity. In any case, it must have been flattering to be taken up by a gentleman whose quality was above one's own, who spent hundreds of pounds at the gaming-table as though it were nothing, who wore fine silk stockings, lace cuffs, and kid gloves. The gentlemen were liberal with their presents and finery; and given the fact that libertinism was the social norm of the theatrical world, it must have seemed madness to resist in the name of a chastity that the wits claimed had long gone out of fashion. It was difficult for a young woman to resist falling into the norm: "as hard a matter for a pretty woman to keep herself honest in a theatre," wrote one of the wits, "as 'tis for an apothecary to keep his treacle from the flies in hot weather; for every libertine in the audience will be buzzing about her honey-pot, and her virtue must defend itself by abundance of fly-flaps, or those flesh-loving insects will soon blow upon her honour, and when once she has a maggot in her tail, all the pepper and salt in the kingdom will scarce keep her reputation from stinking." [38]

That actresses were more or less expected to supplement their professional earnings with what could be garnered from gentlemen is borne out by the fact that their salaries were substantially lower than those of the men of the company, sometimes by more than half. An actor who had had some experience and was reasonably successful might be paid about fifty shillings a week, but even leading ladies rarely managed to earn over thirty shillings—and that with considerable pressure on the owners of the theater. A young actress who had demonstrated her ability and attained a certain popularity, normally was paid between ten and fifteen shillings a week. Charlotte Butler, who acted in several of Aphra Behn's plays and was a favorite of the stage, left the London theater in a fury to star in the newly revived Dublin theater in 1692 because she was refused an addition of ten shillings a week to her pittance of a salary. A few years after she played Mrs. Flirt in Aphra's *The Widow Ranter* (1689), the popular Katherine Corey was still making only thirty shillings a week—after twenty-eight years in the theater. Elinor Leigh, who was married to the actor Anthony Leigh, got a raise from twenty to thirty shillings when her husband died in 1692, presumably because she was now expected to support herself. Even Elizabeth Barry, universally acknowledged to be the most gifted actress of her age, was paid only fifty shillings a week, in addition to the proceeds from an annual benefit performance.[39] This was hardly enough to keep oneself in any ordinary circumstances, much less in the style that a career in the theater demanded. An actress was expected to glitter both on and off the stage, but ten or twenty or even thirty shillings a week would not go far toward the purchase of silk stockings at fifteen shillings; gloves at two to ten shillings; a seat in the pit at two shillings; or in the upper boxes of the theater from six pence to four shillings—or even an orange from Orange Betty at three pence. Necessaries like petticoats and underwear, which were often very expensive, were beyond the reach of their small salaries. Sometimes actresses were tempted to embezzle their costumes to wear out of the theater for an evening on the town after the performance was over—an offense for which they were fined a week's pay.

The introduction of women to the English stage might have provided a profession that would permit a woman to lead an independent, autonomous life—in the same way that Aphra Behn saw living by her pen as a means to her freedom. Instead, the fact that the double standard was applied to their salaries and that the very act of exposing themselves on the stage placed them outside the class of respectable women made survival dependent on their ability to capitalize on beauty and feminine wiles. The innovation of actresses was therefore all too easily integrated into the existing structure of Restoration society. The actress was vilified because she behaved the same way that "Ladies of quality" did, only outside the sacrament of marriage. Aphra Behn was attacked because she was an anomaly: she introduced a new element that challenged established paradigms for feminine behavior.

CHAPTER TEN

War Between the Sexes: Independence and Desire

Who can be happy without love? for me I never numbered those dull days amongst those of my life, in which I had not my soul filled with that soft passion. . . .

—Aphra Behn

A woman must never write anything but posthumous works . . . for a woman under fifty to get into print, is submitting her happiness to the most terrible of lotteries; if she has the good fortune to have a lover, she'll begin by losing him.

—Stendhal

Pan, grant that I may never prove
So great a Slave to fall in love,
And to an unknown deity
Resign my happy liberty.

—Aphra Behn, "Song"

We women are always in danger of living too exclusively in the affections; and though our affections are perhaps the best gifts we have, we ought also to have our share of the more independent life. . . .

—George Eliot

I

If Aphra Behn had courted immodesty on a symbolic level merely in the act of staging her plays or the publishing of her writing, she openly embraced it in what she wrote. She frankly addressed the question of sex and was not afraid to bring it onto the stage. Her second play, *The Amorous Prince* (1671), opened on a seduction scene which had just been brought to fruition—the couple rising from their love-making. According to the stage directions, she is dressed in her "night attire" (probably a loose *robe de chambre*) and he is dressing himself; the setting is her bedroom. Not only has the act taken place outside the sanctity of marriage, but the gallant in question is not even the young lady's fiancé.

By seventeenth-century definition, the scene was at least racy, and for a great many, it was out-and-out scandalous. Without a doubt, the English stage had never seen a scene like this from the pen of a woman. This was indeed a vast departure from the chaste friendships of Katherine Philips or the platonic gallantries of Mlle. de Scudéry. Aphra's version of the pastoral ideal did not portray shepherds and shepherdesses exchanging elevated vows without ever so much as touching each other; she believed that physical passion was an inseparable part of love and ought to be acknowledged as such. Women as well as men, she held, experience desire and are equally as capable of its intense expression. A song she wrote for her third play, *The Dutch Lover* (1673), made her sexual stance quite clear:

> Amyntas led me to a grove,
>   Where all the trees did shade us;
> The sun itself, though it had strove,
>   It could not have betrayed us:
> The place secured from human eyes,
>   No other fear allows,
> But when the winds that gently rise,
> Do kiss the yeilding boughs.
>
> Down there we sat upon the moss,
>   And did begin to play
> A thousand amorous tricks, to pass
>   The heat of all the day.
> A many kisses he did give:
>   And I returned the same

Which made me willing to receive
That which I dare not name.

His charming eyes no aid required
To tell their softning tale;
On her that was already fired,
'Twas easy to prevail.
He did but kiss and clasp me round,
Whilst those his thoughts expressed:
And layed me gently on the ground;
Ah who can guess the rest?

Within the stiff form of pastoral convention, she was taking a position that was revolutionary for a woman writer of her time. Not only was such direct acknowledgment of her own desire considered unfeminine in a woman, but her equal activity in sexual advance—"and I returned the same"—must have been disconcerting even to the rakehell fops and seducers who pretended a disregard for female honor. Aphra's poem, called "The Willing Mistress," was putting a period to the "Coy Mistress." She had taken a position for sexual freedom, for women as well as for men, that would make her name a scandal to be reckoned with for three centuries. Aphra's views were, of course, more complicated than a simple advocation of feminine sexual liberty: she was, first, very much aware of the practical difficulties of such a position, and second, too much subject to the conventional wisdom about women that was part of her education and upbringing to avoid equivocation. But the fact remains that she boldly ventured her stand, however much she might later attempt to elude the consequences.

II

Perhaps Aphra might not have had the courage or stamina to defend such a position had the Restoration not created a favorable climate. It was generally acknowledged among both proponents and opponents that there had been what might be called a "sexual revolution" in the 1660s. Charles II's return to the throne effected an abrupt and deliberate reversal of Puritan ethic. His need to distinguish himself in every way from his predecessors—added to his natural inclination—created an atmosphere in which promiscuity, systematic frivolity, and extravagance were adhered to as a social norm almost as dogmatically as the more severe of the Puritan party had adhered to godliness. Part of the point, of course, was to demonstrate one's loyalty to the royal cause: Francis North was advised that his sobriety might call his political sympathies into question and was counseled to "keep a whore," because he was "ill-looked upon [at Court] for want of doing so."[1] Adultery was part of the calling of a gentleman, as essential to his place in society as fluency in French, a wig, or a sword at his side. The King set the tone by openly keeping several mistresses, carrying on numerous chance affairs, and bestowing titles, estates, and fortunes on his women and bastards. Royal libertinism does not necessarily engender promiscuity in the population at large—in fact the King may bring disapproval and disrespect upon himself; but there seems to have been a particularly vocal group that imitated Charles II's precedent. The movement primarily affected the fashionable society of London—the court and aristocratic circles, the playhouse, the taverns, coffeehouses, and ordinaries—but, as these were both the most visible and the most influential groups, they seemed to dominate the rest. The Whiggish City merchants who were the moral and political inheritors of Puritanism were, as the constant taunting of Restoration dramatists (including Aphra Behn) indicates, very much in opposition to the Tory libertines, but it is hard to tell to what extent the new immorality filtered down to the rest of the population. Statistics indicate a slight rise in bastardy and prenuptial pregnancies during this period, and there seems to have been a remarkable increase in prostitution as well at the end of the seventeenth century; but those figures may just as well have been influenced by economic considerations and other changes in the social fabric as by revolutions in sexuality.[2] However widespread the practice of sexual freedom actually was in Restoration society as a whole, it was so much in evidence in the capital that even those contemporaries who disapproved often believed themselves to be in the minority—lonely voices of reason in an unruly and wicked age.

The new sexual freedom was very much the fashion in the circles that Aphra Behn moved in—the courtiers, wits, poets, theatergoers, fops, actors, and actresses. A character in her play *The Amorous Prince* (1671), remarks that "there is nothing but foutering* in this

---

* fornicating

town"—a play on words that covered both the sexual sense and also meant, in the slang of the day, to waste time and tongue doing nothing. There are several references to the vogue for libertinism and the new breed of wild gallant who seduces wherever he likes. At one point, the hero chastises a lady he is trying to persuade to bed by telling her that her concern for her reputation is out-of-date: *"Fy, fy, Laura,"* he says, *"a Lady bred at court, and yet want complaisance enough to entertain a gallant in private! This coy humour is not à-la-mode. . . ."* Another hesitant young lady in a poem of Aphra's called "The Invitation" is informed *"this nicety's out of fashion."*

Countless other references to the universality of the "modern" social mode fill the poetry, plays, tracts, diaries, letters, and other documents of the period. A minor playwright named Joseph Arrowsmith even wrote a play (*The Reformation,* 1673) in which a mock Society for the Reformation of Male-Female Relations was created—to the purpose of assuring greater sexual freedom. Outside of the context of a general movement in that direction, the joke would not have been funny. The Earl of Rochester, who was a friend and patron of Aphra's, a man whose wit and poetry she greatly admired, wrote a poem called "A Ramble in St. James's Park" describing the fashionable scene of London in the early 1670s:

> *Much wine had passed, with grave discourse*
> *Of who fucks who, and who does worse*
> *(Such as you usually do hear*
> *From those that diet at the Bear),* *
> *When I, who still take care to see*
> *Drunkenness relieved by lechery,*
> *Went out into St. James's Park*
> *To cool my head and fire my heart.*
> *But though St. James had th' honor on 't,*
> *'Tis consecrate to prick and cunt. . . .*
> *Nightly now beneath* [the] *shade* [of the trees there]
> *Are buggeries, rapes, and incests made.*
> *Unto this all-sin-sheltering grove*
> *Whores of the bulk and the alcove,*
> *Great ladies, chambermaids, and drudges,*
> *The ragpicker, and heiress trudges.*

*The Bear was a tavern on Drury Lane, near the Theater Royal; it was frequented by the wits and the theatrical milieu.

Carmen, divines, great lords, and tailors,
Prentices, poets, pimps, and jailers,
Footmen, fine fops do here arrive,
And here promiscuously they swive. * [3]

Rochester's poem was passed around in manuscript, copied, and sent to relatives and friends in the country to amuse them with the latest goings-on in London. No doubt some were offended by the grossness of the verses, but Rochester and the avant-garde wits only laughed at prudery. The Court, wits, players, and gentry flocked to Spring-Gardens, to Hyde Park and St. James, where they promenaded, flirted, told the newest gossip, looked over, and were looked over. Obscene poems were much in vogue, and wits tossed off lines conjuring their mistresses to be "kind," (i.e., compliant), and insulting them if they refused. They wrote each other satires making fun of their more sober contemporaries, laughing at the women they had seduced and dropped, and recounting their "last night's rambles" in search of satisfaction. A wit's reputation rested on his notoriety for sexual conquest: if you wish to be excused in society, wrote Lord Buckhurst, "say that cunt detained thee." [4]

The Restoration rake was the hero of most of the plays staged at the Theater Royal or the Dorset Garden Theater; he was never serious, frequently drunk, and systematically lusty, capricious, wild, and jesting. Above all, he was anti-romantic. He subscribed to the philosophy that based its rejection of the spiritual on the materialism of Hobbes and Lucretius and placed body over mind, sense over soul. Preoccupation with morality or the metaphysical were better left to Puritans; wits would chose, as Rochester put it, "the readiest way to Hell." The only principle that existed for them was the pleasure principle: "For why should mankind live by rule and measure," said Sir Francis Fane, "since all his virtue rises from his pleasure?" [5] Any lie a gallant might tell in the pursuit of that pleasure was only a part of the game. When one character expresses surprise that the hero of Crowne's *The Country Wit* (1675), appropriately named "Ramble," has sworn up and down on his soul, and then casually broken his word and followed his own desires, another character tells him: ". . . Ramble thinks he has a soul! Alas good man, he seldom sets his thoughts on those affairs: he loves his soul, but as he loves his bawd,†

* fornicate
† prostitute

only to pimp for pleasures for the body, and then, bawd-like it may be damned, he cares not." [6]

Charles II himself had a reputation for cynicism and was skeptical of anyone who pretended to act out of any other motive than self-interest. According to Gilbert Burnet, he "had a very ill opinion both of men and women; and did not think there was either sincerity or chastity in the world out of principle." [7] Even in Aphra Behn's first play, there is a passing reference to what was regarded as the general dissolution of morals: *"Art thou honest?"* Philander asks Alcander, and the latter replies, *"As most men of my age. . . ."* The heroine of her play *The Amorous Prince* is warned by her own brother not to believe anything her lover might say to get her into bed: *". . . beware of men,"* he tells her in a letter, *"for though I myself be one, yet I have the frailties of my sex, and can dissemble too. Trust none of us, for if thou dost, thou art undone. We make vows to all alike we see, and even the best of men . . . is not to be credited in an affair of love."* The lover, a typical Restoration gallant, has promised to marry her and successfully made love to her on that condition, without the slightest intention of keeping his word.

III

Good God! What an age is this, and what a world is this! that a man cannot live without playing the knave and dissimulation.
—Samuel Pepys

The sexual "revolution" and Restoration cynicism had made love obsolete. Charles II, in 1664, wrote to his sister, Minette, in France: "I find the passion love is very much out of fashion in this country . . ." [8] Earlier poets of the seventeenth century had placed their mistresses on the Petrarchan pedestal: their eyes were idealized to starry orbs, lips to coral, breasts to snow, cheeks to roses, teeth to pearls. . . . The unrequited lover of platonic convention threatened to expire from despair alone if his mistress would not condescend to return, even for a minute, his worshipping look. But the Restoration wits would have nothing of idealized love: any pretense of love at all they deemed nothing more than shallow hypocrisy. Their mistresses were advised to give up such ridiculous romantic daydreaming and deliver up their "charms." Women who demurred or protested modesty were as likely as not told that their beauty was not worth the pursuit when there were other women more easily to be had. Etherege wrote that a man was an "ass" to "sigh and whine" for a woman; "if she be not as kind [in the sexual sense] as fair, but peevish and unhandy," he counseled, "leave her, she's only worth the care of some spruce Jack-a-dandy."[9] Wycherley, whose mistress evidently wanted him to declare his love before she would consider sleeping with him, told her: "Fantastic Phillis! cease to please,/Or else consent to give me ease [i.e., make love]/ Pox! of your dull platonic schemes/ 'Tis wasting life in idle dreams/ And quitting solid joys, to prove/ What crowns the fairy land of love."[10]

Libertine philosophy held that love was merely an illusion—an elaborate myth to cover what was really no more than sexual desire pressing to be satisfied. Rochester mocks the tradition of love songs written to women under the guise of a pastoral name, saying: "A song to Phyllis I perhaps might make,/ but never rhymed but for my pintle's* sake." A pamphlet describing the *Character of a Town Gallant* (1675), stated that "his trade is making-of-love, yet he knows no difference between that and lust. . . ."[11] The same wisdom is repeated over and over again by contemporaries, including the gallants and wits themselves, who were not in the least averse to making their attitudes public. Sir George Etherege, writing to Lord Buckhurst in a verse letter that was circulated to the amusement of all, tells of his sexual adventures and philosophically remarks:

> . . . *This shows love's chiefest magic lies*
> *In women's cunts, not in their eyes:*
> *There Cupid does his revels keep,*
> *There lovers all their sorrows steep;*
> *For having once but tasted that,*
> *Their mysteries are quite forgot.*

Woman's mystery could be reduced to just that. A woman was a "cunt" and any man who was fool enough to respect her for other qualities was missing the point. Poems like the anonymous "No true love between man and woman," proliferated in contemporary collections of verse: "No, no—'tis not love—" the author begins. "You may talk

*slang for penis

till doomsday,/ If you tell me 'tis more than mere satisfaction/ I'll never believe a tittle you say . . .

> *When a man to a woman comes creeping and cringing,*
> *And spends his high raptures on her nose and her eyes;*
> *'Tis Priapus* inspires the talkative engine,*
> *And all for the sake of her lilly white thighs.*
>
> *Your vows and protests, your oaths all and some,*
> *Ask Solon, Lycurgus † both learned and smart;*
> *They'll tell you the place from whence they all come,*
> *Is half a yard almost below the heart."* [12]

If love was an unreasonable expectation on the part of a mistress, then so was fidelity. Desire must find its expression wherever and whenever it arises, the rhetoric went. When the young woman in love with Celladon, the rake hero of Dryden's *Secret Love* (1668), asks him if he could be faithful to one woman alone, he replies: "Constant to one! I have been a courtier, a soldier, and a traveller, to good purpose, if I must be constant to one; give me some twenty, some forty, some a hundred mistresses: I have more love than any one woman can turn her to. . . . Yet for my part, I can live with as few mistresses as any man. I desire no superfluities, only for necessary change, or so, as I shift my linen." [13]

Rochester, in a poem called "Against Constancy" (1676), warns his mistress: "Tell me no more of constancy,/ The frivolous pretence/ Of cold age, narrow jealousy,/ Disease, and want of sense." He further informs her that he intends to change his mistress nightly until he is dead and is changed himself to worms. In another poem, on "Love and Life" (1677), he replies to another young woman, who is evidently reproaching him for his falseness to her, that "If I, by miracle, can be/ This livelong minute true to thee,/ 'Tis all that heaven allows." In still another poem, when a shepherdess accuses her lover of betrayal, he answers that "Since 'tis nature's law to change,/ constancy alone is strange." He explains to her that it is the nature of love itself that once the object of desire is possessed it ceases to hold interest for the man who desired. The "showers" of ecstasy kill the "flame," the shepherd tells the nymph—man's nature is that satisfaction extinguishes love.

* Priapus was the Roman god of procreation.
† Solon and Lycurgus were both Greek philosophers.

A great number of similar poems justifying masculine roving and attacking the ideal of constancy appeared in the miscellanies of the time and were passed from hand to hand. Usually they were written in reply to some demanding feminine voice in the poem who is either accusing the masculine "I" of desertion or attempting to exact some promise of fidelity on his part. Etherege's "To a Lady, asking him how long he would love her," conjures her to refrain from asking for anything more than the pleasure of the moment. "It is not, Celia, in our power/ To say how long our love will last,/ It may be we within this hour/ May lose the joys we now do taste,/ The blessed, that immortal be/ From change in love are only free." Celia is exhorted to sleep with her suitor while he is still in love with her, as his fancy will inevitably pass elsewhere.

The proponent of the "new sexuality" of the 1660s gave his mistress no commitments and no reassurances—except that of his own capriciousness. The only pledge a woman might have in an affair with a wit was the certainty that he would sooner or later abandon her for some fresher adventure and probably prove unfaithful even before. Sir Charles Sedley, in a "Song, to Phyllis," tells her, "I'll dote no longer than I can" and presents her with an ideal of liberated love in which each party, on tiring of the other, is free to part (as freely as they met), "each one possessed of their own heart."[14] One does not know what Phyllis answered, but the lady whom Charles Cotton wrote to charged him with loving her too little:

> . . . She cries I do not love her,
>   And tells me of her honour;
> Then have I no way to disprove her,
> And my true passion to discover,
>   But straight to fall upon her.
>
> Which done, forsooth, she talks of wedding,
>   But what will that avail her?
> For though I am old dog at begging,
> I'm yet a man of so much reading,
>   That there I sure shall fail her.
>
> No, hang me if I ever marry,
>   Till womankind grow stauncher,
> I do delight delights to vary,
> And love not in one hulk to tarry,
>   But only trim and launch her.[15]

Marriage was anathema to the Restoration gallant. To be forced to remain on terms of intimacy with a woman beyond the (avowedly short) term of his desire was an affront to his manhood. Though wives seldom succeeded in exacting any real restraint over their husbands' amorous activities, they could be a nuisance: "A spouse I do hate," wrote Wycherley, "for either she's false or she's jealous." A husband had to take care that he was not being cuckolded by another man and at the same time avoid arousing his wife's jealousy by concealing his own affairs. A wit needed, so the wits said, a woman who would give everything and ask nothing—for he could make no commitments, stand no obligations: "Give us a mate," said Wycherley, "who nothing will ask us or tell us./ She stands on no terms, . . . But takes her kind man at a venture./ If all prove not right,/ Without an act, process or warning,/ From a wife for a night,/ You may be divorced in the morning." [16]

IV

To an exact perfection they have wrought,
The action, love; the passion is forgot.

—Rochester

The multiplicity of feminine voices in the wits' verses complaining of their behavior seems to suggest that there was considerable female discontent with the state of affairs between the sexes. For women, the new sexual liberty, as it turned out, consisted primarily in the freedom to behave as cynically as the men; a woman who failed to understand the rules of the game and to play it to her advantage was likely to end in ruin. Casualties of the sexual ideology that the wits were celebrating in their verses as "free love" were common.

The career of the actress Elizabeth Farley was not unusual. She first appeared on the stage at the opening of the theaters after the Restoration, in the season of 1660–1661. Virginal, young, and reportedly very beautiful, she immediately caught the eye of the King, whose messenger summoned her to his bedchamber shortly thereafter. She held his fancy for a short time, and then he proceeded to other amorous interests—which were many. A few months later, Elizabeth Farley became the mistress of a lawyer of Gray's Inn, James Weaver, who kept her for almost a year. When his desire also began to wander, he threw her out of the house they had been living in together and requested the return of thirty pounds he had given her, for which he had (with what might be called cynical anticipation) previously extracted a written note from her. When his desertion was generally known, the tradesmen who had advanced her credit applied to the Lord Chamberlain for permission to sue her. She was left entirely without resources, and to make matters worse, she was pregnant. Mrs. Farley continued to act with the King's Company as long as possible, but when the fact of her condition could no longer be disguised, she was forced to abandon her only source of income. As long as she was a "servant of the King" (as all members of the King's Company were), she could not be arrested, but after her discharge from the theater, debtor's prison threatened. In desperation, she applied to Charles (who had, after all, originally "ruined" her). Thomas Killigrew, head of the King's Company, was ordered to reinstate her, but his collaborator, Sir Robert Howard, protested that "women of quality" had promised to boycott the stage if such a woman were allowed on it in such a condition. Mrs. Farley weathered her disaster until her bastard was born and quietly took her place in the company again. The scandal had finished her reputation, however, and she was deeply in debt. An actress's salary was little enough to live on, much less to pay off debts. She had become too "common" to attract another wealthy keeper. Hounded by debts and disgrace, she finally vanished into the slums of London when the theaters closed temporarily at the time of the Great Plague in 1665. Years later, Lord Buckhurst mentioned her in a bawdy verse letter to Sir George Etherege—she had become a well-known prostitute. The market value of those ladies in the latter half of the seventeenth century, perhaps because of their rapid increase in number, was notoriously low, and the relatively few years of prosperity a young woman in that profession might have to trade on then gave way to a lifetime of poverty, disease, and abuse. A great many looked like old women before they were thirty-five.

In James Wright's* *Humours and Conversations of the Town* (1693), one woman warns another of the inevitable result of too easily trusting a wit or gallant in an affair of the heart. Once his object

---

*another friend of Aphra Behn's, who contributed a song to one of her plays

(seduction) has been attained, she says, he will find some excuse to break off with you or simply drop you without apology at all. The consequence of such an affair, in addition to a child, perhaps, "is to be cast off by your relations, forced to prostitute yourself for a living, or marry some footman or soldier, follow the camp, and die in a hospital;* at best in an old tattered manto, carrying news about, from one acquaintance to another, for a meals-meat and a glass of wine. If there be anything delightful in the affair, 'tis but short, and full of fatigue, and attended with certain ruin of fortune and fame." [17]

If the end for women of the Restoration game of love was inevitable, the time she could play it was short, only as long as her beauty lasted—"at twenty-five in women's eyes/ Beauty does fade, at thirty dies." [18] Male attractiveness, on the other hand, went far beyond that age, and the libertines seduced girls at a progressively greater distance from their own age, while the young women who had been their contemporaries were discarded as no longer "fresh." This apparently was so widely and unquestioningly accepted that the wits even used it as a "persuasion to enjoy" device in their poems, arguing that a woman ought to take full advantage of her brief moment of beauty, as all too soon she will be no longer desirable. She had to be careful, though, not to take *too* full advantage. Sexual experience reduced the value of a lady even as it served to make a gallant more charming. Too many love affairs inevitably branded her a whore.

The loosening of moral strictures that began in the 1660s had undoubtedly given women of a certain circle (Aphra's and that of fashionable London) a greater freedom of movement and possibility, but it had also split them off from the great majority of other women. The choice was limited: one could become a wife or a mistress. The fact that there was little possibility, financial or social, of a single woman's surviving on her own is supported by an interesting linguistic development that John Evelyn recorded in his diary for 1662—"Miss," which had previously simply indicated a young unmarried woman, came to mean a whore. The actress Roxolana had been taken away to become the Earl of Oxford's "Miss," noted Evelyn, "as at this time they began to call lewd women." [19] Actresses and other women, whether married or not, had to begin to call themselves "Mrs." to avoid scandal.

*a sort of dumping ground for the poor in the seventeenth century

Choosing to be a wife, despite the advantages of social respectability and financial security, usually meant lonely confinement in an isolated country estate for the better part of one's life; it was customary for Restoration gentlemen to leave their spouses safely out of the path of potential cuckolds and themselves free to do as they liked in libertine London, far from the jealous eyes of their wives. This practice became so common that it was even noted as an explanation by the early demographer John Graunt (1696) for the lower birth rate in London than in the surrounding countryside.[20] The ideology that had come into fashion deemed wives hateful burdens and made them the butt of countless jokes, satires, and tirades. Only Presbyterian preachers superseded them as objects of ridicule.

Choosing to be a mistress, however, made one still more dependent, of course—unless one's "keeper" could be outwitted by calculating tactic. In a world where men had grown accustomed to using women with ruthless egotism, the only way for a woman to survive was to behave even more cynically than her man.

Rochester, in "A Letter from Artemesia in the Town to Chloë in the Country" (1679), gives, in the guise of a woman's voice, an account of the gossip of the town ("What loves have passed/ In this lewd town, since you and I met last") and describes the state of affairs between the sexes in London. Artemesia regrets the passing of "that lost thing love" and blames it on feminine manipulation: "Love, the most generous passion of the mind . . . is grown like play,* to be an arrant trade/ The rooks† creep in, and it has got of late/ As many little cheats and tricks as that./ But what yet more a woman's heart would vex,/ 'Tis chiefly carried on by our own sex. . . ." As illustration, she gives the story of Corinna, a young beauty who came to town and was courted, admired, loved and "with presents fed" until she had the misfortune to fall in love with "a man of wit, who found 'twas dull to love above a day;/ Made his ill-natured jest, and went away./ Now scorned by all, forsaken and oppressed,/ She's a *memento mori* to the rest;/ Diseased, decayed, to take up half a crown,/ Must mortgage her long scarf and manteau gown." After six months' scrounging and skimping, Corinna collects the money to buy herself a new gown and sets out to turn the "too dear-bought trick on men." She finds a young heir just come up to town from the country and

* gambling
† cheats

plies him with her charms. She sets up as his mistress, extracts a house (the deed in her own name), money, jewels, and plate,* and then poisons him before he begins to tire of her—having made sure that his will has been revised first.

A successful Corinna, like Rochester's, was not quite as common as he makes her out to be. His description of the circumstances that forced her into such behavior, however, is substantiated by many other texts of the period. Marriage for money had quantified the relationship between men and women, devaluing it as well, and now "free love" had become a "trade." The idea was current that any woman could be bought—it was only a question of price. An anonymous "Song on London Ladies," published right after Aphra Behn's poem "The Willing Mistress"† in *A Collection of Poems by Several Persons* (1673), describes the phenomenon:

> *A World 'tis of pleasure, one necklace or pearl,*
> *Will conjure the richest, or modestest girl.*
> *All trade is for gain, all commodities sold,*
> *Fear not; for thy coin thou mayst justly be bold.*
> *A pox on fine words; the contemplative fool*
> *Talks of love, and of shame; and oh! what misrule*
> *These keep in his heart. . . .*
>
> *Love is banished the world, and vertue is gone,*
> *To some private recess, to lament all alone;*
> *For now she grows barren, and none of her race*
> *Can be found either with, or without a good face;*
> *To the Mall, to the Park, to the Pit, to the Box;*
> *Where you will, you can't miss: there's meat for the cocks.*[21]

In order to survive in such a world, women had to renounce love because it made them too vulnerable in a predatory sexual scheme where the law was to eat or be eaten.

V

What is not a crime in men is scandalous and unpardonable in women . . .

—Mary Manley, 1696

*silver
†See pages 164–65.

The wits had announced the demise of feminine chastity and a fashionable following had ostensibly rejected traditional restrictions, but the influence of modesty had far from departed. It had, in a sense, gone underground. The libertine bent every effort to seduce a lady to his bed, but once she was there, he despised her for it. The expression of desire on the part of a woman still violated too many taboos—the woman who was kind (in both senses of the word) was sure to be rejected: "My love she did retard, prevent,/ Giving too soon, her kind consent," wrote Wycherley. A woman had to be distant in order to be attractive. "The Forsaken Mistress" who speaks in Etherege's poem of that name has understood too late the sexual politics behind the seduction she has given in to: "Tell me, gently Strepthon, why," she begs her lover, "You from my embraces fly?/ Does my love thy love destroy?/ Tell me, I will yet be coy." Whether it was fear of the emotional commitment reciprocal love might involve or the threat that women would actively return desire rather than merely act as its passive instrument that motivated the wits, they generally took flight in the face of feminine response. Ismena, a young woman in Aphra Behn's *The Amorous Prince* (1671), remarks to a typical Restoration rake: ". . . *as most gallants are, you're but pleased with what you have not; and love a mistress with great passion, 'till you find yourself beloved again, and then you hate her.*"

A series of love lyrics exchanged between Rochester and his wife reveals a great deal about the sort of strategies this fact forced women to adopt. Rochester, in the first verses, pleads with his wife to be "kind." Her answer (still preserved in manuscript) reminds him that when she was kind, he only rejected, scorned, and abandoned her: "I, to cherish your desire,/ Kindness used, but 'twas in vain./ You insulted in your slave;/ To be mine you soon refused. . . ." The only way to keep his love, she concludes, is to feign "scorn and rigour." Of course it might be argued that this phenomenon was by no means confined to Restoration sexuality but is universal. In that period, however, this mode of masculine perversity seems to have so marked relations between the sexes that contemporaries commented on it repeatedly.

Despite their profession of sexual liberty, the promiscuous gallants still more or less unconsciously held on to the very ideas about woman's modesty they had loudly repudiated. This double impulse put women in an impossible position. Aphra Behn, in a poem "To Alexis, in answer to his Poem against Fruition," complained:

> *Since Man with that inconstancy was born,*
> *To love the absent, and the present scorn,*
> *Why do we deck, why do we dress*
> *For such a short-liv'd happiness?*
> *Why do we put attraction on,*
> *Since either way 'tis we must be undone?*
> *They fly if honour take our part,*
> *Our virtue drives 'em o'er the field.*
> *We lose 'em by too much desert,*
> *And Oh! they fly us if we yeild.*
> *Ye Gods! is there no charm in all the fair*
> *To fix this wild, this faithless, wanderer?*

Wycherley wrote of another lady who protested similarly in "A Song sent to a Lady, who gave the subject for it, by complaining of the hard fate of Women; who, for refusing love [i.e., sex], must be hated, yet for granting it, despised." After listing all the lady's complaints, Wycherley twists them into an argument for sleeping with him—on the ground that she cannot win no matter what she does, so she may as well have the temporary satisfaction of sex. He does not say that he intends to treat her any differently from the other men she complains of.

The contradictory position that the demands of modesty had always put women in needed no external reinforcement from men, however, for whatever libertine ideology might proclaim, the "fair sex" was still very much subject to them. Women of Aphra Behn's generation had been educated to modesty, and it remained a powerful force whether they chose to conform to its dictates or defy them. Countless remarks in letters, poetry, and drama suggest that it was rare for a woman to renounce entirely at least the appearance of feminine virtue—Wycherley's reference in a preface to one of his plays to that "mask of modesty" all women "promiscuously wear in public," is characteristic. This self-image was so deeply ingrained that often even women of notorious reputation made an attempt at pretense. If they acknowledged their own sexuality and acceded to it, they violated the essential element of what they had been brought up to believe was their femininity: virtue. On the other hand, if they held to honor, they sacrificed desire. Numerous poems written by the wits and libertines record this ambiguity on the part of their women—Wycherley's "A Song to an incredulous dissident Mistress, who said, she was resolved to keep her reputation, in spite of her love," among them.

Since few seventeenth-century ladies discussed such matters in personal correspondence, it is difficult to document fully the feminine point of view, but what little survives testifies to the toll this conflict took on women. Aphra Behn herself wrote at the end of her life in one of the last works she composed, published posthumously, of the mind/body split that the feminine education of her age necessarily produced: ". . . 'tis the humour of our sex to deny most eagerly those grants to lovers, for which most tenderly we sigh, so contradictory are we to ourselves, as if the deity that made us with a seeming reluctancy to his own designs; placing as much discord in our minds, as there is harmony in our faces. We are a sort of airy clouds, whose lightning flash out one way, and the thunder another. Our words and thoughts can ne'er agree."

Aphra was not alone in her perception of the underlying structure of women's experience. About the time she wrote these lines, her fellow poetess the anonymous author of *Sylvia's Complaint of her Sex's Unhappiness* (1688) wrote of the very same impulse:

> Hence 'tis, our thoughts like tinder, apt to fire,
> Are often caught with loving kind desire;
> But custom does such rigid laws impose,
> We must not for our lives the thing disclose.
> If one of us a lowly youth has seen,
> And straight some tender thoughts to feel begin;
> Which liking does insensibly improve
> Itself to longing fond impatient love,
> The damsel in distress must still remain,
> Tortured and wracked with the tormenting pain:
> Custom and modesty, much more severe,
> Strictly forbid our passion to declare.
> If we reveal, then decency's provoked,
> If kept, then we are with the secret choked.[22]

The scarcity of evidence itself argues that it was modesty, not passion, that emerged dominant in the struggle; if it did not always

1. Aphra Behn, engraving of portrait attributed to Mary Beale.

2. (*Above left*) Aphra Behn, portrait by Sir Peter Lely.

3. (*Above right*) Aphra Behn, engraving from a portrait by John Riley.

4. (*Left*) Anne Finch, Countess of Winchelsea.

5. (*Opposite*) Aphra Behn's biography by "One of the Fair Sex."

THE
HISTORY
OF THE
LIFE and MEMOIRS
OF
Mrs. *BEHN.*

Written by one of the Fair Sex.

MY Intimate Acquaintance with the admirable *Aftrea*, gave me naturally a very great Efteem for her; for it both freed me from that Folly of my Sex, of envying or flighting Excellencies I could not obtain, and infpired me with a noble Fire to celebrate that Woman, who was an Honour and Glory to our Sex: and this reprinting her incomparable Novels, prefented me with a lucky Occafion of exerting that Defire into Action.

B   **She**

9. Charles II.

Opposite:

6. (*Above left*) Thomas Scot, regicide and father of William Scot.

7. (*Above right*) Francis, Lord Willoughby.

8. (*Below*) Surinam, about the time Aphra Behn went there.

11. The Earl of Arlington.

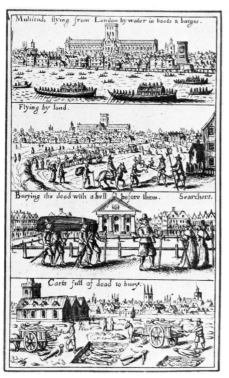

Multituds flying from London by water in boats & barges.

Flying by land.

Burying the dead with a bell before them. Searchers.

Carts full of dead to bury.

10. (*Left*) The Great Plague of 1665–1666.

12. (*Below*) Thomas Killigrew.

13. The Dutch attack on the
Thames (1667).

14. Aphra Behn's letter to
Killigrew, written before going
to debtor's prison (1668).

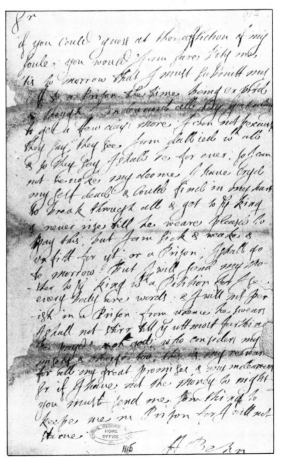

15. Thomas Otway.

Opposite:

16. (*Above left*) John Dryden.

17. (*Below left*) Thomas Betterton.

18. (*Above right*) The Dorset Garden Theater.

19. (*Below right*) Elizabeth Barry.

Opposite:

20. (*Above*) William Wycherley.

21. (*Below left*) Charles Sackville, Earl of Dorset.

22. (*Below right*) George Villiers, Duke of Buckingham.

24. John Greenhill.

25. A London coffee house.

26. Nell Gwyn.

27. (*Below left*) The Earl of Shaftesbury.

28. (*Below right*) William Howard, Viscount Stafford.

See here the Deuils Darling, plotting still
With Blood & Treasons all ye world to fill,
His Romish stratagems, Loe, Non can tell
Who canot fathom to ye Depth of Hell
Nothing but Murder'd Kings can him suffice
And flaming Cityes as a Sacrifice

Yet see behind his chaire Whom Heau'n sent,
Whom God hath made a timely Instrument
Englands intended ruine to prevent

That which, ye Deuil & ye Pope combin'd
Against our King and Protestants design'd
Disclos'd and frustrated by him wee find.

The Emblem Explayn'd

A A the Popes Cabbinett.
B the Pope writing to the Iesuits to
be diligent in the carring on the Plot.
C ye side wherof one lokes more be-
holder & sees all his Contriuances.
D ye Popes Crane whoe cries fryend
Oates is behind you.
E the Pope tilt of Supremacie falling
F downe occasioned by his desire Oates
G gaue him such his Supra fit made him
fall vpon ye work Romans his Letter
scorns ye Oates giues him more fit
for his Head then the former.

Opposite:

29. (*Above left*) Titus Oates and the pope.

30. (*Below right*) James II.

31. (*Below left*) Thomas Creech.

32. (*Left*) The Ice Fair on the Thames (1684).

33. (*Below*) Nathaniel Lee.

34. (*Above left*) Anne Wharton.
35. (*Above right*) Lawrence Hyde.
36. (*Below left*) Jacob Tonson.
37. (*Below right*) Edmund Waller.

actually prevent women from indulging their desires, it at least kept them from talking about them. The one poem published by a woman under her own name (other than Aphra's) in Mrs. Behn's *Miscellany* of 1685 is by an otherwise unidentified Mrs. Taylor, whose contribution begins thus: "Ye virgin powers, defend my heart/ From amorous looks and smiles. . . ." She leaves little doubt that virtue has not been compromised in her case and advises recourse to honor in circumstance of temptation: ". . . if through passion I grow blind/ Let honour be my guide. . . ."[23]

By 1696, when "anon." (female) was writing her *Essay in Defense of the Female Sex,* the bawdy Restoration had passed, and her statement on the subject reflects less conflict than resignation: "Modesty and the rules of decency observed among us, not permitting to us the liberty of declaring our sentiments to those we love, as men may; we dare not indulge a wanton fancy or rambling inclination, which must be stifled in our own breasts, and could only give us a hopeless anxiety. . . ."[24]

Sex in the seventeenth century, given the feminine education of that era, had in recent memory at least always involved a ritual of contradiction between instinct and education; it was part of the way love was carried on. But the new sexual modality of the 1660s had called the traditional structure into question while at the same time tacitly acting on many of its assumptions. The multiplication of conflicts that this engendered added to the real loss of material and emotional security for women and unleashed a war between the sexes that was to be so closely associated with the ethos of the age that it is remembered as one of its most central characteristics. In Restoration drama, a standard scenario of sexual battle is played out over and over: the roving gallant attempts to seduce a young lady, or even several young ladies, without committing himself in any way, while the heroine usually withholds her favors and tries to hold his interest through a series of false promises, disguises, teasings, and other devices, wearing him down to a promise of either constancy or marriage itself before she takes the risk of sleeping with him. There are, of course, variations on the theme and varying degrees of self-consciousness in the action, differing terms on which the women are willing to concede, and more or less cynicism on the part of either the lover or the mistress. The struggle may be light-hearted or intense, but it is inevitably present—the Restoration war between the sexes made it unavoidable.

In addition to unleashing a war between the sexes, the sexual "liberation" of the 1660s and 1670s seems to have set off a series of reactions which ultimately amounted to a counteraction of the original impulse: there was a considerable growth of misogyny, principally directed at those women who had imitated their male partners in their sexual voraciousness. Finally, there is evidence of an increasing disgust with the sexual act itself among the wits and libertines who had initiated the vogue for bawdy. In a sense, the rovers had been alienated by their own promiscuity: "enjoyment dulled the appetite," as Wycherley put it.

The wits had urged their women to cast off old-fashioned coyness, but when they did, the emancipated rakes proved to be among the most threatened. The expression of desire—to say nothing of its realization—evoked disgust. It is apparent in the language itself. "When your lewd cunt came spewing home/ Drenched with the seed of half the town,/ My dram of sperm was supped up after/ For the digestive surfeit water," wrote Rochester, railing at his promiscuous mistress. Her crimes were no more than his, but in a woman they were intolerable. He swears to "plague this woman and undo her." His revenge, he says, will be saved for when she is married; then he will "pelt her with truth or lies/ And her poor cur [husband] with jealousies/ 'Till I have torn him from her breech*/ While she whines like a dog-drawn bitch;/ Loathed and despised, kicked out o' the town/ Into some dirty hole alone,/ To chew her cud of misery/ And know she owes it all to me./ And may no woman better thrive,/ That dares prophane the cunt I swive.†"[25]

Feminine promiscuity, even if it were nothing other than a mirror image of masculine behavior, was intolerable. The wits wrote vicious satires cataloguing the sins of women who had a reputation for lust—including the King's mistresses. The anonymous author of "A Faithful Catalogue of Our Most Eminent Ninnies" called the royal mistresses "a brace of cherubs, of as vile a breed,/ As ever were produced of human seed."[26] Nell Gwyn was called, among other epithets, the "countess of the cockpit," and Louise de Kerouaille,

*i.e., female sexual parts
†fornicate

Duchess of Portsmouth, "the incestuous punk."* Countless satires vilipending the Countess of Castlemaine were passed around or even published, their subject inevitably on this order: "When she has jaded quite/ Her almost boundless appetite/ Cloyed with the choicest banquets of delight/ She'll still drudge on in tasteless vice/ As if she sinned for exercise/ Disabling stoutest stallions every hour,/ And when they can perform no more/ She'll rail at 'em and kick 'em out of door."[27] The wits had cheerfully promised their mistresses that they would do no less, but they did not like to have the tables turned.

The physical repulsion that feminine sexuality inspired in the male poets of Aphra Behn's generation is underlined repeatedly in the way they write about women. Charles Sackville, Earl of Dorset, wrote a mocking poem on Katherine Sedley, mistress of James II and daughter of his friend Sir Charles Sedley, deriding her efforts to disguise incipient wrinkles, "the approaches of decay," with "embroidery, fringe, and lace." He taunts her: "Wilt thou still sparkle in the box,†/ still ogle in the ring?/ . . . So have I seen in larder dark,/ Of veal a lucid loin;/ Replete with many a brilliant spark,/ As wise philosophers remark,/ At once both stink and shine."[28] Aphra had at about the same time written a poem congratulating Dorset on his marriage to a woman twenty years younger than himself; Katherine Sedley was a little over thirty.

The possibility that women might have sexual desires that were independent of their role as passive receptacle of male desire obsessed the wits. Frequent references to feminine masturbation and to the use of dildos testify to this preoccupation. Robert Gould, in *Love Given O'er* (1682), scourges the women of his age and tells how "when into their closets they retire,/ Where flaming dildoes does inflame desire/ And gentle lapdogs/ To whom they are more kind and free/ Than they themselves to their own husbands be./ How curst is man/ When brutes his rivals prove/ Even in the sacred business of love."[29] As the author of "Our Most Eminent Ninnies" warns: "Let no such harlots lead your steps astray./ Her clitoris will mount in open day. . . ." Is it possible, he questions philosophically, that "man be plagued with a severer curse?"

Hardly, said the Earl of Rochester. In his characteristic role of

---

*whore
†of the theater

spokesman for his age, he summed up the view that the gallants and wits of fashionable circles had come to have of women:

> Love a woman? You're an ass!
>   'Tis a most insipid passion
> To choose out for your happiness
>   The silliest part of God's creation.
>
> Let the porter and the groom,
>   Things designed for dirty slaves,
> Drudge in fair Aurelia's womb
>   To get supplies for age and graves.
>
> Farewell, woman! I intend
>   Henceforth every night to sit
> With my lewd, well-natured friend,
>   Drinking to engender wit.
>
> Then give me health, wealth, mirth, and wine,
>   And if busy love entrenches,
> There's a sweet soft page of mine
>   Does the trick worth forty wenches.

Such was the sexual liberation that claimed to free Restoration women from the confines of modesty.

VI

> A pox on foolish politics in love . . .
>
> —Aphra Behn

Aphra, like the wits and libertines who were her friends, subscribed to an ideal of sexual freedom. Like them also, she regarded traditional feminine modesty as oppressive—though, as has been remarked earlier, her attitude in the latter case was not altogether unambiguous; she had spoken of modesty elsewhere with a certain reverence, giving the impression that she regarded it a characteristic essential to femininity. Like Rochester and Wycherley and Etherege, she wrote poetry and plays considered scandalously sexy by the more conservative of their contemporaries. But there the similarity ended. Aphra's conception of the way affairs ought to be carried on between the sexes differed profoundly from that of her male friends and literary peers. Alone, she defended the feminine point of view; but the source of difference between Aphra and the wits was not merely a shift in perspective (male to female)—it had to do with her vision of love itself.

Aphra destested the Restoration "game of love" and passionately desired sincerity. She had a reputation for "plain-dealing" and expected the same from men. In a poem she wrote to a man she was in love with (probably the J. H. of whom we will hear more), she expressed disdain for the sexual politics of the marketplace that Restoration love had become:

> *Take back that heart, you with such caution give,*
>   *Take the fond trifle back;*
> *I hate Love-Merchants that a trade would drive,*
>   *And meanly cunning bargain make.*
>
> *I care not how the busy market goes,*
>   *And scorn to chaffer for a price:*
> *Love does one staple rate on all impose,*
>   *Nor leaves it to the trader's choice.*
>
> *A heart requires a heart unfeigned and true,*
>   *Though subtly you advance the price,*
> *And ask a rate that simple love n'er knew,*
>   *And the free trade monopolize.*

Aphra's lover, according to her, had asked *"more for his heart than 'twas worth."* His condition was that she remain faithful to him, while he reserved the liberty to make love to other women. She was to give herself entirely, while he fit her into the interstices of his other affairs. *"Every hour still more unjust you grow,/ . . . freedoms you my life deny,"* Aphra protests. She does not herself feel either need or desire for the same promiscuity that he claims as his privilege, but she will not be denied equal possibility in principle. Free love demands equality, she tells him: *"Be just, my lovely swain, and do not take/ Freedoms you'll not to me allow;/ Or give Amynta so much freedom back:/ That she may rove as well as you./ Let us then love upon the honest square,/ Since interest neither have designed,/ For the sly gamester, who ne'er plays me fair,/ Must trick for trick expect to find."*

Exploitation, said Aphra, had forced the sexes into a merry-go-round of self-interest: men using women who used men. Furthermore, the double standard imposed on women pressed them into still more degrading hypocrisy and deceit: *"this unlucky restraint on our sex makes us all cunning,"* says one of her female characters. Aphra partly blamed social convention for this state of affairs; but that she also saw men as having a large responsibility in the reinforcement of that convention—despite their rhetoric—is clear from many statements she made in her literary and other texts. *"In vain, dear youth, you say you love,/ And yet my marks of passion blame,"* she wrote in answer to a lover who had sent her *"some verses on a discourse of love's fire."* He had evidently given her notice that it was man's nature to let his fancy wander where it might and that it was not woman's place to object. Her answer implies that he is merely using other women to escape from an intense involvement with her. The "loves fire" he is offering her is only a pale imitation of the real thing: *"A fancy strong may do the feat,"* she tells him; *"Yet this to love a riddle is,/ And shows that passion but a cheat;/ Which men but with their tongues confess."*

For Aphra, sexual desire was naturally a part of love's expression, but if isolated from feeling, it atrophied into an endless repetition. Sexual freedom, without love, was no freedom at all, to her mind. The social modes of the 1660s and 1670s had produced a new sort of narcissism—the highest form of which was a phenomenon which Aphra called *"the fop in fashion."* Incapable of any real passion or feeling outside of self-adoration, *"hardened and incorrigible,"* the fop valued only the constant change of fashion. Aphra, in a caustic aside, describes the way a Restoration fop behaved himself in a love affair: *". . . by a dire mistake, conducted by vast opiniatrety [sic], and a greater portion of self-love . . . he believes that affectation in his mein and dress, that mathematical formality in every action, that a face managed with care, and softened into ridicule, the languishing turn, the toss, and the back-shake of the periwig, is the direct way to the heart of the fine person he adores . . . the glass* is every moment called to counsel, the valet consulted and plagued for new invention of dress, the footman and scrutore perpetually employed . . . [he adjusts] himself in the most amorous posture he can assume, his hat under his arm, while the other hand is put carelessly into his bosom, as if laid upon his panting heart; his head a little bent to one side, supported with a world of cravat-string, which he takes mighty care not to put in disorder. . . . Thus, with a thousand other little motions and formalities, all in the*

---

* mirror

common place of foppery, he takes infinite pains to show himself to the pit and boxes, a most accomplished ass. This is he, of all human kind, on whom love can do no miracles. . . . Perhaps it will be urged, that since no metamorphosis can be made in a fop by love, you must consider him one of those that only talks of love . . . wanting fine sense enough for the real passion. . . ." A fop was a silly imitation of a wit—but an accurate reflection nevertheless of fashionable behavior. Aphra's conclusion makes the connection clear: these pretenses of love, she says, *"reach the desire only, and are cured by possessing, while the short-lived passion betrays the cheat."* Fashion had left love form without substance.

The vision of free love that Aphra opposed to the wits' libertinism was based on a philosophical system that underlies much of her writing: social convention, she held—whether the convention of modesty or that of liberated conformity—had denatured instinct. Aphra's moral system defined what was right as what came naturally. Society and its morality, based on false assumptions, were responsible for the corruption of relations between the sexes.

This logic is very much present in *The Amorous Prince,* Aphra's second play. The heroine is a young woman, Chloris, who has been brought up in the country, away from all society, in perfect innocence. She is seduced by a prince, Frederick, who promises to marry her but leaves on the excuse that business at court requires him. Chloris is so naïve that she is not even aware she has done anything wrong. When another young woman friend asks her whether she has given up her "maidenhead," Chloris replies: *"What's that?"* *"A thing young gallants long extremely for,"* the worldly-wise Lucia tells her, *"and when they have it too, they say they care not a daisy for the giver."* Indeed, it very soon appears that the prince is the model of a Restoration gallant—he has cynically used Chloris and now moves on to other seductions. What is more, he looks down on her because she has neither title nor fortune to barter for marriage. He repents his hard-hearted behavior, however, when he receives the false information that Chloris has committed suicide. Once he believes her dead, his affection blossoms. When she makes an unexpected and sudden return, the Prince is prevailed upon by her brother to marry her. The moral of the story is stated in the epilogue. Addressing the women of the audience, Chloris makes an apology of her lack of modesty: *"Ladies, the Prince was kind at last,/ But all the danger is not past;/ I cannot happy be till you approve/ My hasty condescension to his love./ 'Twas want of art, not virtue, was my crime;/ And that's, I vow, the author's fault, not mine./ She might have made the women pitiless,/ But that had harder been to me than this:/ . . . simple nature never taught the way/ To hide those passions which she must obey."* Aphra's point is that Chloris's virtue is actually far superior to that of her lover, who has after all only acted according to its customs.

Love, as Aphra defined it, existed as an ideal state of freedom. Her poem "The Golden Age" envisioned a precivilized state in which both men and women give themselves freely, without thought of modesty, money, or class:

> *The lovers thus uncontrolled did meet,*
> *Thus all their joys and vows of love repeat:*
> *Joys which were everlasting, ever new*
> *And every vow inviolably true:*
> *Not kept in fear of Gods, no fond religious cause,*
> *Nor in obedience to the duller laws.*
> *Those fopperies of the gown were then not known,*
> *Those vain, those politic curbs to keep man in,*
> *Who by a fond mistake created that a sin;*
> *Which freeborn we, by right of nature claim our own.*
> *Who but the learned and dull moral fool*
> *Could gravely have foreseen, man ought to live by rule?*
>
> *Oh cursed honour! thou who first did damn,*
> *A woman to the sin of shame;*
> *Honour! that rob'st us of our gust, . . .*
> *Honour! that put'st our words that should be free*
> *Into a set formality.*
> *Thou base debaucher of the generous heart,*
> *That teachest all our looks and actions art.*

Aphra Behn was well aware that the ideal love of her imagination was not likely to survive in the society she was a part of, nor did she desist from encouraging women to defend themselves in the battle of the sexes by whatever means their disadvantage allowed them. But she nevertheless held on to her ideal. For her, love was a first principle, its influence the only purifying effect in a society dominated by power struggles and ambitions. *"As love is the most noble and divine passion of the soul,"* she said, *"so it is that to which we may justly attribute all the real satisfactions of life; and without it man is unfinished and unhappy."*

Aphra's character was given to extremes, and her radical imagination could accept no less than the total submission of self to passion: *"What would love signify, if we did not love fervently?"* she wrote, and added, *". . . in matters of love, excess is a virtue, and all other degrees of love are worthy of scorn alone. . . ."* So one more paradox was added to Aphra's long list: love was freedom, but it was also tyrant.

VII

Love in fantastique triumph sat,
Whilst bleeding hearts around him flowed,
For whom fresh pains he did create,
And strange tyranick power he showed.

—Aphra Behn, ca. 1676

How did Aphra's ideal of love translate into experience? Few details of her less than fortunate association with William Scot are known, and it cannot even be said for certain whether the friendship with Jeffrey Boys was ever actually a love affair. In any case, neither relationship seems to have involved the obsessive, all-consuming passion she was to experience later. The only man she wrote of in this way was the J. H. to whom she addressed so many of her poems, the only man identified by initials as her lover. The circumstances and history of their relationship are referred to again and again in the poems, and he is clearly recognizable under three other pseudonyms: she calls him Amyntas, Lysander, and Lycidus; she is Astrea or Amynta. It is difficult to assign an exact chronology to their relationship, but it seems to have occupied the years when Aphra's career was at its height, the years of her thirties.

J. H. was John Hoyle, a lawyer of Gray's Inn, a wit-about-town and, like William Scot, the son of a regicide. His father, Thomas Hoyle, had been Alderman, Lord Mayor, and Member of Parliament for the city of York during the first part of the Commonwealth. One of the most committed of the Puritan party, he sat on the Parliamentary Committee with Thomas Scot. Alice Thornton, whose family lived in the vicinity of York during the Civil War, says that Alderman Hoyle was "a great stickler in the Committee and Parliament

house . . . and of so daring and confident an humour for this rebellion, that he had too great a share in the King's blood . . . Hoyle sat
with them, and had a great vote, being a man thorough paced in
their practices, and a deep presbyterian."[30] The pastor of the little
church at Kirklington, the small village where Alice Thornton lived,
one Mr. Siddall, had called upon a friend of his, who was Thomas
Hoyle's nephew, to ask his powerful uncle to intercede in his behalf
in Parliament. Alderman Hoyle piously replied that under no circumstances could help be extended to any whose loyalty to the cause or to
the true church might be in any way suspect.

Despite the staunchness of his Parliamentarian principles,
Thomas Hoyle evidently found the beheading of Charles I a greater
burden to his Englishman's conscience than he could bear. He was of
the council who voted to kill the King, but once the deed was actually done, he was staggered. He began to be haunted by visions of the
dead King following him remorselessly, holding his bloody head in
his hands, and moaning. The hallucinations became more and more
persistent until finally he went altogether mad. Mrs. Thornton felt
that Hoyle's fate was no more than just retribution: "After that horrid
murder," she wrote in her autobiography, "he being one of the
deepest in his actings and consent, yet when his conscience flew in his
face for his wickedness, was never quiet night or day, but still cryed
out, 'He saw the king follow him without a head,' and said he had no
hand in his blood; but sometimes looked back, and said, 'I am
damned for the blood of the King,' and, as we were truly informed,
died in this manner as if distracted, but never could find ease, nor
repentence, or comfort, tho' all the godly clergy was about him. God
deliver us from blood guiltiness, and this above all."[31]

On January 30, 1650, a year to the day after Charles I was
beheaded, Thomas Hoyle hanged himself in his garden in Westminster at the very hour that the King had died.[32] John Shaw, a
kinsman whose daughter had stayed with Hoyle's family in York,
wrote that he "was generally accounted a very good man, but before
his death he grew excessively melancholy (as his lady is at this
present)."[33] It is hardly surprising that such an event would have a
depressing effect on Mrs. Hoyle, as it must also have had on her
children. Thomas Hoyle remained a name that stuck in people's
minds for some time, his suicide pointed to by Royalists as the grisly
reward of rebellious crimes. In 1662, after the Restoration, when

John Hoyle was a young man just beginning his career in London, a miscellany of satirical poems called *The Rump: or an exact collection . . . relating to the late times* was published with a stinging verse, "On the happy Memory of Alderman Hoyle that hang'd himself." Whatever John Hoyle's memory of his father, the legend of madness was a heavy inheritance for a young man to bear.

John Hoyle entered Emmanuel College, Oxford, on May 14, 1658. As the normal age for entry varied from about sixteen to nineteen, he must have been born more or less at the same time as Aphra Behn, around 1640. On February 27, 1660, he was admitted to Gray's Inn as a lawyer, which would argue for his being a year or two older than Aphra. It seems that Hoyle continued to espouse republican principles after the Restoration, though he remained considerably less faithful to the religious spirit of the Puritan era. His rebel politics were well known; both contemporary satires that mention him refer to his treasonous philosophy. "A Faithful Catalogue of Our Most Eminent Ninnies" (February 1688), a lampoon which may have been written by Charles Sackville, Earl of Dorset, calls Hoyle "The learned advocate, that rugged stump/ Of old Nol's honor, [who] always loved the Rump."[34] Old Nol was Oliver Cromwell. Sir Charles Sedley portrays Hoyle holding forth on his favorite subject one drunken evening at the Devil's Tavern in Fleet Street:

> *A learned lawyer, at the last,*
> * No Tory, as I'm told,*
> *Began to talk of tyrants past,*
> * In words both sharp and bold.*
>
> *He touched a little on our times,*
> * Defined the power of Kings,*
> *What were their virtues, what their crimes,*
> * And many dangerous things.*[35]

Even those who sneered at Hoyle's republican convictions had to admit his formidable articulateness. He was indeed "learned": he read at least seven languages, including Greek, Hebrew, and Latin, and the catalogue of his library that was sold after his death in 1692 covers an impressive range of classical as well as contemporary philosophy and literature.[36] Aphra, in a verse letter written to Thomas Creech, who had translated *De Rerum Natura,* was eager to introduce

him to Hoyle, on the ground that they shared the same intellectual
interests:

> *To honest H[oy]le I should have shown ye,*
> *A wit that would be proud t'have known ye,*
> *A wit uncommon, and facetious,*
> *A great admirer of Lucretius.* [37]

Despite his republicanism (in the minds of his contemporaries,
dissociable from the Puritanism of the Commonwealth), Hoyle's religion was Epicurean. Like many of the wits, he took as his moral
code the Hobbesian materialism that denied the existence of any experience other than sensuous.

If John Hoyle was a Puritan in political stance, he was unquestionably a Restoration rake in lifestyle. Part of the coterie of wits and
gallants who frequented the playhouses, bawdyhouses, coffeehouses,
and taverns of London, he knew poets, actors, actresses, and playwrights. He was witty and cynical and had the reputation of a libertine. Whitelocke Bulstrode, who had been chaplain to Cromwell
during the Commonwealth—and was also, incidentally, Lord Willoughby's brother-in-law—called Hoyle an "atheist, a sodomite professed, a corrupter of youth, and a blasphemer of Christ." [38] Given
what is known of Hoyle's character, this appears to be no over-
statement. He was a man to match even Aphra's contradictions.

How or exactly when Aphra met Hoyle cannot be said for certain. He may have been a friend of Jeffrey Boys's: they were both
sons of Parliamentarian fathers, they were admitted to Gray's Inn
about the same time, and both apparently led the life of men-about-
town and wits. The first time Aphra mentions John Hoyle is in her
poem "Our Cabal." He is among the number of friends who form her
circle. The Aphra writing then was in love with J.B. (who may well
have been Jeffrey Boys) but was still not altogether insensible to the
charms of Mr. Hoyle: *"His eyes are black,"* she wrote, *"and do tran-*
scend/ All fancy e'er can comprehend." She is wary of him, though,
perhaps perfectly aware of what he is: a tiger in the pastoral cabal. He
is handsome, arrogant, confident in his charm. His reputation is for
seduction and betrayal: *"poor Doris, and Lucinda too,/ And many more*
whom thou dost know/ Who had not the power his charms to shun,/ Too late

to find themselves undone." He is surrounded, Aphra says, by *"sighing beauties"* to whom he *"barely returns civility."*

Stories about Hoyle's female conquests had evidently been staple gossip in Aphra's group for some time: the fact that his *"devices"* and *"falsehood"* were current knowledge does not seem to have impeded the rapid succession of affairs. According to Aphra, he was irresistible to women. She disapproves of him, but is fascinated nevertheless. At the end of "Our Cabal," she speaks of a female friend whom she calls "Chloris," who is, despite herself, beginning to fall in love with Hoyle. *"I have often heard you vow,"* Aphra warns, *"if any could your heart subdue . . . it must be him, or one like him . . . your heart that can no love admit, will hardly stand his shock of wit."* Perhaps Chloris is merely a thin disguise for Aphra herself. Whether this was, consciously or unconsciously, the case, Aphra's attraction to the *"agreeable infidel"* is clear.

A poem addressed "To Lysander at the Musick-Meeting" says she fell in love with him under the effect of the music. Music-meetings had been initiated by the composer John Bannister on December 30, 1672, at his house next to the George Tavern in Whitefriars.[39] Bannister was a friend of Aphra's and had set some of her songs to music; he often worked in the theater, and his concerts drew the fashionable audience of that milieu. If this Lysander is indeed John Hoyle, who fits the description to a particular, then their affair cannot have begun before 1672. If the *Muses Mercury* of 1707 that claimed to reprint a series of manuscript poems written by Aphra to John Hoyle is correct in that attribution, then the liaison must date from the first months of 1673, as one of the songs she is supposed to have written originally for him she then included in her play *The Dutch Lover* and reprinted in a miscellany of 1673.[40] The dating would fit well with the identification of J. B. of "Our Cabal" with Jeffrey Boys, who mentions his friendship with Aphra in 1671. If Aphra has not yet fallen in love with J. H. but is just about to, then the poem would date to that year or the year after, 1672. The pieces seem to fit. Though of course it cannot be proven, it seems reasonable to assume that Aphra Behn's love affair with John Hoyle began sometime in the early or middle 1670s.

The passion that Lysander inspired in Aphra at the music-meeting was not of the order of platonic gallantry portrayed in Mlle de

Scudéry's romances or celebrated in Katherine Philips's chaste verses. It was frankly and undeniably a passion of the senses: the combination of the music and the sight of him, she says, *"raised the pleasure even to extasy: so ravished lovers in each others arms, faint with excess of joy."* The rapture of music has transformed her perception and made her vulnerable to a sensual attraction that she experiences like a crescendo. Hoyle, unaware of her presence, is listening to the music with an intensity that is communicated to Aphra. It is as though she has understood something about his capacity for pleasure that she has not fully taken in before. She had thought him handsome and charming in "Our Cabal" and was fascinated by his renowned facility with women, his wit, and forcefulness, but what was happening to her now passed on an entirely other level:

> *Your body easy and all tempting lay,*
> *Inspiring wishes which the eyes betray,*
> *In all that have the fate to glance that way:*
> *A careless and lovely negligence,*
> *Did a new charm to every limb dispense.*

Even knowing what she knew about him, she was helpless to resist the strength of her own desire. Aphra saw the relationship from the beginning as a power struggle, aware, as she was, of the cynical way he habitually behaved with women. She confesses to a female friend in "A Ballad on Mr. J. H. to Amoret, asking why I was so sad":

> *. . . he could at his pleasure move,*
> *The nymphs he liked to fall in love,*
> *Yet so he ordered every glance,*
> *That still they seemed but wounds of chance.*

> *He well could feign an innocence,*
> *And taught his silence eloquence:*
> *Each smile he used, and got the force,*
> *To conquer more than soft discourse:*
> *Which when it served his ends he'd use,*
> *And subtly thro' a heart infuse.*

> *His wit was such it could control*
> *The resolutions of a soul;*
> *That a religious vow had made,*
> *By love it n'er would be betrayed.*

Amoret, commonly identified as the actress Elizabeth Barry, who later acted in many of Aphra's plays and remained an intimate of hers for many years, was among the friends of "Our Cabal." She was therefore well acquainted with Hoyle's character and practice and apparently chided Aphra for getting involved with him. It was too late, however, for as Aphra tells her, *"to me much passion he did vow. . . ./ I strove in vain to guard my heart/ And ere the night our revels crost,/ I was entirely won and lost."* Aphra's play on "lost" alludes to her having forfeited, in the terms of her century, the most highly valued commodity a woman possessed: her honor. But what was much more important to Aphra, however, was the loss of her independence. She had resolved, she affirmed, that no man would have that kind of power over her, that no love would violate her self-determination.

Apparently her passion took her entirely by surprise. Until now, she had not understood her own sexual nature, said Aphra. Her poem "On Desire" evokes that discovery of her senses:

What are thou, oh! thou new-found pain?
From what infection dost thou spring?
Inform me by what subtle art,
  What powerful influence,
You got such vast dominion in a part
Of my unheeded, and unguarded heart
That fame and honour cannot drive ye hence.
Oh! mischievous usurper of my peace;
Oh! soft intruder on my solitude,
  Charming disturber of my ease,
Thou hast by nobler fate persued.

Thou haunt'st my inconvenient hours;
The business of the day, nor silence of the night,
That should to cares and sleep invite,
Can bid defiance to thy conquering powers.
Where hast thou been this live-long age
  That from my birth till now,
Thou never could'st one thought engage,
Or charm my soul with the uneasy rate
That made it all its humble feebles know? . . .

Tell me, thou nimble fire, that dost dilate
  Thy might force thro every part,
What God, or human power did thee create
  In my, till now, unfacil heart? . . .

> *Yes, yes tormentor, I have found thee now;*
> *And found to whom thou dost thy being owe,*
> *'Tis thou the blushes dost impart . . .*
> *When e're I touch the charming swain*
> *When e're I gaze, when e're I speak,*
> *Thy conscious fire is mingled with my love. . . .*

Aphra is quite conscious of the territory she is violating, because the next lines take up the question whether she is alone in her feelings or other women also feel the same passion but hide it in the *"needful fraud"* of modesty. If other women do feel so, then, *"Oh tell me,"* she asks, *"how do you remain discreet?"* It can only be that women who remain modest are unacquainted with the real pleasure of making love, their chastity merely the effect of ignorance, she concludes. If any doubt could remain that Aphra's discovered desire existed only in her mind, untranslated into Lysander's arms, she explicitly tells the reader in the last line of the poem that she had yielded him *"her heart and bed."*

The identity of the man to whom Aphra wrote so many of her poems was apparently no secret to her contemporaries. She herself confirmed as much in a poem written "On Mr. J. H., in a fit of sickness," in which she says:

> *Astrea, whom from all the sighing throng,*
> *   You did your oft-worn garlands give:*
> *For which she paid you back in grateful song:*
> *Astrea, who did still the glory boast,*
> *To be adored by thee, and to adore thee most.*

Having publicly declared her affair with Hoyle, she set herself up for lampoon, ridicule, censure, and humiliation. As her literary stance demonstrated, she was more than capable of defending a position she had taken—but protecting herself from John Hoyle was another matter.

Although Aphra had given herself entirely to the passion she had conceived for Hoyle, she disliked her sense of powerlessness. She was proud, too, and could not bear the idea of his being in control. Hoyle demanded that she love him without any reciprocal commitment on his part. He was jealous of her, but forbade her to object to his own activities. He kept her under his power by withholding his affection and approval, by holding her on the edge of rejection.

In a series of letters "to a Gentleman," whom she addresses as Lycidus, Aphra describes a chronology of feeling which so perfectly matches the one in the poems written to Hoyle that it is difficult to believe Lycidus was anyone but him. In fact, he is often referred to by that name elsewhere. There are many specific character traits mentioned in the letters that correspond precisely with those detailed in the poems: among others, his tendency to lecture, his preference for silent communication through long, intense looks, his fear of publicity. The fact that the man to whom the letters were written has complained of Aphra's making their affair public, taken with the fact that she herself says she *"did in glory boast,/ To be adored by thee, and to adore thee most,"* further confirms the identification of Lycidus with Hoyle. Indeed, he is the only man repeatedly mentioned as her lover by her contemporaries.

The first letter in the series finds Aphra already in a state of vacillation: she has proscribed his visiting her for a time, but wishes he had disobeyed her. He has written to her instead, saying that on that evening he intends to go dancing. Aphra is jealous, but trying to restrain herself. She does not want to write a begging letter, and so begins: *"You bid me write, and I wish it were only the effect of complaisance that makes me obey you. I should be very angry with myself and you, if I thought it were any other motive: I hope it is not, and will not have you believe otherwise. I cannot help however wishing you no mirth, nor any content in your dancing-design; and this unwonted malice in me I do not like, and would have concealed it if I could, lest you should take it for something which I am not, nor will believe myself guilty of. May your women be all ugly, ill-natured, ill-dressed, ill-fashioned, and unconversable; and, for your greater disappointment, may every moment of your time there be taken up with thoughts of me (a sufficient curse) and yet you will be better entertained than me, who possibly am, and shall be uneasy with thoughts not so good. Perhaps you had eased me of some trouble, if you had let me seen you, or known you had been well: but these are favours for better friends, and I'll endeavour not to resent the loss, or rather the miss of 'em. It may be, since I have so easily granted this desire of your's, in writing to you, you will fear you have pulled a trouble on—but do not. I do by this send for you—you know what you gave your hand upon; the date of banishment is already out, and I could have wished you had been so good-natured as to have disobeyed me. Pray take no-*

tice therefore I am better natured than you. I am profoundly melancholy since I saw you, I know not why: and should be glad to see you when your occasions permit you to visit

Astrea"

Aphra fretted while Lycidus went dancing. Writing to her of his intention had its calculated effect. It is impossible to know how long he kept her waiting (if at all) before he went to see her as she asked, but it seems they had made up before the next letter, when they were fighting again. Hoyle has come to Aphra's house with a letter for her but, finding a crowd of company there, has perversely taken it away with him again. All evening long he has shown Aphra his distance and refused to recognize her signs to him to stay. *"You may tell me a thousand years, my dear Lycidus,"* she writes to him, *"of your unbounded friendship; but after so unkind a departure as that last night, give me leave (when serious) to doubt it; nay, 'tis past doubt, I know you rather hate me. What else could hurry you from me, when you saw me surrounded with all the necessary impossibilities of speaking to you? I made as broad signs as one could do who durst not speak, both for your sake and my own. I acted even imprudently to make my soul understood, that was then (if I may say so) in real agonies for your departure. 'Tis a wonder a woman so violent in all her passions as I, did not (forgetting all prudence, all considerations) fly out into absolute commands, or at least entreaties, that you would give me a moment's time longer. I burst to speak with you to know a thousand things; but particularly, how you came to be so barbarous, as to carry away all that could make my satisfaction. You carried away my letter, and you carried away Lycidus . . . I am ashamed to tell you this; I know your peevish vertue will misinterpret me. But take it how you will, think of it as you please; I am undone, and will be free; I will tell you, you did not use me well: I am ruined and will rail at you—Come then, I conjure you, this evening, that after it I may shut those eyes that have been too long waking. I have committed a thousand madnesses in this; but you must pardon the faults you have created. Come and do so; for I must see you tonight, and that in better humour than you were last night. No more; obey me as you have that friendship for me you profess. . . ."*

Hoyle seems to have been constantly counseling Aphra "prudence" and "discretion"—evidently her lack of modesty disturbed him. He frowned on her unrestrained avowal of her passion and at the same time frequently elicited it. She complained of his constantly lecturing her and inflicting punishments when she did not behave according to his prescription. He has refused to sit next to her (perhaps at the play; she does not say where), accusing her of loving him less than before: she is "changed," he tells her. *"When shall we understand each other?"* she answers him in her next letter. The change that John Hoyle objected to seemed to be that Aphra had begun to criticize his own behavior. She was far from passively accepting whatever way he chose to treat her. She was outspoken; she made demands; she wrote him "tedious" letters. He accused her of aggression and she replied: *"Who grows cold first? Who is changed? And who the aggressor? 'Tis I was first in friendship, and shall be last in constancy."* Mr. Hoyle, the letter implies, has chastised her for arguing with him: she is stubborn, he maintains, and will not admit herself in the wrong. She is troublesome and cannot hold her tongue. *"I scorn to guard my tongue,"* Aphra answered, *"yet I can with much ado hold it, when I have a great mind to say a thousand things I know will be taken in all ill sense."*

Perhaps Aphra was too much for John Hoyle. Her desire threatened him and her tongue threatened him—according to her. She was torn between her instinct for independence and her desperate need to hold on to him. She swings from fury at his treatment of her to a pleading reassurance of her love. Her doubleness of impulse no doubt would have appeared sooner or later in any relationship with a man of her time, but Hoyle most certainly aggravated it. He could neither commit himself to her nor let her go; he told her he loved her and constantly distanced himself at the same time. *"Take your course,"* she told him bitterly, *"be a friend like a foe, and continue to impose upon me, that you esteem me when you fly me. Renounce your false friendship, or let me see you give it entire to*

Astrea."

Hoyle's equivocal behavior and perpetual posing of conditions had considerably restrained Aphra's initial flight of ecstasy. She was forced into an alternation of attack and defense that she was only too aware was destroying the very thing she so desired. What is more, she knew that the learned lawyer's refusal to commit himself put all the power in his hands—a situation which he would protect at all cost. *"I had rather,"* she told him, *"set myself to write to any man on earth than you; for I fear your severe prudence and discretion, so nice,* may

* exacting, quibbling

make an ill judgment of what I say. Yet you bid me not dissemble; and you
need not have cautioned me, who so naturally hate those little arts of my sex,
that I often run on freedoms that may well enough bear a censure from people
so scrupulous as Lycidas. Nor dare I follow all my inclinations neither, nor
tell all the little secrets of my soul: why I write them, I can give no account;
'tis but fooling myself, perhaps, into an undoing . . . I may come off unhurt,
but cannot be a winner: why then should I throw an uncertain cast, where I
hazard all, and you nothing. Greedy Lycidus! Unconscionable and ungen-
erous! You would not be in love for all the world, yet wish I were so. Un-
charitable! —Would my fever cure you? or a curse on me make you blessed?
Say Lycidus, will it? I have heard, when two souls kindly meet 'tis a vast
pleasure, as vast as the curse must be, when kindness is not equal; and why
should you believe that necessary for me, that will be very incommode for you?
. . . So much for loving."

There were reconciliations, however—apparently when Aphra
acceded to Hoyle's terms. Fears that she would cuckold him (for
which there seemed to be no foundation, though it is true we have
only her side of the story) seem to have been very much in his mind.
He evidently made her promise on several occasions to see no one else
but him, friends or lovers equally. She kept her vow and was rewarded by his "kindness": *"though it be very late,"* she wrote to him
after he left her, *"I cannot go to bed, but I must tell thee I have been very*
good ever since I saw thee, and have been a writing, and have seen no face of
man, or other body, save my own people [servants]. *I am mightily pleased*
with your kindness to me to-night . . . My Lycidus says, he can be soft and
dear when he please to put off his haughty pride, which is only assumed to see
how far I dare love him ununited. Since then my souls delight you are, and
may be ever assured I am, and ever will be yours, befall me what will; and
that all the devils of hell shall not prevail against thee. . . ."

Aphra was happy to be reconciled with Hoyle, but only on the
condition that he cease his perverse behavior. He deserves her heart
only if he is willing to love her honestly and openly, she tells him:
"There is nothing so grateful to God or man, as plain-dealing." Whether
Aphra provoked Hoyle's jealousy, and so broke the temporary peace,
or whether he himself could not resist the pleasure he seemed to take
in reprimanding her, the truce evidently did not last long. Once
again he was accusing her of flirting, lying, dissembling, and perhaps
more. Aphra was compelled to justify herself. *"I stayed after thee to-*
night, till I had read a whole act of my new play; and then he had me over

all the way, saying, Gad you were the man: And beginning some rallying love-discourse after supper, which he fancied was not so well received as it ought, he said you were not handsome, and called Philly to own it; but he did not, but was of my side, and said you were handsome: so he went on a while, and all ended that concerned you. And this, upon my word, is all."

Evidently, in addition to his jealousies, Hoyle was also afraid of what Aphra might say about him to other people. He began giving her orders again and she felt rebellious: *"you, my dearest Lycidus, have prescribed me laws and rules, how I shall behave myself to please and gain you. . . . Your articles I have read over, and do not like them; you have sworn or sealed 'em; that is, they are writ with reserve. . . . I grow desperate fond of you, and would fain be used well; if not, I will march off. But I will believe you mean to keep your word, as I will forever mine. Pray make haste to see me tomorrow; and if I am not at home when you come, send for me over the way, where I have engaged to dine, there being an entertainment on purpose tomorrow for me. . . . Do not shame me with your perpetual ill opinion; my nature is proud and insolent, and cannot bear it. I will be used something better, in spite of all your apprehensions falsely grounded."*

Aphra's threats and protests seem to have had little effect on Hoyle, who continued to put himself at a distance in every way while at the same time accusing her of not loving him enough. It is clear, too, that he is making love to other women: *"You went to joys,"* she writes him in her next letter, *"and left me to torments! You went to love alone, and left me love and rage, fevers and calentures, even madness itself!"* Although she loves him most passionately, she says, to the exclusion of every other man, she warns him that his behavior is paralyzing her. Her rage at his manipulation matches her love: *"My soul is ready to burst with pride and indignation; and at the same time love, with all his softness, assails me, and will make me write, so that I can express neither as I ought. What shall I do to make you know I do not use to condescend to so much submission?"*

The conflict must finally have been too much for Aphra, because in the next (and last) letter, evidently written after an interval of separation, it is apparent that she has broken off with Hoyle. He has written to her to protest the silence, and she takes it unkindly that he has once again disturbed *"that repose I have resolved to pursue."* She reminds him how he mistreated her, how calculating he has proved, and how he has made her suffer. She recalls all the little tortures he has inflicted on her: insulting her by saying that his business would permit him to visit her every night but his "inclinations" would not, and finally even *"passing by the end of the street where I live and squandering away your time at any coffee-house rather than allow me your . . . dear dull melancholy company."* His manner, she continues, is maddening. If he loves her, *"Why this neglect, then?"* And if he does not, why won't he leave her in peace? When she attempts to withdraw, he says she has betrayed him.

So ends the last letter, giving no further information than that she expects him Thursday next.

What happened next or how long the affair went on is hard to piece together. Alexander Radcliffe's poem *The Ramble: News from Hell,* published in 1682, indicates that their connection was still very much the subject of contemporary gossip. Rumor had it that Hoyle was the author of all her plays.

> *Amongst this heptarchy of wit*
> *The censuring age have thought it fit*
> *To damn a woman, 'cause 'tis said,*
> *The plays she vends she never made,*
> *But that a Gray's Inn lawyer does 'em,*
> *Who unto her was friend in bosom,*
> *So not presenting scarf and hood**
> *New plays and songs are full as good.* [41]

The poem, though published in 1682, must have been written before January 1680, when Hoyle transferred from Gray's Inn to the Inner Temple. He and Aphra were evidently still on friendly terms as late as February 1684, when she offered to introduce Thomas Creech to him. In 1685, she dedicated the second half of her *Miscellany* to "Lysander," but the man behind the pseudonym, as his description in the dedication evinces, can be none other than John Hoyle. He is still giving her copious instructions how to behave, and she once again complains of his *"wise reproofs"* and *"the loss and destruction of many an honest hour which might have been passed more gaily if you had pleased."* She sarcastically refers to their continuous quarrel and his angry response to her criticisms of him: *"I would give you my sentiments on the whole, but that I am afraid of showing myself a critick; but no matter, I am*

---

* The bridgegroom presented a scarf and hood to the bride.

so used to be impertinent in Lysander's company that 'twill appear no more strange than what he is entertained with every time I have the happiness of seeing him . . . for which I have many times met with wise reproofs, as 'tis very likely I may now, and which will as little work upon the temper of a woman of my humour, as mercy to a hardened Whig."

Two poems published in *Lycidus* (1689) document the end of the affair. In "On the first Discovery of falseness in Amintas," Aphra attempts to persuade herself to leave a man who has betrayed her. Think how the *"infidel"* is at this very moment with another woman, she tells herself; *"Think how the faithless treated thee last night,/ And then, my tortured soul, assume thy flight."* In the early poem "Our Cabal," J. H. had been the *"agreeable infidel";* now the term only conjures up the painful memory of his faithlessness to her. In the poem "To Damon," also in the 1689 volume, she proclaims that she has finally succeeded in dissociating herself: *"Ere since Amintas proved ingrate,"* she has freed herself from the "storms of love." She has bid good-bye to all that with a sense of relief, but also with regret: *"For when the mind so cool is grown/ As neither love nor hate to own,/ The life but dully lingers on."*

Why John Hoyle? Why would Aphra choose, and so persistently pursue, a man whom she knew from the beginning would reject her? The very first time she mentions him, in "Our Cabal," she observes and records the perverse way J. H. behaves with women. She quite clearly sees his consistent unwillingness to give himself while demanding total immersion of self from the other.

She also knew that he was a homosexual. Even before she had involved herself with him, she had mentioned that in addition to the bevy of women he had seduced and discarded, he was also having an affair with a young man named "Mr. Ed. Bed." In "Our Cabal," Aphra evinces neither approval nor disapproval, perhaps because in the 1670s and 1680s sexual experimentation was very much in fashion. In one well-known salon, sado-masochists were whipped, and the wits said they practiced buggery when a woman was not at hand. Hoyle's homosexuality seems, however, to have been more than casual randiness. The authorities certainly thought so when they arrested and indicted him on February 26, 1687. He was accused of buggering a poulterer, a William Bistow of Gracechurch Street. The grand jury, Narcissus Luttrell wrote in his diary, returned a verdict of *igno-*

ramus, and Hoyle was discharged. Probably there was not enough evidence to convict him. Such an arrest was a serious matter, as the legal penalty for sodomy was death.

Hoyle's sexual proclivities became a sort of joke among his contemporaries. The "Faithful Catalogue of Our Most Eminent Ninnies" refers to his adventure as though it were common currency:

> *Which made the wiser choice, is now our strife;*
> *Hoyle his he-mistress, or the Prince his wife.*
> *Those traders, sure, will be beloved as well*
> *As all the dainty birds they sell.* *
> *The learned advocate, that rugged stump*
> *Of Old Nol's honour, always loved the Rump* †
> *And 'tis no miracle, since all the hoiles* **
> *Were given, they say, to raise intestine broils.* [42]

It seems likely that the love affair between Aphra and Mr. Hoyle was over by the time of his arrest. What effect his homosexuality had on the relationship itself cannot be said. The only hint of sexual difficulties is a poem that Aphra's friend Tom Brown said she wrote for Hoyle, "The Disappointment." The poem begins, as "The Willing Mistress" does, with a shepherdess's being led to a *"lone thicket made for love"* by her shepherd, who begins by kissing her, then moves his hand to her *"swelling snowy breast,/ While she lay panting in his arms."* The hand, *"by swift degrees advancing,"* finally reaches *"that fountain where delight still flows,/ And gives the universal world repose."* At this point, utterly carried away by desire, the shepherdess stretches herself out on the moss, only to find that she is to be disappointed: *"In vain he toils, in vain commands;/ The insensible* †† *fell weeping in his hand."* Once she has understood, the shepherdess runs away in shame, embarrassment and, no doubt, frustration. Her *"resentments none but I/ Can well imagine or condole,"* concludes Aphra. To add insult to injury, Lysander blames the shepherdess, or her "charms," which he says, *"had damned him to the hell of impotence."*

Aphra, it seems, had sent the poem to Rochester, as it was among the manuscripts published by mistake with his in the pirated

* a reference to Hoyle's poulterer-lover
† a pun on the Parliament and the buttocks
** hoiles—Hoyles
†† the penis

edition of his work brought out after his death. He, too, had written a poem on impotence, but of course from a different point of view. Aphra's treatment of the subject was unique.

If Aphra Behn understood even before her affair with John Hoyle began that he would keep her at a distance, perhaps that was, in a sense, what she wanted. She might have chosen a man who was not a wit, but none of the forms that a conventionally reciprocated relationship took in her age would have permitted her the freedom she required. Had she been a wife, she would have had to worry about compromising the family honor by her writing; and even as a mistress, she would have had to play the sort of feminine games she detested. Loving a man who loved her wholly in return would have made it much more difficult to oppose him. In choosing John Hoyle, she could give herself entirely to her passion without bearing the usual consequences, maintain her ideal of love without living it out in social convention.

There is reason to believe that whatever the logic of her affair with Hoyle, the intensity of the pain and disappointment it caused considerably lessened her desire to repeat the experience. "To Damon" implies that after "Amintas proved ingrate," Aphra gave up men. Whether this assertion was made in passing anger, or held true for the few remaining years of her life is impossible to establish. Along with two poems in *Lycidus* (1688) that attest her renunciation of Hoyle, there is another which suggests that she might have transferred her sexual interest to women. "To the fair Clarinda, who made love to me, imagined more than woman" begins by addressing *"a fair lovely maid,"* and then corrects it to *"a name that more approaches truth . . . lovely charming youth."* Aphra goes on to observe that two women may love each other without being suspected of immodesty: *"In pity to our sex sure thou wer't sent,/ That we might love, and yet be innocent:/ For sure no crime with thee we can commit;/ Or if we should—thy form excuses it."* No one suspects women of sexual longings independent of men, she says. The last stanza of the poem eulogizes Clarinda as a *"beauteous wonder of a different kind"*—male and female joined—and ends: *"We the noblest passions do extend/ The love to* Hermes, Aphrodite* *the friend."* Aphra's play on words is triple—Hermes, trickster among the gods,

* Aphra Behn's emphasis here

and Aphrodite, goddess of love; Hermaphrodite, the two sexes joined; and "Aphra," hidden in "Aphrodite." Her playful tribute to her own sex has none of the consuming passion she exhibits for J. H., however. The only other hint of any involvement with women is in the unfinished "Verses designed by Mrs. A. Behn to be sent to a fair Lady, that denied she would absent herself to cure her love," published posthumously by her literary executor, Charles Gildon. The poem is more vague than that to Clarinda and does not indicate Aphra's "love" for the anonymous fair lady was actually consummated.

It was said that John Hoyle wrote the short and suspiciously dismissive verses on Aphra Behn's tombstone in Westminster Abbey. There is no evidence to determine either for or against this claim, but Hoyle did survive Aphra by three years. If Aphra wished any poetic justice for his treatment of her, she had it posthumously. At two o'clock on Saturday morning, May 28, 1692, John Hoyle died ignominiously in a knife fight after a drunken brawl in the Young Devil Tavern on Fleet Street. When his murderer was tried before the Grand Jury some months later, it was asserted that Hoyle had begun the quarrel by "railing against all government." Several witnesses testified that "Mr. Hoyle in his lifetime, was a person much addicted to quarrelling, etc." The murderer was judged guilty only of self-defense.

CHAPTER ELEVEN

Success and Attack

Poetry, the supreme pleasure of the mind, is begot and born in pleasure, but oppressed and killed with pain. So that this reflection ought to raise our admiration of Mrs. Behn, whose genius was of that force, like Homer's to maintain its gaiety in the midst of disappointments, which a woman of her sense and merit ought never to have met with.

—Charles Gildon,
preface to A. Behn's *Works* (1696)

I, a woman, cannot be exempt from the malice and aspersion of spiteful tongues, which they cast upon my poor writings.

—Margaret Cavendish, Duchess of Newcastle

The penalties and discouragements attending the profession of an author fall upon women with a double weight; to the curiosity of the idle and the envy of the malicious their sex affords a peculiar incitement: arraigned, not merely as writers, but as women, their characters, their conduct, even their personal endowments become subjects of severe inquisition. In detecting their errors and exposing their foibles, malignant ingenuity is active and unwearied.

—*Public Characters*, Anonymous, 1801

I

All my life is nothing but extremes. . . .

—Aphra Behn

The staging of Aphra's tragedy *Abdelazer* in July 1676 marked the end of a three-year literary silence. No play had appeared under her name since the foundering of *The Dutch Lover* in 1673. Perhaps she was still smarting from the attacks launched against her on that occasion; or perhaps she was writing plays that were only to be staged later. A third possibility is that she was very much preoccupied by the initial intensity of her love affair with John Hoyle. The play *Abdelazer* opened with a song which was to become one of her most famous lyrics. It was called "Love Armed" and began thus:

> *Love in fantastique triumph sat,*
> *Whilst bleeding hearts around him flowed,*
> *For whom fresh pains he did create,*
> *And strange tyranick power he showed.*
> *From thy bright eyes he took his fire,*
> *Which round about, in sport he hurled,*
> *But 'twas from mine he took desire,*
> *Enough to undo the amorous world.*

Aphra then describes the *"languishments and fears"* she has suffered from this cavalier lover who remains cruelly remote while she undergoes the pain of attachment: *"My poor heart alone is harmed,/ Whilst thine the victor is, and free."* Whether or not the poem was actually written for Hoyle and then inserted in her play cannot be definitely ascertained, but it certainly described their relationship. It may also have reflected something of Aphra's current state of mind, for the subject of *Abdelazer* is obsessional passion. The tragedy was adapted from an anonymous play called *Lust's Dominion; or, the Lacivious Queen,* which had been published in 1657. The story centers on the overwhelming desire that the (fictional) Queen of Spain has conceived for Abdelazer, a Moor like Othello, to whom she sacrifices husband, son, country, and eventually, of course, herself. He has only used her to acquire power and has her assassinated when she no longer serves his purpose.

Whatever personal fascination this theme may have had for Aphra, it is also likely that she chose it with the idea of making her return to the stage a commercial success. Nathaniel Lee had recently made his dramatic debut with two ranting, furious tragedies that had met with great popularity. Sex, horror, and madness were all the rage, and Aphra's *Abdelazer* had the right ingredients. Early in the play, Abdelazer sets the tone of what is to come: " *'Tis now dead time of night, when rapes and murders are hid beneath an horrid veil of darkness."*

As Aphra had calculated, the play was a success. Her friend Nell Gwyn supported her by coming and bringing a substantial party from the Court with her. Ordinarily, the presence of such a celebrity was enough to fill the theater with curious onlookers who were eager to catch a glance of the royal mistress even if they cared nothing for the play itself. The play would probably have been financially remunerative even without Nell Gwyn's help, as Aphra had astutely estimated what the public wanted to see. In artistic terms, however, *Abdelazer* is unquestionably among the worst of her plays. Despite the fact that she herself was given to extremity, fustian tragedy was evidently not her gift. The play reeks of melodrama, and Aphra's normally lively dialogue is flat and artificial. She must have realized this because, except for *The Young King,* actually written much earlier in her career, she never attempted the genre again. She found the full expression of her talent in the series of comedies she immediately turned to writing next.

After the performance of *Abdelazer* in July 1676, Aphra retired to the countryside for a brief rest. But peace and quiet were not to be had. Emily Price, a young actress with the Duke's Company who was shortly afterward to act in Mrs. Behn's *Sir Patient Fancy,* wrote from London to tell Aphra that the town was once again talking about her: this time her critics were accusing her of plagiarism. Aphra expressed small surprise at the attack but felt hurt that Thomas Otway had not dealt entirely straightforwardly with her. He had been gossiping unkindly behind her back.

"My dear," she wrote to Emily Price. *"In your last* [letter] *you informed me that the world treated me as a plagiary, and I must confess, not with injustice. But that Mr. Otway should say, my sex would not prevent my being pulled to pieces by the critics, is something odd, since whatever Mr. Otway now declares, he may very well remember when I last saw him, I received more than ordinary encomiums on my* Abdelazer. *But every one knows Mr. Otway's good nature, which will not permit him to shock any one of our sex to their faces. But let that pass. As for being impeached of murdering my Moor, I am thankful, since, when I shall let the world know, whenever I take the pains next to appear in print, of the mighty theft I have been guilty of; but, however, for your own satisfaction, I have sent you the garden from whence I gathered, and I hope you will not think me vain, if I say, I have weeded and improved it. I hope to prevail on the printer to reprint* Lust's

Dominion, *that my theft may be the more public. But I detain you. I believe I shan't have the happiness of seeing my dear Amilla 'till the middle of September. But be assured I shall always remain as I am,*

> *yours,*
> A. Behn" [1]

Aphra refused to be drawn into a quarrel with Thomas Otway, whom she had so generously supported and whose company she took great pleasure in. She probably preferred to take his remark as a response to his own difficulties with the critics rather than as a manifestation of spite or literary jealousy. In any case, it had been demonstrated to her for some time that not only would her sex fail to "prevent her being pulled to pieces by the critics," as Otway had said, but it would more or less *ensure* that she would be. Experience had taught her this much so far, though it had not yet taught her how to deal with the pain and anger such attacks inevitably drew from her.

The accusation of plagiarism was hardly worth serious consideration. It was standard practice to rewrite earlier material for the Restoration stage, and there was hardly a playwright of Aphra Behn's generation who had not at one time in his career based his work on someone else's play. For the most part, the plays that were used for raw material in this way were very much inferior. Often the dialogue of the "rewritten" play was almost entirely original, and several scenes and characters were added. The "plagiary" consisted of little more than using an old plot, usually rather conventional in any case, as a framework for something new. Such literary borrowing was not generally considered much of a sin. Aphra was well aware that she was being singled out for punishment. For the time being, though, she chose to ignore the scandal as best she could and enjoy the rural quiet, perhaps remembering the pastoral Kentish countryside where her childhood had been spent. She tried to explain that pleasure to Emily Price, writing: *"In your last, you admired how I could pass my time so long in the country; I am sorry your taste is so depraved, as not to relish a country life. Now I think there's no satisfaction to be found amidst an urban throng (as Mr. Bayes * calls it)."* Aphra included some verses in her let-

---

* Mr. Bayes-Dryden. The phrase *urban throng* is a reference to Buckingham's burlesque of him in *The Rehearsal* (1671), in which Aphra was also satirized.

ter, praising the peace and green of meadows, woods, and groves and telling her friend to *"fly that hated town, / Where's not a moment thou canst call thy own."* [2]

II

It's a mad age we live in. . . .

—Aphra Behn, 1676

Aphra Behn may have been unappreciated by John Hoyle, but she was, at this point in her career, a success in society. She kept company with Court wits like Buckhurst (later the Earl of Dorset), Sedley, and most particularly Buckingham. She pleased Charles II and gained the patronage of his brother, James, the Duke of York, as well as the friendship of his mistress, Nell Gwyn. She was respected and admired by her fellow playwrights and sought out by gallants, literati, fops, and hangers-on.

The patron and friend she seems to have valued most, though, was the Earl of Rochester. The year before Aphra returned to the stage with *Abdelazer,* Rochester had taken three of her closest friends under his protection. He had given Thomas Otway a great deal of encouragement, some of it financial, and had seen to it that his first play, *Alcibades,* was produced by the Duke's Company in 1675. Rochester was also midwife to Nathaniel Lee's literary debut in the same year, and the latter dedicated his play *Nero* to the Earl in gratitude. Rochester's patronage of Elizabeth Barry took another form. The actress's first appearance on the stage, a short time before, had been an unqualified disaster. It was decided by both players and management that she was without talent and that no amount of coaching could make her an actress. Seeing an amusing challenge, Rochester offered to bet that in six months he could train her to be one of the most applauded performers on the stage of the Dorset Garden Theater.

The wager engaged, he took her off into the countryside and taught her to control her gestures and movement, to modulate her voice according to dramatic purpose, and "to seize the passions." This last involved a certain personal instruction. They rehearsed night and day, repeating scenes as many as thirty times over, until the young woman was ready to collapse from fatigue. Rochester easily won his wager, and Elizabeth Barry went on to become one of the greatest actresses of her day. Her new skills were first tried in Otway's *Alcibades,* and a short time later she played in Aphra Behn's *Abdelazer.* To all appearances, she and Aphra remained close friends for the rest of their lives. As far as the cast lists that are extant indicate, Mrs. Barry was to have a part—often a leading role—in almost every play Aphra Behn wrote for the rest of her career.

Rochester's association with Mrs. Barry, as may well be imagined from his reputation, did not remain merely professional. She became his mistress sometime around 1675, and the attachment lasted several years—longer than most of the fleeting affairs he was known for. One of his friends said that she was the woman he had loved most passionately in his life, and the letters he wrote to her bear out that statement. Otway was also in love with Elizabeth Barry, and Aphra must have been much involved in the little incestuous circle of friendship, dependence, and patronage that evolved in the season of 1675–1676. Rochester was apparently a frequent visitor to the Dorset Garden Theater in the first part of 1676, but in the last week of June, the public outrage occasioned by one of his drunken "witty pranks" forced him from London to exile in Oxfordshire, at Woodstock, where he was Ranger of the Royal Park.

He remained there in disgrace all summer, but to amuse himself invited company from London to stay at the High Lodge of Woodstock Park—an isolated spot where they might be as witty or debauched as they liked without observation. He wrote to Harry Savile in August to join him and may also have invited some of his theater friends. If he did so, a hint in Aphra's letter to Emily Price, written at about exactly that time, indicates that she may have been among them. Aphra says she was staying in the countryside where the rivers Thames and Isis join, which would place her somewhere near Oxford and consequently in the neighborhood of Woodstock. The precise coincidence of time and place make her presence among the wits at High Lodge quite likely. If she was indeed there, she was privy to yet another scandal. It was rumored in London that Rochester and his companions had engaged in the "beastly prank" of running naked in Woodstock Park. The gossip was in this case quite true; Rochester himself confirmed it in a letter written a year later to Harry Savile: "Be pleased to call to mind the year 1676, when two large fat nudities* led the coranto round fair Rosamund's fountain,† while the poor violated nymph wept to behold the strange decay of manly parts, since the days of her dear Harry the Second: Prick ('tis confessed) you shewed but little of, but for ass and buttocks, (a filthier ostantation! God wot) you exposed more of that nastiness in your two folio volumes, than we all together in our six quartos."[3]

Whether or not Aphra actually participated in this little pastoral frolic, or what she thought about it, is difficult to say. Rochester's attitude toward women, sex, and love represented everything that she opposed. But at the same time she genuinely admired him and found him attractive. That Aphra could hold two very different attitudes simultaneously, however, is quite in character. If she felt the tension of any contradiction in her feeling about Rochester, she gave no indication of it. The financial and professional advantages of having such a patron were clear, but Aphra's attachment to Rochester went far beyond such considerations.

She saw him as a kind of ideal representation of the age, the epitome of the wild hero celebrated in so many of her plays. It was Rochester more than anyone else who lived out the fantasy of his generation: to take as one's calling the unmitigated pursuit of pleasure and wit; to follow that course with all the intensity of one's powers, no matter what the risk and no matter what the end. He was generally acknowledged to be the model for Dorimant, the paragon of Restoration fashion who was the hero of Sir George Etherege's *The Man of Mode* (produced in March 1676). According to the critic John Dennis, "all the world was charmed with Dorimant, and it was unanimously agreed that he had in him several qualities of Wilmot, Earl of Rochester, as, his wit, his spirit, his amorous temper, the charms that he had for the fair sex, his falsehood, and his inconstancy."[4] It was also said among the wits and in society that Mrs. Behn's most famous hero, Willmore of *The Rover,* resembled Rochester enough to have been his double.

Rochester was considered the wittiest man of his day. His clever remarks were repeated at Court, stories of his caprices were recounted with great amusement, and the satires, lampoons, and occasional

---

* Harry Savile was considerably overweight.

† Rosamund was the mistress of Henry II, who was said to have kept her out of sight of his wife, hidden in a labyrinth in Woodstock Park. The fountain was named for her.

verse he wrote were circulated widely in manuscript. After he was dead, Nathaniel Lee, who based still another romantic protagonist on his memory of Rochester, gave him perhaps the most accurate characterization: "If he were dying, with his veins cut, he would call for wine, fiddles and whores, and laugh himself into another world." [5] Rochester himself who was in fact very ill in the summer of 1678, wrote to Savile: "It is a miraculous thing (as the wise have it) when a man, half in the grave, cannot leave off playing the fool, and the buffoon." [6] Extravagance had broken his health, and on his deathbed two years later, he told Gilbert Burnet that "for five years together he was continually drunk. . . . This led him to say and do many wild and unaccountable things [related Burnet], by this, he said, he had broke the firm constitution of his health, that seemed so strong, that nothing was too hard for it. There were two principles in his natural temper, that being heightened by [drink] carried him to great excesses: a violent love of pleasure, and a disposition to extravagant mirth. [He thought] nothing diverting which was not extravagant." [7]

Even as early as 1676, the extravagance of the era had begun to claim its victims: a mutual friend of Rochester's and Aphra's died that year. On May 19, John Greenhill was returning from a drunken debauch at the Vine Tavern in Covent Garden with his companions from the theater when he fell into a "kennel." * Unconscious, he was carried to his lodgings in Lincoln's Inn Fields and died that very evening at the age of thirty-two. His untimely demise was blamed on the dissolute style of life he kept up, which had destroyed both his constitution and his talent. Greenhill had come to London from his native Salisbury in 1662 at eighteen and had been apprenticed to Sir Peter Lely, the most famous portrait painter of the age. He had proved to be Lely's most gifted pupil; his progress was so rapid that even the master began to show signs of jealousy. Charles II sat for him, as did the Duke of York, Shaftesbury, Locke, Sir William Davenant, and many others. Greenhill had worked hard in the first few years of his residence in London, but after a time his love for the theater led him, as the *Dictionary of National Biography* says, "to associate with many members of the free-living theatrical world, and he fell into irregular habits."

Greenhill's death jolted Aphra. He belonged to her world and

---

*This was a wider and considerably more filthy canal than today's gutter.

its intoxication had killed him—so they said. She grieved his absence and wrote the only known elegy of him. In it, she describes him as a kind of sensuous idol: *"love and wine"* were sacred to him, she says, deliberately ignoring the reputed cause of his end. Gossip had it that Greenhill was one of Aphra's lovers, and the *Dictionary of National Biography* claims they "kept up an amorous correspondence," but there is no evidence either to support or deny the contention. Hints in Aphra's poem indicate that he may have been, like Hoyle, bisexual: *"for he had all that could adorn a face,/ All that could either sex subdue."* She also describes him as *"soft and gentle as a love-sick maid."* There is a kind of wistful envy in the elegy: in a way, she saw him as one of the lucky ones. Dying young, he was saved from *"the injuries of age and time."* Like the beauties he painted, he was preserved in the *"sweetness of* [his] *prime."*

Aphra must have sent a manuscript copy of the elegy to Rochester, who also knew Greenhill well, for it, like her poem "The Disappointment," was published among his own works in the pirated edition of his writings that appeared after his death.

Still another of Aphra's friends was suffering from a malady that had its origin in Restoration lifestyle. In her poem "A Letter to a Brother of the Pen in Tribulation," she teasingly berated a fellow playwright whose *"interlude of whoring"* had left him with an uncomfortable case of syphilis. He had promised her a prologue for her play, then disappeared from circulation and failed to deliver. Pretending to retire to write, he was actually taking the cure for his disease in Mrs. Roberts's sweating tubs in Leather Lane (or another similar establishment), where Rochester and Savile often repaired for the same reason. The most likely candidate for the miscreant "brother of the pen" is Edward Ravenscroft, who was one of the few fellow playwrights to sign a prologue written for one of Aphra's plays. Given the nature of the company Mrs. Behn kept, however, the suffering poet might have been any one of a number of her fellow writers. *"Poor Damon! Art thou caught? Is't even so?"* she taunts him sarcastically. *"Pox on't that you must needs be fooling now,/ Just when the wits has greatest need of you . . . Is this thy writing plays? Who thought thy wit/ An interlude of whoring would admit?/ To poetry no more thou'lt be inclined,/ Unless in verse to damn all womankind."*

Aphra might have done well to refrain from passing judgment, for sometime later she herself was to be afflicted with the same indisposition. The ubiquitousness of venereal disease among libertines of the day was well known, and it seemed more or less inevitable that she would eventually be its victim as well, once she had taken John Hoyle as her lover. When she wrote the poem, though, there was no indication yet of the ill health that was later to plague her.

III

If certain of Aphra's friends had already begun to burn themselves out, she herself was rapidly moving into literary stardom and giving every indication that she had now mastered her craft. In the second half of the 1670s she was at the height of her powers. Plays issued from her pen at a remarkable rate: little more than a month after the production of *Abdelazer, The Town Fop* was staged (September 1676). Just six months later, in March 1677, *The Rover* went on the boards, followed by *Sir Patient Fancy* in January 1678. *The Feigned Curtezans* was produced in March 1679, and *The Young King* in September of that year. In addition, there were two plays said to have been of Mrs. Behn's authorship which came out anonymously: *The Debauchee* in February 1677, and *The Counterfeit Bridegroom* in September 1677.

In just a little over three years, Aphra Behn had produced six, and possibly eight, plays which were staged by the Duke's Company at the Dorset Garden Theater. Most of them were at least moderately successful—with the exception of the old-fashioned tragicomedy *The Young King*. *The Rover* was so popular that it had numerous repeat performances. The royal party was so taken with it that a full two years after it had first appeared at the Dorset Garden Theater, the play was performed at Court by special request. Later, when Aphra was on somewhat less certain financial ground, she attempted to reproduce her success by writing a sequel to *The Rover*. She dedicated it to the Duke of York and thanked him for *"the incouragement your Royal Highness was pleased to give The Rover at his first appearance."* Perhaps, in addition to her handsome box-office returns, he had given her some financial reward at the time.

The Town Fop; or Sir Timothy Tawdrey, coming so suddenly on the heels of the lugubrious *Abdelazer,* marked a sharp reversal in dramatic mode and effect. The ready wit, swift and easy pacing of the scenes, visual humor, rapid-fire repartee, comic intrigue, and general waggery of Aphra's new play would become the trademarks of the comedies that were her most successful works. Her handling of social satire in particular was so accurate in its language, social reference, and theatrical timing that it must have sent even the sophisticated Restoration audience howling. Mrs. Behn's parody of the way a would-be man of wit went about courting a young lady was gifted caricature; the tics and pretensions of the fashionable creature she is making fun of were common currency of the time and clearly recognizable to contemporary theatergoers. Her exaggeration of the exaggerated made very good theater:

"I'm the Son of a Whore, if you are not the most belle Person I ever saw," the young man begins, *"and if I be not damnably in love with you; but a pox take all tedious courtship, I have a free-born and generous spirit; and as I hate being confined to dull cringing, whining, flattering, and the Devil and all of foppery, so when I give an heart, I'm an infidel, Madam, if I do not love to do't frankly and quickly, that thereby I may oblige the beautiful receiver of my vows, protestation, passions, and inclination . . . Upon my reputation, Madam, you're a civil well-bred person, you have all the agreemony of your sex, la belle taille, la bonne mine, & reparteee bien, and are toute oure toore,* * *as I'm a Gentleman, fort agreeable . . . Well, if I do not hold out, Egad, I shall be the bravest young fellow in Christendom."*

Out of the context of a carefully built up, complicated structure of events, it is difficult to grasp the full comic effect of the scene, but Mrs. Behn's use of language as social touchstone comes through. The parody is in this case a joke within a joke, because the young gallant in question, Wittmore, is deliberately trying to make himself as absurd as possible so that the young woman he is courting (Isabella) will be sure not to fall in love with him. Wittmore's wooing is actually a pretext to insinuate himself into the pious household of Sir Patient Fancy, Isabella's father, so that he may make love to her young step-mother. Lady Fancy is in fact Wittmore's former mistress, forced by financial duress to marry the old Sir Patient Fancy, a City merchant whose hypocritical obsession with godliness makes him entirely deserving of the deception constantly practiced on him. Mrs. Behn twists the plot into more and more intricate configurations, until fi-

---

* *Tout autour . . . fort agréable;* a pun on her general agreeable character and her evidently agreeable physique.

nally Wittmore, who has been *"towsing"** Lady Fancy in her bed-room, is nearly discovered by her husband. She pushes her lover, half-dressed, under the bed and hides his clothes just a moment before Sir Patient intrudes. A letter of assignation addressed to Witt-more has been found—written, of course, by Lady Fancy—and Sir Patient is under the mistaken impression that his daughter has sacri-ficed her virginity to the man he believes to be her suitor. Rushing into Lady Fancy's bedroom, he commences a rant in which the au-thoress plays verbal and visual humor off against each other in an in-credible burlesque:

SIR PATIENT: *Oh, I am half killed, my daughter, my honour—my reputation.*
LADY FANCY: *Good heavens, Sir, is she dead?*
SIR PATIENT: *I wou'd she were, her portion and her honour would then be saved. But oh, I'm sick at heart, Maundy, fetch me the bottle of Mirabilis in the closet,—she's wanton, unchaste.*
        {Enter Maundy with the bottle.}
Oh, I cannot speak it; oh, the bottle—[Drinks.] *she has lost her fame, her shame, her name.—Oh,* [Drinks.] *that is not the right bottle, that with the red cork* [Drinks.] [Exit Maundy.] *and is grown a very t'other-end-of-the-town creature, a very apple of Sodom, fair without and filthy within, what shall we do with her? she's lost, undone; hah!* [Enter Maundy.] *Let me see,* [Drinks.] *this is* [Drinks.] *not as I take it—*[Drinks.]*—oh, how you vex me—*[Drinks.] *No, no here.* [Gives her the bottle.]
MAUNDY: *You said that with the red cork, Sir.* [Goes out.]
SIR PATIENT: *I meant the blue;—I know not what to say.—In fine, my Lady, let's marry her out of hand, for she is fall'n, fall'n to perdi-tion; she understands more wickedness than had she been bred in a profane nunnery, a court, or a playhouse.* [Drinks.]*—therefore lets marry her instantly, out of hand.*

Proper Sir Patient, intoxicated by the supposedly "medicinal" mirabilis with which he has so liberally punctuated his discourse, now begins to look lecherously at Lady Fancy and bolts the door against interruption. Wittmore, still hiding under the bed, is now prevented from making any silent escape and furthermore forced to

* petting

listen to the ridiculous baby talk Sir Patient is plying Lady Fancy with. He chases her around the room, repeating *"catch her, catch her, catch her," "my little ape's face," "you little mungrel,"* and *"my little harlot"* with idiotic persistence until finally, falling in a drunken stupor on the bed, he sleeps. Seizing the opportunity, Wittmore creeps out from under the bed, but he knocks over a chair in the process. Sir Patient awakens and the lover runs to his hiding place again. Lady Fancy forcibly holds her husband down, explaining that it was she who had tripped over the chair. Calmed, he sleeps again. Wittmore then crawls toward the door and nearly escapes when the alarm on his watch goes off and Sir Patient is once again aroused. Lady Fancy throws herself weeping onto him and reveals that the alarm comes from a death-watch that has been in her family for more than a hundred years, which mysteriously rings just before the death of anyone close to her. After one more failed escape, Wittmore next gets as far as the dressing table, overturning it while trying to stand up. Lady Fancy sits down on his back as though he were a stool, pretending to faint. Claiming to be at the door of death, she sends Sir Patient for help, and finally her lover is able to slip out undiscovered. On stage, the scene was hugely successful. Such farce was becoming increasingly dominant in Restoration theater, no doubt partly because it was broad enough to capture the attention of the rowdy, self-absorbed audience.

Aphra owed at least some of her popularity to her consummate skill in this aspect of the theater, but she was equally famous for her repartee. She even ventured to make literary jokes on occasion. When the fatuous Sir Timothy Tawdrey, in *The Town Fop,* defends himself from attack by an insubordinate nurse by informing her that he is a "Gentleman, and a Knight," she replies:

NURSE: *Yes, Sir, Knight of the ill-favor'd countenance is it?*
SIR TIMOTHY: *You are beholding to Don Quixote for that, and 'tis so many ages since thou couldst see to read, I wonder thou hast not forgot all that ever belonged to books.*
NURSE: *My eyesight is good enough to see thee in all thy colours, thou Knight of the burning pestle thou.*
SIR TIMOTHY: *Agen, that was out of a play—Hark ye, Witch of Endor, hold your prating tongue, or I shall more well-favourdly cudgel ye.*

NURSE: *As your friend the hostess has it in a play too, I take it, ends which you pick up behind the scenes, when you go to be laught at even by the player-women.*

Defeated by a woman's wit, Sir Timothy sourly remarks: *"The Devils in her tongue, and so 'tis in most women's of her age; for when it has quitted the tail, it repairs to the upper tire."*

IV

Children are so much the goods, the possessions of their parents, that they cannot, without a kind of theft, give away themselves without the allowance of those that have the right in them.

Richard Allestree,
The Whole Duty of Man, 1663

Aphra's plays *The Town Fop, The Rover,* and *Sir Patient Fancy* all took up in various forms a critique of the social practice of marriage in her time and its destructive effects on both men and women—particularly the second sex. Mrs. Behn had initiated the attack on matrimony in her very first work to be staged, *The Forced Marriage* (1671), and developed the theme through nearly every one of her plays, even those whose principal thrust was political.

The property-marriage system had been a firmly entrenched custom for many generations before Aphra was born, and most children were educated to an unquestioning acceptance of the tradition as a fact of life. Primary matrimonial considerations under this system were the financial and political advantages of the union and the social status of the family that was to be married into. For the most part, little attention was paid to the desires or inclinations of the parties concerned. When Henry Oxinden's twelve-year-old daughter steadfastly refused to marry the man he had chosen for her, Oxinden wrote to his wife in a fury: "Let her know from me she has undone herself; and more assuredly she has. Let her know I shall never again desire to see her face: let her like Cain wander as a vagabond and a runagate; it shall move no heart of mine; let her know I shall never count her among the number of my children, and am resolved when I come home to send her out of my sight." [8] It certainly would have been difficult for a twelve-year-old girl to stand up to such pressure. And of course her father could actually force her to do as he wished if he so chose.

It was standard procedure for parents to agree first on a match and then inform their offspring of a *fait accompli*. Often negotiations were in an advanced state or the contract already signed when the bride or groom were told of their impending wedding; sometimes they were even the last to learn. The manner in which Samuel Pepys—as an intermediary party—negotiated an "alliance" between the son and daughter of two high-ranking officials of the Navy, the Earl of Sandwich and Sir George Carteret, in 1665 seems to have been fairly commonplace. Pepys, as he recorded in his diary, was asked by Lady Sandwich to make the necessary approaches to another intermediary, Dr. Clerk, who would discreetly propose the match and terms to the Carteret family. After some bartering, it was agreed that Jemima, the Earl of Sandwich's daughter, was to bring to the merger a portion of five thousand pounds, to be paid over to the groom's family in exchange for a jointure of eight hundred pounds a year. Once the monies had been agreed upon, the King and the Duke of York, High Admiral of the Navy, were asked for their permission and the marriage contract signed. In all the five months of dickering, the bride-to-be was totally unaware that her fate was being decided for her. Only after the legalities had been concluded was she brought up to London to meet her future husband, whom she had never laid eyes on until that moment.

Aphra Behn's assault on the property-marriage system takes the form of satire in *The Town Fop*. As the play opens, the pompous and undesirable Sir Timothy Tawdrey has just arrived in London from his country estate to claim a bride he has never met. He by chance encounters her brother, Friendlove, who is horrified to learn that his sister, Celinda, is to be married off to such a fool. Sir Timothy smugly informs Friendlove how he came into possession of the prize: *"Your father (according to the method in such cases, being certain of my estate) came to me thus—Sir Timothy Tawdrey,—you are a young gentleman, and a Knight, I knew your father well, and my right worshipful neighbour, our estates lie together; therefore, Sir, I have a desire to have a near relation with you, etc."* When Friendlove objects to this sacrifice of his sister, Sir

Timothy dully reminds him: *"The old people have adjusted the matter, and they are the most proper for a negotiation of that kind, which saves us the trouble of a tedious courtship."*

To find Sir Timothy a half-wit is bad enough, but worse still, it now comes out that he has foppish ambitions. Tawdrey unthinkingly mouths all the current clichés about the way marriage was lived among the fashionable; collectively, they add up to a devastating portrait of the cynicism that Aphra Behn saw inevitably grow out of this sort of arbitrarily arranged marriage. The would-be "man-of-mode" explains to his two "witty" companions, Sham and Sharp, his reason for marrying Celinda.

TAWDREY: *The wench I never saw yet, but they say she's handsome— But no matter for that, there's money, my boys . . . money in abundance, or she were not for me . . . my whole design is to be master of myself, and with part of her portion to set up my Miss* [Mistress], *Betty Flauntit; which, by the way, is the main end of my marrying . . . ready money, ye rogues! What charms it has! makes the waiters fly, boys, and the master the cap in hand—excuse what's amiss, gentlemen—Your Worship shall command the best—and the rest— How briskly the box and dice dance, and the gay wench consults with every beauty to make her agreeable to the man with ready money! In fine, dear rogues, all things are sacrificed to its power; and no mortal conceives the joy of argent content. 'Tis this powerful God that makes me submit to the Devil, matrimony; and then thou art assured of me, my stout lads of brisk debauch.*
SHAM: *And is it possible you can be tied up to a wife? Whilst here in London, and free, you have the whole world to range in, and like a wanton heifer, eat of every pasture.*
SIR TIMOTHY: *Why, dost think I'll be confined to my own dull enclosure? No, I had rather feed coarsely upon the boundless common; perhaps two or three days I may be in love, and remain constant, but that's the most.*

Tawdrey has not even met Celinda and already he is spending her portion, in his mind, on his mistress. Not that he truly loves Betty Flauntit either, but simply sees her as a necessary concession to fashion. The acceptance of a corrupted form, as Aphra presents it, has so divorced him from any feeling that his one remaining instinct is exploitation. Aphra draws Tawdrey as an absurd figure through his ridiculous use of language, but beneath the buffoonery, there is a strong current of revulsion in her dramatic treatment of him.

The construction of *The Town Fop*'s byzantine plot is designed to further demonstrate the deleterious effects of marriage as it was then institutionalized. Celinda, awarded without her knowledge to Tawdrey, has secretly contracted herself to Bellmour, a friend of Friendlove's, who is in turn in love with Diana, Bellmour's cousin. The two cousins are both wards of their uncle, Lord Plotwell, who decides to marry them—to each other. Having already pledged himself to Celinda, Bellmour rejects his uncle's proposition. The latter, as it turns out, has the power to alienate Bellmour's fortune as the price of disobedience in the matter of marriage, according to his father's will. It seems that Plotwell's brother has specified that his son (Bellmour) must marry for *family interest* and not *"imprudently"* according to his own inclination—i.e., for love. The unhappy Bellmour asks his uncle, *"Sir, can you think a blessing can e'er fall upon that pair, whom interest joins, not love?"* But Plotwell is not to be persuaded and summarily has his ward arrested for payment of ten years' maintenance. Legally, he was well within his rights. *The Lawes Resolution . . .* (1632) stated that "If any heir . . . shall marry himself without greeing {agreeing} with his Lord . . . where the Lord offered him a convenient marriage, and without disparagement, there it shall be lawful to hold the inheritance until and after the full age of twenty-one years, by so long time as shall suffice to reap and receive the double value of the marriage." [9]

When he realizes that without the requisite finances he will never be allowed to marry Celinda, Bellmour hopelessly gives in and goes through the forced marriage to his cousin Diana. The shame of having broken his vow to Celinda drives him mad, and he rushes off into a fanatic debauch in which half of the fortune gained is spent, leaving Diana, his benefactress, undeflowered on her wedding night. Celinda attempts suicide; her brother tries to kill Bellmour; Diana swears vengeance on the husband who has scorned her. Finally, Lord Plotwell realizes that his misdirected government has led to the destruction of all. He relents and agrees to do his best to obtain a divorce for the unmatched wards.

The ending is not as improbable as it might seem, since Mrs. Behn was playing on a technicality of English Common Law. A pledge to marry, pronounced by both parties in the presence of witnesses—which was Bellmour and Celinda's case—was considered a *spousal de præsenti* by ecclesiastical courts and constituted a valid marriage contract. The court could compel such a contract to be solemnized in church. A subsequent marriage, even if preceded only by contract without ceremony, could be annulled on the grounds that it was bigamous. Aphra Behn used this device in several other plays as well—perhaps she meant it to be read as prescriptive for young lovers seeking a way out of forced marriage.

It was much more rare for a young man to find himself in Bellmour's position than for young women. Because of the high mortality rate in the seventeenth century, a man might be in possession of his fortune at quite an early age, and usually in that case there were few restrictions to tie him down. Also a young man who was still under parental control and had taken a fancy to a lady of sufficient fortune and position might be able to take some initiative in the matter and succeed in his purpose, unless his parents had some overwhelming aversion to the match.

It was much more difficult for a young woman to do the same: if modesty did not prevent her, the societal insistence on female obedience would probably do so. The Marquis of Halifax, in his *Advice to a Daughter* (1700), remarked that the duty to conform to parents' wishes in the matter of matches particularly applied to women: "It is one of the disadvantages of your sex," he wrote, "that young women are seldom permitted to make their own choice."[10] The author of the *Defense of the Female Sex* (1696) refers to the same double standard of custom, complaining, "thus we women are debarred the liberty of choosing for ourselves."[11]

The heroine of Aphra's first play, *The Forced Marriage,* passively accepted this condition, though her despair was so intense that she contemplated suicide. Subsequent heroines were already beginning to manifest signs of rebellion by the time her third play, *The Dutch Lover,* came out two years later. The assertiveness of the feminist "Epistle to the Reader" which prefaces the play is matched by the force of the heroine's declaration in the first act: *"I am contracted to a man I never saw, nor I am sure shall not like when I do see, he having more vice and folly than his fortune will excuse, tho' a great one; and I had rather die than marry him."* She boldly goes out and finds a lover of her own choice. Aphra makes a slight retreat from her point at the end of the play, when her heroine's chosen lover turns out to be the very one her father had designed for her, effectively evading the problem.

The young women who speak the first lines of *Sir Patient Fancy*, Lucretia and Isabella, are still more "forward" than the heroine of *The Dutch Lover*. They choose to enjoy each other's company rather than that of the unwelcome suitors who *"are the precious things our grave parents still chose out to make us happy with, and all for a filthy jointure, the undeniable argument for our slavery to fools."*

ISABELLA: *Custom is unkind to our sex, not to allow us free choice; but we above all creatures must be forced to endure the formal recommendations of a parent, and the more insupportable addresses of an odious fop; whilst the obedient daughter stands—thus—with her hands pinned before her, a set look, few words, and a mein* [look] *that cries—Come marry me; out upon't.*

LUCRETIA: *I perceive then, whatever your father designs, you are resolved to love your own way.*

ISABELLA: *Thou mayst lay thy maidenhead upon't, and be sure of the misfortune to win.*

It was a bold act for a girl educated in the seventeenth-century manner to affirm that she intended to *decide for herself*, but trafficking her way through the battle of the sexes and dealing with the consequences her decision was likely to bring upon her presented considerable difficulties. In *The Rover*, Aphra Behn set forth what was perhaps her most thorough articulation of the dilemma young women like these faced in seeking their freedom. As in *Sir Patient Fancy*, the first scene opens on a private conversation between two girls—Hellena and Florinda, sisters—mutinously discussing how to outwit the intentions of their father, who has decided the fate of each with the customary disregard for their wishes or feelings. Florinda has been promised in marriage to an elderly but wealthy nobleman whom she despises; Hellena, *"designed for a nun,"* proposes that they slip out into the carnival crowd disguised as gypsies, by which means she intends to find *"some mad companion or other that will spoil my devotion** . . . *though I ask first."* Florinda, though sympathetic, is somewhat taken aback by this open declaration of sexual design: *"Art thou mad to talk so?"* she

---

* She cannot take her religious vows if her virginity is "spoiled."

asks Hellena. *"Who will like thee well enough to have thee, that hears what a mad wench thou art?"*

"Like me!" Hellena answers. *"I don't intend every he that likes me shall have me, but he that I like."*

The he she tangles with is of course Willmore, the Rover—so called because he was one of the banished Cavaliers forced into exile with Charles II when the Parliamentarians were in power, and like his King, he has wandered disinherited all over Europe in search of adventure or fortune. Willmore is also a rover in a second sense—his sexual fancy passes from woman to woman as randomly as he chances to meet another, and he is faithful to none. Aphra's Rover is the very pattern of a libertine hero; he is witty, extravagant, irresistibly attractive to women, and promiscuous. Rochester was the most evident model, but another, less publicly visible, likeness was of course John Hoyle.

Willmore's behavior is to the letter that of a Restoration rake: there can be no question of what he means when he tells his companion, Belvile: *"Thou know'st there's but one way for a woman to oblige me."* He has a wit's horror of marriage and subscribes to the "liberated" dismissal of feminine "virtue": *"What the devil should I do with a virtuous woman?—a sort of ill-natured creatures, that take a pride to torment a lover. Virtue is but an infirmity in women, a disease that renders even the handsome ungrateful* [distasteful].

The "mad" heroine realizes from the very first moment what "freedom" she has tangled with and how it will limit her own; but it is precisely this in the Rover's nature that attracts her to begin with. *"How this unconstant humor makes me love him,"* she mutters to herself when she sees he has already betrayed her only an hour after swearing the contrary. The young woman is split between her own desire for sexual freedom and her instinct that it will make her his victim. So she tricks him, frustrates him, and outwits him until finally they negotiate a settlement:

WILLMORE: *Since we are so well agreed, let's retire to my chamber . . .*
HELLENA: *'Tis but getting my consent, and the business is soon done; let but old gaffer hymen* * *and his priest say Amen to't, and I dare lay*

* marriage

my mother's daughter by as proper a fellow as your father's son, without fear or blushing.

WILLMORE: *No, no, we'll have no vows but love, child, nor witness but the lover; . . . Hymen and priest wait still upon portion, and jointure; love and beauty have their own ceremonies. Marriage is as certain a bane to love, as lending money is to friendship. . .*

HELLENA: *And . . . what shall I get? A cradle full of noise and mischief, with a pack of repentance at my back? Can you teach me to weave incle* to pass my time with?*

In the end, he agrees to marry her, but only because she threatens to leave him altogether. Hellena does not believe in marriage any more than her Rover, nor does she care a fig for feminine virtue, but she has understood that withholding her favors is the only way she can survive in the battle of the sexes. Hellena clearly recognizes the crucial difference between the *givens* of her sexuality and her lover's: she is the one who will be left with *"a cradle full of noise and mischief,"* a ruined reputation, and most likely poverty as well. She may be in ideological agreement with Willmore about the oppressiveness of marriage, but her attitude must be practical because she pays a very different price for the "joys" of free love.

Of course Hellena's chosen means of survival was not the only solution for a woman of her time. Mrs. Behn wrote another female character into the play who represents a second avenue of possibility. She is Angelica Bianca, the whore. Willmore, only a very short time after he first meets Hellena, comes across Angelica Bianca's portrait hanging on a balcony and learns that she is to be auctioned for a vast sum of money. As a penniless Cavalier in exile he cannot bid for her, so instead he rails at her mercenary attitude toward love. Angelica replies with infallible logic: since men cannot be depended upon in love, *"I'm resolved that nothing but gold shall charm my heart."* She further reminds him that men are guilty of the same marketplace attitude, for they always choose a wife not for her qualities or beauty but for her fortune.

Despite the resolve to protect herself, Angelica yields to the Rover, who promptly leaves her after he has satisfied his urges. She finds to her horror the virtuous Hellena preferred and finally realizes

---

* linen thread woven into a tape—domestic handiwork of the seventeenth century

what Willmore does not know himself—that despite his disdain for honor in a woman, it is still the only element that can command his love and respect. Her clear view of the social realities governing sexual affairs has not prevented her from falling into the trap of the "ruined" woman: *"In vain I have consulted all my charms,"* she laments, *"in vain this beauty prized, in vain believed my eyes could kindle any lasting fires. I had forgot my name, my infamy, and the reproach honor lays on those that dare pretend a sober passion here. Nice reputation, tho it leave behind more virtues than inhabit where that dwells, yet that once gone, those virtues shine no more."*

V

What an age do we live in, where 'tis a miracle if in ten couple that are married, two of them live so as not to publish to the world that they cannot agree.

—Dorothy Osborne, ca. 1653

The hypocrisy of arranged marriage was a standard theme in Restoration drama, but the violence of Aphra's systematic and persistent attack on the institution was special. Generally, Mrs. Behn's fellow dramatists adopted a more cynical attitude than hers—though exceptions may be argued, and Aphra herself was quite capable of writing against what she had declared elsewhere to be her position.

In life, most of the wits who protested matrimony so vigorously nevertheless married—and clearly wed for "interest." The Earl of Rochester, having been left with a sadly reduced estate by his improvident father, sought to repair his fortune by choosing to pursue one of the richest heiresses in England—at the King's suggestion. After the marriage, it seems he eventually did conceive a certain affection for her, but his original motives were calculatingly financial. Once in possession of the fortune, he left her to the isolation of the country while entertaining mistresses in London. Rochester's booncompanion, the Duke of Buckingham, had, in the last years of the Commonwealth, married the daughter of a Parliamentary General in order to regain his sequestered estates. After the Restoration, he more or less treated her as though she had ceased to exist and lived openly with the Countess of Shrewsbury. The dramatist Etherege married a rich old widow, and Wycherley tried to secure his financial situation in the same way by marrying the widowed Countess of Drogheda, whose ferocity turned out to be as great as her wealth. The witty Buckhurst, Earl of Dorset, married in succession two wealthy ladies of noble birth, both said to be beautiful but evidently also chosen for their dowry and social position.

Neither Rochester nor Buckingham nor Etherege nor Wycherley nor Buckhurst was forced by parents to marry as he did; they were all at their own disposal. Their objections to marriage might be seen, then, in the most unfavorable light, as reluctance to be tied to any woman who could not be as easily discarded as a whore or a mistress and who might even believe that he had some responsibility to her.

Aphra Behn's attack on marriage and the property-marriage system, on the other hand, was part of a much more comprehensive philosophical stance. She was, in principle, opposed to the intrusion of "interest" into intimacy of whatever sort between men and women—whether it be marriage or love; whether that interest be property, title, money, ambition, or other. This was her definition of "free-love." In a poem she wrote to the Earl of Dorset on the occasion of his second marriage, she made the following statement: *"Too often and too fatally we find/ portion and jointure charm the mind,/ The very soul's by interest swayed,/ And nobler passion now by fortune is betrayed;/ By sad experience this I know,/ And sigh, Alas! in vain because 'tis true."* It was a strange remark to have made to a patron from whom she was probably expecting a much-needed reward. But she was apparently unable to refrain from it; perhaps she felt herself a voice against the tide. Her poem "On Desire" seems to indicate that even in the face of opportunity she had never been able to force herself to make love to a man for his position or his money, though everywhere *"interest did all the loving business do."* Speaking to her perversely retreating "desire,"

> *When interest called, then thou wert shy,*
> *Nor to my aid one kind propension brought,*
> *Nor woud'st inspire one tender thought,*
> *When princes at my feet did lie.*
> *When thou could'st mix ambition with thy joy,*
> *Then peevish phantom thou wer't nice and coy.*

She half regrets; her life might have been easier. Still, her overriding feeling is pride in independence and, through all the confusion of her conflicting impulses, a steadfast rejection of the values she sees as false:

> *Take back your gold, and give me current love,*
> *The treasure of your heart, not of your purse . . .*
> *According to the strictest rules of honour,*
> *Beauty should be the reward of love,*
> *Not the vile merchandise of fortune,*
> *Or the cheap drug of a church-ceremony.*
> *She's only infamous, who to her bed*
> *For interest takes some nauseous clown she hates;*
> *And though a jointure or a vow in public*
> *Be her price, that makes her but the dearer whore.*
> *All the desires of mutual love are virtuous.*

There were other voices who had begun to speak out against marriage-for-money in Aphra's time, but few took the logical conclusions of such a stance as far as she did, nor elaborated it as part of a larger, politics of sexuality. Aphra was, though of course she did not know it, at the beginning of a "sentimental revolution" that would eventually revise England's idea of marriage. Though it was clear Aphra's generation was witnessing a disintegration of the old form, the counsel Francis Osborne gave in his *Advice to a Son* (1656) was still uppermost in men's minds: "He that takes a wife wanting money is a slave to his affections, doing the basest of drudgeries without wages."[12] Charles II confirmed this reality when, in 1664, he wrote to his sister that "a handsome face without money has but few gallants, upon the score of marriage."[13]

It would not be until the next century that history would catch up to Aphra's vision.

VI

> *Envy, malice, and all uncharitableness, —these are the fruits of a successful literary career for a woman.*
>
> —Laetitia Landon, 1836

Aphra Behn's astounding rate of dramatic production in the later part of the 1670s, her repeated successes, and increasing fame were continual irritants to her literary competitors and the aspiring lesser wits who fiercely resented that a woman had achieved what they had failed to. In addition, her emancipated attitude and spirited defense of self-determination excited their animosity still further. One of her poems is a reply to a playhouse "friend" who has informed her that she does not know her place: *"Since you'll have it so,"* she says, *"I grant I am impertinent./ And till this moment did not know/ Through all my life what 'twas I meant;/ Your kind opinion was the unflattering glass,/ In which my mind found how deformed it was./ Impertinence, my sex's shame,/ (Which has so long my life persued,)/ You with such modesty reclaim/ . . . To so divine a power what must I owe,/ That renders me so like the perfect— you?"*

Though she often put up a front of saucy reply to her detractors, Aphra was in truth far from indifferent to the siege of criticism and insult. She had complained privately to Emily Price about the charges of plagiarism over *Abdelazer* and in that letter dismissed their importance, but finally the accusation was persistent enough to cause her professional damage. In a postscript to *The Rover,* Aphra publicly protested that this kind of malicious gossip had caused her publishers to delay printing the play. Her statement clearly identified literary jealousy as one of the principal motivations behind the reports: *"Had* [the play] *succeeded ill, I should have had no need of imploring justice from the critics, who are naturally so kind to any that pretend to usurp their dominion."*

The imputation of plagiarism, though, was a minor theme in the diatribe directed against Aphra. The principal charge was that she had failed in feminine modesty—or as it was more commonly put, that she was a whore. A poem by William Wycherley, addressed "To the Sappho of the Age, Supposed to Lye-In* of a Love-Distemper, or a Play," was evidently written when Aphra was at the height of her theatrical success. Wycherley nastily comments on her growing "public" fame—punning on the double sense of the word as it was applied to feminine sexuality at that time. "Once, to your shame, your parts to all were shown," he claims—demonstrating his own "parts" with the clever double entendre on the word, which then meant *wit,* but also slyly implied *private* parts. "But now," Wycherley goes on, "(tho' a more public woman grown,)/ You gain more reputation in the

---

*give birth to; also in the slang sense of "to lay"

town;/ Grow public, to your honor, not your shame,/ As more men now you please, gain much more fame;/ . . . Barren wits, envy your head's offsprings more,/Than barren women, did your tail's* before." The logic Wycherley's joke rested on was well known to everyone: it was the old adage that in gaining "fame," a woman lost it. What was so funny was that there were some "barren wits" gullible enough to see Aphra's reputation shining instead of stinking as it ought.

In a sense, Aphra herself had set up the structure for Wycherley's satire: her very first prologue, it will be remembered, had declared that women, who had formerly pleased by beauty, were now attempting wit as a superior means of conquering the other sex. She had been half-serious and half-playful, but Wycherley used the pretext to drag her through the mud: "Thus, as your beauty did, your wit does now,/ The women's envy, men's diversion grow;/ Who, to be clap'd, or clap you, round you sit,/ And, tho' they sweat for it, will crowd your pit;/ Since lately you lay-in, (but as they say,)/ Because, you had been clap'd another way;/ But, if 'tis true, that you have a need to sweat,/ Get, (if you can) at your new play, a seat."

The slander is couched in a wily series of double meanings: "clap" in the sense of applause, but also as slang for venereal disease; "sweating" from overcrowding the theater, but also as the cure for the "clap" (a reference to the sweating-tubs); and the "pit" of the theater, but also a woman's sexual parts. The last line of the poem seems to suggest a certain envy; though Wycherley was himself undeniably a success, his literary output was small compared to the rush of plays from Aphra's energetic pen—in the end, he wrote only four to her seventeen. In view of the experience of other, far less provoking, women writers, it seems inevitable that the slurs on Aphra's sexuality would come whether there was any basis for them in her life or not. It seems possible that at one time Aphra might indeed have had a succession of lovers, but to be castigated for it by a libertine like Wycherley, however, was ridiculous.

Another contemporary satire written in 1676—anonymously— included Aphra among the leading playwrights of her day competing for the title of Poet Laureate, but in these terms:

> . . . *The poetess Aphra next showed her sweet face*
> *And swore by her poetry and her black ace†*

Tail was slang for a woman's sex.
†seventeenth-century slang for the female sexual parts

> *The laurel by a double right was her own*
> *For the plays she had writ and the conquests she's won.*
> *Apollo acknowledged 'twas hard to deny her,*
> *But to deal frankly and ingeniously by her,*
> *He told her, were conquests and charms her pretence,*
> *She ought to have pleaded a dozen years hence.* [14]

Aphra was then about thirty-six years old. The verses, passed around in manuscript in all the coffeehouses and taverns the wits frequented and then in the Court itself, must have caused her some pain.

Aphra chose to ignore the traducement of her personal life, but was not about to let the remarks pass unanswered when they were directed at her professional capacity. In another "Preface to the Reader," printed at the beginning of her play *Sir Patient Fancy*, she defends herself: "*I printed this play with all the impatient haste one ought to do, who would be vindicated from the most unjust and silly aspersion, woman could invent to cast on woman; and which only my being a woman had procured me;* That it was Bawdy, *the least and most excusable fault in the men writers, to whose plays they all crowd, as if they came to no other end than to hear what they condemn in this:* but from a woman it was unnatural . . . (Aphra's emphases)." It was bad enough to have to take squibs and lampoons and open hostility from men, Aphra contended, but to find herself under attack from the sex whose rights she had been trying to uphold was severely disappointing. *"The play had no other misfortune but that of coming out for a woman's,"* her manifesto went on, *"had it been owned by a man, though the most dull unthinking rascally scribler in town, it had been a most admirable play. Nor does its loss of fame with the ladies do it much hurt, though they ought to have had good nature and justice enough to have attributed all its faults to the authors unhappiness, who is forced to write for bread and not ashamed to own it, and consequently ought to write to please (if she can) an age which has given several proofs it was by this way of writing to be obliged, though it is a way too cheap for men of wit to pursue who write for glory, and a way which even I despise as much below me."*

Did Aphra feel that her gift had been deformed by the necessity of making a living by her writing? She was, she says, forced by necessity to write to the fashion of the age—i.e., to write as the other (male) playwrights did; to write "like a man." Is she saying that she might have written differently had she been free from this demand?

The answer must be speculative—but perhaps this might in part explain the double voice in Aphra's work.

Mrs. Behn's argument that what she wrote was no more salacious than her male colleagues' plays was quite correct. That she was the victim of a literary double standard is confirmed by a letter of John Dryden's to Elizabeth Thomas, a young woman who had confided her literary ambitions to him. "You, who write only for your diversion," he wrote, congratulating her intention not to *publish* anything she wrote, but to keep it private, "may pass your hours with pleasure in it, and without prejudice, always avoiding (as I know you will) the licenses which Mrs. Behn allowed herself, of writing loosely, and giving (if I may have leave to say so) some scandal to the modesty of her sex. I confess, I am the last man who ought, in justice to arraign her, who have been myself too much a libertine." [15] At least Dryden had the grace to admit the hypocrisy of attacks on Mrs. Behn. But the letter was written only after she was dead. The age had reversed its social stance on the issue, and Dryden himself, having recently converted to Catholicism, was primarily apologizing for his own libertine past rather than excusing Mrs. Behn for having scandalized the modesty of her sex.

However she might have been hurt by the aspersions cast on her character and her plays, Aphra's epilogue to *Sir Patient Fancy* in no uncertain terms told her critics she did not intend to be daunted:

> *I here and there o'erheard a coxcomb cry,*
> *Ah, Rot it—'tis a woman's comedy,*
> *One, who because she lately chanc'd to please us,*
> *With her damn'd stuff, will never cease to tease us.*
> *What had poor woman done, that she must be*
> *Debarred from sense, and sacred poetry? . . .*
> *As for you half-wits, you unthinking tribe,*
> *We'll let you see, what e'er besides we do,*
> *How artfully we copy some of you:*
> *And if you're drawn to th' life, pray tell me then,*
> *Why women should not write as well as men.*

The epilogue was spoken by "Mrs. Gwin." Recent scholars have said that the actress cannot have been the famous Nell Gwyn, as she had retired from the stage several years before, when she became the

King's mistress. There is, however, a contemporary engraving depicting her speaking the lines, which seems to argue otherwise. It does seem possible that the jolly Nell might have thought it amusing to return to her former profession once or twice—particularly as she was known for her generosity and it would certainly have given a boost to Aphra's career. The fact that Aphra's very next play, *The Feigned Curtezans,* performed about two months later, is dedicated to Nell Gwyn seems to support the possibility. It was Aphra's first dedication to any of her plays, and she might well have thought it a good opportunity to thank the actress for the support she had given. Mrs. Behn praises Mrs. Gwyn for her beauty, charm, and sweetness, but most of all for her wit—commenting that her example *"ought to make your sex vain enough to despise the malicious world that will allow a woman no wit . . . [and] shame those boasting talkers who are judges of nothing but faults."*

CHAPTER TWELVE

Politics; Plots; Poverty

A Pox of the statesman that's witty,
Who watches and plots all the sleepless night:
For seditious harangues, to the Whigs of the city;
And maliciously turns a traitor in spite.
Let him wear and torment his lean carrion:
  To bring his sham-plots about,
  Till at last King, Bishop and Baron,
For the public good he have quite rooted out.

—Aphra Behn,
"The Cabal at Nickey Nackeys," 1681

I want to be doing something with the pen, since no other means of ac-
tion in politics are in a woman's power.

—Harriet Martineau

Long may [Astrea] scourge this mad rebellious age,
And stem the torrent of fanatic rage,
That once had almost overwhelmed the stage.
O'er all the land the dire contagion spread . . .
But while that spurious race imployed their parts
To alienate their Prince's subjects' hearts,
Her loyal muse still turned her loudest strings,
To sing the praises of the best of kings.

Anonymous (female), 1684

Poverty's the certain fate
Which attends a poet's state.

—Jane Barker,
Poetical Recreations, 1688

I

The world ran mad, and each distempered brain,
Did strange and different frenzies entertain:
Here politick mischiefs, there ambition swayed;
The credulous rest, were fool and coward-mad.

—Aphra Behn

At the end of the 1670s, when against and beyond all expectation Aphra Behn had undeniably achieved literary prosperity, the world began to fall apart again. The heavens had been unusually active in the year 1678; three eclipses of the sun and two of the moon disturbed astrologers enough to predict "frenzies, inflammations and new infirmities proceeding from cholerick humours" in the near future.[1] Such prophecy alone was enough to excite seventeenth-century distemper, and the season, a hot summer like the summer of the Great Plague, no doubt encouraged the mood. It is difficult to understand the madness that erupted into what was known as the Popish Plot in any other way; it was the collective delirium of a people whose credence still instinctively included the supernatural. Such a population was easily manipulated into believing the most incredible tales the plotters behind "the Plot" could invent.

On August 13, 1678, early in the morning, before Charles II departed for his daily constitutional in St. James Park, Christopher Kirby, an obscure chemist working in the royal laboratory, rushed up wild-eyed to report that the King was in imminent danger of assassination by the perpetrators of a "horrid" plot against him and the country. The King, for whom news of conspiracy was everyday stuff, informed Kirby that he would prefer to proceed in his walk without further disturbance, but would listen to his story on returning. Kirby, who was only a tool for two much more clever and convincing plotters, brought to the palace that evening an indictment detailing the intrigue in an impressive forty-three articles. The plot was this: the Pope, Innocent XI, had lent his supreme authority to the Jesuits, who were commanded to dispose of the King of England and take over the government; to this end, two Jesuits had been deputed to shoot Charles, four Irish ruffians hired to knife him, and the Queen's physician, Sir George Wakeman, engaged to poison him discreetly. Named as conspirators were the King of France and his confessor, le père La Chaise, the Archbishop of Dublin, the General of the Jesuits, and five Catholic English Lords—Arundel, Powys, Petre, Stafford, and Belasyse. Under the direction of these last, an army of Catholic fanatics was to rise up at a signal, massacre the Protestants of London, and burn the city to the ground. The popish Duke of York would succeed to the throne and rule according to Jesuit instructions. The plan, the indictment charged, had been worked out and ratified at a meeting of the Jesuits at the White Horse Tavern in the Strand on April 24, 1678.

The authors of the document revealing this "hellish design" were Titus Oates and Ezerel Tonge. The first, an Anglican clergyman temporarily out of work, had converted to Catholicism and been admitted into the Jesuits in order, so he said, to penetrate further into their secrets. In only a few months he acquired a spurious doctorate of divinity from the Spanish University of Salamanca and was hired (at his own suggestion) by the Jesuits of St. Omer to poison Ezerel Tonge, the translator of an antipapist tract—and also Oates's coconspirator in the revelation of the Popish Plot.

The King listened incredulously to Oates's story on that first evening at Whitehall; summarily passed on the forty-three articles of accusation to Danby, the Lord Treasurer; and without another thought left for Windsor the next day. Danby took the matter less lightly than the King, however, and called a meeting of the Privy Council to examine all the evidence. The "plot" might still have fizzled into nothing except for a mysterious and sinister event that set off a general panic. Oates and Tonge, early in September, had given depositions attesting the truth of their story to a prominent London magistrate named Edmund Berry Godfrey. On October 12, he disappeared from his home near the Strand and five days later was found lying facedown in a deserted part of Primrose Hill, a sword through his back. No money had been stolen, and there were strange bruises on his face and throat indicating that he may have been beaten, strangled to death, or even hanged; the sword, apparently, had been inserted after he was dead.

Various theories of the motives behind Godfrey's murder were propounded, but the public immediately assumed it to be the work of the papists. In the interval between the depositions and the murder, it was discovered that one of the accused, Edward Coleman, who was secretary to the Duchess of York and former secretary to the Duke, had indeed been carrying on a treasonous correspondence with various papist powers abroad, among them La Chaise. With the naïve enthusiasm of a recently converted Catholic, he outlined various possibilities for increasing the influence of the Duke of York, to the general end of regaining England for the Catholic faith. He had written many of his letters in cipher and kept a copy of each. There was no evidence that anyone took his pompous grand schemes seriously or that he was indeed acting at anyone else's instigation, but the air of secrecy and his vague reference to "the grand design"—presumably that of spreading the faith—seemed to confirm Oates's accusations. Added to this was the fact that Edmund Berry Godfrey had been on friendly terms with Coleman, and on hearing the depositions of Oates and Tonge, had warned him of their content.

If the incredible claims put forth by Titus Oates had hitherto aroused any suspicions, the unearthing of Coleman's correspondence and Godfrey's murder dismissed them in the national mind. London was thrown into a state of terror. Crowds marched through the streets chanting "No popery!" A flood of pamphlets was published denouncing the foreign menace; coffeehouses brimmed over with partisans debating the subject and eagerly awaiting the latest newssheet. "The press abounds with all sorts of pamphlets and libels," wrote Narcissus Luttrell in his diary, "one side running down the papists and upholding the dissenters; the other crying down both . . . public intelligences* abounding, every day spawning 'two, sometimes three, filling the town and country with notorious falsehoods." [2]

Priests, suspected recusants, even innocent bystanders were arrested and thrown into prison, and houses of known Catholics were broken into and searched for weapons or religious articles. Any popish books or evidence of worship that the mob could lay hands on was publicly burned. One enterprising merchant advertised special daggers for Protestants to protect themselves with, which were inscribed REMEMBER THE MURDER OF EDMUND BERRY GODFREY on one side and REMEMBER RELIGION on the other. In a single day, he sold three thousand. On October 30, a proclamation was issued ordering all popish recusants to leave London; but it is to be imagined that by then any who believed they risked discovery and had a means of escape would have already done so. Three weeks later a reward of twenty pounds was offered to anyone who could find a popish priest or Jesuit.

* newspapers or newssheets

The Royal opposition in Parliament, meanwhile, were exploiting the situation to the utmost. Under the leadership of Shaftesbury and the Country Party (later called Whigs), numerous committees were set up to pursue investigation and prosecute those found guilty. On October 31, 1678, the Commons voted the following official resolution: "That there has been and still is a damnable and hellish plot, contrived and carried on by popish recusants for the assassinating and murdering the King and for subverting the government and rooting out and destroying the Protestant religion."[3] Both houses passed a bill excluding all Catholics from sitting in Parliament—including several members of the Howard family—and five popish Lords were committed to the Tower. One of them was William Howard, Viscount Stafford, whom Aphra had known in Antwerp and whose son she had remained friendly with.

Still more informers presented themselves. A reward of five hundred pounds had been offered to the man who could point to Godfrey's murderers, and a William Bedloe—claiming, falsely, to be *Captain* Bedloe—introduced himself into the plot. On November 8, he testified that he, too, like Titus Oates, had gained the Jesuits' trust by feigning a conversion. He had been hired by them, he said, to murder Godfrey and afterward set fire to London. A Catholic named Prance had been arrested on very little evidence. Bedloe, on seeing him at the Parliamentary committee meeting, claimed to recognize him as one of Godfrey's murderers. Prance, according to Sir Roger L'Estrange's account, was put into solitary confinement at Newgate and terrified into a confession, in which he implicated three other men as accomplices—Green, Berry, and Hill. He then recanted, but was repersuaded with the promise of a pardon.

On December 3, 1678, Edward Coleman was hanged, drawn, and quartered. In the new year, Green, Berry, and Hill were executed, along with eight Jesuits and a barrister. By then Titus Oates was living comfortably on a state pension in Whitehall Palace, under a heavy guard for protection from the "vengeful papists."

II

The Popish Plot put an abrupt end to the merry days of the Restoration: wits, pranks, and the prosperity of the theater were all to vanish in the atmosphere of universal hysteria and accusation. One recent writer compared it to the stock market crash of 1929—a disaster that would determine the fate of an entire decade to follow.

Aphra's survival, of course, was dependent on that of the playhouses, and the theater was in serious trouble. The Duke's Company had produced eighteen new plays a season in the two years preceding the plot, but in 1678–79, it staged only six. The King's Company, suffering from internal disputes, closed down altogether during much of 1678 and 1679. A good many people had fled London in terror of the purges; the King had gone to Newmarket, and many of those who were left were too much taken up with troubles or excitement to care to amuse themselves at the theater as they used to. In the epilogue to *The Feigned Curtezans,* produced in March 1679, Aphra complains of the pitifully reduced audience: *"So hard the times are, and so thin the town,/ Though but one playhouse, that must too lie down;/ And when we fail, what will the Poets do?"* In the prologue, she unequivocally declares her own political position and lashes out at the purveyors of what she is convinced are invented plots: *"The Devil take this cursed plotting age,/ 'T has ruin'd all our plots upon the stage;/ Suspicions, new elections, jealousies,/ Fresh informations, new discoveries,/ Do so employ the busy fearful town,/ Our honest calling here is useless grown:/ Each fool turns politician now, and wears/ A formal face, and talks of state-affairs."*

Titus Oates was still at the height of his power when Aphra wrote her prologue. Anyone who doubted his word, and there were not many, was immediately suspected of harboring popish allegiance. Even the King, despite his own conviction that the plot was a sham, found it more expedient not to declare it so openly. In this light, Aphra's statement seems all the more bold. As if in further provocation, she set her play in Rome—anathema to antipapists—and liberally sprinkled it with Italian words, phrases, and songs. One of the central characters is a foppish young squire from Kent, who has come to Rome with his puritanical tutor, Mr. Tickletext, in order to refine his education. When the young man calls his dull English servingman "Giovanni" instead of "Jack," in an effort to show his breeding, Tickletext steadfastly replies: *"Sir, by your favor, his English Protestant name is John Pepper,* and I'll call him by ne'er a Popish name in Christendom."*

---

* Was there a private joke here in Aphra's Kentishman named John (Cul)Pepper?

Titus Oates and his party of informers had little sense of humor, and Aphra was teasingly calling attention to her point when she wrote in the prologue: "[Each fool] *makes acts, decrees, and a new model draws/ For regulation both of Church and Laws:/ Tires out his empty noddle to invent/ What rule and method's best in government:/ But wit, as if 'twere Jesuitical,/ Is an abomination to ye all./ To what a wretched pass will poor plays come?/ This must be damn'd, the plot is laid in Rome."*

In addition to greatly reducing the audiences, the tumult of the Popish Plot had created an atmosphere of querulousness in the theater. A few months after the production of Aphra's *The Feigned Curtezans,* John Verney wrote to Sir Ralph Verney that "On Saturday, at the Duke's Theater, happened a quarrel between young Bedloe* and one of the novices of St. Omer's,† and many swords were drawn, but as yet I have not heard whether any blood was shed in this religious quarrel."[4] Later, *The True News; or Mercurius Anglicus* reported "a great dispute in the Duke's Playhouse."[5] A number of drunken antipapist gentlemen, it appears, had entered the pit in the course of a play, thrown lighted torches at the actors, and insulted the Duchess of Portsmouth—the King's "Catholic whore," as she was called by most of London then. The "disorders" so infuriated the King that he ordered the Duke's Theater closed until further notice, and the disorderly were arrested as "ryotters." Aphra's provocative statements and topical barbs cannot have failed to elicit a reaction in such a tinderbox.

The prologue to Aphra's next play, *The Young King* (produced in September 1679), recounted a falling-out in the pit which seems to have had its origins in sheer irascibility rather than political struggle. Young Jack Churchill, later to become famous as the Duke of Marlborough, took exception to something in a transaction with Orange Betty** and proceeded to beat her savagely. Thomas Otway, who gallantly could not witness such treatment of even an "orange wench," challenged Churchill and in the ensuing fight emerged triumphant. It was Churchill's first and last defeat in battle and Otway's only victory in that field. Otway was in low spirits, however, and Aphra Behn's lampoon of Churchill in her prologue may have cheered

* an informer
† The Catholic college Titus Oates had attended, which he pretended had been part of the plot.
** The woman who sold oranges in the pit of the Duke's Theater

him up: *"Cudgel the weapon was, the pit the field;/ Fierce was the hero, and too brave to yield./ But stoutest hearts must bow; and being well caned,/ He crys, Hold, hold, you have the victory gain'd./ All laughing call—/ Turn out the Rascal, the eternal blockhead;/ —Zounds, crys Tartarian,* I am out of pocket:/ Half crown my play, sixpence my orange cost."*

Aphra had every reason to be in low spirits herself. Her financial base was crumbling, her beloved King was besieged, the world had exploded as though all the furies had been released. In November 1679, her friend Henry Neville (Payne), a well-known Catholic, was arrested. On the seventeenth of that month, Queen Elizabeth's Accession Day, which had always to some extent commemorated the triumph of Protestantism over Queen Mary's Catholicism, was celebrated by a massive mock-popish procession that recreated the "horrid Plot." The crowd was parted for the solemn cortege by six whistlers and a bell ringer intoning "Remember Justice Godfrey," followed by a horseman carrying a dead body dressed as Sir Edmund Berry Godfrey, bloodied in the appropriate places. Next was a Cardinal offering pardons and indulgences for the murders of Protestants, and behind him came a bevy of menacing Jesuits armed with daggers. Next were four Bishops in full regalia, and finally, the Pope himself, riding on a throne with the Devil whispering in his ear.[6] The citizens of London filled the streets carrying torches, swords, and cudgels: it was said that as many as two hundred thousand of them participated in this mob hysteria. The procession ended at the statue of Queen Elizabeth, where all the popish vestments and an effigy of the Pope himself went up in an enormous bonfire.

A year later, on December 8, 1680, a similarly vengeful crowd watched the beheading of the elderly William Howard, Viscount Stafford. He had been convicted of treason by Parliament itself for his imaginary involvement in the fictional plot.

If it was true that Aphra was, as she said, once *"designed for a nun,"* and had indeed had some sort of Catholic upbringing, she had good cause to be nervous on her own account. The very fact that she had so many Catholic connections would have created suspicion even if nothing further had been known. Though her violent attack on the

---

* Churchill

Protestant party inevitably placed her on the side of the papists, her statements were political in nature rather than religious. To have declared herself a papist in such times would have been sheer madness, but what Aphra did say seems to indicate that if she had been a Catholic, she had probably lapsed. For the most part, she seems to have taken the wits' attitude toward religion: *"Who would have thought* [religion] *would have been the occasion of any contest in an hopeful nation?"* A poem she wrote in the last year of her life, speaking of the plot fever, which had been over for several years, seems to indicate some identification with the faith, however:

> *The Lord of life, his image rudely torn,*
> *To flames was by the common-hangman born.*
> *Here noble Stafford fell, on death's great stage,*
> *A victim to the lawless peoples rage.*
> *Calm as a dove, receiv'd a shameful death,*
> *To undeceive the world, resign'd his breath,*
> *And like a God, dy'd to redeem our faith.* [7]

In the midst of all the furor, Rochester died at Woodstock on July 26, 1680. He was thirty-three years old. On his deathbed, he recanted his libertine philosophy and swore to the Reverend Gilbert Burnet that it was the decadence of the life he had led that had broken his health and his mind. It was an ending unworthy of Aphra's gay, careless hero. She chose to remember him as he had been; in the long elegy she wrote, she recalls his wit, his beauty, and his fatal charm for "the fair sex": *"Mourn, all ye beauties,/ The truest swain that e'er adored you's gone;/ Think how he loved, and writ, and sighed, and spoke,/ Recall his mein, his fashion, and his look."*

Another woman poet—or aspiring poet—answered Aphra. She was Anne Wharton, Rochester's cousin. The verses she herself wrote in her elegy on Rochester's death were probably the first she had ever made public: those she wrote to Aphra Behn thanking her for "what she writ of the Earl of Rochester" were almost certainly the second. Mrs. Behn, she said, had been an inspiration to her and indeed an example to all women, with only one exception: in the question of modesty. Of Aphra's "fame" she wrote:

> *May yours excel the matchless Sappho's name;*
> *May you have all her wit, without her shame:*

'Tho she to honour gave a fatal wound,
Employ your hand to raise it from the ground. . . .
Scorn meaner themes, declining low desire,
And bid your Muse maintain a Vestal fire. *
If you do this, what glory will insue,
To all our sex, to poesie, and you? [8]

Anne Wharton was the author of a handful of poems; Aphra had more than ten years' professional experience behind her. Mrs. Wharton's presumption in telling Mrs. Behn how to write may be somewhat excused by the fact that she was married to Thomas Wharton, older than she and reputed to be one of the most promiscuous men of his generation—which, given the competition, involved a considerable commitment of time and energy. Apparently it was a "forced marriage," and she was disapproving and unhappy.

Aphra Behn replied in more verses "To Mrs. W[harton] On her Excellent Verses (Writ in Praise of Some I had made on the Earl of Rochester) Written in a Fit of Sickness." She generously praised Anne Wharton's poem and encouraged her literary efforts, but ignored the remarks about her "honour" and declined to reject the "desire" she saw as a central part of Rochester's character. Mrs. Wharton seems to have been pleased nevertheless, and must have spoken of the praise from Aphra to Gilbert Burnet, with whom she maintained a pious correspondence. He answered her reprovingly: "Some of Mrs. Behn's songs are very tender; but she is so abominably vile a woman, and rallies not only all religion but all virtue in so odious and obscene a manner, that I am heartily sorry she has writ anything in your commendation." [9]

III

Out of the confusion of the Popish Plot emerged a set of political distinctions which ultimately gave birth to the modern party system. Whigs and Tories came into being. The "plot" simply catalyzed an evolution which had been developing for years. The Whigs, in their advocacy of Parliamentary independence were the political inheritors of the men who had made the Commonwealth. They also carried on

* Mrs. Wharton undoubtedly had the Vestal Virgins in mind.

the Puritan hatred of Roman Catholics and the wish to purge all things popish from England. Since the Restoration, a continuous battle had raged between King and opposition over religious toleration and alliances with France—a country not only thoroughly Catholic but also under an absolute monarchy. When James, Duke of York, openly declared himself a papist, the agitation fixed on the growing fear that he would, upon inheriting the throne, attempt to impose Catholicism and, with the aid of his cousin Louis XIV, rule without consulting Parliament. Shaftesbury, leader of the Country Party (as opposed to the Court Party), later the Whigs, had already understood in 1674 that the only way to combat the Duke of York successfully was to stir up public fear of popery: in that year he made an inflammatory speech before Parliament declaring that there were sixteen thousand Catholics around London ready to rise in arms at any moment.

The explosion of the Popish Plot five years later provided a perfect opportunity to bring the question of exclusion to a head. The King, though not fond of his brother, firmly believed in principle that the royal succession must be kept intact. Between February 1679 and February 1681, Charles II called the third and fourth Parliaments of his reign; in both, the House of Commons passed a bill excluding the Duke of York from the throne, and both were dissolved by the King before they could complete the action. In the fierce debate of the issues, the party platforms defined themselves. The Whigs advocated a Parliamentary monarchy: the King would have no powers of taxation nor any revenue not accorded him by Parliament, and his power to prorogue or dissolve that body at will would be limited by law. In addition, they argued that the King must represent and uphold the Protestant religion and protect England from foreign manipulation in that domain. James's character as well as his avowed religion made him unsuitable for this kind of monarchy, and the Whigs wished to exclude him from the throne in favor of either William of Orange, who was married to James's daughter, or Monmouth, Charles II's illegitimate son.

To Tories, the succession was sacred. They demanded absolute allegiance to the King, who governed by divine right. To question, let alone attempt to limit that right, was heresy. The King as father was a constant Tory theme and obedience to him must be absolute.

The Whig conception of monarchy as social contract was considered seditious as well as heretical.

Aphra Behn remained relatively quiet during 1680, though she supported the royal cause. *The Rover* was performed at Court for the King in February and *The Feigned Curtezans* in March. In June, a comedy called *The Revenge; or, A Match in Newgate* was staged at the Dorset Garden Theater. It was printed anonymously, but Narcissus Luttrell, who bought a copy of the printed version a month after the performance, inscribed the name of "Mrs. Ann Behn" as author.

In 1681, Aphra once again took up her political polemic on the stage with a vigor few other playwrights could imitate. In the year and a half between January 1681 and May 1682, she produced five plays. In January, a sequel to *The Rover* went on the boards; November saw *The False Count;* December, *The Roundheads.* In March 1682, *Like Father, Like Son* (an unpublished play of which only prologue and epilogue are extant) was acted, and in May, *The City Heiress.* Aphra was working very quickly indeed; she herself speaks of having written *The False Count* in only five days. Perhaps it was the energy of her anger driving her pen, or perhaps the pressure of increasing financial difficulties in the theaters—probably it was both.

She dedicated *The Rover II* to the Catholic Duke of York, who had been forced into exile for the second time and was then abroad. On his return from the first exile, he had spent the night with Lady Willoughby's relative James Cecil, the Earl of Salisbury—also a Catholic, related to the Howard family. Aphra apparently knew the Earl of Salisbury well. When three years later she dedicated her *Voyage to the Isle of Love* to him, an unfounded rumor went around that she had been his mistress.

Aphra's dedication to the Duke of York, however, is strongly political: she fulminates against the *"sanctified faction"* who had first made his father, Charles I, its victim and now dared to attack the Duke, rather than expiate the sin of regicide *"by an entire submission."* She parallels James with her *Rover,* exiled by the forefathers of *"this again gathering faction, who make their needless and self-created fears* [i.e., the Popish Plot], *an occasion to play the old game over again* [i.e., the Parliamentary rebellion]."

In the prologue to *The Rover II,* Aphra aims at her fellow playwright Elkannah Settle, who had taken up for the Whigs: *"In vain we labour to reform the stage,/ Poets have caught too the disease o' th' age,/ That pest, of not being quiet when they're well,/ That restless fever, in the brethren, Zeal;/ In public spirits call'd, good o' th' Commonweal./ Some for this faction cry, others for that,/ That pious mobile* for they know not what:/ So tho' by different ways the fever seize,/ In all 'tis one and the same mad disease."* In her epilogue, she scorns the other writers who have betrayed their royal patron *"and write against their consciences, to show/ How dull they can be to comply with you./ They've flattered all the mutineers in the nation. . . ."* Parliament had just voted to deny the King funds until the Exclusion Bill was passed, and Aphra's epilogue ends with a plea for the gentlemen of those houses not to let the *"King of Poets"* (i.e., Charles II) go begging like the faithless playwrights who have recanted their *"loyal principle."*

Aphra's next play, *The False Count,* carried on the battle with a sarcastic pretense of conversion to Whiggery in the prologue:

> *Know all ye Whigs and Tories of the Pit,*
> *(Ye furious Guelphs and Gibelins of Wit,*
> *Who for the cause, and crimes of Forty-One †*
> *So furiously maintain the quarrel on)*
> *Our author, as you'll find it writ in story,*
> *Has hitherto been a most wicked Tory;*
> *But now, to th' joy o' th' brethren be it spoken,*
> *Our sister's vain mistaken eyes are open;*
> *And wisely valuing her dear interest now,*
> *All-powerful Whigs, converted is to you.*

Aphra's list of her Tory sins makes it clear that she had not confined her political activities to the stage but had also been busy writing lampoons and satires—most likely anonymous—and perhaps even pamphlets. Tory poets were encouraged to do so by the King, who felt some reply needed to be made to the avalanche of antipapist and Whiggish literature: *"'Twas long she did maintain the Royal cause,/ Argu'd, disputed, rail'd with great applause;/ Writ madrigals and doggerel on the times,/ And charg'd you all with your fore-fathers crimes;/ Nay, con-*

* mob

† 1641 was the year the English Civil War began. Aphra is emphasizing the political resemblance between Whigs and Puritans here.

fidently swore no plot was true,/ But that so slyly carried on by you;/ Rais'd horrid scandals on you, hellish stories,/ In conventicles how you eat young Tories."

In her preface to *The Dutch Lover*, Aphra had argued that plays ought not to have a moral end—but then she was setting herself against those who wanted her women and her plots dressed up decently in the cloak of modesty. Now she changed her tack; for political morality she made an exception. Drama not only could, Aphra later said in a dedication, but *ought* to be political when the times call for commitment. Plays, she contended, *"are secret instructions to the people, in things that 'tis impossible to insinuate into them any other way. 'Tis example that prevails above reason or DIVINE PRECEPTS. (Philosophy not understood by the multitude;) 'tis example alone that inspires morality, and best establishes vertue, I have myself known a man, whom neither conscience nor religion cou'd perswade to loyalty, who with beholding in our theatre a modern politician set forth in all his colours, was converted, renounc'd his opinion, and quitted the party. . . . Plays and public diversions were thought by the greatest and wisest of states, one of the most essential parts of good government, and in which so many great persons were interested. . . .*

Aphra dedicated her third play of 1681, *The Roundheads*, to Henry Fitzroy, Duke of Grafton—an illegitimate son of Charles II who was, incidentally, married to Arlington's daughter. Aphra undoubtedly had Monmouth, Charles's disloyal illegitimate son, in mind when she exhorted Grafton to *"become the great example of loyalty and obedience, and stand a firm and unmovable pillar to monarchy, a noble bullwark to majesty; defend the sacred cause, imploy all that youth, courage, and noble conduct which God and nature purposely has endued you with, to serve the Royal interest: You, Sir, who are obliged by a double duty to love, honor, and obey his Majesty, both as a father and a King! O undissolvable knot! O sacred union! what duty, what love, what adoration can express or repay the debt we owe the first, or the allegiance due to the last, but where both meet in one, to make the tie eternal. . . ."* Her enthusiasm seems so excessive here as to appear ridiculous, but another remark she makes in the dedication indicates that she is feeling heavily besieged: *"This play, for which I humbly beg your Grace's protection, needs it in a more peculiar manner, it having drawn down legions upon its head, for its loyalty—'what, to name us' cries one, "tis most abominable, unheard of daring,' cries another—'she deserves to be swing'd,' cries a third; as if 'twere all a libel, a scandal impossible to be prov'd, or that their rogueries were of so old a date their reign were past remembrance or history; when they take such zealous care to renew it daily to our memories."*

The Roundheads was the most explicitly partisan play she had written yet: she posited as a mirror for the times the events of 1659, when the members of the governing Committee of Safety were vying for control after Cromwell's death. She used the real names of the people involved—Fleetwood, Lambert, Desbro, and even Whitelocke, Lord Willoughby's brother-in-law—but imposed an absurd comic plot that made their political maneuverings look like so much bumbling. It was odd that she should have chosen that year and those characters for her satire: Thomas Scot, whose name does not appear in the play, was also on the Committee of Safety, and it was in 1659 that Lady Willoughby betrayed Lord Willoughby and the Royalist plot to him. None of these are mentioned either, but Desbro, who figures prominently, had been one of the rebels Aphra and William Scot spied on in Antwerp. Was Aphra drawing on her own past in the plot or was it simply now so distant that she no longer remembered or felt any connection?

Although *The Roundheads* was well received, it is in the end not a very good play, the clumsy combination of politics and comedy betraying, perhaps, over-hasty composition. Mrs. Behn repaired her errors, however, in *The City Heiress; or, Sir Timothy Treatall,* which achieves a perfect balance. The play is a viciously funny political caricature of the Whig leader Shaftesbury (Sir Timothy). It was dedicated to Henry Howard, whose great-uncle William Howard, Viscount Stafford, had been beheaded in the heat of the Popish Plot. Thomas Otway wrote a prologue for the play, and both he and Aphra were soon under fire in an anonymous lampoon, probably by Shadwell, on "The Tory Poets": "Poetess Aphra, though she's damn'd today,/ Tomorrow will put up another play;/ And Otway must be pimp to set her off/ Lest the enraged bully scowl, and scoff,/ And hiss, and laugh, and give not such applause/ To Th' City Heresy as The Good Old Cause."[10]

Even political assault had to take up the old accusation of immodesty: but then after all what could be more "public" than politics? Another satirist who wrote of her on the same occasion ignored altogether her political statement and concentrated his vituperation on the theme Aphra was so familiar with: "That clean piece of wit/ *The*

City Heiress by chaste Sappho writ,/ Where the lewd widow comes with brazen face,/ Just seeking from a Stallion's rank embrace,/ T'acquaint the Audience with her filthy case.*/ Where can you find a scene for juster praise,/ In Shakespeare, Jonson, or in Fletcher's Plays?"[11] There was indeed a "loose" widow in the play, but everyone knew that the "lewd widow" was also Aphra, Mrs. Behn.

Her political efforts came to an abrupt end a few months later when she overstepped her domain an inch too far. In an epilogue written for an anonymous play called *Romulus and Hersillia* (August 1682), she pilloried Monmouth for desertion of his father. Charles, who was at once enraged by his son's rebellion and very fond of him, acted on the second feeling and promptly had Aphra and Lady Slingsby, the actress who had spoken the derogatory lines, arrested by the Lord Chamberlain—Arlington. The charges read thus: "Whereas the Lady Slingsby and Mrs. Aphra Behn have by writing and acting at his Royal Highness's Theatre committed several misdemeanors and made abusive reflections upon persons of quality, and have written and spoken scandalous speeches without any license or approbation of those that ought to peruse and authorize the same, these therefore to require you to take into your custody the said Lady Slingsby and Mrs. Aphra Behn and bring them before me to answer the said offence, and for so doing this shall be your sufficient warrant. Given under my hand and seal this 12th day of August, 1682. To Henry Legatt Messenger of his Majesty's Chamber, etc."[12] Though the arrests were reported in the *Newdigate Newsletter* and the *True Protestant Mercury*, those newssheets do not indicate how long the ladies remained in custody. If they were even actually imprisoned for the offense, the incarceration was brief, for both were publicly in evidence not long after.

Aphra at least was considerably chastened. She produced no new plays for four years. The lines that had occasioned Mrs. Behn's disgrace were these: *"Of all treasons, mine was most accurst;/ Rebelling 'gainst a KING and FATHER first./ A sin, which Heaven nor man can e'er forgive."* Though Aphra's immediate aim had been to castigate Whiggish Duke of Monmouth, such a statement nevertheless seems strangely inconsonant with the personal politics she had defended from the outset of her career as a writer. To present rebellion against a *father* as the highest moral sin was out of character indeed when the

---

*seventeenth-century slang for a woman's sexual parts

whole of her literary work was implacably committed to the promotion of disobedience to parents, particularly to fathers, in the matter of marriage.

Tory doctrine of course assumed the identification of kingly authority with paternal right, but Aphra's Tory politics were never elaborated to a sufficient degree of sophistication to reveal the contradiction. She fiercely threw herself into the spirit of doing battle without considering the ideological implications of the stance she took. Like most Tories, she characterized Whigs as sniveling, pious Puritans and mercenary City traders. Aphra's prejudice makes emotional sense when her advocacy of free sexuality and her hatred of interest are considered. The incompatibility of her social and political ideas, however, proved even more apparent when, a short time later, she began to expand her attack on the society that enslaved young men and women through forced marriage.

IV

Those who with nine months toil had spoil'd a play
In hopes of eating at a full third day,
Justly despairing longer to sustain
A craving stomach from an empty brain,
Have left stage-practice, chang'd their old vocations,
Attoning for bad plays, with worse translations;
And like old sternhold, with laborious spite,
Burlesque what nobler muses better write.

—Anonymous,
"A Satyr on the Modern Translators," 1684

A few months after Aphra's arrest, the King's Company and the Duke's Company merged to become the United Company (November 1682). The King's Company had been on hard times for more than four years; at the end of 1677 a play by Dryden, its principal dramatist, brought in only a few shillings more than twenty-eight pounds. The house was less than half full.[13] When the company closed for part of 1678–1679, Dryden promptly went over to the rival company. His defection no doubt contributed still further to the decline. It must have been clear that the King's Company could not survive much longer when, in the spring of 1681, box-office receipts for nineteen days fell below the basic operating expenses. On May 11, 1681, the takings were three pounds, fourteen shillings, and six pence while the house rent alone came to five pounds, fifteen shillings.[14] The Duke's Company had been doing much better than the King's Company but its prosperity was only relative: many playwrights were complaining of the slender returns of their trade. *"Lord what a house is here, how thin 'tis grown,"* Mrs. Behn herself remarked in the prologue to her play *Like Father, Like Son,* which went on the boards about March 1682.

Even the combined resources of the two companies could not bring back the full audiences of the 1660s and 1670s. Worse still for the playwrights, the United Company now adopted a policy favoring the revival of old plays rather than the production of new ones. There were two reasons for this. First, it was more economical: no author's benefits had to be paid to a dead playwright. The second reason was that the actor/manager of the Duke's Company, Thomas Betterton, had now come into possession of the rights to act countless roles he had for years envied the King's Company.

The professional writers who had depended on the theater were in desperate need. Even the Poet Laureate, Dryden, was having a hard time staying solvent. In a letter to Lawrence Hyde, first Earl of Rochester, probably written in 1683, he begs for a half year's salary, pleading an impossible burden of debt, fear of arrest, and chronic ill health: "It is enough for an age to have neglected Mr. Cowley and starved Mr. Butler."[15] In December 1683, Dryden was given a small government post at a salary of five pounds a year, possibly at Hyde's suggestion. The other poets fared worse: "Otway can hardly guts from jail preserve,/ For though he's very fat, he's like to starve."[16] Wycherley, after having tried unsuccessfully to borrow twenty pounds from the printer of his play *The Plain Dealer* to meet obligations, was languishing in debtor's prison.

The hungry "tribe" began to cast about for other ways to add to their income. They dunned wealthy noblemen with dedications and composed eulogistic verses in their honor, which often brought concrete rewards.[17] During the Plot fever, political doggerel had been most profitable, but that trade had now fallen off to some extent. Fortunately, a new vogue for translation provided another outlet for eager pens. Already in 1680 a collective translation of Ovid's *Epistles* had come out with a preface by Dryden, who was also one of the

translators. Among the other collaborators were Thomas Otway, Elkannah Settle, Samuel Butler, Nahum Tate, Thomas Rhymer, and
Aphra Behn. In 1683, a young scholar (he was twenty-three) named
Thomas Creech created a sensation with a translation of Lucretius.
Aphra had befriended Creech and attempted to further his career
as she had Otway's; her generous praise prefaced the volume, along
with verses by Otway, Duke, and Evelyn.

Aphra Behn was very much at a disadvantage in this literary
game because, as she reminds Thomas Creech, her sex had excluded
her from classical training. She was forced to work from a rough literal translation done by someone else. Aphra had a literary precedent
for her procedure in Cowley's theory that "imitation" was more original than translation; and she thought it more interesting anyway to
"make the poem her own." Either out of a sense of fairness to the
reader or in expectation of criticism, she asked Dryden to mention her
ignorance of the language she was translating in his preface. He
complied gracefully: "I was desired to say that the author, who is of
the fair sex, understood not Latin. But if she does not, I am afraid she
has given us occasion to be ashamed who do." [18]

Even Dryden could not protect her from the inevitable attack,
which came in "A Satyr on the Modern Translators" (1684) and lam-
pooned "our blind translatress Behn":

> The female wit, who next convicted stands,
> Not for abusing Ovid's verse but Sand's;
> She might have learn'd from the ill-borrow'd grace,
> (Which little helps the ruin of her face)
> That wit, like beauty, triumphs o'er the heart
> When more of nature's seen and less of art:
> Nor strive in Ovid's letters to have shown
> As much of skill, as lewdness in her own.
> Then let her from the next inconstant lover,
> Take a new copy for a second Rover.
> Describe the cunning of a jilting whore,
> From the ill arts herself has us'd before;
> Thus let her write, but paraphrase no more. [19]

Aphra had used her "paraphrasing" freedom to introduce into Ovid's
Epistles an attack on the hypocrisy of sexual codes applying to feminine behavior, so in a sense she had brought the epithet "whore" on

herself. Her presentation of the issue was one of abstract principle, but she might well have expected to have her own life dragged into the satire, as it always had been. To accuse her of sexual adventuring and at the same time draw attention to the "ruin of her face"—past forty and far beyond the age of beauty in seventeenth-century eyes— seems gratuitously cruel.

In addition to her "translating," Aphra was in 1683 gathering up poems she had written over the years and working on a longer piece called *Voyage to the Isle of Love,* which she intended to publish in one volume. Beset by financial difficulties, she was having trouble finishing and wrote to her publisher, Jacob Tonson, asking him to increase her advance by just five pounds. It is the only letter extant which gives an idea of Aphra's literary dealings. Apparently Tonson had mediated some quarrel involving Dryden and Thomas Creech.

Deare Mr. Tonson,

I am mightly obliged to you for the service you have don me to Mr. Dryden; in whose esteeme I wou'd chuse to be rather then any bodys in the world; and I am sure I never, in thought, word, or deed merritted other from him, but if you had heard what was told me, you wou'd have excus'd all I said on that account. Thank him most infinitly for the honor he offers, and I shall never think I can do any thing that can merritt so vast a glory; and I must owe it all to you if I have it. As for Mr. Creech, I would not have you afflict him with a thing can not now be help'd, so never let him know my resentment. I am troubled for the line that's left out of Dr. Garth, and wish your man wou'd write it in the margent, at his leasure, to all you sell.

As for the verses of mine, I shou'd really have thought 'em worth thirty pound; and I hope you will find it worth twenty-five; not that I shou'd dispute at any other time for 5 pound wher I am so obleeged; but you can not think what a preety thing the Island will be, and what a deal of labor I shall have yet with it: and if that pleases, I will do the 2nd Voyage, which will compose a little book as big as a novel by it- self. But pray speake to your Brother to advance the price to one five pound more, 'twill at this time be more then given me, and I vow I wou'd not loose my time in such low gettings, but only since I am about it I am resolv'd to go throw with it tho I shou'd give it. I pray go about

*it as soone as you please, for I shall finish as fast as you can go on.
Methinks the Voyage shou'd com last, as being the largest volume. You
know Mr. Couly's David is last, because a large poem, and Mrs.
Philips her Plays for the same reason. I wish I had more time, I wou'd
ad something to the verses yet I have a mind too, but, good deare Mr.
Tonson, let it be 5 pound more, for I may safly swere I have lost the
getting of 50 pounds by it, tho that's nothing to you, or my satisfaction
and humour; but I have been without getting so long yet I am just on
the poynt of breaking, especiall since a body has no creditt at the
Playhouse for money as we used to have, fifty or 60 deepe, or more; I
want extreamly or I wo'd not urge this.*

Yours
A.B.

*Pray send me the loose papers to put to these I have, and let me know
which you will go about first, the songs or verses or that. Send me an
answer to-day.*

Aphra, whose successful plays of five or six years had brought
her from fifty to a hundred pounds for each production from box-
office receipts alone, must have been hard pressed indeed to quibble
over five pounds. Whether Tonson gave it to her is unknown. He was
renowned for his stinginess to authors, but on June 30, 1683, he nevertheless forwarded eleven pounds to the starving Thomas Otway.
Still, Tonson's revenues were not enormous, and at this point he was
supporting the whole crew of scribblers. He became known as the
"Muse's midwife," and his bookshop was a center for literary friendships, disputes, and the mediation of both. Tonson had published
Dryden's *Miscellany* and in 1685 came out with one by Mrs. Behn.
She included several poems of her own, as well as others by Rochester, Thomas Otway, Dorset (Buckhurst), Henry Neville (Payne),
Thomas Brown, Henry Crispe, Anne Wharton, a "Mrs. Taylor," and
an anonymous "Lady of Quality." Henry Crispe was Thomas Culpepper's young cousin, a native of Canterbury. The "Lady of Quality,"
who contributed the poem called "The Female Wits," remains unidentified, and nothing more is known of Mrs. Taylor other than the
text of her poem, which calls on "ye virgin powers" to protect her
from thought or act of immodesty. This last makes it unlikely that
she was merely a pseudonym for Mrs. Behn.

Sheer necessity had created a sort of literary coterie among the

professional writers and poetasters that must have been a sorry replacement for the high fun of the disbanded wits, but Aphra nevertheless attempted to keep up the spirit, despite the ruin of her face
and purse. She apparently carried on a witty correspondence with
Thomas Creech, for in the *Miscellany* of 1685 she printed a verse letter to him, "written in the Last Great Frost":

> *Daphnis, because I am your debtor,*
> *(And other causes which are better)*
> *I send you here my debt of letter.*
> *You should have had a scrap of nonsense,*
> *You may remember left at Tonson's.*
> *(Tho by the way that's scurvy rhime, Sir,*
> *But yet will serve to tag a line, Sir.)*
> *A billet deux* I had designed then,*
> *But you may think I was in wine then;*
> *Because it being cold, you know*
> *We warmed it with a glass—or so,*
> *I grant you that the wine's the devil,*
> *To make ones memory uncivil;*
> *But when 'twixt every sparkling cup,*
> *I so much brisker wit took up;*
> *Wit, able to inspire a thinking;*
> *And make one solemn even in drinking;*
> *Wit that would charm and stock a poet;*
> *Even instruct——who has no wit;*
> *Wit that was hearty, true, and loyal,*
> *Of wit, like Bayes' Sir, that's my trial;*
> *But say 'twas most impossible,*
> *That after that one should be dull.*
> *Therefore because you may not blame me,*
> *Take the whole truth as——shall fa' me.*

The winter of 1684 had been the coldest in memory, so icy that
the Thames froze over to a depth that would hold not only horses and
carriages, but tents, shops, and even a printing press. On January 6,
John Evelyn wrote: "I went across the Thames on the ice, now become so thick as to bear not only whole streets of booths, in which
they roasted meat, and had divers shops of wares, quite across as in a

---

*billet doux—a love letter

town, but coaches, carts and horses passed over."[20] On subsequent days, he noted the continuance of this frost, and on January 24 described the fair on the Thames with its sleds, skating, a bull-baiting, horse and coach races, puppet shows and interludes, cooks, tippling—a bacchanalian revel.

The merry carnival brought back memories of happier days before the Plot—spoiled for Aphra by a nasty accident. As she was returning from Whitehall Palace, her coach overturned on the slippery ice and she was prevented from keeping her appointment at Tonson's with Creech, where she intended to introduce him to "a wit uncommon and facetious"—John Hoyle. Her injuries were multiple, she told Creech in her letter: *"The scribbling fist was out of joint,/ And every limb made great complaint . . ./ Who saw me cou'd not chuse but think/ I looked like brawn in sowsing drink."* But her greatest loss, she maintained, was Thomas Creech's company.

The pleasure garden on the ice was the last celebration of Restoration spirit. The next winter, on February 6, King Charles was dead and with him closed an era. Aphra's beloved theater was operating in severely reduced circumstances; her means of income was seriously theatened; her world had been torn apart by political strife; her generation was quickly passing—dead or dying, starving, burned out, or simply given up to staidness. Sedley had retired to complacent middle age and domestic content in the country; Etherege was living a lonely exile in a foreign court and had ceased to write plays; Wycherley was helpless in debtor's prison. Buckingham, in ill health and political disgrace, was described by a contemporary letterwriter as "worn to a thread with whoring."[21] Rochester had been dead nearly five years: the deathbed confession in which he denied the validity of the life he had lived had been published and had gone through several editions already, as an example to other "sinners." It had been only three years or so since his cousin Anne Wharton thanked Aphra for her elegy on Rochester, but now she was dead too, only a few months after the King.

Aphra Behn's friend Nathaniel Lee, who like many of the playwrights found himself in a precarious financial position, began to suffer intervals of madness as early as 1682. His fits grew worse and worse until finally two years later he lost his mind altogether. In September 1684, according to Anthony Wood, he was committed to

Bethlehem Hospital for the insane—known to Londoners as Bedlam. Reactions to madness in the seventeenth century ranged from curiosity to ridicule, revulsion to censure, and its erratic treatment reflected those responses. Apparently Lee was for a time exhibited as a freak to fashionable ladies and gentlemen: *"that thy want of wit may be their sport."* Later, he was treated as though he were a common criminal. His fine head of hair was shorn, to his great shame and embarrassment when, in lucid moments, he missed it. He was chained to a wall and left in darkness for long periods. In an effort to "discipline" him out of his insanity, he was whipped and even starved. Wycherley callously played on this paradox in a poem whose argument was that Lee fared better safe in Bedlam than abroad in a mad and savage world: "You, but because you starved, fell mad before,/ Now starving does your wits to you restore."[22] For Nathaniel Lee, there could be no escape—starving was both cause and cure of his lunacy.

Aphra's "foster brother," Thomas Culpepper, was behaving strangely too: without any warning, he assaulted the Earl of Devonshire, who was standing at the entrance to His Majesty's bedchamber. The King, having witnessed the entire scene along with the diarist John Evelyn, ordered Culpepper incarcerated in the Marshalsea prison on the spot. He was afterward sentenced to have his hand cut off, but was saved through the intervention of his wife. The occasion of Culpepper's quarrel with the Earl of Devonshire was a piece of property the former laid claim to—on completely unreasonable grounds, as the courts to which he had applied had repeatedly told him. Culpepper was desperate for money, however, having sold his own estate ten years before and dissipated what small inheritance had fallen to him.

Perhaps most painful of all for Aphra was the gradual decline and final degradation of her brother of the pen Thomas Otway. She had first helped him on the stage, then encouraged and supported his career. In return, he had defended her publicly, kept up a close friendship, and shared countless witty adventures. Lacking Aphra's capacity for voluminous and rapid literary production, he had never been able to eke out more than subsistence from the theater, and in the past few years his revenues had clearly fallen even below that level. Like Greenhill and Rochester, he also seems to have impaired his health by systematic inebriation: "He never writes a verse but when he is drunk,"[23] wrote one contemporary.

Heavily in debt, Otway had retreated to the slums of Tower Hill early in 1685 to avoid joining Wycherley in prison. One account has it that he died of a fever contracted in his sordid surroundings; another, that he choked on a piece of bread he had begged after several days with nothing to eat. A narrative drawn from contemporary sources asserts that Mrs. Behn was the last of Otway's literary friends ever to see the playwright and poet. The Duchess of Portsmouth, Thomas Betterton, and some of Otway's theater friends had advanced him a sum of money to live on, with the provision that he go to Hampshire, a cheap place to live where he could presumably stay sober, and write another play. "Otway seemingly complied," the narrative continues, "[but] his friends were very uneasy at not hearing from him for some time, when in about three months they were informed that he had been seen in the outskirts of the town in a very mean garb. This they soon found to be true, on the receipt of some petitionary letters from him, which they were too much displeased with him to answer. He had now no resource but to apply to Mrs. Behn for the loan of five pounds, to enable him, as he termed it, to finish his play, which she generously advanced; but how agreeably was she surprised with the style and pathetical distress of four Acts of it almost finished which he shewed her! In her judgment it was superior to anything he had before written. The story was that of Iphigenia: she advised him to shew it to Mr. Betterton, adding, that she was sure it would compromise all differences. This he modestly declined till he had completed the whole. It is probable that at this time he went to his lodgings on Tower Hill. However, Mrs. Behn acquainted Mr. Betterton with this interview, who immediately made all possible enquiry after him, till about a month afterwards he was informed of his death on Tower Hill."[24] Like Rochester, Thomas Otway was only thirty-three years old when he died.

Aphra Behn could ill afford her generosity to the dying Otway; she may even have had to borrow five pounds herself to give him. Otway died in April 1685; on August 1, Aphra wrote to a moneylender who was obviously dunning her, trying to put him off for a while longer: *"Whereas I am indebted to Mr. Baggs the sum of six pound for the payment of which Mr. Tonson has obleged himself. Now I do hereby empower Mr. Zachary Baggs, in case the said debt is not fully discharged before Michaelmas next, to stop what money he shall hereafter have in his hands of mine, upon the playing my first play 'till this aforesaid debt of six pound be discharged."*[25]

Aphra was indeed reduced to narrow means if she could not hope to come by six pounds between August and Michaelmas. Apparently, she could no longer borrow from Thomas Betterton, whose interest lay in her survival as a writer. The decline in box-office receipts had made such advances impracticable, and now Aphra was in debt to a moneylender, a low species not remembered for understanding or generosity. In a dedication written at about this time, she complained that she had escaped being torn to pieces by her political enemies only *"to starve more securely in my own native province of poetry."* [26]

Aphra had written a wistful elegy on Charles II's death, and on James's accession she reiterated the loyalty she had many times before professed in a lengthy state-poem celebrating his coronation. No doubt she was hoping for some return for her poetic evocation of the "glorious light" of his monarchy. In an aside, she reminded him how tired, overworked, and impecunious his faithful servant was (whose only pleasure was the "sunshine" of his presence):

> *How e're I toil for life all day,*
> *With what e'er cares my soul's opprest,*
> *'Tis in that sunshine still I play,*
> *'Tis there my wearied mind's at rest.*

James may have helped her on this occasion, but he was far too oppressed with his own cares of state during most of his reign to worry about a poet's dilemma.

In addition to her poverty, Aphra was beginning to be chronically unwell. Her answer to Anne Wharton had been written *"in a fit of sickness,"* and the pain she spoke of then seems to have worsened. An anonymous attack on Aphra, probably written about 1686, viciously describes her miserable condition: "Doth that lewd harlot, that poetic queen/ Fam'd through Whitefriars, you know who I mean,/ Mend for reproof, Others set up in spight,/ To flux, take glisters, vomits, purge and write./ Long with sciatica she's beside lame,/ Her limbs distortur'd, nerves shrunk up with pain,/ And therefore I'll all sharp reflections shun,/Poverty, poetry, pox, are plagues enough for one." [27]

Mrs. Behn had already demonstrated herself a woman of extraordinary resource, however, and the last years of her life were to prove perhaps the most creative in her career—and certainly among the most important in terms of her contribution to the evolution of the novel in English literature.

CHAPTER THIRTEEN

Double Binds;
or, the Male Poet in Me

All I ask, is the privilege for my masculine part, the poet in me . . .
—Aphra Behn, 1686

What in strong manly verse I would express,
Turns all to womanish tenderness within.

—Aphra Behn, 1682

Monstrous! A woman *of the* masculine *gender.*

—Henry Fitzgeffrey, 1617

You may try—but you can never imagine, what it is to have a man's force of genius in you, and yet to suffer the slavery of being a girl.
—George Eliot, 1876

Mrs. Behn's verses are natural and cordial, written in a masculine style, yet womanly withal.

—Leigh Hunt, 1847

Thou wonder of thy sex! Thou greatest good!
The ages glory, if but understood.

—George Jenkins,
"To the Divine Astrea," 1686

I

Soft winning language will become you best;
Ladies ought not to rail, tho' but in jest.

—Lady Mary Chudleigh,
The Ladies Defence, 1701

Arrest, indisposition, poverty, and the difficulty of getting new work performed might discourage Aphra, but could not definitively exile her from the stage. In April 1686, four years after *The City Heiress* was acted, her play *The Lucky Chance* went on the boards of the Drury Lane Theater. A production of the United Company under Thomas Betterton, it was the only new play put on that month— among a paltry three, one of which was a private performance for the Court. Despite everything, Mrs. Behn's reputation for writing good theater drew a full house on the third day and she was well satisfied with her author's receipts. Her triumph also drew the by-now customary invective and character assassination from the self-appointed critics who still assembled at Will's Coffee House after the play to make or break its "fame" in the town. The abuse, as before, centered on Aphra's sex and it made her angrier than ever. She had proved herself over and over as a writer and still had to put up with being treated like an upstart—an impertinent female.

When the play was published in 1687, she added a manifesto to the text, defending herself from the old charges and demanding equal rights as a woman writer: *"The little obligation I have to some of the witty sparks and poets of the town, has put me on a vindication of this comedy from those censures I heartily excuse, since there is a sort of self-interest in their malice, which I should rather call a witty way they have in this age, of railing at every thing they find with pain successful, and never to shew good nature and speak well of any thing; but when they are sure 'tis damn'd, then they afford it that worse scandal, their pity. And nothing makes them so thorough-stitcht an enemy as a full third day, that's crime enough to load it with all manner of infamy; and when they can no other way prevail with the town, they charge it with the old never failing scandal—that 'tis not fit for the ladies: As if (if it were as they falsely give it out) the ladies were obliged to hear indecencys only from their pens and plays and some of them have ventured to treat 'em as coarsely as 'twas possible, without the least reproach from them . . . never taken notice of, because a man writ them, and they may hear*

that from them [which] *they blush at from a woman . . . Right or wrong*
[my plays] *must be criminal because a woman's; condemning them without
having the Christian charity to examine whether it be guilty or not, with
reading, comparing or thinking; the Ladies taking up any scandal on trust
from some conceited sparks, who will in spite of nature be wits and* beaus;
*then scatter it for authentic all over the town and court, poisoning of others
judgements with their false notions, condemning it to worse than death,* loss
of fame."

Foreseeing that she would be attacked on grounds of immodesty,
Aphra contends that before allowing the play to be acted, she took
the precaution of having it read by Davenant, Sir Roger L'Estrange
(who licensed it), Thomas Killigrew, the major players of the company, and *"several Ladies of very great Quality, and unquestioned fame."*
Since none of the aforementioned had signaled any indecency in the
play, the author felt confident, she said, in submitting her work to
the public. Continuing her justifications, Aphra catalogued the male
playwrights of her generation, naming scenes from the most ac-
claimed plays which might, according to the terms being applied to
her play, be called obscene. Indeed there are far more offending
scenes, she claims, in Etherege's *The Man of Mode* or Rochester's adaptation of *Valentinian* (the posthumous performance of which was
prefaced by her own prologue). But, as she notes with the acrimony
of experience, *"such masculine strokes in me must not be allowed."*

"Had I a day or two's time," Aphra continues, *"as I have scarce so
many hours to write this in (the play, being all printed off and the press
waiting), I would sum up all your beloved plays, and all the things in them
that are past with such silence by, because written by men . . . But 'tis in
vain by dint of comparison to convince the obstinate critics, whose business is
to find fault, if not by a loose and gross imagination to create them, for they
must either find the jest, or make it; and those of this sort* [i.e., the "immodest" sort] *fall to my share, they find faults of another kind for the men
writers. And this one thing I will venture to say, though against my nature,
because it has a vanity in it: That had the plays I have writ come forth
under any mans name, and never known to have been mine; I appeal to all
unbiased judges of sense, if they had not said that person* [herself] *had made
as many good comedies, as any one man that has writ in our age; but a
Devil on't, the Woman damns the poet."*

Many other women who came after, even when the figure of the
woman writer was a firmly established fact of the literary landscape,

would choose the expedient Aphra had disdained—that of signing a man's name to one's writing. It was her politic to defend herself rather than seek the protection of invisibility. Still, she could not prevent herself from feeling hurt and betrayed when even her close men friends behaved like all the rest:

"I cannot omit to tell you, that a wit of the town, a friend of mine at Will's Coffee House, the first night of the play, cry'd it down as much as in him lay, who before had read it and assured me he never saw a prettier comedy."

The logic of Aphra's argument has a strange contour: she posits first that the "obscenities" in her plays are no worse than any in those written by her male contemporaries, but then asserts that there is nothing immodest whatsoever in her writing. She maintains her *"conversation* * not at all addicted to the indecencies alleged . . . I would much less practice it in a play, that must stand the test of the censoring world . . . I must want common sense, and all degrees of good manners, renouncing my fame, all modesty and interest for a silly, saucy, fruitless jest, to make fools laugh, and women blush, and wise men ashamed; myself all the while, if I had been guilty of this crime charged to me, remaining the only stupid, insensible. Is this likely, is this reasonable to be believed by anybody, but the wilfully blind?"*

The Lucky Chance was, of course, as bawdy as any other play of the age—and both Aphra and her audience knew it well. What is more, its author had repeatedly affirmed her opposition in principle to the censorship of modesty; had published undeniably "indecent" poems; had been a scandalous friend to the libertine wits; and had made little attempt to hide her affair with John Hoyle. She was now in her mid-forties and had, as she said in a dedication written at about this time, lived through *"all the torments of love, before dully living without it."* [1] What interest or motive could she have in claiming "modesty" at this point?

First, there was her anger at what she had finally understood to be the impossible structure under which she must operate; that no matter what she had written, though it be only the chastest of dramas, the very fact that she had appeared so often on the "public" stage was alone sufficient to place her under the rubric of "immodest." But it also seems that however much she might reject the constraints

---

Conversation had a double meaning, covering both verbal and sexual intercourse.

of modesty, it nevertheless continued to function as a controlling ideology. No matter how radical her vision of a different reality, Aphra could not entirely cut herself off from the associations and ordering of her seventeenth-century feminine education.

The final plea of Aphra's manifesto conspicuously reflected this split consciousness: *"All I ask, is the privilege for my masculine part, the poet in me, (if any such you will allow me) to tread in those successful paths my predecessors have so long thrived in, to take those measures that both the ancient and the modern writers have set me, and by which they have pleased the world so well: If I must not, because of my sex, have this freedom, but that you will usurp all to yourselves; I lay down my quill, and you shall hear no more of me, no not so much as to make comparisons, because I will be kinder to my brothers of the pen, than they have been to a defenceless woman; for I am not content to write for a third day only. I value fame as much as if I had been born a Hero; and if you rob me of that, I can retire from the ungrateful world, and scorn its fickle favours."* The transversion of reference and category in this statement is complex: though Aphra was undoubtedly ironic in her reference to "the masculine part, the poet" in her, she was also quite serious. From the very beginning, she had acknowledged the definitions of her time in assigning beauty to the feminine domain and wit to the masculine. Elsewhere she maintained that it was women's education and not their innate capacities that excluded them from the field of wit, but a part of Aphra persisted in seeing herself as divided between the woman admired for her beauty, and the "masculine part," the writer. In doing so, she refused the woman writer whose rights she was defending, a literary "identity": if the activity of writing belonged to man's province, then the Aphra who wrote was a masculine self in a woman's body.

Mrs. Behn's half-conscious identification with the other sex in her capacity as a writer is further demonstrated by her stated desire *"to tread in those successful paths my predecessors have so long thrived in."* As a female playwright, she *had no predecessors*—in the prologue to *The Forced Marriage* she herself acknowledged the intrusion on a tradition that had been hitherto dominated by men. Still more remarkable was Aphra's declaration that she valued *"fame as much as if I had been born a Hero."* She is speaking of fame in its manly sense of "glory," as though the feminine sense—fame as synonymous with modesty—did not apply to her.

———— •

Most of the laudatory poems that preface the various collections of verse and translation that Aphra Behn published during her lifetime refer to her unique position astride two spheres and eulogize her as a masculine/feminine. "To Astrea on her Poems," by J. C., an encomium prefacing Mrs. Behn's *Poems upon Several Occasions* (1684), asserted that the authoress's poetry showed "the beauties of both Sexes joined."[2] John Adams, a minor poet who had contributed to both Dryden's and Mrs. Behn's poetical miscellanies, wrote of Aphra: "Neither sex do you surpass alone,/ Both in your verse are their glory shown,/ . . . While in the softest dress you wit dispense,/ With all the nerves of reason and of sense./ In mingled beauties we at once may trace/ A female sweetness and a manly grace."

A third poem in the same volume repeats the conventional equation of women with beauty, and men with mind in commendation of Mrs. Behn's gifts: "Oh, wonder of thy sex! Where can we see,/ Beauty and knowledge joined except in thee?/ Such pains took nature with your heavenly face,/ Formed it for love, and moulded every grace;/ I doubted first and feared that you had been/ Unfinished left like other she's within:/ I see the folly of that fear, and find/ Your face is not more beauteous than your mind./ . . . Never was soul and body better joined."

Evidently, Aphra's fellow poets felt it incumbent upon them to praise her beauty even though the purpose at hand was to recommend her poetry. If one remembers that Mrs. Behn was by now far past the age at which her contemporaries still considered a woman beautiful, and that she was no doubt further aged by her relentless work, poverty, and illness, the insistence on her physical charms in these poems seems almost perverse. It is true that Mrs. Behn had been considered most beautiful in younger days, but J. C. and John Adams were writing of the present. Probably they saw their assertions as a kindness to Aphra, but the constant reference to beauty was also a cultural tic: tribute to a woman could not ignore what society deemed praiseworthy in her (and modesty was quite out of the question in Aphra's case). By the same token, Aphra's detractors unvaryingly felt they must disparage her looks.

Interestingly enough, it is the poetry written in *appreciation* of Aphra that speaks of her "masculine" part; the satires and lampoons written against Aphra concentrate their attack on her femininity—portraying her as a "lost woman."

Daniel Kendrick, a poet and physician, went so far as to pompously report her a sex unto her own in his poem affixed to her *Lycidus* (1688):

> *Hail, beauteous Prophetess, in whom alone,*
> *Of all your sex Heaven's masterpiece is shown.*
> *For wondrous skill it argues, wondrous care,*
> *Where two such stars in firm conjunction are,*
> *A brain so glorious, and a face so fair.*
> *Two Goddesses in your composure joyn'd,*
> *Nothing but Goddess could, you're so refined,*
> *Bright* Venus Body *gave,* Minerva Mind.
> *How soft and fine your manly numbers flow . . .*
> *Ah, more than Woman! more than man she is.* [3]

Even for Aphra Behn's literary friends and admirers, she was still—as a woman writer—a "thing out of nature." They twisted what most of Aphra's world saw as a contradictory double into a combination that was complementary, but the essential vision nevertheless followed the traditional division of masculine and feminine spheres. That definition of what was proper to each sex, of course, would have said Aphra ought not to be writing at all. Aphra herself, as the history of her declarations well documents, vacillated between tacit acceptance of that definition, violent rejection of it, guilt at her transgression, and denial that she had violated any codes at all.

The Young King, which Aphra said was the first play she had ever written, dramatizes a strange sequence of sexual metamorphoses in which a young woman changes from male to female identity and back again—with the resulting confusion of "spheres." Aphra's heroine, Cleomena, has been brought up as an Amazon by her mother, the Queen of Dacia. [4] Cleomena has a brother who ought to be heir to the throne, but a prophesy has declared that terrible things will come to pass if he becomes King. Consequently, his sister has received the *"masculine"* education he was to have had; she is taught to be a *"Hero"* and trained in all the *"arts of war."* The Dacian courtiers are very much discontented at this perversion of nature and complain that the Amazon's mother, the Queen, *"breeds her more like a general than a woman. Ah, how she loves fine arms! a bow, a quiver! . . . if it were not for her beauty, one would swear* [she] *were no woman, she's so given to noise and fighting."* Cleomena's martial upbringing excludes the possibility of weakness or sentiment—"feminine" characteristics.

The Dacians, whom the Amazon princess is to lead to glory, are at war with the Scythians. Thersander, the Scythian prince, penetrates disguised into the enemy camp, where he falls in love with Cleomena—precisely because *"she scorns the little customs of her sex."* When in return she discovers herself in love with the prince, a symbolic transmutation of sex takes place: she finds she is *"all woman."* The (former) Amazon's lady-in-waiting, who is not yet aware of the transformation, has just been berating her mistress for "masculine" behavior, which she says is unnatural, even deformed, in a woman: *"I would excuse you, if you should now fall in love, here's* substance; *but that passion for fame alone, I do not like."* Fame is used here in its masculine sense, a synonym of the glory that heroes seek.

The princess replies: *"You charge me with the faults of education, that cozening* form that veils the face of nature, but does not see what's hid within . . . I have a heart all soft as thine, all woman . . . Oh Semiris! there's a strange change within me."*

Indeed. Falling in love with a man has transformed the Amazon into a woman. Her masculine "courage" vanishes, and she remarks with amazement: *"I find I am a perfect woman now, and have my fears and fits of cowardice."* A confusion of disguise leads her to believe that her lover has been assassinated, however, and the process is rapidly reversed: his murder, she says, *"creates me man."* She dresses up in his clothes and goes to fight the duel he was to have fought—except that through a mistake it is her own lover she wounds, believing him to be the murderer. In the end, the lovers rediscover each other, proper identities are assigned, and: *"The god of love o'ercomes the god of war."*

A special set of associations emerges from Mrs. Behn's vocabulary. Quite traditionally, love and war are opposed as feminine and masculine principles; but then "love" is defined as a natural state and "war" a deformation. Mrs. Behn takes the distinctions no further than this vague equation in *The Young King* but already in this earliest work there were the seeds of an idea she was to develop more clearly later on.

In a poem Aphra Behn published in her collection of 1684, en-

---

* false, deceiving

titled "A Farewell to Celladon, On his going into Ireland," she sets up a similar polarity, only in this case "love" is presented as the absolute value of an ideal state of nature. The verses were evidently written to a friend of hers—definitely *not* William Scot, the *former* Celladon—who had been sent by the King, whom she calls "Caesar," on some governmental or military errand to Ireland. In the guise of a pastoral farewell, Aphra elaborates a system of values that opposes the occupations of nature and those of society: until drafted by the *"mighty"* Caesar, Aphra's friend Celladon had *"unambitiously"* concerned himself with no other *"power than love."* This, Aphra remarks, is the state of innocence that the *"first man in Paradise"* knew. But Celladon, motivated by *"false ambition,"* has traded his paradise for a mess of pottage: *"though for empire he did Eden change;/ Less charming was, and far less worth."*

Celladon's natural virtue, contends Aphra, has been corrupted to *"cunning policy"* by his seduction into the world of State: *"Business debauches all his hours of love;/ Business, whose hurry, noise and news/ Even natures self subdues;/ Changes her best and first simplicity,/ Her soft, her easy quietude/ Into mean arts of cunning policy,/ The grave and drudging coxcomb to delude."* Don't let *"ambition,"* the poetess begs her friend, destroy *"nature's first intent."* She knows her plea is in vain, however, because he will not refuse the honor "Caesar" has conferred on him—but she is reminding him nevertheless of the other self, the other sphere he has chosen to forego.

The dialectic of opposing spheres in Aphra's poem in certain respects resembles the conventional division between masculine and feminine universes. Love, naturally, had been by tradition the primary occupation of women and only entered men's lives as a passing interest, or as one interest among others. This commonplace was still a cliché a century later, when Mary Wollstonecraft termed "feeling the only province of woman, at present," and her younger contemporary Byron wrote: "Man's love is of man's life a thing apart,/'Tis a woman's whole existence."

If one separates the vocabulary of Aphra's poem according to the "spheres" that are antithesis, the principle of division becomes clear: *"mighty," "ambition," "empire," "business," "statesman," "false," "dictates," "great,"* and *"world,"* are opposed to *"plain," "unambitiously," "simplicity," "nature," "carelessness," "joy," "groves," "soul," "beauty," "love."* Mrs. Behn's antipodal categories draw on contemporary conceptions of masculine and feminine domains insofar as the first represents the business of the world and empire and the second the "business" of love and beauty. But Aphra has tied the spheres to a parallel set of definitions: society/nature; corruption/innocence; deception/truth. She has in effect assigned value judgements, but in so doing reverses the order of importance: the lesser "feminine" principle of love is revalued over the "masculine" empire. Aphra does not, however, exclude men from her paradise, but invites them to give up *"false ambition"* and enter.

Aphra's vision of an ideal state of nature in which love is the key to freedom runs through much of her work, but its fullest articulation is in her poem "The Golden Age." The latter, as she described it, was a perfect epoch of precivilization: *"The stubborn plough had then,/Made no rude rapes upon the virgin earth;/ Who yielded of her own accord her plentious birth."* Civilization is rape here; and the act is performed upon the female body of the earth, who before the denaturing influence, had yielded *"of her own accord."* In fact in that *"unsullied age,"* Aphra continues:

> *Then no rough sound of wars alarms,*
> *Had taught the world the needless use of arms:*
> *Monarchs were uncreated then,*
> *Those arbitrary rulers over men:*
> *Kings that made laws, first broke 'em, and the gods*
> *By teaching us religion first, first set the world at odds.*

Ambition was unknown then, and each man was *"lord o'er his own will alone"*: his innocence served for religion and law. No external restraints were needed before society polluted man's natural goodness. Aphra's men of nature shared equally in all necessaries plentifully supplied by the green world they lived in. It was the "civilizing" influence, she says, that divided up the earth and set each man against the other.

> *Right and property were words since made,*
> *When power taught mankind to invade:*
> *When pride and avarice became a trade;*
> *Carried on by discord, noise and wars,*
> *For which they bartered wounds and scars;*
> *And to inhance the merchandize, miscalled it, fame,*
> *And rapes, invasions, tyrannies,*
> *Was gaining of a glorious name:*

Styling their savage slaughters, victories;
Of the ill-natured busy great,
Nonsense, invented by the proud . . .
Thou wert not known in those blest days.

Aphra has drawn an astoundingly radical connection of conclusions from her original premise. In enumerating society's disfigure-
ments she has attacked war, monarchy, religion, laws, competition,
property, money, trade, and honor. According to her, the source of
all these evils is in the struggle for power: the corrupting desire to
dominate another human being. All crimes (rapes, invasions, tyranny)
are committed in the interest of establishing this hierarchy, which is
maintained through the institutions of *"right and property"* and the
false ideologies of *"fame," "name,"* and *"honor"*—war as chivalry;
family or title as social status; filial obedience as moral duty.

The next section of Aphra's poem translates the political position
taken to the question of power struggle between the sexes. In the first
state, she asserts, women were not bound by the dictates of modesty.
Free love was the rule. It was the concept of honor that made love a
sin: *"Honour! thou who first didst damn,/ A woman to the sin of shame."* A
principle foreign to feminine instinct, states Aphra's poem, this cir-
cumscription has been imposed on the fair sex as a correlative to property and inheritance.

The implication of Aphra's contention seems to be that the
despoiling of natural goodness may be laid at the door of the "masculine" principle of aggression and acquisition as well as the oppressive
social machinery that this process has spawned. The principle is only
masculine in its symbolic provenance, however, for it can be said to
exploit men as well a women. If the female sex is the more obviously
confined, men like Aphra's "Celladon" are nonetheless deprived as
well in a different way.

Aphra Behn propounded her revolutionary attack on the concepts of social hierarchy, property, and repressive sexual codes with
just as much sincerity as she had given to her advocacy of Toryism.
The former was gradually developed over a period of time as a theme
that appeared first episodically and then more insistently in her work
and was not fully articulated until the end of her life, whereas the latter was dogmatically defended party allegiance in the context of an
immediate political dispute. In the fervor over the Popish Plot, fam-

ily alliances and emotional ties were often more important than the ideological issue at hand. Nevertheless, no two philosophical systems could be more opposed than Aphra's revolutionary and Tory thinking: once again, she was at odds with herself.

Aphra's questioning of the property system has much more in common with the convictions of Gerrard Winstanley, a radical Puritan, than with those of the Royalists, who represented first and foremost the interests of the landed aristocracy. Winstanley held that all property was theft, as God had given the earth to all mankind in common: "the earth was not made purposely for you to be lords of it," he told the landowners of England in 1649, "and we to be your slaves, servants and beggars; but it was made to be a common livelihood to all, without respect to persons."[5] Despite the wide difference in style and expression, Winstanley's idea was very close to Aphra's, though she would certainly have been irritated by the association. The sources of Winstanley's thought were fundamentally different from Aphra's, however: his text was the Bible and hers nature itself. The concept of original sin was central to Puritanism, and that premise was precisely what Aphra Behn was rejecting. What she and Winstanley shared was a radical impulse toward freedom and a demand for the right of human beings to act according to individual conscience.

Few of Aphra's contemporaries realized the latent revolutionary implications in her theory of man's original goodness—no doubt partly because her early elaboration of it was couched in language and imagery that drew heavily on the clichéd pastoral tradition. But it was also an idea very much in advance of the times. Englishmen were busy working out a division of power between Parliament and the King: few would have been sympathetic to a questioning of the validity of power or property altogether. It was not until more than half a century later that Jean Jacques Rousseau's working-out of the philosophy would provide the impetus for the unprecedented reversal of social order that was the French Revolution.

II

If Aphra Behn had begun to develop strangely un-Tory-like political theories near the end of her life (all the while maintaining emotional loyalty to the royal cause), she also took a new direction in her writing. In 1684, the same year she published "The Golden Age," Aphra ventured a fictional enterprise that was to become known as a "novel": a word which had not yet taken on its later meaning and for many of Aphra's contemporaries still simply meant "news" or "new." Her fiction, called *Love Letters from a Nobleman to his Sister,* was in fact an extraordinarily accurate account of real events. Mrs. Behn supplied the imagined details of scene and dialogue, but the plot drew upon a scandal that was on the tongue of every gossip in London.

In August 1682, a nobleman named Lord Grey of Werke absconded with Lady Henrietta, fifth daughter of the Earl of Berkeley, whom he removed from the safety of her father's estate near Epsom. The young lady was his sister-in-law. Lady Henrietta was at the time less than eighteen years old, but the affair had been going on for three or four years already. The legitimate Lady Grey, Henrietta's older sister, had been involved in a previous scandal in 1680, when it was rumored that she had been carrying on an affair with one of Lord Grey's closest friends, the Duke of Monmouth. Lord Grey publicly refused to admit that his friend would compromise him, but nevertheless ordered Lady Grey to leave London for their country estate, giving her only a day's notice to pack.

It may have been that Lord Grey used this incident to blackmail his wife into accepting his "incestuous" love affair; Henrietta, however, was under the impression that she had successfully deceived her older sister. Shortly before the elopement, her mother, Lady Berkeley, discovered the younger daughter writing to Grey: "My sister . . . did not suspect our being together last night, for she did not hear the noise." [6] Apparently they were making love right under the wronged sibling's nose.

This piece of evidence was presented in the trial when, on November 23, 1682, Lord Grey was accused before the King's Bench of debauching the unmarried Lady Henrietta Berkeley, whom he presumed to call "my dear Lady Hen" before the Lord Chief Justice himself. The Earl of Berkeley demanded that his daughter be returned to him, and Lady Henrietta publicly declined to go. It was then revealed that Lord Grey, having foreseen this eventuality, had taken the precaution of marrying his mistress to a factotum of his, a Mr. Turner. This new information provoked a series of violent eruptions between father and daughter in court, which read like dialogue in one of Aphra Behn's plays:

EARL OF BERKELEY: "Hussy, you shall go home with me."
LADY HENRIETTA: "I will go with my husband."
[Supposedly she meant Mr. Turner.][7]

Lord Grey was found guilty and the rebellious Lady Henrietta imprisoned in the Marshalsea for one whole night, but no sentence was ever passed, as the Earl of Berkeley had reconsidered the wisdom of pressing charges to their ultimate end.

Less than half a year later, Lord Grey was once again the talk of London when he was implicated with the Duke of Monmouth, Algernon Sidney (Thomas Culpepper's uncle and Thomas Scot's fellow republican, it will be remembered), and Lord William Russell in a plot to assassinate King Charles on his way home from meeting Parliament in Oxford at the end of March 1683. Unlike the invented Popish Plot, this scheme was no fiction: it was afterward called the Rye House Plot, named for the house in which the conspirators met to execute their plan. Algernon Sidney was executed on Tower Hill for his part in the plot, but Lord Grey managed to escape through a disguise and shortly afterward sailed to the continent with Lady Henrietta.

It was exactly the sort of story to appeal to Mrs. Behn—romance, parental disobedience, defiance of social codes, political intrigue, incest, disguise, escape, betrayal. Added to which, it was a subject very much in the public imagination and therefore capable of having some salutary effect on Mrs. Behn's tenuous finances, if it could sell a good number of copies. The particulars of what happened between Lord Grey and his sister-in-law had been liberally brought out at the trial in 1682, and the rest Aphra logically inferred. The characters were disguised under type-names common to the romances and pastoral poetry of the day (Caesario for the Duke of Monmouth; Philander for Lord Grey; Myrtilla for Lady Grey; Sylvia for her sister Henrietta; Brillard for Mr. Turner; and Hermione for Monmouth's mistress, Lady Wentworth).

Contemporary readers had little difficulty identifying the characters. The original owner of one of the copies of the novel, now in the

Bodleian Library, Oxford, had carefully inscribed the date of Lord Grey's elopement with Lady Henrietta on the title page, and in an elegant seventeenth-century script assiduously supplied the real names of all the personages mentioned in the text. *Love Letters from a Nobleman to his Sister* indeed proved popular, and Mrs. Behn wrote two more parts in the course of the next four years, continuing the narrative as it developed in reality. All the evidence indicates that Mrs. Behn's audience took it quite simply as real, despite some of the high-flown language of romance (which would not have been regarded then as utterly out of the ordinary). The characters were accurately drawn—for instance, the Duke of Monmouth's obsession with astrology and naïve credence in magic is well documented by historical sources.

The first part of *Love Letters from a Nobleman to his Sister* was written in the form of a series of letters between Lord Grey and Lady Henrietta—Philander and Sylvia—in which the history of her resistance to seduction, on the grounds of honor and fear that she will be rejected once "spoiled," is recounted. She finally gives in, and after a while Philander, true to his Cavalier name and character, tires of her and wanders to other female conquests. When Sylvia discovers his infidelity, she is at first crushed, but shortly takes up defense by imitating him. While Philander is away on business, Sylvia charms a wealthy young man who is ignorant of her history and whom she schemes to marry. At the last moment, he chooses to become a monk and eludes her. Mrs. Behn does not disguise her revulsion at her heroine's grasping mercenary motives: *"She was not of a nature to die for love; and charming and brave as Octavio was, it was perhaps her interest, and the loss of his considerable fortune, that gave her the greatest cause of grief . . . for she had this wretched prudence, even in the highest flights and passions of love, to have a wise regard to interest."* Aphra, as her life and work well documented, had little but scorn for women who valued money over love.

Another woman in the novel is actually punished because she demands five hundred pistoles for her favors—and doesn't even need it, as she is married to a rich man and lives in luxury. The young man, her suitor, who has been in love with her until he discovers that she can be had only for money, is disgusted and shows his disdain by making love to her maid, almost within her hearing. The maid gives herself freely simply because she is attracted to her mistress's suitor, and her lady is spurned and humiliated.

At the same time, Mrs. Behn's disapproval of Sylvia's attitude toward money is somewhat mitigated by a consciousness of her vulnerable position. The young woman's hard-heartedness is very much connected to objective circumstance: *"She considers her condition in a strange country, her splendor declining, her love for Philander quite reduced to friendship, or hardly that,"* and comes to the conclusion that she must exercise her charms while they last. *" 'Twas a loss of time her youth could not spare."* The example of Hermione, *"whose charms of youth were ended, being turned of thirty,"* was warning enough. The latter was forced to *"fortify her decays with all the art her wit and sex were capable of."*

The first part of *Love Letters* was in epistolary form, but the two subsequent parts were narrated by a first person, whose "I" entered the story periodically to describe certain events or fill in information for the reader. One such intrusion is particularly interesting: Aphra—"I"—gives a lengthy and densely described account of Octavio's ordination into the Order of St. Bernard. *" 'Twas upon a Thursday this ceremony began, and as I said, there was never anything beheld so fine as the church that day was, and all the Fathers that officiated at the High-Altar . . . for my part, I confess, I thought myself no longer on earth; and sure there is nothing gives us an idea of real heaven, like a church adorned with rare pictures, and those other ornaments of it, with what can charm the eyes; and music, and voices to ravish the ear; both of which inspire the soul with unresistable devotion; and I can swear for my own part, in those moments a thousand times I have wished to die; so absolutely had I forgot the world, and all its vanities; and fixed my thoughts on heaven."* Aphra goes on to narrate the ordination, filling in precisely the visual, aural, tactile, and material details she observed: boys in white, bearing silver censers, cast incense all around; other boys strewed flowers upon the inlaid pavement; the spectators were silent; the whole order of St. Bernard came in, two by two, went up to the altar, and then retired to their gilded stalls. Next, fifty singing boys proceeded in, dressed in white cloth of silver, with golden wings and rosy droplets. Finally Octavio himself entered the sanctuary, attended by two young noblemen and dressed also in white cloth of silver, embroidered with gold, lined with rich cloth of gold and silver flowers, buttoned with diamonds.

As Aphra earlier explains, the Order of St. Bernard was special in that it did not require a vow of austerity, like the Jesuit or other orders, but only a vow of chastity and retreat from the world; the aristocrats who made up the greater part of the Bernardines were allowed to live in luxury that at least moderately resembled what they had formerly been used to. Aphra's extensive knowledge of the elaborate ceremonies, orders, and furniture of the Catholic Church was indeed unusual, given the public mood of her time. It is utterly impossible that she should have observed such a ritual in England, which raises the question whether she had actually done so on the Continent. In a later work, *The Fair Jilt,* she says she frequently visited the Franciscan friars in Antwerp, where she may have gained some knowledge of the Bernardines as well though the two orders were very different.

However she came by her knowledge, the mere recitation of it would certainly have classed her as a rabid papist in many minds. But perhaps it was not given serious notice, since Mrs. Behn's identification with the atheists was well established. Nor did she, like Dryden, ever make any public statement of conversion or belonging to the Church outside of the very strong hints presented under the cover of "fiction."

The third and last part of *Love Letters,* published in 1687, followed Monmouth's life to its end and reported in accurate particular his meetings on the Continent with Lord Grey, their plottings of rebellion against the newly-crowned James II, and the final defeat of hope at the Battle of Sedgemoor in 1685. Lord Grey commanded the cavalry of the Whig forces, which fled in disorder before the more highly trained and better equipped Royal troops. Monmouth, it is said, accused his friend of cowardice and, worse, betrayal at the crucial moment. It is difficult to tell whether the loss of the battle can be actually laid at Lord Grey's door, but the fact that Monmouth was condemned to die while the wily Lord Grey once again escaped execution to live to a prosperous old age hardly makes him look a hero.

Aphra's account is borne out by historical evidence—even to the detail of her representation of the begging letters Monmouth wrote to his uncle, James II, and the Dowager Queen Catherine, hoping for a reprieve.

III

Men have had every advantage of us in telling their own story. . . .
Education has been theirs in so much higher a degree; the pen has been
in their hands.

—Jane Austen,
Persuasion

Love Letters from a Nobleman to his Sister was Aphra Behn's first published novel, but a reference in a later narrative, *The Fair Jilt* (1688), seems to indicate that she may have been working toward this transformation of both personal and collective history into literary form for some time. When Aphra mentions the "Journal-Observations" she kept during her residence in Antwerp in 1666, she implies that it is the particulars and events recorded therein from which she has constructed her story. She speaks of this journal as though keeping it were a habitual exercise; perhaps it was written with the idea of garnering material for future literary use. The process of turning experience into fiction can clearly be seen in Aphra's "letters" from Antwerp, which One of the Fair Sex reprinted in her biography of Mrs. Behn (as opposed to her official spying letters preserved in the Public Record Office). The story told in the "letters" is clearly based in part on real events and the characters drawn from William Scot and Thomas Corney, but the narrative itself resembles an early, unsophisticated version of the later novels. Perhaps it might even have been a rough draft of a story Mrs. Behn intended to rework and publish, which One of the Fair Sex fell heir to among her literary remains. In any case, it illustrates a stage in the evolution of Aphra Behn's fiction from source to form.

Aphra wrote fourteen novels, counting the three parts of *Love Letters,* but published only six during her lifetime: *The Fair Jilt, Oroonoko,* and *Agnes de Castro* in 1688; *The Lucky Mistake* and *The History of the Nun* in 1689, the year she died. Posthumously published were *The Adventure of the Black Lady, The Court of the King of Bantam, The Unfortunate Happy Lady, The Nun; or the Perjured Beauty, The Wandering Beauty, The Unfortunate Bride, The Dumb Beauty; or the Force of Imagination,* and *The Unhappy Mistake.* Even considering that these early fictions were much shorter than the length we now expect of novels (except for the prolix *Love Letters*), this was an astounding output if, as seems probable, none was actually written in final form before the last few years of Mrs. Behn's life.

Composition of the posthumously published *The Court of the King of Bantam* can be dated definitely to a period between 1683 and 1685, and internal evidence also places the writing of *The Black Lady* and *The Unfortunate Happy Lady* before 1685. Why Mrs. Behn failed to publish these at the time they were written, when she was so desperately in need of money, is hard to understand. Publishers may have been wary of a new medium that was for the most part untried.[8] The topical scandal behind *Love Letters* was sure to sell copies, and long romances had a wide audience; but the strange fictional creations Aphra Behn was beginning to produce were not yet quantifiable.

In writing plays and poetry, Aphra Behn was stepping into a tradition whose language, form, and metaphors had already been shaped. It was a literary heritage she could not have the same access to as the male writers of her generation who were educated in universities did. As poetry increasingly modeled itself on classical prototypes, Mrs. Behn's disadvantage in that field became more noticeable than it might have been otherwise. Even so, poetry presented at least a possibility of individual direction because of its private character; whereas the highly conventionalized theater had rules and imperatives that Aphra could not ignore. She had to imitate, though her special concerns nevertheless run through the works as a second, subversive voice that surfaces into statement from time to time, like an underground stream bubbling up.

The very novelty of the "novel," however, presented Aphra with an opportunity to define and construct her own literary universe. Though she drew on some of the formal characteristics of the historical romances her generation read with avidity, the principal architecture of her fictional world grew out of her own experience—which included the vicarious experience of gossip about people she knew or did not know. This association with oral rather than written tradition is quite clear in the opening lines of Aphra's story *The Wandering Beauty:* "*I was not above twelve years old, as near as I can remember, when a Lady of my acquaintance, who was particularly concerned in many of the passages, very pleasantly entertained me with the relation of the Lady Arabella's adventures, who was eldest daughter to Sir Francis Fairname, a gentleman of noble family, and of very large estate in the West of England.*"

This "I" was something new not only in literature but in history. It was a very early example of the growing self-consciousness of the individual, which would, in the next century and a half, develop into a "given" in the way people thought about themselves. Aphra's focus on individual experience and self-expression was historically avant-garde. As historians of autobiography have recently demonstrated, that form of writing did not fully evolve into the personal history we now define it as until the late seventeenth century.[9] Narcissus Luttrell's diary, written while Aphra Behn was alive, is still primarily a culling of his reading of newspapers rather than a record of his own thoughts and feelings. Samuel Pepys, writing only a short time before, was moving toward the new ethos of individualism. His diary, written in a mysterious cipher and unknown to his contemporaries, was, like most works of a "private" nature then, not published until much later. To have had the idea of bringing the private sphere of personal experience into the published domain of fiction was an original achievement—and one that set Aphra far ahead of most of her literary colleagues.

Mrs. Behn was eager to distinguish her texts from the historical romance and emphasize their source in life. *Oroonoko* begins, *"I do not pretend, in giving you the history of this royal slave, to entertain the reader with the adventures of a feigned hero, whose life and fortunes fancy may manage at the poet's pleasure."* This claim to veracity was by no means entirely new. It was a device that romance writers had used in the past; but Aphra fortifies her conception by introducing into the story realistic description, a certain amount of objectively verifiable information, and a number of autobiographical details.

That Aphra's claim to veracity had its roots in a desire to establish the story as part of her own experience rather than in a self-conscious literary device is underlined by her statement in the preface of *The Fair Jilt* (1688), dedicated to Henry Neville (Payne), where she described her "novel," thus: *"It is the truth: truth, which you so much admire. But 'tis a truth that entertains you with so many accidents diverting and moving, that they will need both a patron, and an assertor in this incredulous world. . . . I desire to have it understood that this is a reality, and matter of fact, and acted in our latter age. . . . . Tarquin* [Aphra's hero] *. . . I have often seen, and you have heard of, and* [his] *story is well known to yourself, and many hundred more: part of which I had from the mouth of this unhappy great man, and was an eye-witness to the rest."*

Aphra Behn substantiates her assertion by autobiographically pinning down the action of the story: Prince Tarquin *"arrived at Antwerp about the time of my being sent thither by King Charles,"* she says, and elsewhere mentions that Castel Roderigo was then Governor of Flanders. At the end of the story, Aphra states that *"since I began this relation* (presumably 1687 or 1688), *I heard that Prince Tarquin dy'd about three-quarters of a year ago."*

Modern literary critics, taking their cue from Ernest Bernbaum's statement that Aphra Behn was "lying," have commonly described the hero of *The Fair Jilt* as an outrageously romantic invention, just as they have denied that Aphra ever went to Surinam. The historical evidence for her presence in that place and for the accuracy of her description has since been well documented. As for Prince Tarquin, it has recently been pointed out that not only did Prince Tarquin really exist, but certain events in the narrative—which critics have used to illustrate Mrs. Behn's reputedly uncontrolled taste for the fantastic— were actually reported in *The London Gazette* at about the time she maintained they took place. Her spying letters in the Public Record Office supply further testimony to the fact that she certainly was in Antwerp and in a position to observe what she said she had seen.

What is particularly interesting about these revelations is that there was some truth to her claim to truth: she was not, like other writers, merely repeating a story-telling convention, but signaling a new kind of relation of writer to narrative.

The value and nature of Aphra Behn's contribution to the novel form has been the subject of much dispute among scholars. It is generally held that the first literary works in the English language that may properly be called novels were Daniel Defoe's *Robinson Crusoe* (1719) and Samuel Richardson's *Pamela* (1740). The first is so considered because of its unity of theme and its realistic recreation of the world through description, and the second because of its development of character in which inner reality is important. Aphra Behn began to write her "novels" thirty-six years before *Robinson Crusoe* and more than half a century before *Pamela;* and the innovative elements that each of these later novels is known for are unquestionably present in her work.

Ian Watt, in *The Rise of the Novel,* defines the most important characteristic distinguishing the novel from the other forms of romance or epic as "the production of what purports to be an authentic account of the actual experience of individuals."[10] Flaubert describes this transcription of real life as *"le réel écrit."* One of the ways novelists have of supporting this verisimilitude is by anchoring the story in space and time through reference and description. Though Aphra by no means does this systematically, her conscious attempt to supply these elements in her stories is evident. The accretion of particulars and description that forms the fictional world Oroonoko moves in has been already detailed, but many of the novels set in England also contain references to commonly known—and therefore verifiable—facts or places. A character in Aphra's *The Court of the King of Bantam* lives, when he comes to town, in the Strand, somewhere near Charing Cross; another character takes lodgings in Germain Street (now Jermyn) and sends a note to *C—d,* the goldsmith at Temple-Bar; the company dines at Locket's and on two separate occasions attends the plays *A King and No King* and Ravenscroft's *The London Cuckolds.* Any contemporary of Aphra could have easily dated the action of the story even if she herself had not said it took place in 1683. Precise chronology is very much part of the material reality of the narrative; the author often gives the day of the week, the hour of the day, and the amount of time elapsed between one event in the story and another.

The argument that Aphra Behn's novels have strong elements of the romance in them are not without foundation. She was perfectly capable of inserting some unlikely coincidence or outrageously improbable event in the midst of her efforts to establish a realistic narrative, and one or two of her stories clearly belong to the category of romance rather than novel—*Agnes de Castro,* for example. As in much of Aphra's work, the contradiction between her elaboration of a new form and her concurrent repetition of the rejected convention is present in her novels.

One qualifying factor must be noted in the debate over the extent to which Aphra's novels may be said to be "realistic." Realism, says one literary historian, depends on the "correspondence between the literary work and the reality which it imitates." It must be remembered that the world Aphra Behn was describing was only beginning to apply scientific criteria to the examination of evidence: the separation between the natural and supernatural, reality and magic, miracle and fact, had not yet entirely taken place, as it had by the time eighteenth-century novelists were writing. A document written by William Byam, Deputy Governor of Surinam (whom Aphra mentions in *Oroonoko*), published in London in 1665 under the title *An Exact Relation of the most Execrable Attempts of John Allin Committed on the Person of His Excellency Francis Lord Willoughby, etc.*, amply illustrates the way in which the improbable was taken for granted as real.

Byam's relation served more or less as an official report of an assassination attempt made on Lord Willoughby by one Mr. Allin. In giving the defendant's background, he states that "on the 15th of Feb., 1659, [Allin] was accused and tried for horrid blasphemy, cursing the most blessed redeemer of the world, with expressions unfit to be named but by devils; at the instant recital of which . . . the very foundation of the house wherein they sat (I being then an auricular witness) gave a fearful crack, to the terrible annoyement of the trembling auditors." There was no doubt in the minds of any that this was, as Byam says, a "dreadful signal of divine displeasure."[11]

If some of the events in Aphra Behn's novels which the twentieth century terms "improbable" or "romantic" in fact mirror this reality, then they must at least be considered realistic according to seventeenth-century lights.

Whether or not one agrees that Aphra Behn's novels fulfill enough of the requirements in the definition of that genre to be considered "the first"—displacing *Robinson Crusoe* and *Pamela* and making Aphra initiator rather than precursor—it is nevertheless historically agreed that the advent of the novel more or less coincides with the entry of the woman writer into literature. It is also true that the novel was to prove the most important field in which lady writers would choose to exercise their pens: even though there were certainly novels written by men, it was a genre that, at least in the first two centuries of its life, would be identified with the fair sex. In addition to the large number of women writing novels in the eighteenth century, the readership was overwhelmingly female. Virginia Woolf, in *A Room of One's Own*, speculates that novel writing was taken up by women writers partly because it was a new domain and consequently one that they could make their own; whereas poetry had long belonged to the other sex, who had forbade them literature.

But there were other aspects of the genre that tied women to it: they had been the principal readers of its literary progenitor, the romance, whose principal subject was love. A great many men had scorned romances as "silly" works, preoccupied with concerns of lesser importance in "the world"—principally love. As the novel developed, it more and more came to focus its attention on the examination of relationships between people, on *feeling*—"the only province of woman," as Mary Wollstonecraft said. As the scientific revolution continued to widen the gap between subjective and objective, the subjective—or emotional—fell increasingly into feminine domain. In this way, the definition of fictional domain came to resemble closely what was tacitly considered the feminine sphere. Added to this, the practice of gossip—which under its most favorable definition may be understood as the collective examination of social relationships—has been traditionally the property of women. In this light, it seems perfectly logical that Samuel Richardson would choose to pretend that he was merely the editor of letters that had been written by a young woman named Pamela, in the same way that, nine years earlier, the French writer Marivaux presented his epistolary novel *La Vie de Marianne* (*1731*) as of feminine authorship. These writers evidently associated the sort of "inner reality" they were portraying as naturally belonging to a feminine world.

Of course Aphra Behn's "I" was necessarily feminine, but the importance of her sex in the narrator's point of view seems nevertheless to be quite deliberate. As the titles of her novels announce, they are, with only one or two exceptions, dominated by female protagonists. Aphra calls attention to the feminine perspective even in the dedication to Part Three of *Love Letters*, addressed to Robert Spencer, son of the Earl of Sunderland. She refers to Spencer's black reputation in the town and discounts its importance, except when his libertinism has proved injurious to her own sex. *"The women's quarrel to your Lordship has some more reasonable foundation, than that of your own sex,"* she writes. "[Women] *cannot but complain on that mistaken conduct of yours . . . squandering away that youth and time on many, which might be more advantageously dedicated to some one of the fair; and . . . rob 'em of all the hopes of conquest over that heart which they believe can fix nowhere . . .* [so that] *they are still upon their guard with you."*

This feminine quarrel with men is repeated by one of Aphra's heroines in a later novel through a peculiarly literary metaphor: *"Women enjoyed are like romances read,"* she tells her lover, who she is sure will leave her. " 'Tis expectation endears the blessing . . . when the plot's out you have done with the play, and when the last act's done, you see the curtain drawn with great indifferency." The "last act" was of course the sexual act—the curtain drawn on an enclosed, four-poster seventeenth-century bed.

The incapacity to give oneself entirely to another, or even to love in more than a passing fashion, is not limited to men, Aphra admits in *The History of the Nun; or the Fair Vow-Breaker* (1689). But women have been taught to practice deception by men, she contends: *"Perhaps, at first, by some dear false one, who had fatally instructed her youth in an art she had ever after practised in revenge . . . [to] conquer [men] at their own weapons."* The cynical attitude adopted by some women of her generation, Aphra says, is merely a form of self-defense, *"for without all dispute, women are by nature more constant and just than men, did not their first lovers teach them the trick of change. . . . But customs of countries change even nature herself, and long habit takes her place; the women are taught, by the lives of men, to live up to all their vices, and are become almost as inconstant. . . ."* Once again, Aphra is connecting natural goodness with the feminine and denaturing corruption with masculine "custom" and society.

If one makes an inventory of Aphra Behn's fiction, the central elements of most of the novels will be found within the definition of feminine sphere: the preoccupations are love, marriage, and the contingent negotiation of both between the sexes. Generally, the novels may be said to delineate a map of feminine possibility and limitation. As in Aphra's plays, there is a strong protest against the custom that denies young women the right to choose for themselves. *The History of the Nun* protests the two extremes of parental control over daughterly sexuality—forced marriage or the nunnery: *"I could wish,"* Aphra says, *"for the prevention of abundance of mischiefs and miseries, that nunneries and marriages were not to be entered into, till the maid, so destined, were of a mature age to make her own choice; and that parents would not make use of their authority to compel their children, neither to the one or the other."*

What appears still more persistently in the stories is the degrading intrusion of economic consideration into relations between the sexes—an old familiar theme of Aphra's, which she now put forth with all the force and precision of social realism. She is careful to name exact sums: in *The Unhappy Mistake*, Miles Hardyman, with an estate of four thousand pounds a year, whose sister Lucretia will have a portion of ten thousand pounds a year, cannot marry the young woman he loves, Lady Constance, because she has at her disposal only two thousand pounds for a dowry. Lucretia Hardyman, in love with Lady Constance's brother, is not permitted to entertain thoughts of marrying him: his estate is only twelve hundred pounds a year. *"(O the unkind distance that money makes, even between friends),"* comments narrator Aphra in parentheses. *"You are guilty of a foolish lazy passion,"* Miles Hardyman's father tells him; *"in love with one who can no way advance your fortune, family, or fame. 'Tis true, she has beauty, and o' my conscience she is virtuous too; but will beauty and virtue, with a small portion of two thousand pounds answer to the estate of nearly four thousand a year?"* This oppressive attitude causes the young man in question years of deprivation, misery, and exile before he finally achieves a happy ending.

In her equation of economic survival and marriage for young women and portrayal of their negotiation of possibility, Aphra Behn prefigured not only Richardson's *Pamela,* but the principal subject of Jane Austen's novels more than a century later. In *Pamela,* however, there is no real questioning of values: marriage is the ultimate reward; whereas Aphra Behn, though she sometimes allows her characters to marry happily, ultimately sees the institution as a corrupting force. In a novel like *Pride and Prejudice,* Jane Austen's irony exposes the savage struggle for survival in the marriage market that is masked by social politeness, but she views marrying *well* as the final and proper good. Her novels are a unified movement toward that goal, while Aphra's vacillate in the double structure of necessity and rebellion.

IV

L'homme est né libre et partout il est dans les fers.
> —Jean-Jacques Rousseau, *Le Contrat Social,*
> 1751

Oroonoko stands in a category by itself among all Aphra Behn's other novels. It is alone in having as its protagonist a man. Secondly, its subject matter, at least in appearance, is widely different from the love-and-marriage novels. Furthermore, its architecture is more complicated than Mrs. Behn's other fictions.

At the very outset of *Oroonoko*, Aphra returns to her theme of the natural goodness of man in a perfect state of nature. She describes the native Indians whom she had been able to observe firsthand in Surinam: *"These people represented to me an absolute idea of the first state of innocence, before man knew how to sin: and 'tis most evident and plain, that simple nature is the most harmless, inoffensive, and virtuous mistress. 'Tis she alone, if she were permitted, that better instructs the world, than all the inventions of man. Religion would here but destroy the tranquillity they possess by ignorance; and laws would but teach 'em to know offences, of which they now have no notion. . . . They have a native justice, which knows no fraud; and they understand no vice, or cunning, but when they are taught by the white men."*

It has been argued that this evocation of the virtues of "natural man" is simply an awkward digression inserted into a story whose principal interest lies elsewhere—in the hero, Oroonoko, who is not an untaught noble savage but has been educated as a European prince would have been, by European tutors. The interaction of these two ideals—symbolized by the "civilized" Oroonoko and the noble savage is essential to the story. However, they both serve to point up the corruption of the society that pretends to be more civilized than they are. Oroonoko's education in the chivalric tradition and his adherence to those standards ironically presents a degraded society with the very model of virtue to which it pretends to subscribe. In this sense, the novel corresponds to a kind of literature which was not to find its full expression until the Romantic revolt a century later. This phase in the history of the novel belongs primarily to the nineteenth century, however; hardly to Aphra Behn's seventeenth-century England.

Another element in the novel brings out the connection between the two themes defined above and ties it to Aphra's other fiction. *Oroonoko* is divided into two parts: the first takes place in Africa and focuses on the love affair between Oroonoko and Imoinda; the second shifts the focus to the hero's enslavement and efforts to gain his freedom in Surinam. Even after he rediscovers his beloved Imoinda in that country, they find they cannot be happy in slavery.

The protest against slavery clearly articulates the evil of regarding human beings as property to be bought and sold. In Oroonoko's stirring speech against slavery, he describes the moral savagery of such a system: *And why (said he) my dear friends and fellow-sufferers, should we be slaves to an unknown people? . . . No, but we are bought and sold like apes and monkeys, to be the sport of women, fools and cowards; and the support of rogues and runagades, that have abandoned their own countries for rapine, murders, theft and villanies. Do you not hear every day how they upbraid each other with infamy of life, below the wildest savages? And shall we render obedience to such a degenerate race, who have no one human virtue left, to distinguish them from the vilest creatures? Will you, I say, suffer the lash from such hands? They all reply'd with one accord, 'No, No, No'."*

Oroonoko's words could easily be extended to Aphra's attack on the social system that regarded women as property and promoted marriage for money. Love cannot exist without freedom, she would have said, and true freedom of love cannot survive in a world where men and women, feeling and desire, are subordinated to "interest" and the moral system that safeguards that material status quo.

Aphra's impassioned attack on the condition of slavery and defense of human rights in *Oroonoko* is perhaps the first important abolitionist statement in the history of English literature. There were a few other obscure voices raised in objection to the institution at the time, in the main marginal elements like religious dissenters (the Quaker George Fox for example). Certainly no other major literary figure producing work for a popular audience attempted such a subject until much later. *Oroonoko* was reprinted repeatedly in the eighteenth century and, along with the popular theatrical adaptation by Thomas Southerne, eventually became a rallying point for the abolitionist movement that grew into a political force more than a century after Aphra's death. In France, *Oroonoko*'s revolutionary implications were sooner recognized; first translated in 1745, it went through new editions in 1751, 1755, 1756, 1769, 1779, 1788, and 1799. A study of the catalogues of private libraries between 1750 and 1780 shows that it was one of the most popular books in eighteenth-century France—though now altogether unremembered.

Aphra's *Oroonoko* also was the beginning of another important connection: the historical alliance of abolitionism and feminism. In the nineteenth century, during the years that led up to the Civil War in America, the feminists agitating for women's rights were closely tied to, and in fact worked within, the groups fighting for the abolition of slavery. The progression from one to the other is logical, and on reflection, it is not surprising that women—who had so few rights themselves, who were considered the "property" of their husbands by the legal system—should best understand and sympathize with the position of slaves. The language of "slavery" was applied to the case of women very early on by feminist writers who came on the heels of Aphra's pioneering. The anonymous female author of the 1696 *Defense of the Female Sex* explicitly stated: "Women, like our Negroes in our western plantations, are born slaves, and live prisoners all their lives."[12] Mary Astell, in *Reflections on Marriage* (1706) wrote: "If all men are born free, how is it that all women are born slaves?"[13] That many women of the eighteenth century had come to feel that marriage, as it was defined and ordered by their society, resembled the deplorable state of slavery in which Negroes found themselves is confirmed by a letter Lady Mary Wortley Montagu wrote to her future husband: "People in my way are sold like slaves; and I cannot tell what price my masters will put on me."[14]

V

Thus died this great man, worthy of a better fate, and a more sublime wit than mine to write his praise. Yet, I hope, the reputation of my pen is considerable enough to make his glorious name to survive all ages.

—Aphra Behn,
Oroonoko, 1688

In addition to the impressive number of novels Aphra wrote in the last years of her life, she continued to produce a steady stream of verse on occasions of state, translations, and even an essay on prose translation. In 1686, *La Montre; or the Lover's Watch,* a translation from the French, was published; in 1687, a new comedy called *The Emperor of the Moon* went on the boards; Aphra wrote verses for Barlow's edition of Aesop, a long pindaric to Christopher, Duke of Albermarle, and a eulogy on the death of her old friend the Duke of Buckingham. 1688 saw the publication of two congratulatory poems on the birth of an heir to James II, a poem to Sir Roger L'Estrange, an attack on an anti-Royalist scribbler named John Baber, translations of Tallemant's *Lycidus* and Fontenelle's *History of Oracles* and

Discovery of New Worlds, to which a lengthy essay on the theory of translation was appended.

Despite her impressive literary output, Aphra's health was rapidly failing, and few of her friends remained who might offer her some relief from now chronic illness and poverty. On October 21, 1687, the poet Waller died. She had much admired him and evidently his daughter-in-law had asked her for some verses for a commemorative volume. Aphra gracefully complied, but in the accompanying letter excused whatever weakness they might betray thus: *"I am very ill and have been dying this twelve month, and (my verses) want those graces and spirit which possible I might have dressed 'em in had my health and dulling vapors permitted me."*[15] The poem began with these lines to Waller:

> *How, to thy sacred memory, shall I bring*
> *(Worthy thy fame) a grateful offering?*
> *I, who by toils of sickness, am became*
> *Almost as near as thou art to a tomb?*

A pitiful postscript was added to Aphra's letter, saying, *"I humbly beg pardon for my writing Madam for 'tis with a lame hand scarce able to hold a pen."*

Mrs. Behn continued to write at breakneck speed all through 1688, even through the disfiguring pain of her illness. In December of that year, the last Stuart, James II, first ignominiously fled in secret before the tide turned against him and then, after a brief return to London, was finally ordered into exile by the succeeding William of Orange. When he took ship for France on the day before Christmas, he ended the monarchy to which Aphra had remained so loyal even against her own interests. She sent a congratulatory poem to Queen Mary, who at least had Stuart blood, but on the subject of Parliament's crowning of William III she remained silent. Gilbert Burnet, despite the disparaging remarks he had made when Anne Wharton praised Aphra, now wrote her to ask if she did not wish to write a eulogy of the new King—who would no doubt return the compliment with a substantial reward. Aphra sent him some other verses instead, explaining that her loyalties would not permit her to turn her pen whichever way the prosperous wind blew: *"The breeze that wafts the crowding nations o're,/ Leaves me unpity'd far behind/ On the forsaken barren shore."*

She was already thinking of posterity and could not concern herself further with material survival in the world she knew she was leaving. Her essay on translation (1688), which cannot have brought her much financial return for the effort expended, was surely composed partly out of a desire to leave a "learned" treatise from the pen of a woman. The dedication to the Earl of Drumsberry begins: *"I hope your Lordship will pardon* [this] *in a woman, who is not supposed to be well versed in terms of philosophy, being but a new beginner in that science."* But she added with her old spirit, *"if any body think it worth their pains to quarrel with my boldness, I am able to defend myself."*

In the first few months of 1689, Aphra translated the sixth book of Abraham Cowley's *Sex Librii plantarum* (*Six Books of Plants*), and as she comes to the laurel tree, digresses under this note in the margin: *"The translatress speaks in her own person"*:

> *After the Monarchs, poets claim a share*
> *As the next worthy thy prized wreaths to wear.*
> *Among that number, do not me disdain,*
> *Me, the most humble of thy glorious train.*
> *Let me with Sappho and Orinda be*
> *Oh ever sacred nymph, adorned by Thee;*
> *And give my verses immortality.*[16]

Aphra Behn died a few months later, on April 16, 1689. One of the Fair Sex tells us that "her death was occasioned by an unskillful physician," but we know from Aphra herself that she had been dying for some time. The two "wretched verses" on her tombstone in Westminster Abbey, said to have been written by John Hoyle, did not augur well for posterity:

> *Here lies a proof that wit can never be*
> *Defence against mortality.*

The history of Mrs. Behn's posthumous demise had begun.

Appendix

Brief Chronology of Aphra Behn's Life and Works

ca. 1640   Aphra Behn born

1663   Trip to Surinam; returns to London ca. May 1664

ca. 1664   Marriage to Mr. Behn

1666   July, Aphra goes to Antwerp as a spy for Charles II; returns in the spring of 1667

1668   Aphra imprisoned for debt

1670   September, literary debut; *The Forced Marriage* produced at Lincoln's Inn Fields

1671   February, *The Amorous Prince* produced at Lincoln's Inn Fields

1672   Aphra may have edited *The Covent Garden Drollery,* a collection of poems

1673   February, *The Dutch Lover* produced at the Dorset Garden Theater

1676   July, *Abdelazer,* Dorset Garden; ca. September, *The Town Fop,* Dorset Garden

1677   February, *The Debauchee,* attributed to Aphra Behn, Dorset Garden; September, *The Counterfeit Bridegroom,* attributed to Aphra Behn

1678   January, *Sir Patient Fancy,* Dorset Garden; Summer, the Popish Plot panic begins

1679   ca. March, *The Feigned Curtezans,* Dorset Garden; ca. September, *The Young King,* Dorset Garden

1680   ca. June, *The Revenge,* attributed to Aphra Behn; July, the Earl of Rochester dies

1681   ca. January, *The Rover II,* Dorset Garden; November, *The False Count,* Dorset Garden; ca. December, *The Roundheads,* Dorset Garden

1682   ca. March, *Like Father, Like Son,* performed at Dorset Garden, but never published; ca. May, *The City Heiress,* Dorset Garden; August, Aphra Behn arrested for her epilogue to *Romulus and Hersilia,* in which she attacked the Duke of Monmouth, illegitimate son of Charles II and leader of the Whig opposition; November, the King's Company and the Duke's Company merge to become the United Company

1684   *Poems upon Several Occasions* published, as well as the first part of *Love Letters between a Nobleman and his Sister,* a fictional narrative

1685   February, death of Charles II and accession of his brother, James II; April, Thomas Otway dies; Aphra publishes a poetical *Miscellany* and three state poems: *A Pindaric on the Death of Our Late Sovereign; A Poem . . . to . . . Catherine Queen Dowager; A Pindaric Poem on the Happy Coronation*

1686   April, *The Lucky Chance,* Theater Royal; *La Montre, or The Lover's Watch,* a translation from the French of Balthazar Bonnecorse

1687   March, *The Emperor of the Moon,* Dorset Garden; *A Pindaric to . . . Christopher, Duke of Albemarle; To the Memory of . . . George, Duke of Buckingham;* Part III of *Love Letters between a Nobleman and his Sister*

1688   *Oroonoko, The Fair Jilt, Agnes de Castro;* "novels"; *A Congratulatory Poem to . . . Her Most Sacred Majesty; A Congratulatory Poem . . . on the Happy Birth of the Prince of Wales; A Poem to Sir Roger L'Estrange; To Poet Bavius; The History of the Oracles,* a translation from the French of Fontenelle, and *Lycidus,* a translation from the French of Tallemant

1689   *The History of the Nun, The Lucky Mistake:* "novels"; *Of Plants,* a paraphrase from the Latin of Abraham Cowley (Book VI of *Sex Libri plantarum); A Congratulatory Poem to . . . Queen Mary; A Pindaric Poem to the Reverend Dr. Burnet.* April 16, Aphra Behn dies and is buried in Westminster Abbey

Posthumous Publications and Productions

November 1689, *The Widow Ranter,* produced at the Drury Lane Theater; February 1696, *The Younger Brother,* Drury Lane. Novels: *The Adventure of the Black Lady, The Unfortunate Happy Lady, The Wandering Beauty, The Nun, or the Perjured Beauty, The Court of the King of Bantam, The Unfortunate Bride, The Dumb Virgin, The Unhappy Mistake.*

Notes

A fully documented social history of women in Aphra Behn's century could easily fill several volumes, but as the purpose of the "social" in this biography is to establish a context in which Mrs. Behn may be seen either to imitate or oppose contemporary standards, I have limited supporting evidence to a minimum. The conclusions reached here are based on a wide sampling of diaries, letters, etiquette manuals, literature, and other documents; only those which most articulately address issues of importance to Aphra have been used as illustration. Many more might have been cited. I have listed a few of these in the bibliography, in the hope that it may prove useful to readers who wish to pursue the subject further.

Abbreviations used in the notes are as follows:

Bodleian	Bodleian Library, Oxford
BM	British Museum, London
C.S.P. Col.	Calendar of State Papers, Colonial America and the West Indies
C.S.P. Dom.	Calendar of State Papers, Domestic
H.M.C.	Historical Manuscripts Commission
L.C.	Lord Chamberlain's Records, Public Record Office, London
PMLA	Publications of the Modern Language Association
P.R.O.	Public Record Office
S.P.	State Papers, manuscript in Public Record Office

All quotes from Aphra Behn are from Montague Summers's edition of her *Works* (London, 1913), unless otherwise noted.

Chapter 1

1. That is, she was the first woman to actually support herself by writing. Of course it is true that the professional writer was only just coming into

being as a social phenomenon in the latter half of the seventeenth century, and that few men before that had managed to eke out a living from books or plays or poetry. It is also true that Aphra Behn was by no means the "first woman writer." Numbers of women wrote and even published before her, but Aphra's demand to be considered a literary professional alongside her male peers is unprecedented, as is her determination to create a financial basis for her independence.

I have, aside from the mention of a few important influences, confined my discussion to English literature and tradition, though there are a few women of other literatures who might arguably lay claim to Aphra Behn's title of "the first." The most notable example is her contemporary, the French writer Madeleine de Scudéry, whose enormously successful (if interminable) historical romances recovered the failing family fortunes and supported her brother and herself. She published under her brother's name initially, however, and firmly denied authorship of her own works even after widespread public knowledge made the assertion ridiculous. To the end of her life, she continued to claim that she only wrote to amuse herself, as other ladies made verses or played the harpsichord. The idea of writing as a profession was profoundly at odds with what she considered proper to a lady.

2. Virginia Woolf, *A Room of One's Own* (London, 1928, repr. 1963), p. 65.

Chapter 2

1. Since this was written, a full-length biography of Aphra Behn by Maureen Duffy has been published. As will be seen in the following text, we disagree, occasionally to a considerable extent, on certain biographical details. Our approaches and points of view are also at variance and have led us to conclude two very different biographies of Aphra. Perhaps there could be no more appropriate homage to her. Aphra's play *The Rover* has also been revived recently and her work has begun to be reprinted often in anthologies.

2. Aphra's novel *Oroonoko* seems to be the single exception: reprinted over and over again, it became a classic whose foresight and power were recognized more than a century and a half later by the abolitionist movement.

3. "History of the Life and Memoirs of Mrs. Behn, by One of the Fair Sex," in *All the Histories and Novels Written by the Late Ingenious Mrs. Behn* (London, 1696, repr. 1705), pp. 1–2.

4. Ibid., p. 51.

5. Anne Finch, Countess of Winchelsea, *Poems,* ed. Myra Reynolds (Chicago, 1903), p. 92.

6. Edmund Gosse, "Mrs. Behn," *Athenaeum,* 2 (1884), p. 304. Gosse

also wrote the biography of Mrs. Behn included in the *Dictionary of National Biography*, based on his discovery. The manuscript of the Countess of Winchelsea's poem is now in the Folger Library, Washington, D. C.

7. Ernest Bernbaum, "Mrs. Behn's Biography, a Fiction," *PMLA,* 28, (1913), pp. 432–453; and "Mrs. Behn's *Oroonoko,*" in *Anniversary Papers by Colleagues and Pupils of George Lyman Kittredge* (Boston, 1913), pp. 419–435.

8. Charles Gildon, "An Account of the Life of the Incomparable Mrs. Behn," prefacing *The Younger Brother* (London, 1696), unpaginated.

9. A. Purvis, "Mrs. Aphra Behn," *Amateur Historian,* 1, no. 9, (1953–1954).

10. BM, Harleian Ms. 7588, fol. 426b.

11. James Rodway and Thomas Wyatt, *Chronological History of the Discovery and Settlement of Guiana* (Georgetown, Demerera), p. 138.

12. "The Apotheosis of Milton," *The Gentleman's Magazine,* vol. 8, (September 1738), p. 469.

13. "Literary Garbage," Anon. rev., *Saturday Review,* 33 (January 27, 1862), p. 109.

14. S. Austin Allibone, *Critical Dictionary of English Literature* (London, 1859–1871).

15. John Doran, "Their Majesties' Servants," in *Annals of the English Stage* (London, 1888), vol. 1, p. 239.

16. Julia Kavanaugh, *English Women of Letters* (London, 1863), p. 7; p. 21.

17. Ernest Baker, introduction to *The Novels of Aphra Behn* (London, 1905), p. 1.

Chapter 3

1. William Lambarde, *The Perambulation of Kent* (London, 1656), pp. 4–5.

2. Thomas Scot, "Confession of transactions in the service of Parliament, 1660," BM, Stowe Ms. 189, fol. 73b.

Chapter 4

1. *The Women's Sharpe Revenge* (London, 1640), pp. 40–42. This militantly feminist text was written in answer to two virulent attacks on women by John Taylor, the Water-Poet, entitled *A Juniper Lecture* and *A Crab-Tree Lecture.*

2. Lady Damaris Masham, *Occasional Thoughts in reference to a Vertuous or Christian Life* (London, 1694), p. 8.

3. *An Essay in Defense of the Female Sex* (London, 1696, repr. 1721), pp.

32–33. This early, anonymous defense of women has been attributed to Mary Astell, but it contains statements that she almost certainly would not have made, and its tone and style are very different from her other published work.

4. Roger Thompson, *Women in Stuart England and America* (London, 1974) p. 192.

5. Abraham Cowley, *Works* (London, 1693), p. 43.

6. Hannah Woolley, *The Queen-Like Closet* (London, 1684), p. 125.

7. Hannah Woolley herself, though she objected to the low state of women's education, does not seem to question their exclusion from universities either.

8. Hannah Woolley, *The Gentlewoman's Companion* (London, 1675), pp. 10–11.

9. Bathusa Makin, *An Essay to Revive the Antient Education of Women* (London, 1673), p. 22.

10. *The Oxinden and Peyton Letters, 1642–1670,* ed., Dorothy Gardiner (London, 1937), p. 128.

11. Ibid., p. 127.

12. *Memoirs of the Verney Family during the Seventeenth Century,* ed. F. P. and M. M. Verney (London, 1925), vol. 1, p. 501.

13. Lucy Hutchinson, *Memoirs of the Life of Col. Hutchinson,* ed. James Sutherland (Oxford, 1973), p. 288.

14. Bathusa Makin, op. cit., p. 26.

15. Lady Damaris Masham, op. cit., p. 197.

16. Charles Gildon, "Epistle Dedicatory," prefacing his edition of Aphra Behn's *Works* (London, 1696), unpaginated.

17. *An Essay in Defense of the Female Sex* (London, 1696, repr. 1721), p. 33.

18. Margaret Cavendish, Duchess of Newcastle, *The World's Olio* (London, 1655), "Preface to the Reader," unpaginated.

19. Richard Brathwaite, *The English Gentlewoman* (London, 1631), p. 89.

20. *An Essay in Defense of the Female Sex,* op. cit., p. 125; p. 101.

21. Sir Thomas Overbury, "The Wife," *The Overburian Characters,* ed. W. J. Paylor (Oxford, 1963), p. 105.

22. Thomas D'Urfey, *Richmond Heiress* (London, 1693), p. 29.

23. Elizabeth Jocelyn, "Treatise of Education," BM, Add. Ms. 27467, fol. 3.

24. John Evelyn, *Diary,* ed. William Bray (London, 1852), vol. 4, pp. 31–32. Letter to Mr. Bohun, January 1672.

25. Anna van Schurman, *The Learned Maid, or Whether a Maid may be a Scholar?* (London, transl. 1641), p. 13.

26. Lady Mary Wortley Montagu, *Complete Letters,* ed. Robert Halsband, (Oxford, 1965), vol. 1, pp. 44–45.

27. Virginia Woolf, *A Room of One's Own* (London, 1928, repr. 1963), pp. 51–52.

28. [Richard Allestree?] *The Whole Duty of Man* (London, 1804), p. 152; Luis Vives, *The Instruction of a Christian Woman*, transl. R. Hyde (1541) f.66ʳ, quoted in Keith Thomas, "The Double Standard," in *Journal of the History of Ideas*, 20 (1959), p. 210. Part of my argument with regard to women as property is based on his.

29. Margaret Cavendish, *The World's Olio* (London, 1655), "Preface," unpaginated.

30. Henry F. Abell, *Kent and the Great Civil War* (Ashford, 1901), pp. 141–42.

31. *Oxinden Letters*, op. cit., p. xxvii.

32. *The Whole Duty of a Woman*, Written by a Lady (London, 1696, repr. 1708), p. 6; p. 3.

Chapter 5

1. If she was indeed an adopted daughter, Aphra would have had no legal claim on her father's fortune in any case if there were no will.

2. C.S.P. Col., 1675–1676, p. 423.

3. C.S.P. Col., 1661–1668, p. 465.

4. Aphra Behn, *Works*, ed. Montague Summers (London, 1913), vol. 5, p. 129. All further quotes are from this edition of *Oroonoko*.

5. H. L. Mencken, "From the Diary of a Reviewer," *Smart Set*, no. 61 (February 1920), pp. 139–40. Mencken was reviewing a book by Paul Elmer More (then editor of *The Nation*) called *With the Wits* (1920). It contained an essay on Aphra Behn in which More devoted a great deal of space to arguing with Bernbaum. I owe this reference to James T. Farrell.

6. See Harrison Gray Platt, W. J. Cameron, J. A. Ramsaran, etc. The last notes, among other arguments, some interesting linguistic evidence: Aphra uses a number of words and expressions native to Surinam which had not yet come into general usage in England. Her mention of "cruel whips they call *cat with nine tails*" in *Oroonoko* antedates the *Oxford English Dictionary*'s "cat-o'-nine-tails" by seven years; and if "backerary" is a variant of "buckra," meaning a white man, Aphra Behn's use of the word antedates the O.E.D.'s by sixteen years. She also casually speaks of osenbrigs, hamaca, savana, pickanninies, paddle, punch, and other words which were still uncommon in England.

7. See illustration 8.

8. Aphra Behn, "Epistle Dedicatory," *Oroonoko* (London, 1689), unpaginated. This epistle appeared in the first edition only.

9. Thomas Southerne, *Oroonoko; A Tragedy* (London, 1696) "Dedication," unpaginated.

10. BM, Sloane Ms. 3662, fol. 40b.

11. Henry Adis, *A Letter Sent from Surinam* . . . (London, 1665), p. 5; p. 7.

12. Sir Josiah Child, *A New Discourse of Trade* (London, 1694), p. 170.

13. The subject of *The Widow Ranter,* which was probably written about the same time as *Oroonoko,* is a rebellion carried out by an obscure figure named Nathaniel Bacon. It took place in Virginia, during 1675–76. Aphra's extremely realistic representation of colonial customs and language in this play has often been remarked by critics, and her knowledge of these attributed to her experience in Surinam. There was, however, another source she might have had for her information in this case: there was a large contingent of Thomas Culpepper's relatives in Virginia at the time, including a John Culpepper who took part in the rebellion. In 1672, the whole territory of Virginia had been jointly granted to Lord Arlington and Thomas, Lord Culpepper and in 1675, the latter had been made Governor of Virginia for life.

14. Carl and Roberta Bridenbaugh, *No Peace Beyond the Lines: The English in the Carribean, 1624–1690* (New York, 1972), p. 394.

15. C.S.P. Col. 1661–1668, pp. 131–32. The grant gives Willoughby the right to "appoint governors and other officers."

16. Ibid., pp. 142–43.

17. H.M.C. 10th Report, App. 4, Bouverie Ms., p. 96.

18. C.S.P. Col., 1661–1668, pp. 166–67.

19. BM Harl. Ms. 7588, fol. 367b; V. L. Oliver, *The Monumental Inscriptions in the Churches* . . . (London, 1915), p. 4; pp. 194–95.

20. H.M.C. 14th Report, App. 2, Portland Ms. 3., p. 280.

21. "History of the Life and Memoirs of Mrs. Behn, by One of the Fair Sex," in *All the Histories and Novels Written by the Late Ingenious Mrs. Behn* (London, 1696, repr. 1705), p. 51.

22. Ibid., p. 2.

23. George Guffey is the most recent proponent of this argument ("Aphra Behn's *Oroonoko:* Occasion and Accomplishment," in *Two English Novelists*) . . . (Los Angeles, 1975). He adduces two sources which apparently contradict Aphra Behn's presentation of West African customs in general, and her description of Oroonoko in particular. It seems quite possible that these accounts are somewhat prejudiced: the first writer goes out of his way to make the inhabitants of Guinea look like savages, describing their towns as "filthy and stinking." The second author, William Bosman, was an advocate of the slave trade and eagerly retailed how lucrative it might be—it would hardly be surprising, then, that he would speak of the people he was enslaving as "cheats and liars." One of Guffey's reasons for not believing in Aphra's knowl-

edge of West Africa is that her physical description of Oroonoko does not correspond to the way Bosman said the people who lived on the Gold Coast looked. There were, in fact, several different races in that part of the world, and recent research has pointed out that Oroonoko's people, the Koromantee, were indeed very different in appearance from the other Africans of the area, as they were descended from a northern desert tribe that had migrated to the Gold Coast. Aphra's Oroonoko, then, corresponded even more precisely to objective reality than has been previously assumed. Both J. A. Ramsaran and the historian David Brion Davis cite a wide range of sources that counter Guffey's evidence.

24. David Brion Davis, *Slavery in Western Culture* (Ithaca, 1966), pp. 474–77.

25. *The Gentleman's Magazine*, 19 (1749), pp. 89–90; *London Magazine*, 18 (1749), p. 94. Quoted in David Brion Davis.

26. H.M.C. 14th Report, App., 2, Portland Ms., III, p. 280.

27. See V. T. Harlow, *Colonizing Expeditions in the West Indies and Guiana, 1623–1667*, Hakluyt Society, 2nd ser., 56 (London, 1923), p. 103, fn.

28. Cf. Lawrence Stone, *The Family, Sex and Marriage in England, 1500–1800* (London, 1977), p. 503.

29. According to the *Oxford English Dictionary*, early travelers and colonists, unfamiliar with the American jaguars or cougars, commonly referred to them simply as "tygers." In Guiana today, natives still refer to any wild cats, jaguars, and pumas as tigers. E. Eggleston, in *Century Magazine* (April 1894), noted that in the North American Carolinas, the panther was long called a "tyger."

30. William Byam, "An exact narrative of the state of Guiana . . . ," Bodleian, Ashmolean Ms., fols. 109–22.

31. C.S.P. Dom., 1659–1660, p. 571.

32. Edmund Ludlow, *Memoirs,* ed. C. H. Firth (Oxford, 1894), vol. 2, p. 234.

33. Robert Sanford, *Surinam Justice* (London, 1662), p. 4; p. 5.

34. Ibid., p. 7.

35. William Byam, "An exact narrative . . . ," op. cit., Ashmolean Ms., fol. 110.

36. Harlow, op. cit., p. 191.

37. H.M.C. 14th Report, App. 2, vol. 3, p. 308.

38. Portland Ms., Univ. of Nottingham. Uncalendared.

39. Harlow, op. cit., p. 192.

40. H.M.C. 14th Report, App. 2, vol. 3, p. 287.

Chapter 6

1. Christopher Hill, *The Century of Revolution, 1603–1714* (London, 1961), p. 24.

2. Gregory King, *Natural and Political Observations* (London, 1696, repr. 1936), p. 31. The accuracy of certain of Gregory King's calculations has been questioned by historians, but most of his critics would agree that even if the exactitude of the figures he produces in this case may be doubted, the validity of his conclusion is confirmed elsewhere.

3. Alice Clark, *The Working Life of Women in the Seventeenth Century* (London, 1919, repr. 1968), p. 80; C.S.P. Dom., 1638, p. 43.

4. Ibid., p. 113.

5. *Hertfordshire Quarter Sessions* (1658–1659), ed. W. J. Hardy, (1905), vol. 3, pp. xxxiv–xxxvi.

6. F. W. Tickner, *Women in Economic History* (London, 1923), p. 104.

7. For example, see T. S. Willan's "A Bedfordshire Wages Assessment of 1684," *Bedfordshire Historical Record Society Publications,* 25 (1947), pp. 135–37. This is also borne out by most of the other local county records I have consulted.

8. Christopher Hill, op. cit., p. 25.

9. Quoted in Roger Thompson, *Women in Stuart England and America* (London, 1974), p. 63.

10. Hannah Woolley, *The Gentlewoman's Companion* (London, 1675), p. 134.

11. Richard Parkinson, *The Life of Adam Martindale,* Chetham Society, 1st series, vol. 4, (1845), p. 8.

12. Jane Barker, *Poetical Recreations* (London, 1688), pp. 12–13; p. 98.

13. Despite the fact that the dominant social ideology made women feel that they were failures if they had not found husbands by the time they were twenty-five, it was very common for women to marry later. A number of economic factors favored late marriage: in the upper classes, many younger sons had to struggle for many years to establish themselves in some profession in order to make a living (some were never able to afford to marry at all); in the lower classes, many young men had to serve lengthy apprenticeships and were not allowed to marry while under this contract. Many other reasons, both economic and demographic, could be cited. Evidence pointed to by Peter Laslett, in *Family Life and Illicit Love in Earlier Generations* (Cambridge, 1977), indicates that for the population as a whole, there was a large percentage of women who married much later than the "ideal." Using demographic samplings ranging from 1599 to 1796 for six English towns, he found that in the age group from 15–19, 98.5% of women were still single; from 20–24, 81% were; from 25–29, 48.1%; and only in the

30–34 age group were 70.9% of women married. The fact that so many women of the period could be called "old maids" for many years of their lives did not seem to have significantly affected the way that category was defined by contemporaries, however.

14. Anne Finch, Countess of Winchelsea, *Poems,* ed. Myra Reynolds (Chicago, 1903), p. xxv.

15. [Richard Allestree?], *The Ladies' Calling* (London, 1673), p. 158.

16. [Mary Astell], *A Serious Proposal to the Ladies for the Advancement of their true and greatest Interest* (London, 1694, repr. 1696), p. 11–12.

17. Alan Macfarlane, *The Family Life of Ralph Josselin* (Cambridge, 1970), p. 129.

18. Ibid., p. 130.

19. *The Lawes Resolution of the Rights of Women* (London, 1632), p. 8. This was a legal handbook written for the ordinary, educated woman, outlining the laws and practice for all the stages of her life: age of legal consent for marriage, inheritance, dowry and jointure, marriage, property, widowhood, etc. Though the author was occasionally apologetic about the very disadvantageous position women of that time held under English Common Law, he counseled them forbearance and reminded that the Bible itself dictated an inherent inferiority.

20. Gregory King, op. cit., p. 22. The numbers of unmarried people in different parts of England could vary a great deal for external reasons. At first glance, Peter Laslett's figures for the town of Clayworth in 1676 seem to directly counter Gregory King's: the percentage of unmarried people in the population was 58.8%. Out of these, however, 38.4% were children and 16.7% servants, leaving only 3.7% who were actually on the marriage "market."

21. Lawrence Stone, *Crisis of the Aristocracy, 1558–1641* (Oxford, 1965), pp. 643–45.

22. *The Oxinden Letters, 1607–1642,* ed. Dorothy Gardiner (London, 1933), p. 144.

23. *Hertfordshire Quarter Sessions,* ed. W. J. Hardy (1905), vol. 3, p. xxxiv.

24. *The Lawes Resolution of the Rights of Women* (London, 1632), p. 124–25.

25. *Sylvia's Complaint of her Sex's Unhappiness, being the second part of Sylvia's Revenge, or a Satyr Against Man* (London, 1688), p. 14.

26. Lady Anne Fanshawe, *Memoirs* (London, 1907).

27. Alice Thornton, *Autobiography,* Surtees Soc., 62 (1873), pp. 164–65.

28. Margaret Cavendish, Duchess of Newcastle, *Sociable Letters* (London, 1664), p. 184.

29. BM, Harl. Ms. 7588, fol. 453*b.

30. H. A. Hargreaves speculates that Aphra's Mr. Behn may have been one Joachim Beene, a merchant from Hamburg, whom he connects with one

John Behn, mentioned in similar circumstances in the Calendar of State Papers, Colonial Series, America and the West Indies. Beene (or Behn) was master of the ship *King David,* which was built in Holland and traded in Barbados and the West Indies, often sailing under a Dutch, Hamburg, or Norwegian flag. There is, of course, no real evidence to connect this Mr. Behn with the man Aphra married, other than he was an eminent merchant who may have been of Dutch descent whom she might have met in Surinam. On the slim evidence that remains about Mr. Behn, however, it is unlikely that he could be definitively identified from contemporary records outside of a statement by someone who actually knew Aphra or knew of her private history.

31.   Samuel Pepys, *Diary,* ed. Robert Latham and William Matthews (London, 1972) vol. 6, p. 120; p. 189; p. 212.

32.   Ibid., pp. 257–58.

Chapter 7

1.   Bathusa Makin, *Essay to Revive the Antient Education of Gentlewomen* (London, 1673), p. 24.

2.   Katherine Philips, *Poems* (London, 1669), p. 1.

3.   Patricia Higgins, "The Reactions of Women, with special reference to Women Petitioners," in *Politics, Religion and the English Civil War,* ed. Brian Manning (London, 1973), pp. 210–11; p. 212.

4.   Ibid., p. 213.

5.   John Dryden, *Of Dramatic Poesy* [1668], ed. George Watson (London, 1962), p. 18.

6.   C.S.P. Dom., 1664–1665, pp. 426–27, June 15.

7.   C.S.P. Dom., 1666–1667, p. 427. Arlington's correspondent had written already on October 1 to say that he had been informed that there was a "fanatic plot" afoot in Yorkshire, with connections in Derby, Nottinghamshire, and Lincoln, but the "party will resolve nothing till they hear from their agents, Washington and Lunn, in Holland" (C.S.P. Dom, 1664–1665, pp. 32–33). Washington was one of the "fanatics" that William Scot was able to give Arlington information about from Holland. On October 21, Arlington received another letter giving the further information that one of the agents of the plotters in Yorkshire was William Sykes, merchant, brother to Richard Sykes, who married the daughter of Thomas Scot— William Scot's brother-in-law. Sykes, said the letter, had been an agent in foreign parts ever since the Restoration. He had been in disguise in England as a spy and recently had requested a license to come home, on pretense of wishing to live quietly in England. It was noted, however, that "he has been

in counsel with Bampfield, Kelsey, and other fugitives; he knows all the secrets of the cabal, and if he be taken, can discover all that has been in agitation against the government for three or four years past" (C.S.P. Dom., 1665–1666, pp. 22–23).

8. C.S.P. Dom., 1664–1665, p. 500.

9. Samuel Pepys, *Diary* (1666), ed. Robert Latham and William Matthews (London, 1973), vol. 7, June 4, p. 149; June 24, pp. 178–80.

10. C.S.P. Col., 1667–1668, p. 465.

11. Pepys, op. cit., vol. 9 (1668), pp. 66–67.

12. These "Memorialls," the series of letters from Aphra Behn and those she forwarded from William Scot, are preserved in the Public Record Office, with Joseph Williamson's State Papers. (He was Arlington's Secretary.) The documents are dated both in Old and New Style; to simplify matters, I have followed William Cameron's example in translating all the dates to the Old Style, which still predominated in England, though not on the Continent.

13. P.R.O., S.P. 29/172, no. 81, I.

14. C.S.P. Dom., 1665–1666, pp. 318, 342, and 358.

15. P.R.O., S.P. 29/167, no. 160.

16. Joseph Bampfield, whose name was to come up so often in Aphra's letters home, and who provided the prime obstacle to her communicating with Scot, would have been a match for the most experienced of agents. He had had a long and checkered career as a spy, which began while he was a Colonel in the King's Army. Charles I noted the young officer's extraordinary talent for intrigue and sent him to London in 1644 in disguise to "penetrate the designs of the two parties in Parliament." In 1654, however, Charles II discovered him to be a double agent, secretly working on the side for the republicans. After his dismissal from the Royalist camp, Bampfield continued working for Cromwell, in association with Thomas Scot, among others. By the Restoration, he was up to his old double-dealing again, having entered into a correspondence with the Royalist agent Sir Anthony Desmarches (who was to be Aphra's confidant). On September 20, 1659—just after Sir George Booth's plot to restore the King—Lord Chancellor Hyde wrote to Sir Anthony to tell him not to trust Bampfield, "who is too crafty."

17. P.R.O., S.P. 29/169, no. 38.

18. P.R.O., S.P. 29/172, no. 81, II.

19. P.R.O., S.P. 29/169, no. 117.

20. P.R.O., S.P. 29/169, no. 118.

21. Ibid.

22. P.R.O., S.P. 29/170, no. 75.

23. *Memoirs of the Verney Family during the Seventeenth Century,* ed. F. P. Verney and M. M. Verney (London, 1925), vol. 2, p. 254.

24. Maureen Duffy identifies this "Sir Thomas" as Sir Thomas Gower,

High Sheriff of Yorkshire. There is, however, no evidence to support this supposition other than the fact that he was one of Arlington's intelligence correspondents—one of his official responsibilities as High Sheriff. In the absence of any document of statement or external evidence actually connecting him with Aphra, I see no reason for assuming that he was her "Sir Thomas."

25. P.R.O., S.P. 29/172, no. 14.

26. Ibid.

27. P.R.O., S.P. 29/172, no. 81.

28. *The Right Honorable Earl of Arlington's Letters,* ed. Thomas Bebington (London, 1701), p. 100. Letter of October 12, 1666.

29. P.R.O., S.P. 29/182, no. 143.

30. Ibid.

31. One of the Fair Sex casts some doubt on her narrative by adding romantic details to her account of Aphra's return. The basic facts, however—the time and place of departure and the fact of the storm—are substantiated by official reports.

32. C.S.P. Dom., 1667, p. 67.

33. Ibid., p. 189; p. 199.

34. Ibid., pp. 185–86.

35. P.R.O., S.P. 29/171, no. 65.

36. Samuel Pepys, op. cit., vol. 7., (1666), p. 339.

37. Ibid., p. 350.

38. "Life and Memoirs of Mrs. Behn, by One of the Fair Sex," in *All the Histories and Novels written by . . . Mrs. Behn* (London, 1696, repr. 1705), p. 7.

39. Ibid., p. 8.

40. William Cameron, *New Light on Aphra Behn* (Auckland, 1961); Ernest Bernbaum, "Mrs. Behn's Biography, a Fiction," PMLA, 28 (1913), pp. 432–53; and Harrison Gray Platt, "Astrea and Celadon: An Untouched Portrait of Aphra Behn," PMLA, 49 (1934), pp. 544–59.

41. Peter Fraser, *The Intelligence of the Secretaries of State, 1660–1668* (Cambridge, 1956), pp. 9–10.

42. Ibid., p. 75, pp. 111–12.

43. P.R.O., S.P. 29/251, no. 91.

44. Ibid., no. 91, I. This letter is reproduced as illustration no. 14.

Chapter 8

1. *Tixall Letters,* ed. Arthur Clifford (London, 1815), vol. 2, p. 60. May 1669 is the date assigned this letter by *The London Stage;* it is approximate.

2. Bodleian Ms. Poet. 195. Bound into this volume is also a manuscript copy of Aphra Behn's play *The Younger Brother,* published only after her death.

3. Elizabeth Polwhele, *The Frolicks,* ed. Judith Milhouse and Robert D. Hume (Ithaca, 1977), pp. 57–58.

4. Frances Boothby, *Marcelia* (London, 1670), "Dedication," p. A 2.

5. Charles Gildon, "An Account of the Incomparable Mrs. Behn," prefacing his edition of *The Younger Brother* (London, 1696), unpaginated.

6. William Oldys, "From Ms. 'Adversaria'," *Notes and Queries,* 2nd series, 11 (London, 1861), p. 201.

7. Leslie Hotson, *The Commonwealth and Restoration Stage* (New York, 1962), pp. 233–235.

8. Samuel Pepys, *Diary,* ed. Robert Latham and William Matthews (London, 1974), vol. 8, p. 72, February 18, 1667.

9. BM, Harl. Ms. 6913, fol. 2.

10. *The Debauchee* (London, 1677), attributed to Aphra Behn. "Prologue," unpaginated.

11. Samuel Vincent, *The Young Gallants' Academy* (London, 1674), pp. 56–58.

12. In Shakespeare's time, playwrights were generally paid a flat fee for the performance of their work. This is documented in Philip Henslowe's *Diary,* ed. W. W. Greg (London, 1904–1908).

13. This record was set by Thomas Shadwell, for *The Squire of Alsatia,* in 1688.

14. George Granville, Lord Lansdowne, *The She-Gallants* (London, 1695), p. 41.

15. Samuel Vincent, op. cit., p. 59.

16. The metaphor of "eyes . . . wounding" is also conventional Petrarchan language. In that tradition, beams from the idealized woman's eyes pierce the lover's heart as arrows. Aphra seems to be playing on this metaphor ironically here, though elsewhere in the play she apparently uses it with no distancing.

17. It was quite frequent for an epilogue to apologize for the play; but in view of the statement made in the prologue and the way it is answered here, this may be considered a special case, more than merely a conventional ending.

18. It might be claimed that in addition to illustrating the misery of arranged marriages in *The Forced Marriage,* Aphra Behn is also attacking the code that censured marriage outside one's social class—a source of the original mishap that led to all the other troubles is the fact that it is inconceivable for Erminia, a commoner, to marry the Prince. One of Erminia's father's arguments for forcing her to marry Alcipius is that she is a fool to believe the

Prince could possibly be serious in his promise to marry her. It would not be out of character for Mrs. Behn to put forth such a critique, but the fact that this romantic situation was very much a cliché makes it difficult to argue that she meant it to serve the purpose of social criticism.

19. John Downes, *Roscius Anglicanus* (London, 1708), p. 34.

20. The performance is on the Lord Chamberlain's lists, but there is no indication of whether or not this was the premiere.

21. Aphra is referring to the proponents of heroic drama, who defended the nobility of tragedy against "low comedy." A "regular" play respected the Aristotelian unities of time, place, and action. Ben Jonson advocated this model and further insisted upon consistency of character in his theory of "humours."

22. John Dryden, *Of Dramatic Poesy, etc.,* ed. George Watson (London, 1962), vol. 1, p. 124.

23. Ibid., p. 46.

24. Richard Flecknoe, "Discourse of the English Stage," prefacing *Love's Kingdom* (London, 1664), unpaginated.

25. Thomas Shadwell, preface to *The Humorists* (London, 1671), unpaginated; Dryden, op. cit., pp. 138–39; p. 145.

26. John Evelyn, *Diary and Correspondence,* ed. William Bray (London, 1852), vol. 4, p. 25. The letter from Mrs. Evelyn is dated January, 1671.

27. Shakespeare's plays had been denigrated by the proponents of the "Ancient" school because they disregarded the requirements of the three unities. The "purists" gave Ben Jonson's work a superior rank for this reason.

28. Gildon, op. cit., unpaginated.

29. Henry Neville (Payne) was an ardent Catholic and later on a firm supporter of James II. He had been a prompter in the theater before making his debut as a playwright.

30. Tom Brown, in a fictional letter to Mrs. Behn from the actress Mrs. Bracegirdle, reproves her for a liaison with "an old poet . . . who went lately off the stage." Ravenscroft was the only literary friend of Aphra's still alive who fit the description in the letter. He had indeed retired from the stage a short time before.

31. *Westminster Drolleries,* ed. Joseph W. Ebsworth (Boston, Lincolnshire, 1875).

32. Thorn-Drury notes that a first edition had appeared under the initials R.B., but the second edition corrected the misprint to A.B.

33. G. Thorn-Drury, introduction to *Covent Garden Drollery* (London, 1672, repr. 1928), p. xviii.

34. Lady Carola Morland's husband, Sir Samuel Morland, was connected to Aphra in a number of strangely incongruent ways: he was, first of all, employed in Thomas Scot's spying network; then, he was converted to the

royal cause and was involved in Booth's rebellion along with Lord Willoughby; thirdly, he was a friend and collaborator of Thomas Culpepper's. Culpepper mentions him in the same "Adversaria" that records Aphra's origins, and in 1667 they were issued a joint patent for the "making of fire hearths." Aphra herself referred eulogistically to Sir Samuel Morland, in her *The Lover's Watch* (1686), as one of the "great inventors of the age."

35. It was Edward Butler who had Aphra confined to debtor's prison for her failure to repay a loan. Is this a second Edward Butler, or had Aphra forgiven the first his unfriendly behavior? Or is it possible that the poem in fact dates from a much earlier period, before her trip to Antwerp?

36. G. J. Gray, "The Diary of Jeffrey Boys of Gray's Inn, 1671," *Notes and Queries* 27 (December 1930), p. 456.

37. Boyses were liberally represented in Hackington, the manor which belonged to Thomas Culpepper. Jeffrey Boys's uncle built a hospital in nearby Sturry, where Culpepper thought Aphra might have been born. There were Boyses distantly related by marriage to Lord Willoughby, as one John Boys married Lady Elizabeth Finch, who belonged to a branch of the same family that the Earls of Winchelsea came from. Lady Elizabeth Finch was the daughter of Sir John Fotherley, who had been Thomas Culpepper's original guardian and was steward of the Earl of Winchelsea.

38. Notations for clothing expenditures are taken from Jeffrey Boys's *Diary* p. 455.

39. Ibid., p. 456.

Chapter 9

1. Katherine Philips, *Letters from Orinda to Poliarchus* (London, 1705), pp. 127–28.

2. Ibid., p. 152.

3. Ibid., pp. 227–29; p. 234.

4. Letter to Dorothy Osborne [Temple], printed in *Martha, Lady Giffard; her Life and Correspondence (1664–1722)*, ed. Julia Longe (London, 1911), pp. 38–42.

5. Katherine Philips, op. cit., p. 232.

6. Margaret Cavendish, Duchess of Newcastle, "A True Relation of my Birth, Breeding, and Life," appended to *Memoirs of the Duke of Newcastle* (London, 1667, repr. 1907), p. 176.

7. Margaret Cavendish, *Sociable Letters* (London, 1664), p. 14.

8. Ibid., p. 225.

9. Margaret Cavendish, "To the Lord Marquis of Newcastle," prefacing *Philosophical Letters* (London, 1664), unpaginated.

10. Margaret Cavendish, *The World's Olio* (London, 1655), "Epistle," unpaginated.

11. Dorothy Osborne [Temple], *Letters,* ed. E. A. Parry (London, 1914), p. 82.

12. Ibid., p. 100; p. 218.

13 [Madeleine de Scudéry], *Artamènes, or the Grand Cyrus: An Excellent New Romance. Written by that Famous Wit of France, Monsieur de Scudéry, and now Englished by F. G. Gent.* (London, 1653), "Dedication," unpaginated.

14. It is true that earlier it had also been considered unseemly in aristocratic circles for a man to publish, but this had to do more with class snobbery than sexual identity. Noblemen who wrote verse usually handed them around in manuscript at Court or among friends—to make them generally available was to break the circle of exclusivity. It was déclassé for a courtier to publish in the same way that it was looked down upon for him to work to earn his living. Men who did not belong to this class were under no restraint at all, whereas this was the case for women of all classes. There are no records of any man suffering as Katherine Philips did over the publication of his literary work. By the Restoration, there were numbers of noblemen who published verse in the popular miscellanies of the time and even wrote for the stage. Though they still scorned writers who "worked" (i.e., wrote) for a living, they were only too happy in the limelight of publication or performance.

15. Lady E[lizabeth] C[arey], *The Tragedy of Mariam, The Fair Queen of Jewry* (London, 1613, repr. Malone Soc., 1914), Act III, unpaginated.

16. *An Essay in Defense of the Female Sex* (London, 1696, repr. 1721), pp. iv–vi.

17. Anna van Schurman, *The Learned Maid . . .* (London, transl. 1641), p. 38.

18. Ibid., "Epistle to the Reader," unpaginated.

19. Anne Wharton, "Love's Martyr; or Witt Above Crowns," BM, Add. Ms. 28,693, fol. 4.

20. Anne Finch, Countess of Winchelsea, *Poems,* ed. Myra Reynolds (Chicago, 1903), p. 92; pp. 4–6. Despite the fact that Anne Finch had renounced literary reputation, she was mercilessly burlesqued in the character of Phoebe Clinket in *Three Hours After Marriage* (London, 1717).

21. Margaret Cavendish, "A True Relation of my Birth . . ." appended to *Memoirs of the Duke of Newcastle* (1667, repr. 1907), p. 178. The Duchess went on to excuse herself further, explaining: "I hope my readers will not think me vain for writing my life, since there have been many that have done the like, as Caesar, Ovid, and many more . . . but I verily believe the censuring readers will scornfully say, why hath this lady writ her own life?

Since no one cares to know whose daughter she was or whose life she is, or how she was bred, or what fortunes she had, I answer that it is true, that 'tis no purpose to the readers, but it is to the authoress. . . ."

22. [Mary Astell], *A Serious Proposal to the Ladies* (London, 1694, repr. 1696), p. 8.

23. Margaret Cavendish, *Sociable Letters* (London, 1664), pp. 183–84.

24. Sir Thomas Overbury, "The Wife," in *Overburian Characters,* ed. W. J. Paylor (Oxford, 1936), p. 105.

25. Hannah Woolley, *The Gentlewoman's Companion* (London, 1675), p. 10.

26. William Walsh, *A Dialogue Concerning Women, being a Defense of the Sex; with a preface by John Dryden* (London, 1691), pp. 97–98.

27. *Sylvia's Complaint of her Sex's Unhappiness* (London, 1688), p. 21.

28. *An Essay in Defense of the Female Sex,* op. cit., pp. 18–19.

29. "To the Excellent Orinda," prefacing Katherine Philips, *Poems* (London, 1669), unpaginated.

30. Lady Mary Chudleigh, *The Ladies' Defense* (London, 1701), p. 16.

31. Lady Mary Chudleigh, *Poems* (London, 1703), p. 23.

32. [Robert Gould], *A Satyrical Epistle to the Female Author of a Poem called 'Sylvia's Revenge,'* (London, 1691), p. 19.

33. Henry Lanier, *The First English Actresses, 1660–1700* (New York, 1931), p. 26.

34. The wives and daughters of actors and managers in the theater were in a different position—their employment on the stage was viewed as a matter of course.

35. Colley Cibber, *An Apology for the Life of Colley Cibber,* ed. R. W. Lowe (London, 1889), vol. 1, p. 75.

36. L.C. 5/141, p. 521.

37. P.R.O., S.P. 29/142, p. 160.

38. Tom Brown, *Letters from the Dead to the Living* (London, 1707), pp. 166–167. This was a fictional letter Tom Brown had written, impersonating Aphra Behn.

39. Lanier, op. cit., p. 66; Allardyce Nicoll, *Restoration Drama, 1660–1700* (Cambridge, 1923), pp. 369–379.

Chapter 10

1. Roger North, *Lives of the Norths* (London, 1826), vol. 2, p. 164.

2. The assumption, says Peter Laslett, "that illegitimacy figures directly reflect the prevalence of sexual intercourse outside marriage, which seems to be made whenever such figures are used to suggest that beliefs, attitudes and

interests have changed in some particular way, can be shown to be very shaky in its foundations." (*Family Life and Illicit Love in Earlier Generations* [Cambridge, 1977], p. 106.)

3. John Wilmot, Earl of Rochester, *Complete Poems,* ed. David Vieth (New Haven, 1968), pp. 40–41. The date of this poem is uncertain, but evidence indicates that it was written sometime not long before March 1673. All further quotes from Rochester's poems are from this edition.

4. George Etherege, *Poems,* ed. J. Thorpe (Princeton, 1963), p. 42. All further quotes from Etherege's poems are from this edition.

5. Sir Francis Fane, *Love in the Dark* (London, 1675), p. 77. Fane was also a friend of Rochester's. In 1689, Aphra wrote commendatory verses for Fane's play *The Sacrifice,* which was published but never performed.

6. John Crowne, *The Country Wit* (London, 1675), p. 8.

7. Gilbert Burnet, *History of My Own Times* (London, 1883), p. 61.

8. Julia Cartwright, *Madame: A Life of Henrietta, daughter of Charles I and Duchess of Orleans* (London, 1900), p. 153.

9. George Etherege, *The Comical Revenge; or Love in a Tub* (London, 1664, repr. 1667), p. 24.

10. William Wycherley, *Works,* ed. Montague Summers (London, 1924), vol. 4, p. 237. All further quotes from Wycherley's plays or poems are from this edition.

11. *Character of a Town Gallant* (London, 1675), p. 2.

12. This was printed in *Chorus Poetarum* (London, 1694), a poetical miscellany edited by Charles Gildon. It contains several previously unpublished poems by Aphra Behn.

13. John Dryden, *Dramatic Works,* ed. Montague Summers (London, 1931–1932), vol. 2, pp. 14–15.

14. Sir Charles Sedley, *Works,* ed. V. de Sola Pinto (London, 1928), vol. 1, p. 6.

15. Charles Cotton, *Selected Poems,* ed. Gregory Grigson (London, 1975), pp. 88–89. Cotton was an admirer of Aphra's and wrote laudatory verses to her which were published in a collection of her poems.

16. From Wycherley's *Love in a Wood,* produced in 1671.

17. James Wright, *Humours and Conversations of the Town* (London, 1693), p. 136.

18. *A New Collection of Poems* (London, 1674), p. 76.

19. John Evelyn, *Diary,* ed. E. S. de Beer (Oxford, 1959), p. 433, January 1662.

20. John Graunt, *Natural and Political Observations on the Bills of Mortality* (London, 1662), p. 62.

21. *A Collection of Poems by Several Persons* (London, 1673), pp. 178–79.

22. *Sylvia's Complaint of her Sex's Unhappiness* (London, 1688), p. 12.

23. Aphra Behn, *Miscellany* (London, 1685), pp. 69–70.
24. *An Essay in Defense of the Female Sex* (London, 1696, repr. 1721), p. 118.
25. There was a tradition going back to the Middle Ages of antifeminist tracts written to demonstrate women's carnal nature and warn unsuspecting male victims of their instability, but this vituperation came from moralists for the most part. What the wits and libertines were writing had a very different source, tone, and vocabulary.
26. *Poems on Affairs of State,* ed. George de F. Lord (New Haven, 1963–1976), vol. 4, p. 192.
27. BM, Harl. Ms. 6913, fol. 36b.
28. Charles Sackville, Earl of Dorset, in *The Works of the Most Celebrated Minor Poets* (London, 1749), p. 131.
29. Robert Gould, *Love Given O'er; A Satyr Against Women* (London, 1682), p. 5.
30. Alice Thornton, *Autobiography,* Surtees Society, 62 (1873), p. 210.
31. Ibid., p. 212.
32. Francis Drake, *Eboracum; or the History and Antiquities of the City of York* (London, 1736), p. 172.
33. *Yorkshire Diaries and Autobiographies in the Seventeenth Century . . . ,* ed., Charles Jackson (Durham, 1877–1886), vol. 1, John Shaw's diary, p. 147.
34. *Poems on Affairs of State,* op. cit., p. 213.
35. Sir Charles Sedley, op. cit., p. 33.
36. *Biblioteca Hoyleana* (London, 1692).
37. Aphra Behn, *Miscellany* (London, 1685), p. 75.
38. Whitelocke Bulstrode, Ms. Commonplace book, quoted by Montague Summers in the introduction to his edition of Aphra Behn's *Works.*
39. *The London Gazette,* no. 742, pp. 26–30, December 1672.
40. The poem was published in the *Muses Mercury* of December 1707, under the title "A Song for J. H." A few months earlier, several other poems by Aphra Behn had been published, introduced by the following notice: "If it were proper to make public what we have learnt of the story of the author of the following verse, 'twould be an unquestionable proof of their being genuine. For they are all writ with her own hand in a person's book who was very much her friend. . . ." That friend was later identified as John Hoyle. It is not improbable that the editors could have come into possession of a manuscript book of poems that had belonged to Hoyle. He had only been dead fifteen years; there were plenty of people alive who had known him; and his library had been sold at public auction in 1692. What makes the claim seem even more plausible is that the editors of the *Muses Mercury* do not seem to realize they are reprinting several poems which had already been published, which would argue that they might well have been printing from a

manuscript they took to be entirely unpublished, without consulting Mrs. Behn's printed works.

41. Alexander Radcliffe, *Works* (London, 1696), pp. 6–7.

42. *Poems on Affairs of State,* op. cit., p. 213.

Chapter 11

1. *Familiar Letters of Love and Gallantry,* ed. Tom Brown (London 1718) vol. 1, pp. 31–32.

2. Ibid., p. 32.

3. *The Rochester-Savile Letters,* ed. J. H. Wilson (Ohio, 1941), p. 46.

4. John Dennis, *A Defense of Sir Fopling Flutter* (London, 1722), p. 19.

5. Nathaniel Lee, *The Princess of Cleves,* in *Works,* ed. Stroup and Cook (New Brunswick, N.J., 1954) vol. 2, p. 218.

6. *The Rochester-Savile Letters,* op. cit., p. 65.

7. Gilbert Burnet, *Some Passages of the Life* [*of*] . . . *the Earl of Rochester* (London, 1680, repr. 1724), pp. 20–21.

8. *The Oxinden and Peyton Letters, 1642–1670,* ed. Dorothy Gardiner (London, 1937), p. 113.

9. *The Lawes Resolution of the Rights of Women* (London, 1632), p. 9.

10. George Savile, Marquis of Halifax, *The Ladies' New Year Gift, or, Advice to a Daughter* (London, 1700, repr. 1934), p. 15.

11. *An Essay in Defense of the Female Sex* (London, 1696, repr. 1721), p. 115.

12. Francis Osborne, *Advice to a Son* (London, 1656), p. 66. Osborne believed the acquiring of a fortune virtually the only recompense for the odious condition of being allied to a woman in marriage. The desire for woman, he said, leads to "madness in some, folly in all: placing, like stupid idolaters, divinity in a silly creature, set by the institutes of nature in a far inferior class of perfection to that which makes it his business to worship and adore it" (p. 49). Apparently the female readers of this widely disseminated text protested Osborne's attitude toward their sex, because in the second edition he included a preface defending himself against their criticisms.

13. Julia Cartwright, *Madame: A Life of Henrietta . . . Duchess of Orleans* (London, 1900), p. 153.

14. "A Session of the Poets," in *Poems on Affairs of State,* ed. George de F. Lord (New Haven, 1693), Vol. 1, p. 355.

15. John Dryden, *Letters,* ed. Charles Ward (Durham, N.C., 1942), p. 127.

Chapter 12

1. Dade, *A prognostication* . . . (London, 1678). The following account of the Popish Plot is based on William Bedloe's *Impartial Discovery of the horrid popish plot* (1679); J. P. Kenyon, *The Popish Plot* (1976); Titus Oates, *A True Narrative of the Horrid Plot* (1679); David Ogg, *England in the Reign of Charles II* (1956); and *A True and Perfect Narrative of the late terrible and bloody murder of Sir Edmund Berry Godfrey* (1678).

2. Narcissus Luttrell, *A Brief Relation of State Affairs* (Oxford, 1857), vol. 1, p. 171.

3. *Common's Journals,* 9, p. 530, October 31, 1678.

4. H.M.C. 7th Rep., Verney Ms., p. 473.

5. *The True News; or, Mercurius Anglicus,* 4–7 Feb., 1679/80.

6. An engraving of this procession is in the British Museum Prints and Drawings Collection.

7. Aphra Behn, *A Poem to Sir Roger L'Estrange on his Third Part of the History of the Times; relating to the death of Edmund Berry Godfrey* (London, 1688), p. 4.

8. Anne Wharton, *The Temple of Death* (London, 1695), pp. 242–44.

9. *Letters Between the Reverend James Granger . . . and many of the most Eminent Literary Men of His Time,* ed. J. P. Malcolm (London, 1805), pp. 234–35.

10. *The Tory Poets* (London, 1682), p. 8.

11. Robert Gould, "The Playhouse, A Satyr," BM, Add. Ms. 30,492, fol. 9.

12. L.C. 5/191; 5/16, p. 118.

13. *The London Stage,* ed. William van Lennep, vol. 1, p. 265.

14. Leslie Hotson, *The Commonwealth and Restoration Stage* (New York, 1962), p. 267.

15. John Dryden, *Letters,* ed. C. Ward (Durham, N.C., 1942), pp. 20–21.

16. Robert Gould, *Poems* (London, 1689), p. 279.

17. Aphra Behn addressed a translation of Sappho to the Duke of Buckingham in 1681, which may have brought her a gift in return.

18. John Dryden, *Of Dramatic Poesy, etc.,* ed. George Watson (London, 1692), p. 273.

19. *A Satyr on Modern Translators* (1684), printed in *Money Masters all Things: or, Satyrical Poems* (London, 1698), pp. 119–120. This has been tentatively attributed to Mathew Prior, but he himself excluded it from his collected *Works*.

20. John Evelyn, *Diary,* ed. E. S. de Beer (Oxford, 1959), pp. 763–64; Jan. 8, 1684.

21. *Ellis Correspondence, 1686–1688,* ed. G. Agar-Ellis (London, 1829), vol. 1, p. 64.

22. William Wycherley, *Miscellany Poems* (London, 1704), p. 301.

23. *The Tory Poets* (London, 1682), p. 7.

24. John Wilkes, *A General View of the Stage* (London, 1762), pp. 245–46.

25. This letter, in Aphra Behn's handwriting, is in the collection of the Folger Library, Washington, D. C.

26. Aphra Behn, *Love Letters from a Nobleman to his Sister* (London, 1696), vol. 2, dedication to Lemeul Kingdon, unpaginated.

27. BM, Harl. Ms. 7317, fol. 59.

Chapter 13

1. Aphra Behn, *Love Letters between a Nobleman and his Sister* (London, 1694), vol. 1, dedication to Thomas Condon, unpaginated.

2. Aphra Behn, *Poems upon Several Occasions* (London, 1684).

3. Aphra Behn, *Lycidus; or the Lover in Fashion* (London, 1688), unpaginated.

4. If, as her statement in the dedication indicates, Aphra Behn indeed wrote this play while a young woman in Surinam, one might speculate that she felt some identification with her Amazon heroine. Aphra was herself referred to as an Amazon by Jonathan Swift in *The Battle of the Books.*

5. Gerrard Winstanley, *The Law of Freedom and Other Writings,* ed. Christopher Hill (London, 1973), p. 99.

6. William Cobbett, ed. *State Trials* (London, 1811), vol. 9, p. 135.

7. Ibid., p. 184.

8. Aphra's publisher Tonson did not publish any of her novels: *Love Letters between a Nobleman and his Sister* was published by J. Hindmarsh, then R. Taylor; *Oroonoko* by W. Canning; and *The Lucky Mistake* by R. Bentley.

9. See P. Delany, *British Autobiography in the Seventeenth Century* (London, 1969), and W. Matthews, *Autobiography in the Seventeenth Century* (Los Angeles, 1973).

10. Ian Watt, *The Rise of the Novel* (London, 1957), p. 27.

11. William Byam, *An Exact Relation of the Most Execrable Attempts of John Allin Committed on the Person of his Excellency Francis, Lord Willoughby* (London, 1665), p. 1.

12. *Defense of the Female Sex* (London, 1696), p. 38.

13. [Mary Astell], *Reflections on Marriage* (London, 1706), pp. 106–7.

14. Lady Mary Wortley Montagu, *Complete Letters,* ed. Robert Halsband (Oxford, 1965), p. 64.

15. The letter to Waller's daughter-in-law is reprinted in Montague Summers's introduction to Aphra Behn's *Works* (London, 1913), pp. i–ii.

16. Abraham Cowley, *Works* (London, 1693), p. 143.

Bibliography

Manuscript Sources

Behn, Aphra. *The Younger Brother,* Bodleian, Rawlinson Ms. Poet. 195.

Byam, William. "An exact narrative of the state of Guiana, as it stood Anno 1665, particularly of the English Colony of Surinam," Bodleian, Ashmolean Ms.

Culpepper, Thomas. "Adversaria," BM, Harleian Ms. 7587–7605.

"The Description of a Poetress," BM, Harleian Ms. 6913.

"An Epistle to Julian," BM, Harleian Ms. 7319.

Gould, Robert. "The Playhouse, A Satire," BM, Additional MS. 30,492.

Jocelyn, Elizabeth. "Treatise of Education," BM, Additional Ms. 27,467.

Polwhele, Elizabeth. "The Faithful Virgins," Bodleian, Rawlinson Ms. Poet. 195.

"Satire Against the Poets," BM, Harleian Ms. 7317.

Scot, Thomas. "Confession," (1660) BM, Stowe Ms. 185.

Scott, John. "The Description of Guiana," BM, Sloane Ms. 185.

"The Session of the Ladies," BM, Harleian 7317.

Wharton, Anne. "Love's Martyr; or, Wit above Crowns," BM, Additional Ms. 28,693.

"The Woman's Complaint to Venus," Bodleian, Rawlinson Ms. Poet. 152.

Primary Sources

The Academy of Complements: or a new way of wooing. London, 1685.

An Account of Marriage. London, 1672.

Adis, Henry. *A Letter sent from Surinam to his Excellency, the Lord Willoughby of Parham* . . . London, 1665.

Advice to the Women and Maidens of London, by one of that sex. London, 1678.

319

Against Marriage. London(?), 1690.

[Allestree, Richard.] *The Ladies' Calling.* London, 1673.

———— *The Whole Duty of Man.* London, 1658.

The Anatomy of a Woman's Tongue. London, 1638.

An Answer to the Character of an Exchange Wench. London, 1675.

An Ape-Gentlewoman, or the Character of an Exchange Wench. London, 1675.

Arlington, Henry Bennet, Earl of. *The Right Honourable Earl of Arlington's Letters,* ed. Thomas Bebington. London, 1701.

The Art of Making Love: or, rules for the conduct of Ladies and Gallants in their Amours. London, 1676.

[Astell, Mary.] *Reflections on Marriage.* London, 1706.

———— *A Serious Proposal to the Ladies for the Advancement of their true and greatest Interest.* London, 1694, repr. 1696.

B., A. *Covent Garden Drollery,* ed. G. Thorn-Drury. London, 1672, repr. 1928.

B., A. *A Letter of Advice Concerning Marriage.* London, 1676.

Bampfield, Joseph. *Colonel Bampfield's Apologie.* The Hague, 1685.

Barker, Jane. *Poetical Recreations.* London, 1688.

Baron and Femme: A Treatise of Law and Equity concerning Husbands and Wives. London, 1700.

Batchilder, John. *The Virgin's Pattern.* London, 1661.

Bate, George. *Lives of the Regicides.* London, 1661.

Bedloe, William. *Impartial Discovery of the horrid Popish Plot.* London, 1679.

Betterton, Thomas. *The Life of Thomas Betterton.* London, 1710.

Boothby, Frances. *Marcelia.* London, 1670.

Brathwaite, Richard. *The English Gentlewoman.* London, 1631.

A Broadside against Marriage. London, 1675.

Brown, Tom. *Letters from the Dead to the Living and from the Living to the Dead.* London, 1702.

———— *Works.* London, 1720.

Burnet, Gilbert. *History of My Own Times.* London, 1883.

———— *Some Passages of the Life and Death of Rochester.* London, 1680, repr. 1724.

Byam, William. *An Exact Relation of the Most Execrable Attempts of John Allin Committed on the Person of his Excellency Francis, Lord Willoughby.* London, 1665.

C., J. *An Elegy upon the Death of the most Incomparable Katherine Philips.* London, 1664.

C[arey], Lady E[lizabeth]. *The Tragedy of Mariam, the Fair Queen of Jewry.* London, 1613, repr. Malone Soc., 1914.

Cavendish, Margaret, Duchess of Newcastle. *Letters of Margaret Lucas to William Cavendish, Duke of Newcastle.* London, 1956.

Hickes, *William. Coffee–House Jests*. London, 1677.

"History of the Life and Memoirs of Mrs. Behn, by One of the Fair Sex," in *All the Histories and Novels written by the late Ingenious Mrs. Behn*. London, 1696, repr. 1705.

Howard, Edward. *The Six Days' Adventure, or The New Utopia*. London, 1671.

———— *The Women's Conquest*. London, 1671.

Hoyle, John. *Bibliotheca Hoyleana*. London, 1692.

Hutchinson, Lucy. *Memoirs of the Life of Colonel Hutchinson*, ed. James Sutherland. Oxford, 1973.

Hyde, Edward, Earl of Clarendon. *The Life of Edward, Earl of Clarendon*. Oxford, 1857.

Jacob, Giles. *The Poetical Register*. London, 1719.

Killigrew, Anne. *Poems*. London, 1686.

Killigrew, Thomas. *Comedies and Tragedies*. London, 1664.

King, Gregory. *Natural and Political Observations and Conclusions upon the State and Condition of England*. London, 1696, repr. 1936.

Lambarde, William. *The Perambulation of Kent*. London, 1656.

Langbaine, Gerard. *An Account of the English Dramatic Poets*. Oxford, 1691.

The Lawes Resolution of the Rights of Women. London, 1632.

Lee, Nathaniel. *Works*, ed. Thomas B. Stroup and Arthur L. Cooke. New Brunswick, 1954.

L'Estrange, Sir Roger. *Brief History of the Times*. London, 1687–1688.

The London Gazette, 1665–1690.

Ludlow, Edmund. *Memoirs*, ed. C. H. Firth. Oxford, 1894.

Luttrell, Narcissus. *A Brief Relation of State Affairs* . . . Oxford, 1857.

Makin, Bathusa. *Essay to Revive the Antient Education of Gentlewomen*. London, 1673.

Mancini, Hortense, Duchess of Mazarin. *Memoirs*. London, 1676.

Manley, Mary de la Riviere. *The Adventures of Rivella: or, the History of the Author of the Atlantis*. London, 1714.

Masham, Lady Damaris. *Occasional Thoughts in reference to a Vertuous or Christian Life*. London, 1694.

Montagu, Lady Mary Wortley. *Complete Letters*, ed. Robert Halsband. Oxford, 1967.

Mordaunt, John. *The Letterbook of Viscount Mordaunt (1658–1660)*, ed. Mary Coate. Camden Society, 3rd. ser., 69, London, 1945.

The Muses Mercury, 1707–1709.

A New Collection of Poems. London, 1674.

Oates, Titus. *A True Narrative of the Horrid Plot*. London, 1679.

Osborne, Dorothy [Temple]. *Letters*, ed. E. A. Parry. London, 1914.

Osborne, Francis. *Advice to a Son*. Oxford, 1656.

Otway, Thomas. *Works*, ed. Montague Summers. London, 1926.

Overbury, Sir Thomas. *The Overburian Characters*, ed. W. J. Paylor. Oxford, 1936.

The Oxinden Letters, 1607–1642, ed. Dorothy Gardiner. London, 1933.

The Oxinden and Peyton Letters, 1642–1670, ed. Dorothy Gardiner. London, 1937.

Pepys, Samuel. *Diary*, ed. Robert Latham and William Matthews. London, 1970–1976.

Philips, Katherine. *Letters from Orinda to Poliarchus*. London, 1705.

———— *Poems*. London, 1669.

———— *Pompey*, a translation. London, 1663.

Poems on Affairs of State, ed. George de F. Lord. New Haven, 1963–1976.

Polwhele, Elizabeth. *The Frolicks, or the Lawyer Cheated*. [1671], ed. Judith Milhous and Robert D. Hume. Ithaca, 1977.

Radcliffe, Alexander. *Works*. London, 1696.

Raillery a la mode Considered . . . London, 1673.

Ralegh, Sir Walter. *The Discovery of the Large, Rich, and Beautiful Empire of Guiana* [1595]. London, 1928.

Remarks on the Humours and Conversations of the Town. London, 1673.

Remarks upon Remarks; or a Vindication of the Conversations of the Town. London, 1673.

Rich, Mary, Countess of Warwick. *Autobiography*. Percy Society, 22, London, 1848.

The Rochester–Savile Letters, ed. J. H. Wilson. Ohio, 1941.

The Rump; or an Exact collection . . . *relating to the late times* (1639–1661). London, 1662, repr. 1974.

Sackville, Charles, Earl of Dorset. *Works of the Most Celebrated Minor Poets*. London, 1749.

Sanford, Robert. *Surinam Justice*. London, 1662.

Satyr on the Modern Translators, [1684] printed in *Money Masters all Things: or, Satirical Poems*. London, 1698.

Savile, George, Marquis of Halifax. *The Ladies' New Year Gift, or, Advice to a Daughter*. London, 1700, repr. 1934.

Schurman, Anna van. *The Learned Maid, or whether a Maid may be a Scholar?* transl. London, 1641.

[Scudéry, Madeleine de]. *Artamènes, or the Grand Cyrus, an Excellent New Romance, Written by that famous Wit of France, Monsieur de Scudéry*. London, 1653–55.

Sedley, Sir Charles. *Works*, ed. V. de Sola Pinto. London, 1928.

Shadwell, Thomas. *The Humorists*. London, 1671.

Swinburne, Henry. *A Treatise of Spousals and Matrimonial Contracts*. London, 1686.

Sylvia's Complaint of Her Sex's Unhappiness . . . the second part of Syliva's Revenge. London, 1688.

Sylvia's Revenge, or, a Satyr Against Man. London, 1688.

Tate, Nahum. *A Present for the Ladies: Being a Historical Account of Several Illustrious Persons of the Female Sex.* London, 1693.

Thornton, Alice. *Autobiography.* Surtees Society, 62, 1873.

Tixall Letters; or the Correspondence of the Aston family . . . during the Seventeenth Century, ed. A. Clifford. London, 1815.

The Tory Poets. London, 1682.

The Town-Misses Declaration and Apology; or, an Answer to the Character of a Town-Miss. London, 1675.

The True News; or, Mercurius Anglicus. London, 1679–1680.

A True and Perfect Narrative of the late terrible and bloody murder of Sir Edmund Berry Godfrey. London, 1678.

The True Protestant Mercury (1680–1682), ed. Thomas Vile.

Verney. *Memoirs of the Verney Family during the Seventeenth Century,* ed. F. P. Verney and M. M. Verney. London, 1925.

Villiers, George, Duke of Buckingham. *The Rehearsal* (1671). London, 1672.

———— *Works.* London, 1715.

Vincent, Samuel. *The Young Gallants' Academy.* London, 1674.

Walsh, William. *A Dialogue Concerning Women, being a Defense of the Sex.* Preface by John Dryden. London, 1691.

Warren, George. *Description of Surinam.* London, 1667.

Westminster Drolleries, ed. J. W. Ebsworth. Boston, Lincolnshire, 1875.

Wharton, Anne. *Temple of Death.* London, 1695.

The Whole Duty of a Woman. London, 1696, repr. 1708.

Wilkes, John. *A General View of the Stage.* London, 1762.

Wilmot, John, Earl of Rochester. *Complete Poems,* ed. David Vieth. New Haven, 1968.

Winstanley, Gerrard. *The Law of Freedom and Other Writings,* ed. Christopher Hill. London, 1973.

The Women's Sharpe Revenge. London, 1640.

Woolley, Hannah. *The Gentlewoman's Companion; or a Guide to the Female Sex . . .* London, 1675.

———— *The Queen-like Closet . . .* London, 1684.

Wright, James. *Humours and Conversations of the Town.* London, 1693.

Wycherley, William. *Works,* ed. Montague Summers. London, 1924.

Yorkshire Diaries and Autobiographies of the Seventeenth and Eighteenth Centuries, ed. Charles Jackson. Surtees Society, Durham, 1877–1886.

Secondary Sources

Abbott, W. C. "English Conspiracy and Dissent," *American Historical Review*, 14, (1909), pp. 503–28.

Abell, H. F. *Kent and the Civil War*. Ashford, 1901.

Adams, Joseph Quincy, ed. *The Dramatic Records of Sir Henry Herbert, Master of the Revels, 1623–1673*. London, 1917.

Adamson, J. W. *A Short History of Education*. Connecticut, 1919.

Alleman, G. S. *Matrimonial Law and the Materials of Restoration Comedy*. Wallingford, 1942.

Allibone, S. A. *Critical Dictionary of English Literature*. London, 1859–1871.

"The Apotheosis of Milton," *Gentleman's Magazine*, (May 1738); (September 1738).

Ashley, Maurice. *Stuarts in Love*. London, 1963.

Bernbaum, Ernest. "Mrs. Behn's Biography, a Fiction," *PMLA*, 28, (1913), pp. 432–53.

———— "Mrs. Behn's *Oroonoko*," *Anniversary Papers by Colleagues and Pupils of George Lyman Kittredge*. Boston, 1913.

Berry, M. *Some Account of the life of Rachael Wriothesley, Lady Russell . . . and letters from Dorothy Sidney, Countess of Sunderland*. London, 1819.

Bridenbaugh, Carl and Roberta. *No Peace Beyond the Lines: The English in the Caribbean, 1624–1690*. New York, 1972.

Bridenbaugh, Carl. *Vexed and Troubled Englishmen*. Oxford, 1968.

Bury, Samuel. *Account of the Life and Death of Mrs. Elizabeth Bury, chiefly collected from her own Diary (1644–1720)*. Bristol 1720.

Cameron, William J. *New Light on Aphra Behn*. Auckland, 1961.

Cartwright, Julia. *Madame: A Life of Henrietta . . . Duchess of Orleans*. London, 1900.

Clark, Alice. *Working Life of Women in the Seventeenth Century*. London, 1919, repr. 1968.

Clay, C. "Marriage, Inheritance, and the Rise of large Estates in England, 1660–1815," *Econ. Hist. Rev.*, 2nd ser., 21, (1968).

Cleveland, Arthur R. *Woman Under the English Law*. London, 1896.

Coate, Mary. *Social Life in Stuart England*. London, 1924.

Cobbet, William, ed. *State Trials*. London, 1811.

Davies, Godfrey. *The Restoration of Charles II, 1658–1660*. London, 1955.

Davis, David Brion. *Slavery in Western Culture*. Ithaca, 1966.

Day, Robert Adams. "Aphra Behn's First Biography." *Studies in Bibliography*, no. 5, 22, (1969).

Delany, Paul. *British Autobiography in the Seventeenth Century*. London, 1969.

Doran, John. *Annals of the English Stage*. London, 1888.

Drake, Francis. *Eboracum; or the History and Antiquities of the City of York.* London, 1736.

Duffy, Maureen. *The Passionate Shepherdess.* London, 1977.

Everitt, A. M. *The Community of Kent and the Great Rebellion.* Leicester, 1966.

Foxon, D. *Libertine Literature in England, 1660–1745.* London, 1964.

Fraser, Peter. *The Intelligence of the Secretaries of State, 1660–1668.* Cambridge, 1956.

Furnivall, F. J. *Education in England.* London, 1867.

Gagen, E. J. *The New Woman: her Emergence in English Drama.* New York, 1954.

Gardiner, Dorothy. *English Girlhood at School.* Oxford, 1929.

Gosse, Edmund, "Mrs. Behn," *Athenaeum,* 2, (1884), p. 304.

Gray, G. J. "The Diary of Jeffrey Boys of Gray's Inn, 1671," *Notes and Queries,* December 27, 1930.

Guffey, George. "Aphra Behn's *Oroonoko:* Occasion and Accomplishment," in *Two English Novelists: Aphra Behn and Anthony Trollope.* Los Angeles, 1975.

Hair, P. *Before the Bawdy Court.* New York, 1972.

Halsband, Robert. *The Life of Lady Mary Wortley Montague.* London, 1961.

Ham, Roswell Gray. *Otway and Lee.* New Haven, 1931.

Hargreaves, Henry A. "A Case for Mr. Behn," *Notes and Queries,* 9,(1962).

Harlow, V. T. *Colonizing Expeditions to the West Indies and Guiana, 1623–1667.* Hakluyt Society, 2nd ser., 56, London, 1923.

Harris, Brice. "Aphra Behn's 'Bajazet to Gloriana,' " *TLS,* (February 9, 1933).

Hartman, Cyril Hughes. *Charles II and Madame.* London, 1934.

Hasted, Edward. *History of Kent.* Canterbury, 1778–1799.

Higgins, Patricia. "The Reactions of Women, with special reference to Women Petitioners," in *Politics, Religion and the English Civil War,* ed. Brian Manning. London, 1973.

Highfill, Philip H., etc. *A Biographical Dictionary of Actors, Actresses, Musicians . . . in London, 1660–1800.* Carbondale, Ill., 1973.

Hill, Christopher. *The Century of Revolution, 1603–1714.* London, 1961.

———— *The World Turned Upside Down.* London, 1975.

Hotson, Leslie. *The Commonwealth and Restoration Stage.* New York, 1962.

Howard, G. E. *History of Matrimonial Institutions.* Chicago, 1904.

Hume, Robert D. *The Development of English Drama in the late Seventeenth Century.* Oxford, 1976.

Jerrold, Walter and Clare. *Five Queer Women.* London, 1929.

Johnson, Edwin D. "Aphra Behn's *Oroonoko,*" *Journal of Negro History,* 10, (July 1925).

Lanier, Henry W. *The First English Actresses*. New York, 1931.

Laslett, Peter. *Family Life and Illicit Love in Earlier Generations*. Cambridge, 1977.

———— "The Gentry of Kent in 1640," *Cambridge Historical Journal*, 9, no. 2, (1948).

Link, Frederick. *Aphra Behn*. Lincoln, Nebraska, 1968.

"Literary Garbage," Anon. rev., *Saturday Review*, 33, January 27, 1872.

The London Stage, 1660–1800, ed. William van Lennep. Carbondale, Ill., 1960–1965.

Kavanaugh, Julia. *English Women of Letters*. London, 1863.

Keith, A. B. *West Africa*. London, 1933.

Kenyon, J. P. *The Popish Plot*. London, 1976.

McArthur, E. A., "Women Petitioners and the Long Parliament," *English Historical Review*, 1909.

MacCarthy, B. G. *Women Writers: their contribution to the English novel, 1621–1744*. Oxford, 1944.

Macfarlane, A. *The Family Life of Ralph Josselin*. Cambridge, 1970.

Malcolm, J. P., ed. *Letters between the Reverend James Granger . . . and many of the most Eminent Literary Men of his Time*. London, 1805.

Matthews, William. *British Autobiographies*. Berkeley, 1955.

"Memorials of Literary Characters—No. XIV," *Gentleman's Magazine*, n.s. 1, (1836).

Mencken, H. L. "From the Diary of a Reviewer," *Smart Set*, no. 61, (February 1920).

Mizener, Arthur. "Poems by Mrs. Behn," *TLS*, May 8, 1937.

More, Paul E. "A Bluestocking of the Restoration," *The Nation*, 103, (1916).

Mundy, P. D. "Aphra Behn, 1640?–1689," *Notes and Queries*, 200, (1955).

Newton, A. P. *European Nations in the West Indies, 1493–1668*. London, 1933.

Nicoll, Allardyce. *Restoration Drama, 1660–1700*. Cambridge, 1923.

Noble, Mark. *Lives of the Regicides*. London, 1798.

North, Roger. *The Lives of the Norths*. London, 1826.

Notestein, Wallace. "The English Woman, 1580–1650," in J. H. Plumb, ed., *Studies in Social History presented to G. M. Trevelyan*. London, 1955.

Ogg, David. *England in the Reign of Charles II*. Oxford, 1972.

Oldys, William. "From Ms. 'Adversaria'," *Notes and Queries*, 2nd ser., 11, (1861).

Outhwaite, R. B. "Age at Marriage in England from the late 17th to the 19th Century," *Transactions of the Royal Historical Society*, 5th ser., 23, (1973).

Parkinson, Richard. *The Life of Adam Martindale*. Chetham Society, 1st ser., 4, (1845).

Platt, Harrison Gray. "Astrea and Celadon: An Untouched Portrait of Aphra Behn," *PMLA*, 49 (1934).

Pope-Hennessy, Una. *Anna van Schurman*. London, 1909.

Powell, Chilton L. *English Domestic Relations 1487–1653*. New York, 1917.

Purvis, A. "Mrs. Aphra Behn," *Amateur Historian*, 1, No. 9, (1953–4).

Ramsaran, J. A. *"Oroonoko:* A Study of the Factual Elements," *PMLA*, 205, (1960).

Reynolds, Myra. *The Learned Lady in England, 1650–1760*. Boston, 1920.

Rodway, James and Wyatt, Thomas. *Chronological History of the Discovery and Settlement of Guiana*. Georgetown, Demerara, 1888.

Rogers, J. E. T. *History of Agriculture and Prices*, Oxford, 1866–1902.

Rogers, P. *The Dutch in the Medway*. Oxford, 1970.

Sackville-West, Victoria. *Aphra Behn*. New York, 1927.

Seeber, Edward D. *"Oroonoko* in France in the XVIII Century," *PMLA* 51, (1936).

Sheffey, Ruth. "Some Evidence for a New Source of Aphra Behn's *Oroonoko*," *Studies in Philology*," 64, no. 1, (1962).

Shorter, Edward. *The Making of the Modern Family*. London, 1976.

Slater, Miriam. "The Weightiest Business: Marriage in an Upper-Gentry Family in Seventeenth–Century England," *Past and Present*, 72, (1976).

Smith, Florence. *Mary Astell*. New York, 1916.

Stenton, Doris Mary. *The English Woman in History*. London, 1957.

Stone, Lawrence. *The Crisis of the Aristocracy, 1558–1641*. Oxford, 1965.

———— *Family and Fortune*. Oxford, 1973.

———— *The Family, Sex and Marriage in England, 1500–1800*. London, 1977.

Thomas, Keith. "The Double Standard," *Journal of the History of Ideas*, 20, (1959).

———— "Women and the Civil War Sects," *Past and Present*, 13, (1958).

Thompson, Roger. *Women in Stuart England and America*. London, 1974.

Thomson, Gladys Scott. *Life in a Noble Household, 1641–1700*. London, 1937.

Tickner, F. W. *Women in English Economic History*. London, 1923.

Ustick, W. L. "Changing Ideals of Character and Conduct in Seventeenth-Century England," *Modern Philology*, 30, (November 1932).

Walker, J. "Dissent and Republicanism after the Restoration," *Baptist Quarterly*, 8, (1937).

Watt, Ian. *The Rise of the Novel*. London, 1957.

Wiley, Autrey. *Rare Prologues and Epilogues*. London, 1940.

Willan, T. S. "A Bedfordshire Wages Assessment of 1684," *Bedfordshire Historical Record Society Publications*, 25, (1947).

Williamson, George C. *Lady Anne Clifford, Countess of Pembroke and Montgomery, 1590–1676, Her Life, Letters and Work*. London, 1922.

Williamson, J. A. *English Colonies in Guiana and on the Amazon, 1604–1668*. Oxford, 1923.

Wilson, J. H. *All the King's Ladies*. Chicago, 1958.

—————— *The Court Wits of the Restoration*. Princeton, 1948.

Woodcock, George. *The Incomparable Aphra*. London, 1948.

Woolf, Virginia. *A Room of One's Own*. London, 1928, repr. 1963.

Wrigley, E. A. *Identifying People in the Past*. London, 1973.